INJUSTICE 2™

INJUS

TOM TAYLOR
writer

BRUNO REDONDO **DANIEL SAMPERE** **XERMANICO**
pencillers

JUAN ALBARRAN **BRUNO REDONDO** **XERMANICO**
inkers

REX LOKUS **GABE ELTAEB** **J. NANJAN** **JOHN KALISZ**
colorists

WES ABBOTT
letterer

TICE™ 2

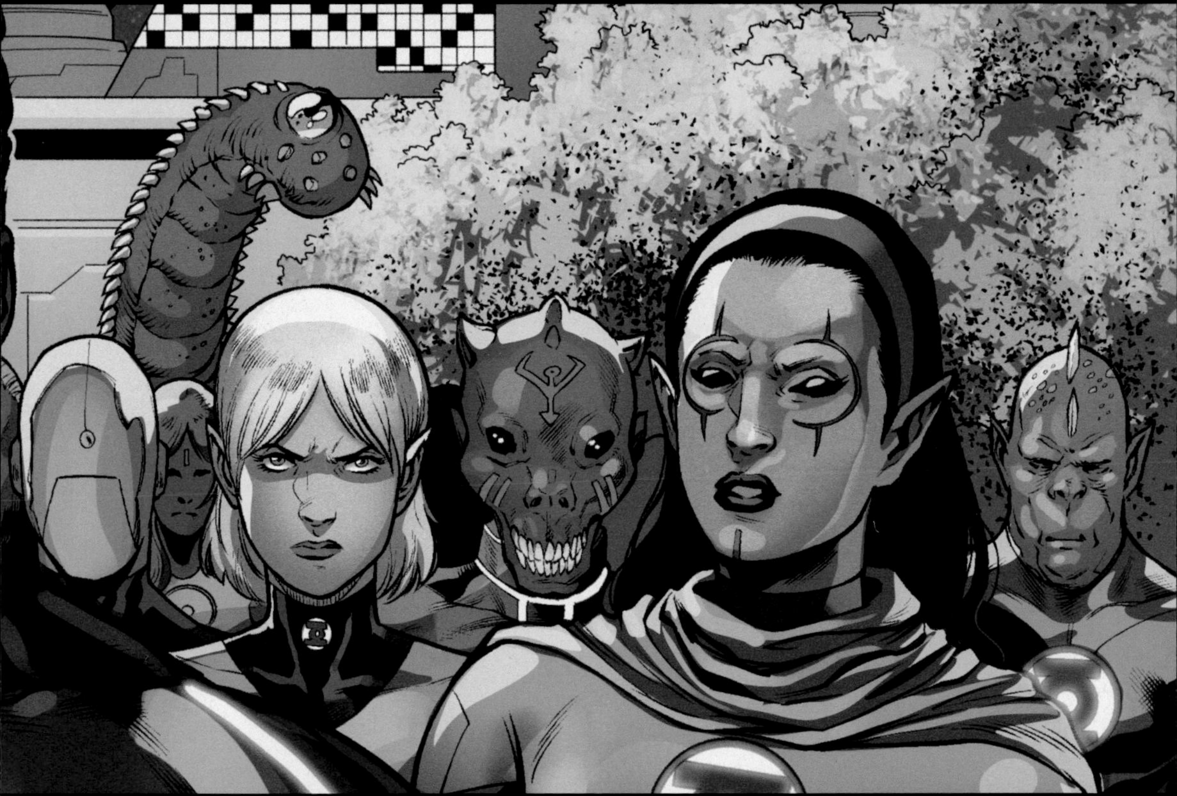

VOLUME 6

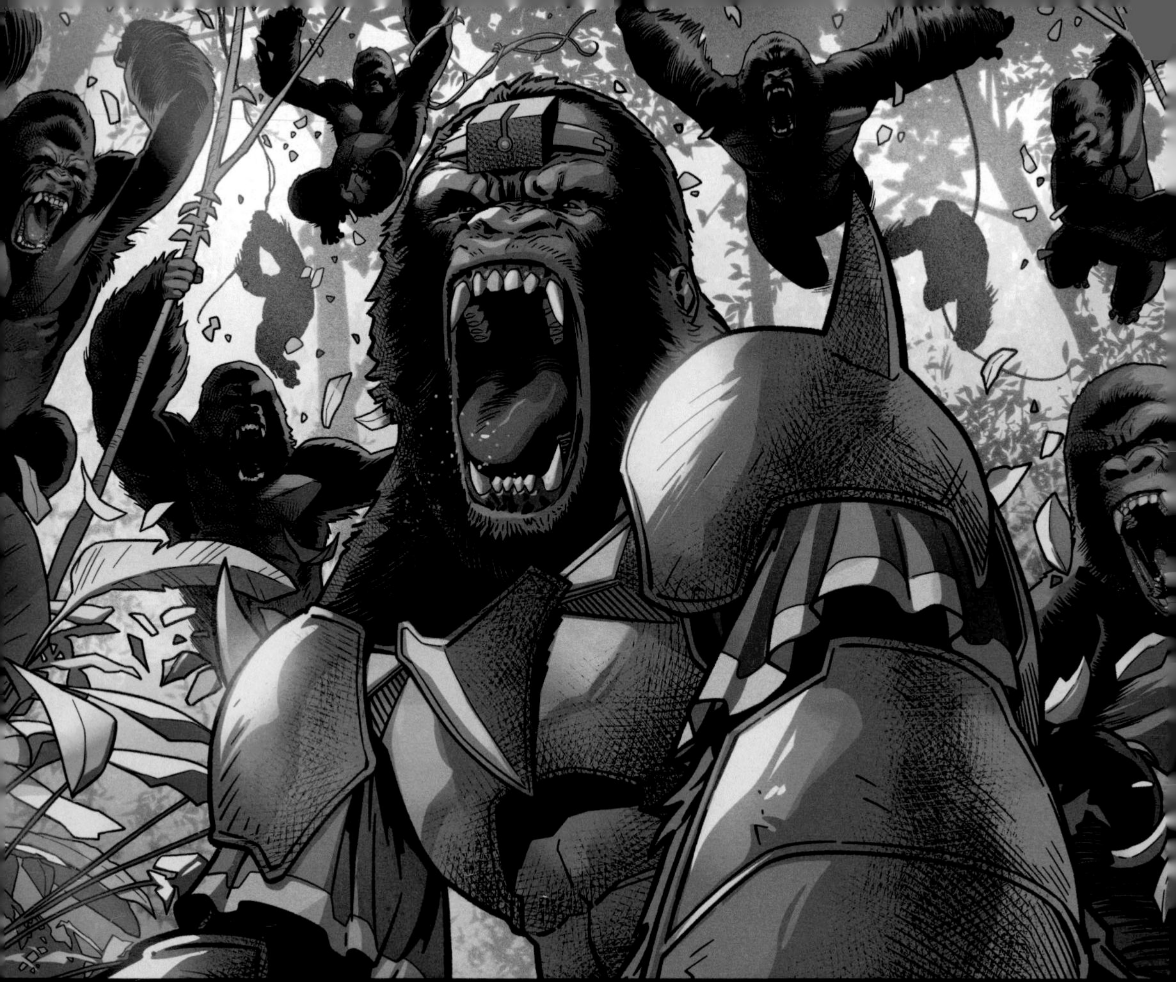

JIM CHADWICK Editor – Original Series
LIZ ERICKSON Assistant Editor – Original Series
JEB WOODARD Group Editor – Collected Editions
ALEX GALER Editor – Collected Edition
STEVE COOK Design Director – Books
MEGEN BELLERSEN Publication Design
ADAM RADO Publication Production

BOB HARRAS Senior VP – Editor-in-Chief, DC Comics
PAT McCALLUM Executive Editor, DC Comics

DAN DiDIO Publisher
JIM LEE Publisher & Chief Creative Officer
BOBBIE CHASE VP – New Publishing Initiatives & Talent Development
DON FALLETTI VP – Manufacturing Operations & Workflow Management
LAWRENCE GANEM VP – Talent Services
ALISON GILL Senior VP – Manufacturing & Operations
HANK KANALZ Senior VP – Publishing Strategy & Support Services
DAN MIRON VP – Publishing Operations
NICK J. NAPOLITANO VP – Manufacturing Administration & Design
NANCY SPEARS VP – Sales
MICHELE R. WELLS VP & Executive Editor, Young Reader

INJUSTICE 2 VOL. 6

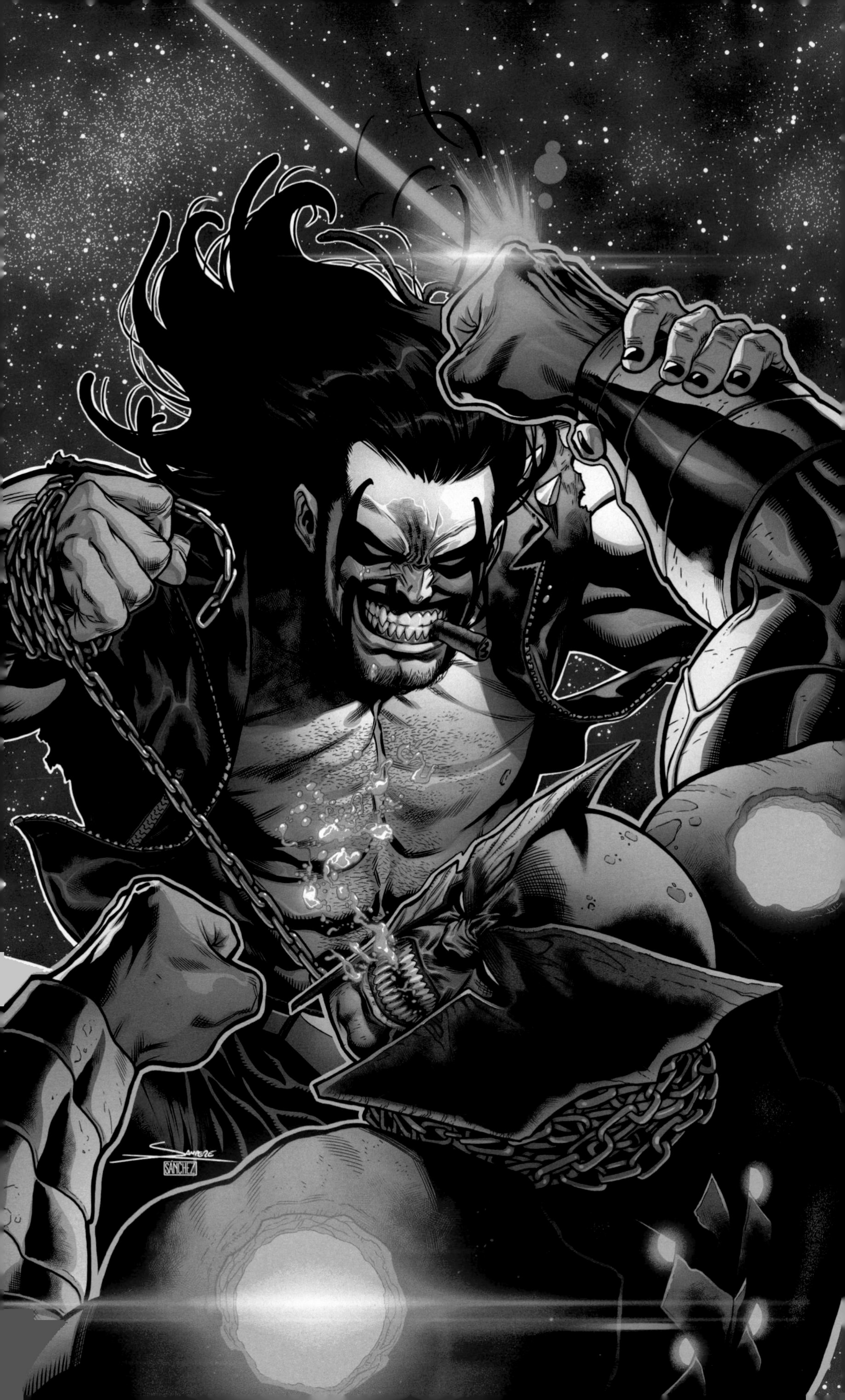
SÁNCHEZ

"Casualties of War"

Tom Taylor Writer **Daniel Sampere** Penciller **Juan Albarran** Inker **John Kalisz** **Rex Lokus** Colorists **Wes Abbott** Letterer

Cover art by **Daniel Sampere** and **Alejandro Sanchez**

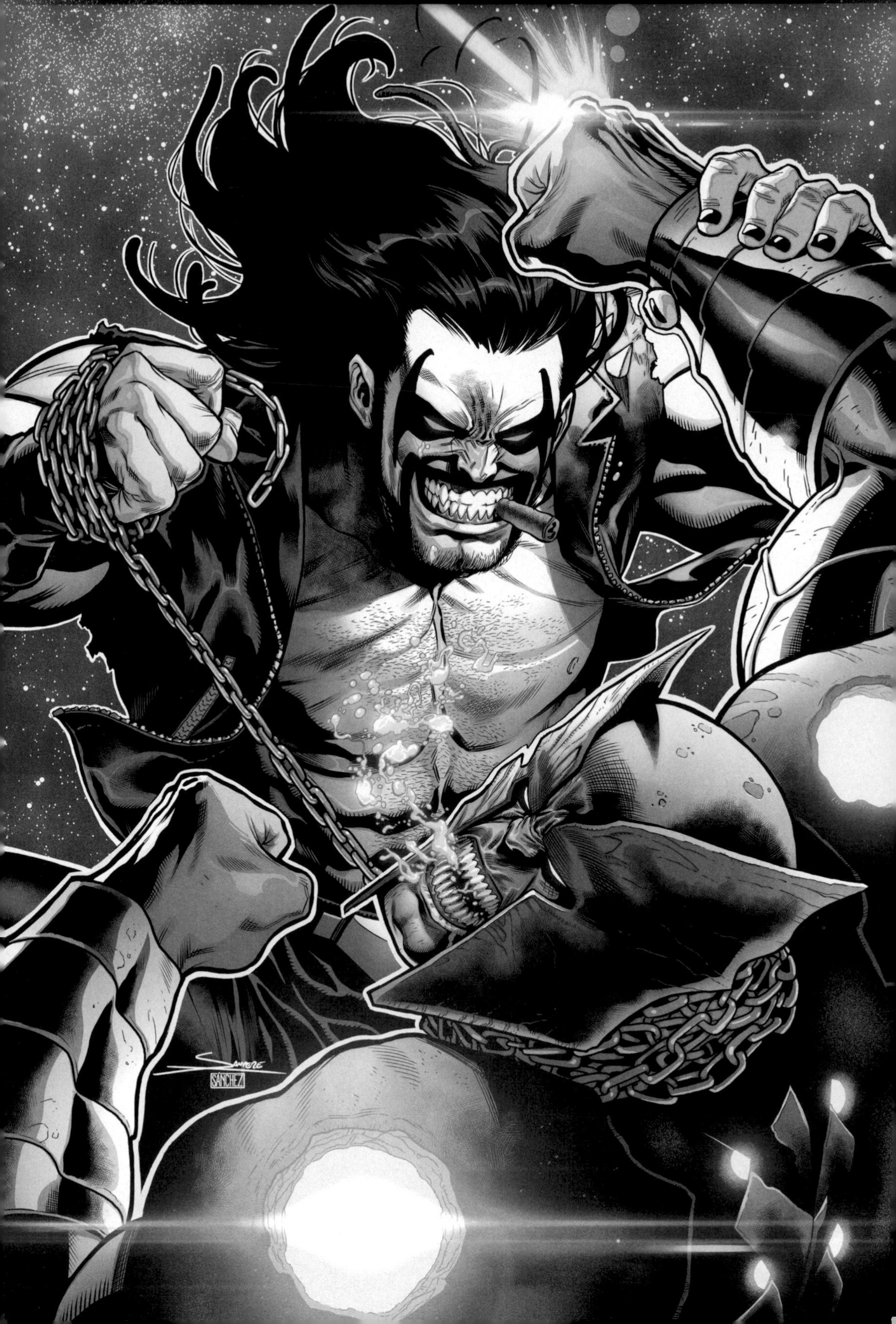

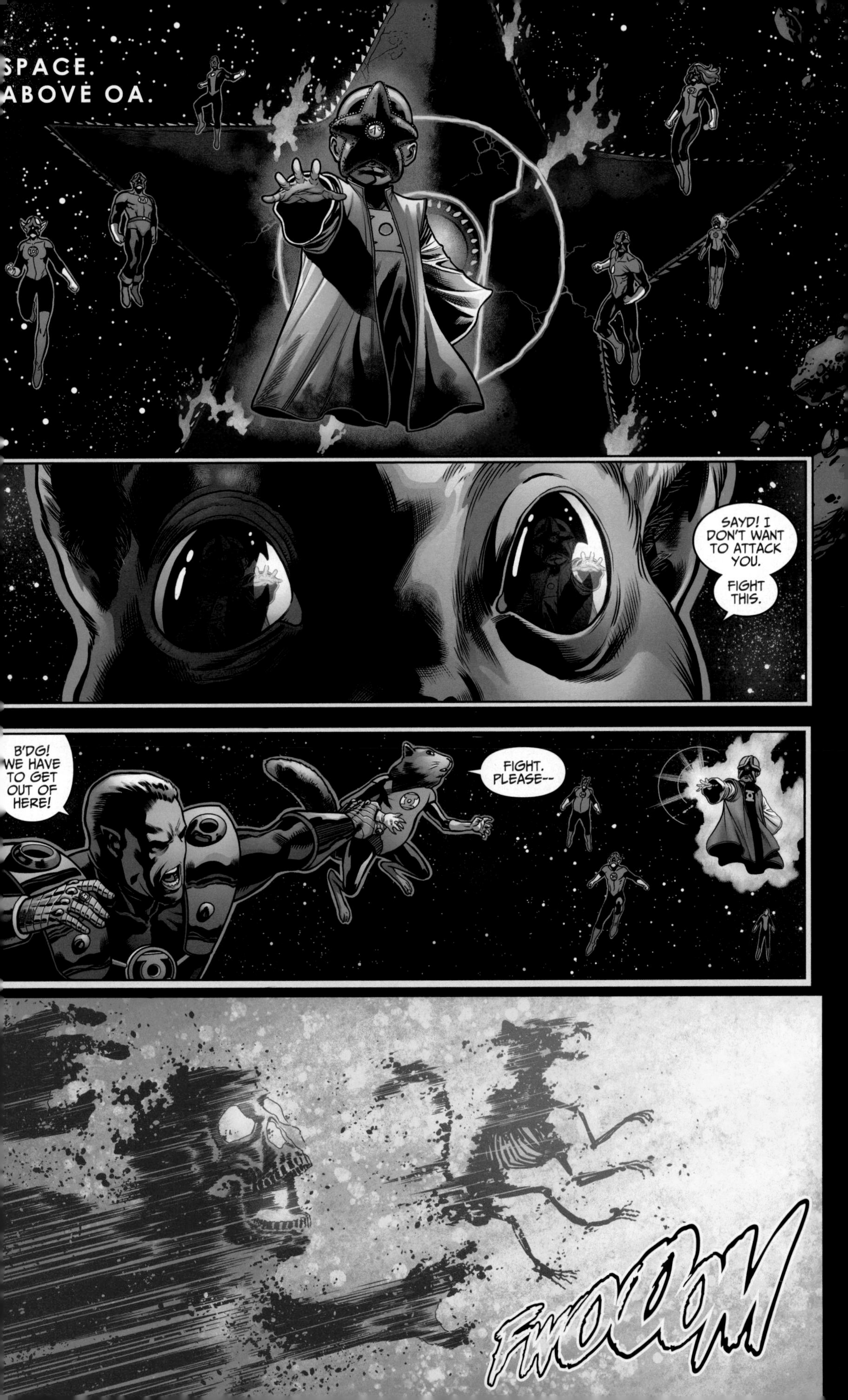
SPACE. ABOVE OA.
SAYD! I DON'T WANT TO ATTACK YOU.
FIGHT THIS.
B'DG! WE HAVE TO GET OUT OF HERE!
FIGHT. PLEASE--
FWOOOM

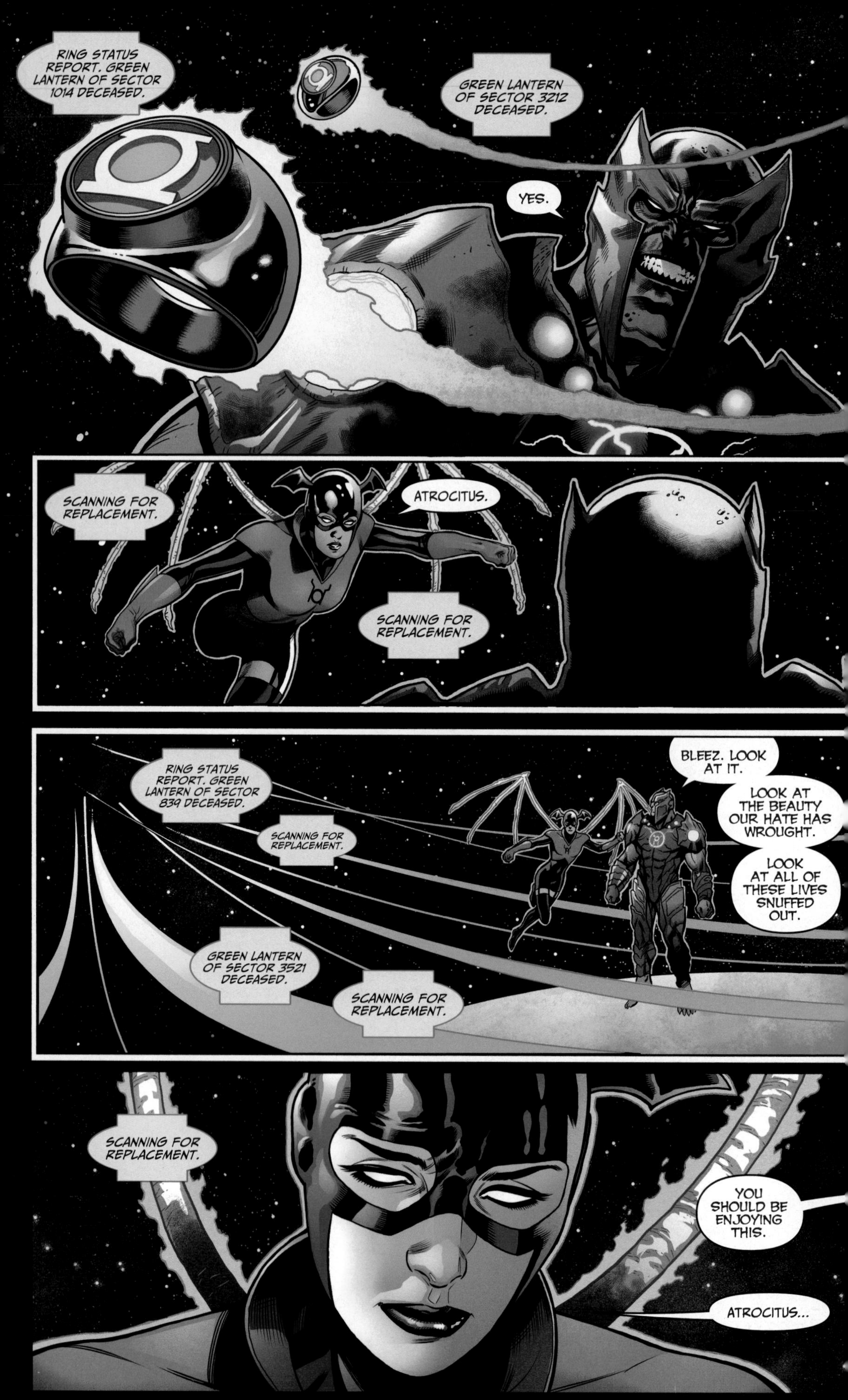
RING STATUS REPORT. GREEN LANTERN OF SECTOR 1014 DECEASED.
GREEN LANTERN OF SECTOR 3212 DECEASED.
YES.
SCANNING FOR REPLACEMENT.
ATROCITUS.
SCANNING FOR REPLACEMENT.
RING STATUS REPORT. GREEN LANTERN OF SECTOR 839 DECEASED.
SCANNING FOR REPLACEMENT.
BLEEZ. LOOK AT IT.
LOOK AT THE BEAUTY OUR HATE HAS WROUGHT.
LOOK AT ALL OF THESE LIVES SNUFFED OUT.
GREEN LANTERN OF SECTOR 3521 DECEASED.
SCANNING FOR REPLACEMENT.
SCANNING FOR REPLACEMENT.
YOU SHOULD BE ENJOYING THIS.
ATROCITUS...

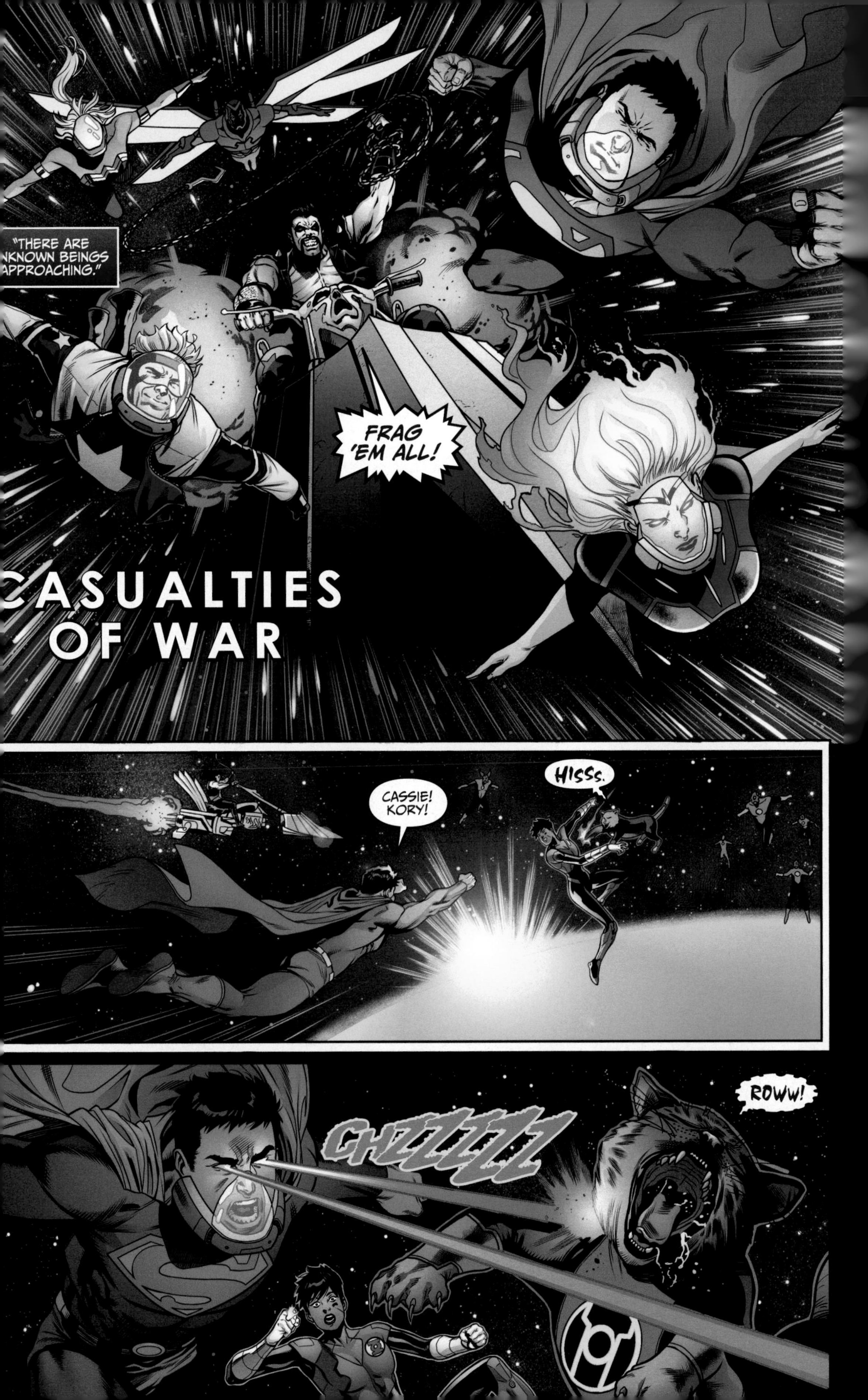
"THERE ARE
NKNOWN BEINGS
APPROACHING."
FRAG 'EM ALL!
CASUALTIES OF WAR
CASSIE! KORY!
HISSs.
ROWW!

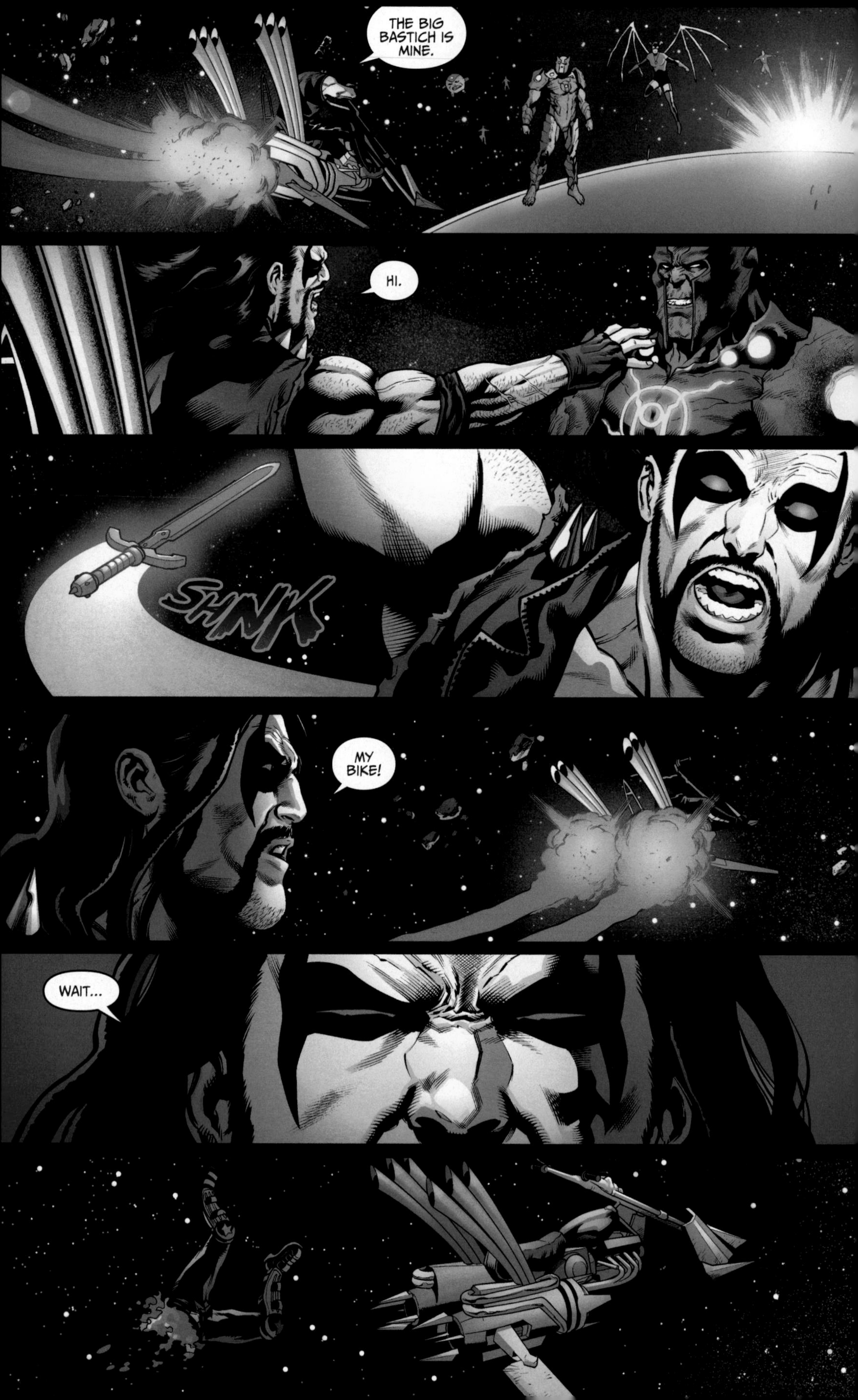
THE BIG BASTICH IS MINE.
HI.
SHNK
MY BIKE!
WAIT...

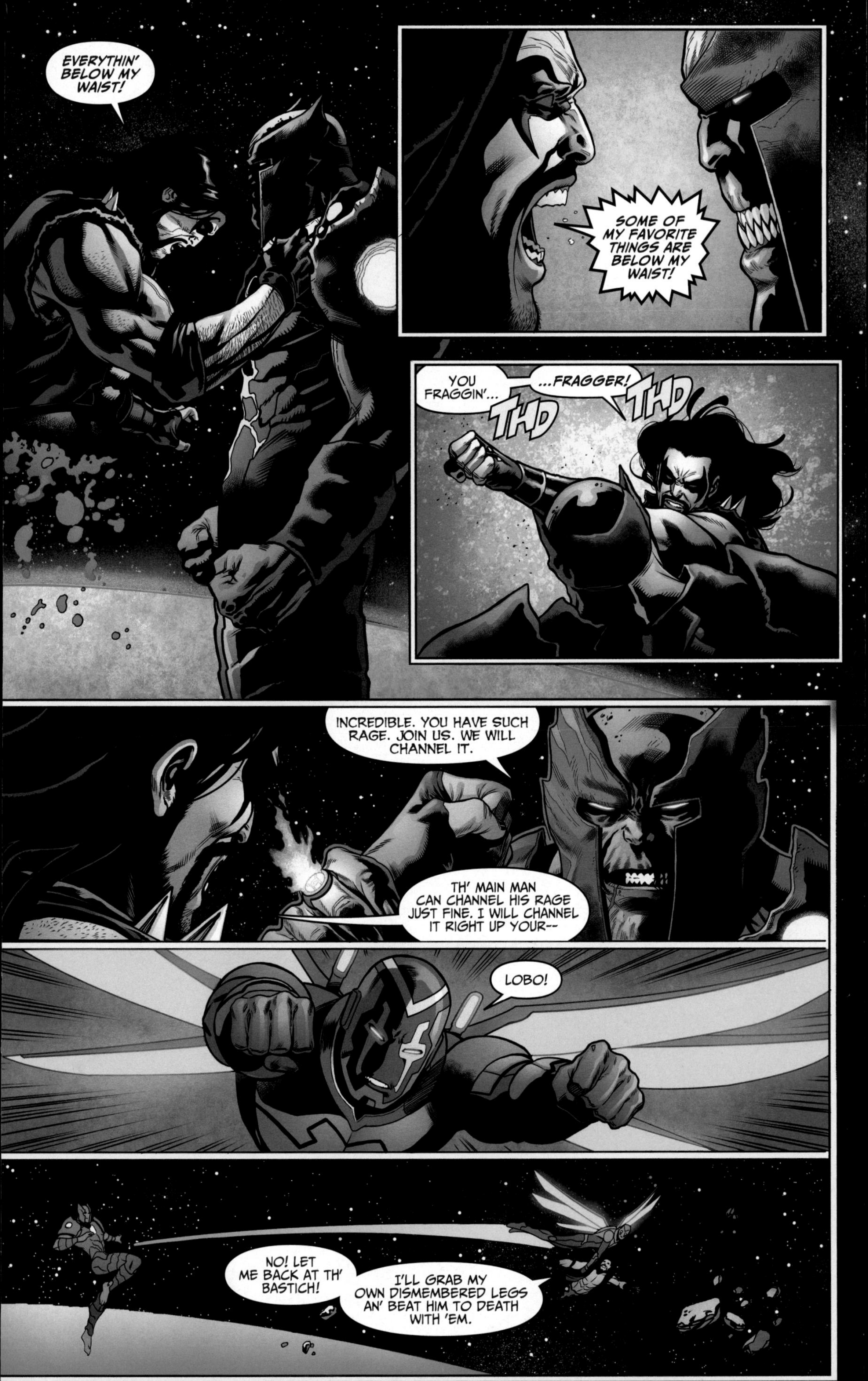

EVERYTHIN' BELOW MY WAIST!
SOME OF MY FAVORITE THINGS ARE BELOW MY WAIST!
YOU FRAGGIN'...
THD
...FRAGGER!
THD
INCREDIBLE. YOU HAVE SUCH RAGE. JOIN US. WE WILL CHANNEL IT.
TH' MAIN MAN CAN CHANNEL HIS RAGE JUST FINE. I WILL CHANNEL IT RIGHT UP YOUR--
LOBO!
NO! LET ME BACK AT TH' BASTICH!
I'LL GRAB MY OWN DISMEMBERED LEGS AN' BEAT HIM TO DEATH WITH 'EM.

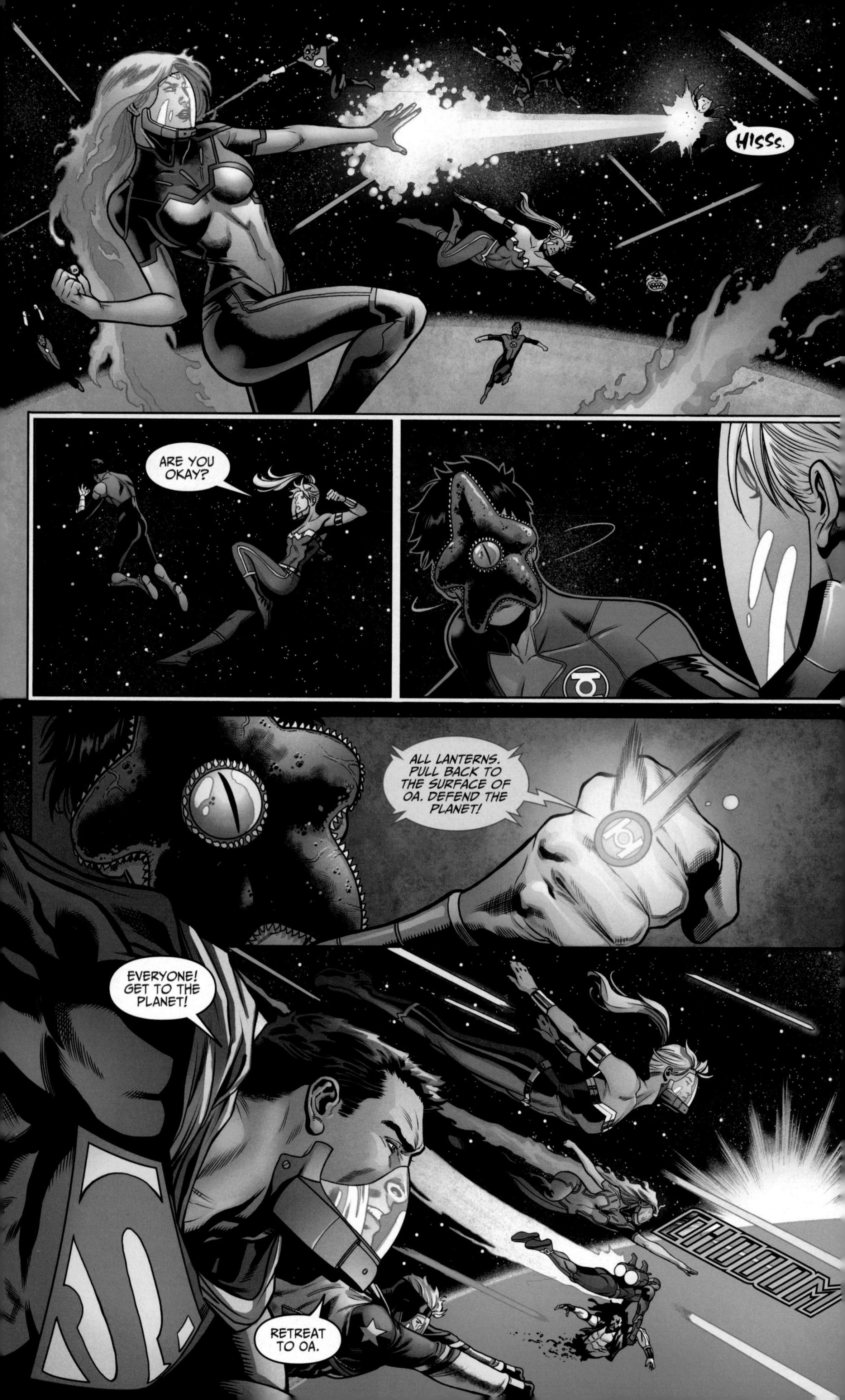
HISSs.
ARE YOU OKAY?
ALL LANTERNS. PULL BACK TO THE SURFACE OF OA. DEFEND THE PLANET!
EVERYONE! GET TO THE PLANET!
CHOOOM
RETREAT TO OA.

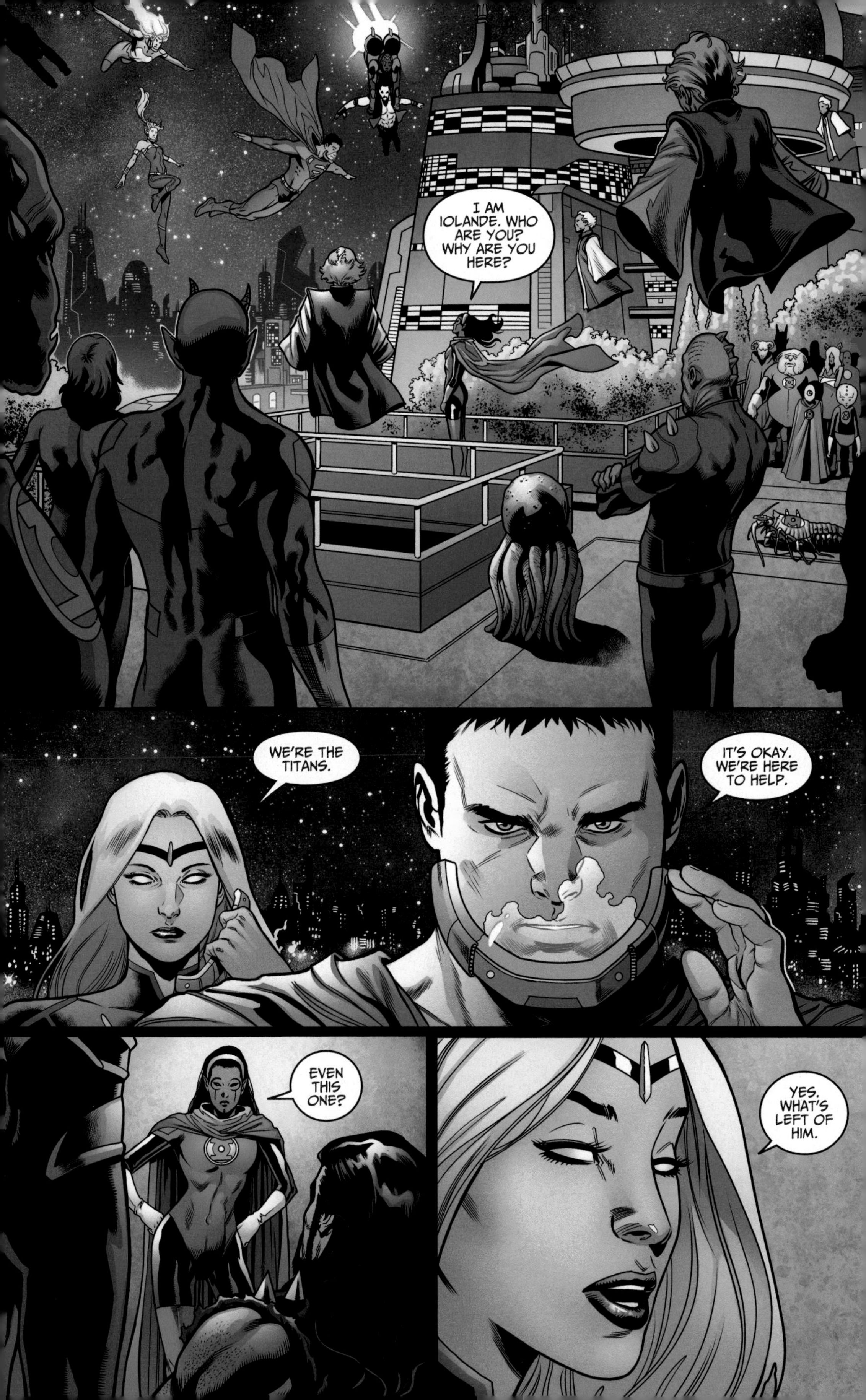
I AM IOLANDE. WHO ARE YOU? WHY ARE YOU HERE?
WE'RE THE TITANS.
IT'S OKAY. WE'RE HERE TO HELP.
EVEN THIS ONE?
YES. WHAT'S LEFT OF HIM.

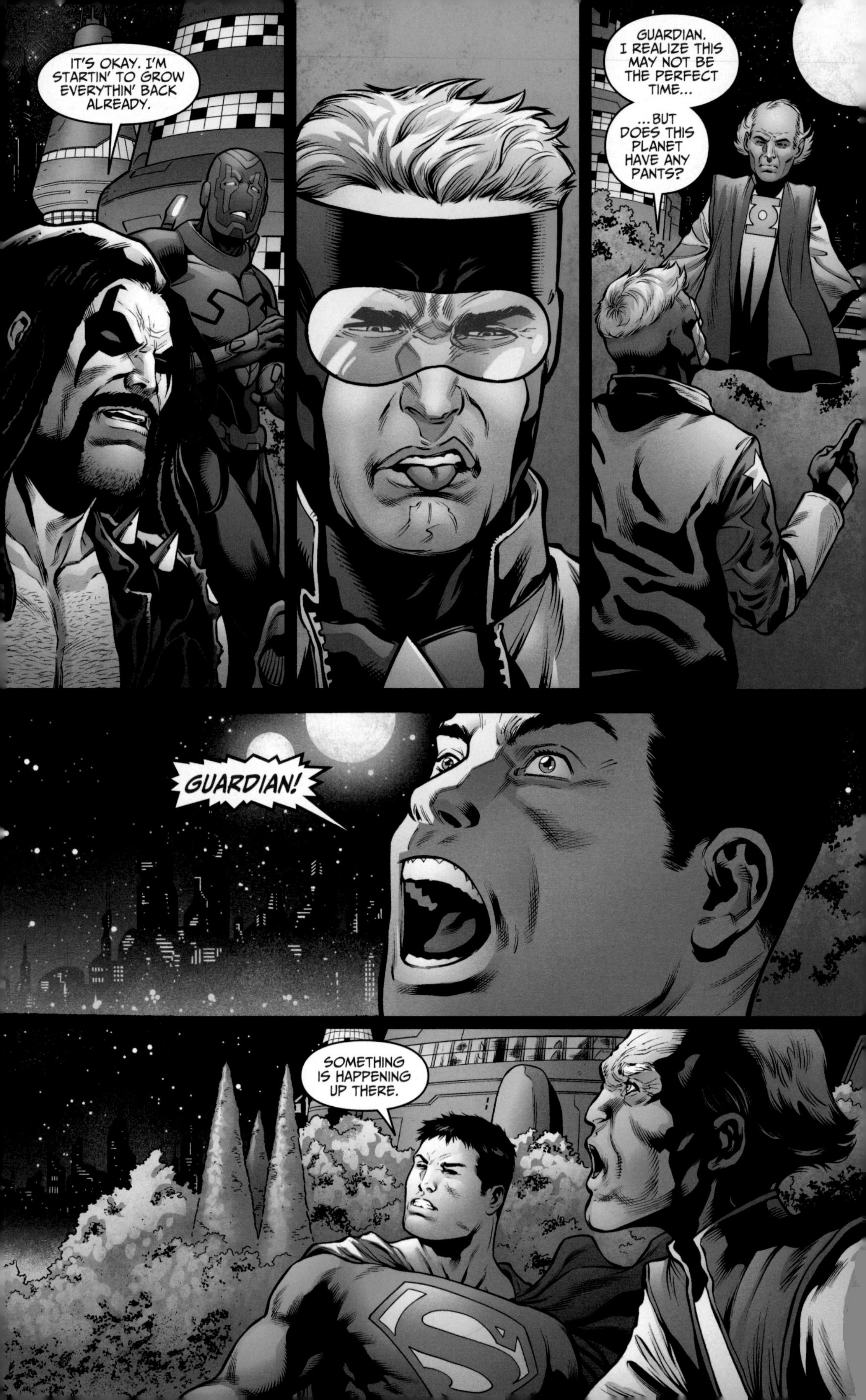
IT'S OKAY. I'M STARTIN' TO GROW EVERYTHIN' BACK ALREADY.
GUARDIAN. I REALIZE THIS MAY NOT BE THE PERFECT TIME...
...BUT DOES THIS PLANET HAVE ANY PANTS?
GUARDIAN!
SOMETHING IS HAPPENING UP THERE.

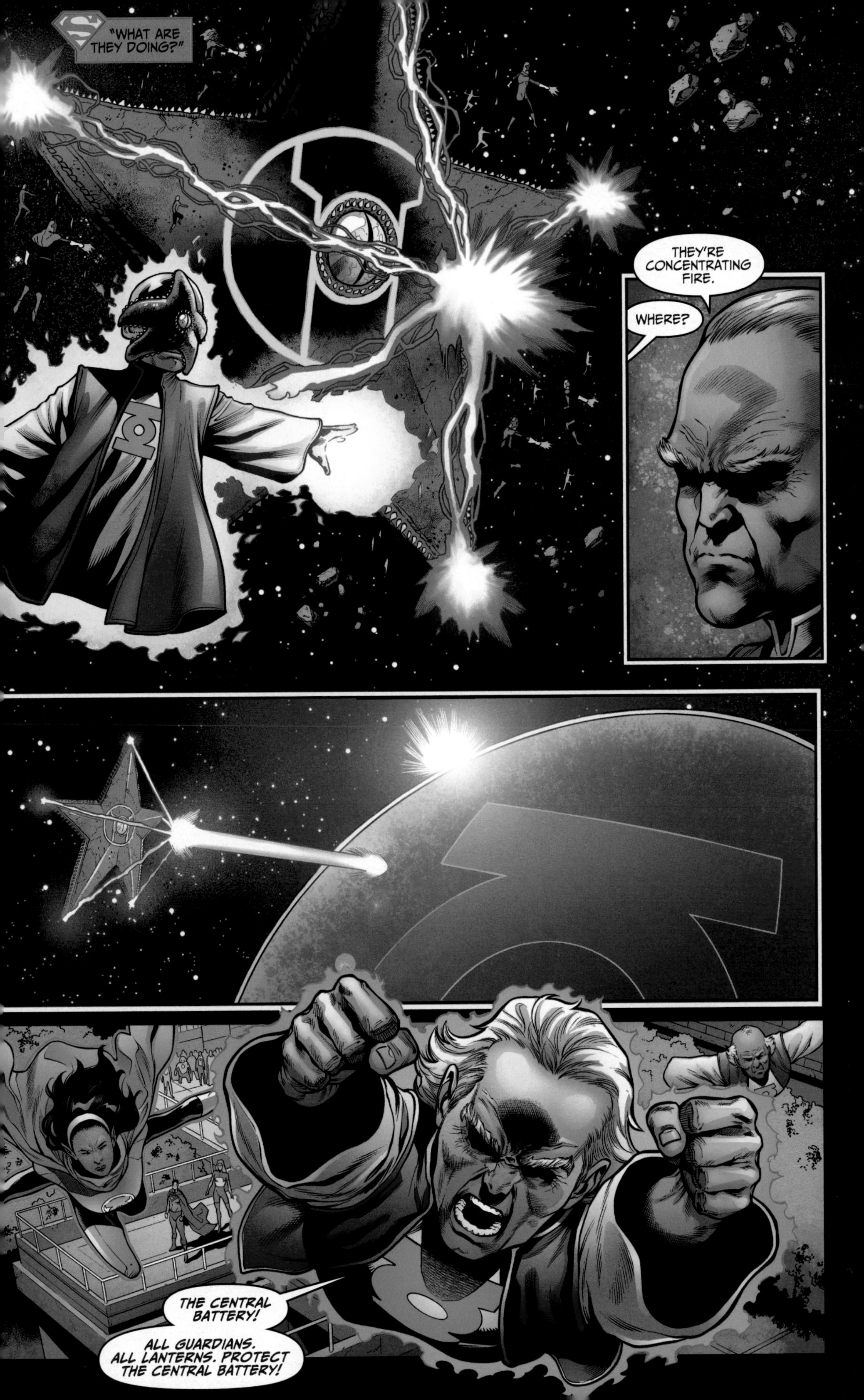
"WHAT ARE THEY DOING?"
THEY'RE CONCENTRATING FIRE.
WHERE?
THE CENTRAL BATTERY!
ALL GUARDIANS. ALL LANTERNS. PROTECT THE CENTRAL BATTERY!

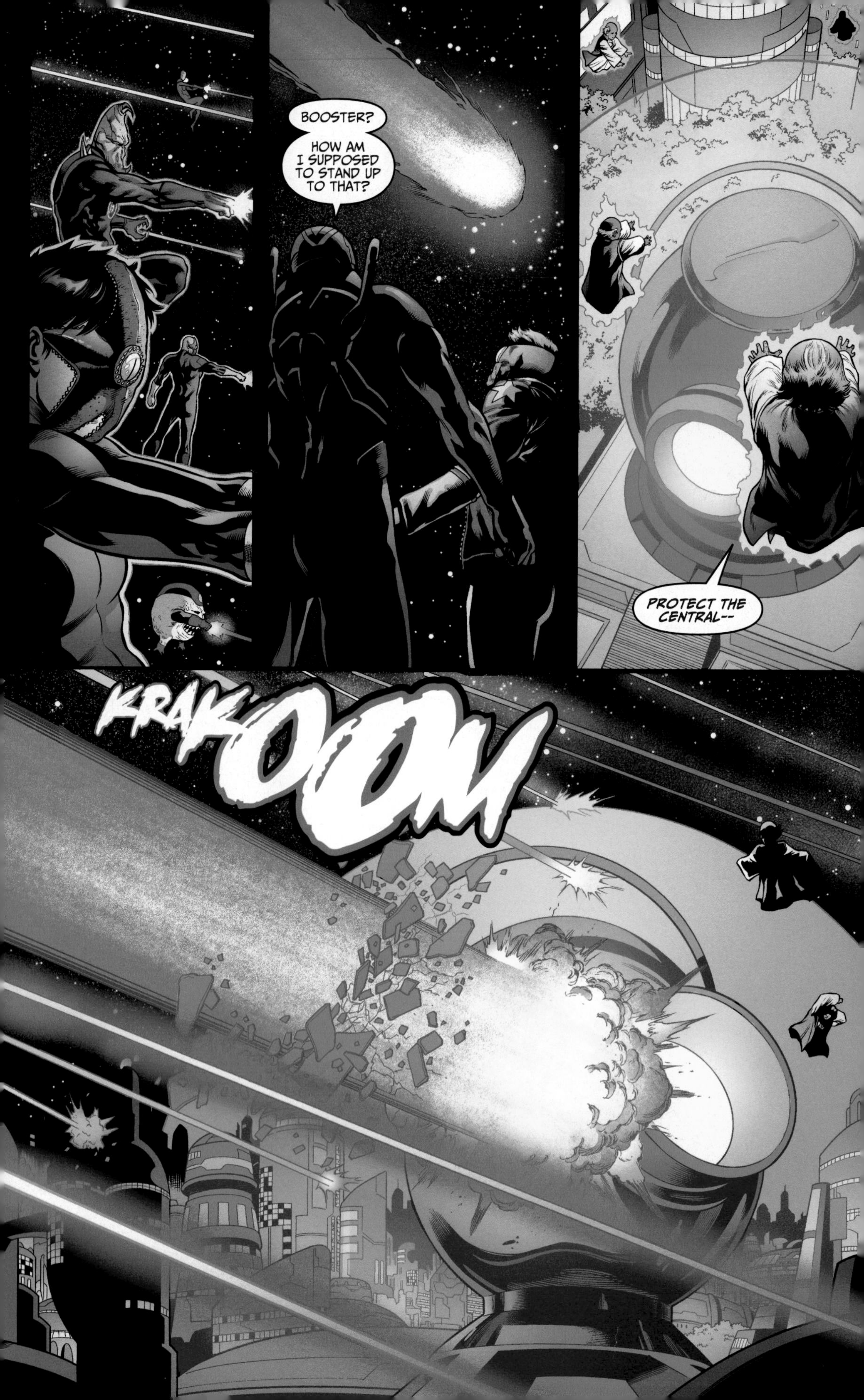
BOOSTER?
HOW AM I SUPPOSED TO STAND UP TO THAT?
PROTECT THE CENTRAL--
KRAKOOOM

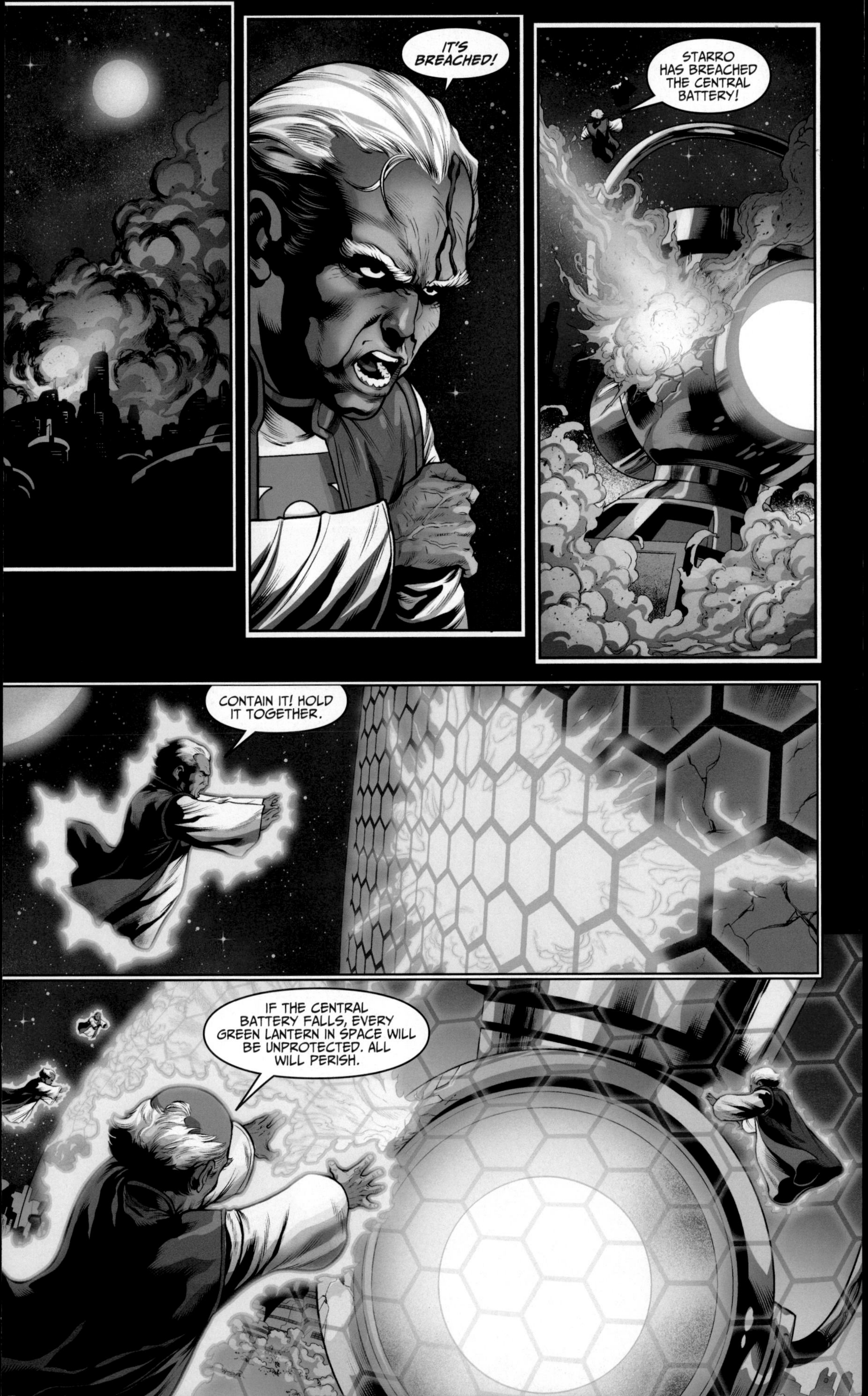
IT'S BREACHED!
STARRO HAS BREACHED THE CENTRAL BATTERY!
CONTAIN IT! HOLD IT TOGETHER.
IF THE CENTRAL BATTERY FALLS, EVERY GREEN LANTERN IN SPACE WILL BE UNPROTECTED. ALL WILL PERISH.

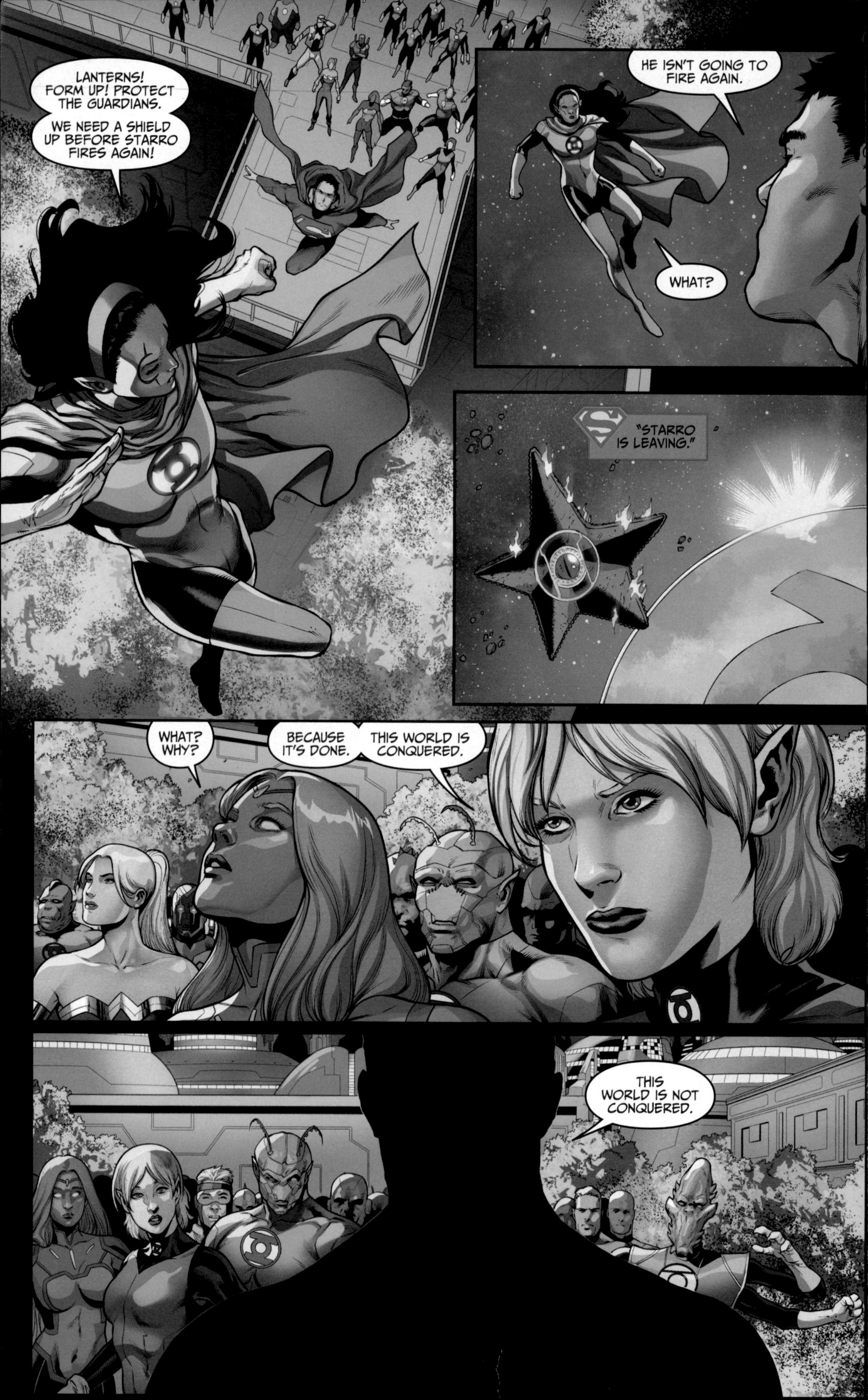
LANTERNS! FORM UP! PROTECT THE GUARDIANS.
WE NEED A SHIELD UP BEFORE STARRO FIRES AGAIN!
HE ISN'T GOING TO FIRE AGAIN.
WHAT?
"STARRO IS LEAVING."
WHAT? WHY?
BECAUSE IT'S DONE.
THIS WORLD IS CONQUERED.
THIS WORLD IS NOT CONQUERED.

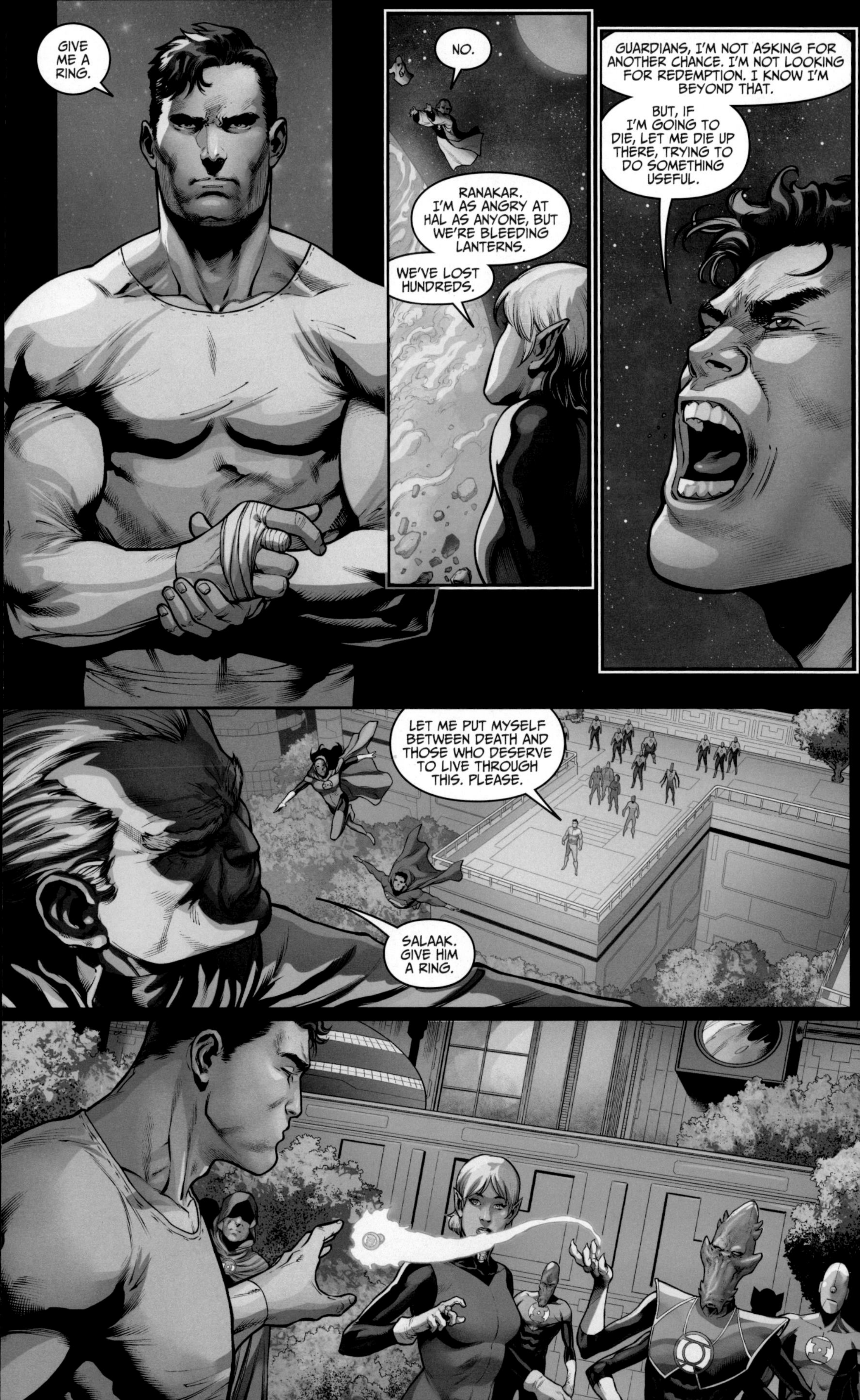
GIVE ME A RING.
NO.
RANAKAR. I'M AS ANGRY AT HAL AS ANYONE, BUT WE'RE BLEEDING LANTERNS.
WE'VE LOST HUNDREDS.
GUARDIANS, I'M NOT ASKING FOR ANOTHER CHANCE. I'M NOT LOOKING FOR REDEMPTION. I KNOW I'M BEYOND THAT.
BUT, IF I'M GOING TO DIE, LET ME DIE UP THERE, TRYING TO DO SOMETHING USEFUL.
LET ME PUT MYSELF BETWEEN DEATH AND THOSE WHO DESERVE TO LIVE THROUGH THIS. PLEASE.
SALAAK. GIVE HIM A RING.

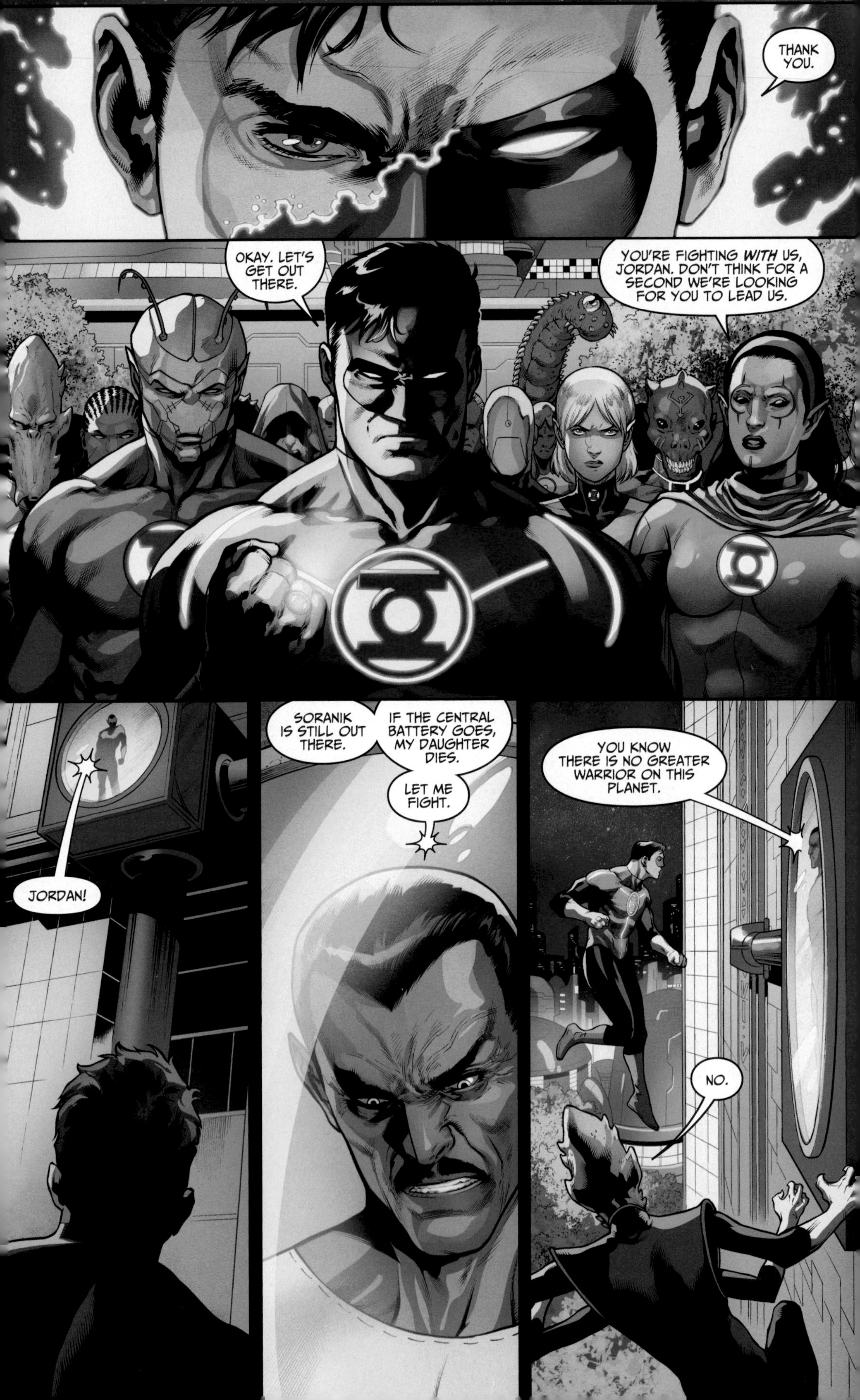
THANK YOU.
OKAY. LET'S GET OUT THERE.
YOU'RE FIGHTING *WITH* US, JORDAN. DON'T THINK FOR A SECOND WE'RE LOOKING FOR YOU TO LEAD US.
JORDAN!
SORANIK IS STILL OUT THERE.
IF THE CENTRAL BATTERY GOES, MY DAUGHTER DIES.
LET ME FIGHT.
YOU KNOW THERE IS NO GREATER WARRIOR ON THIS PLANET.
NO.

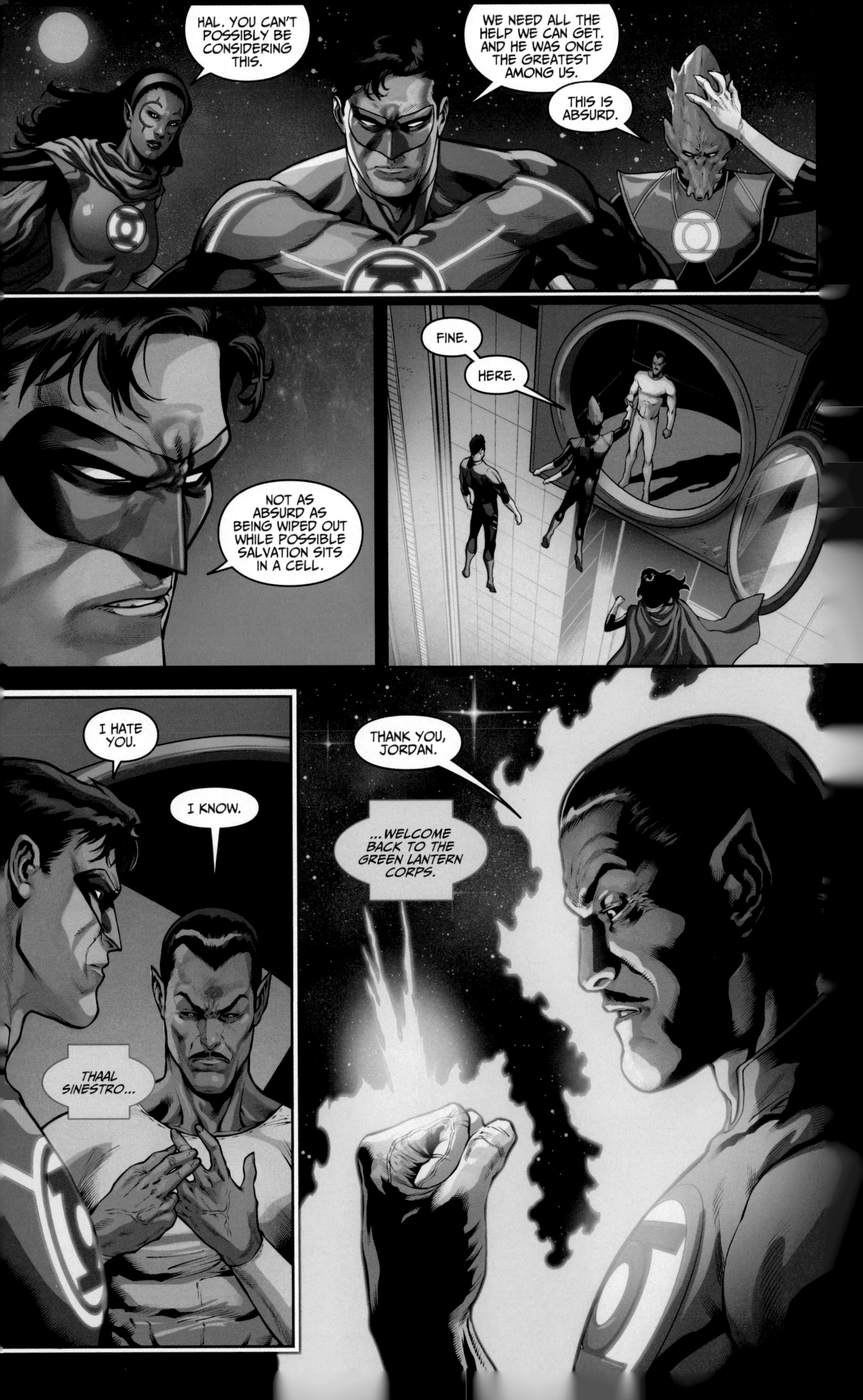
HAL. YOU CAN'T POSSIBLY BE CONSIDERING THIS.
WE NEED ALL THE HELP WE CAN GET. AND HE WAS ONCE THE GREATEST AMONG US.
THIS IS ABSURD.
NOT AS ABSURD AS BEING WIPED OUT WHILE POSSIBLE SALVATION SITS IN A CELL.
FINE.
HERE.
I HATE YOU.
I KNOW.
THAAL SINESTRO...
THANK YOU, JORDAN.
...WELCOME BACK TO THE GREEN LANTERN CORPS.

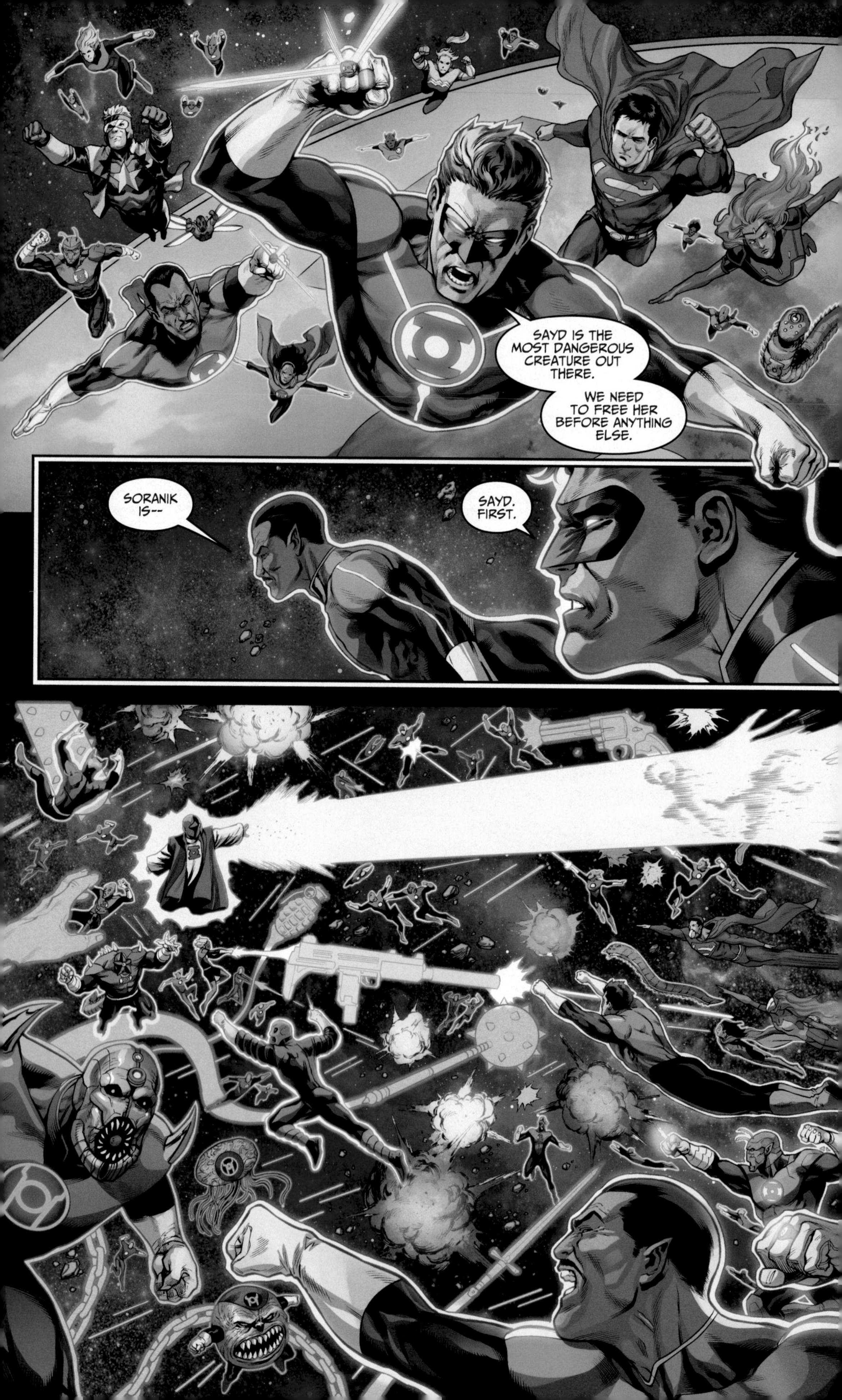
SAYD IS THE MOST DANGEROUS CREATURE OUT THERE.
WE NEED TO FREE HER BEFORE ANYTHING ELSE.
SORANIK IS--
SAYD. FIRST.

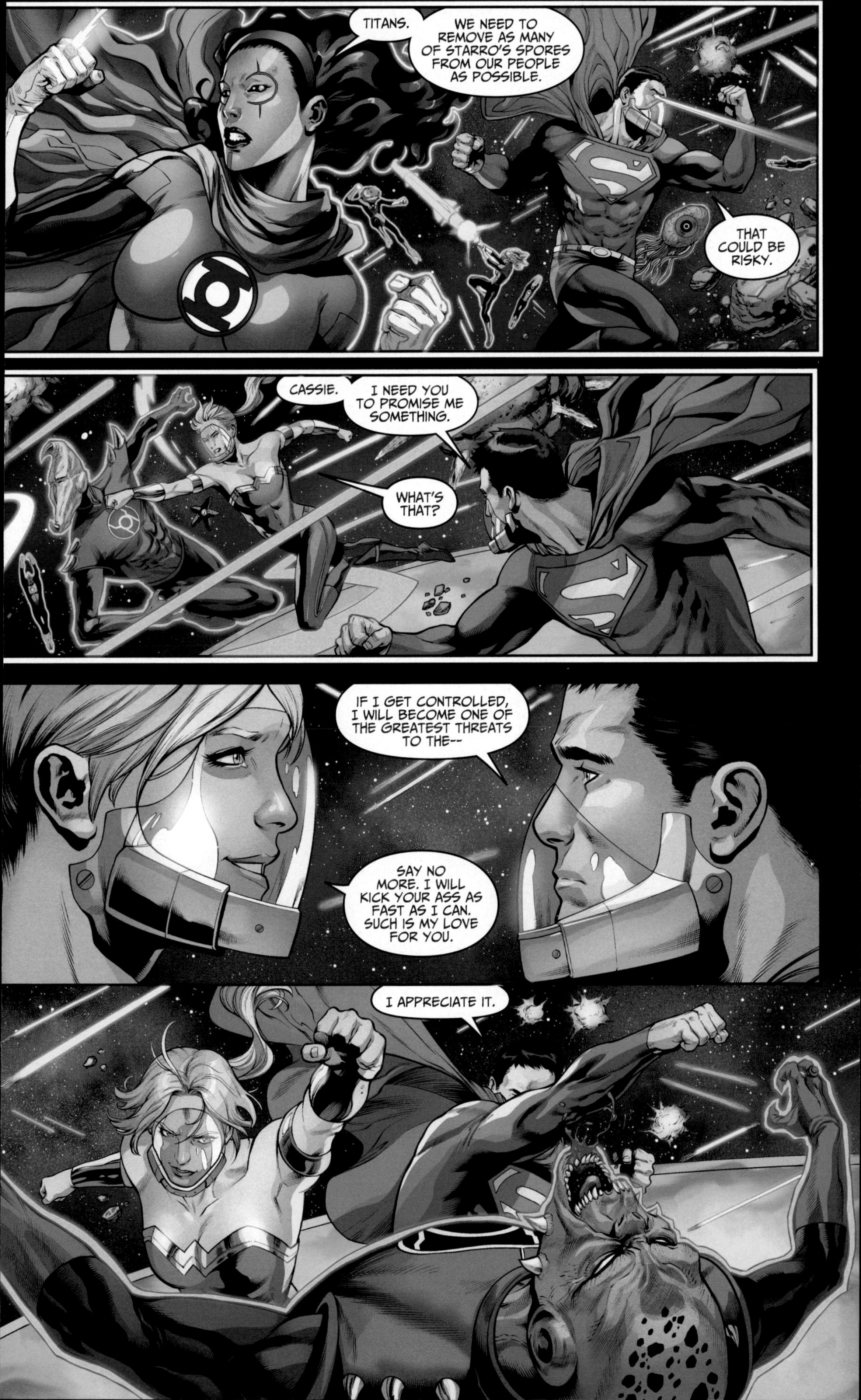
TITANS.
WE NEED TO REMOVE AS MANY OF STARRO'S SPORES FROM OUR PEOPLE AS POSSIBLE.
THAT COULD BE RISKY.
CASSIE.
I NEED YOU TO PROMISE ME SOMETHING.
WHAT'S THAT?
IF I GET CONTROLLED, I WILL BECOME ONE OF THE GREATEST THREATS TO THE--
SAY NO MORE. I WILL KICK YOUR ASS AS FAST AS I CAN. SUCH IS MY LOVE FOR YOU.
I APPRECIATE IT.

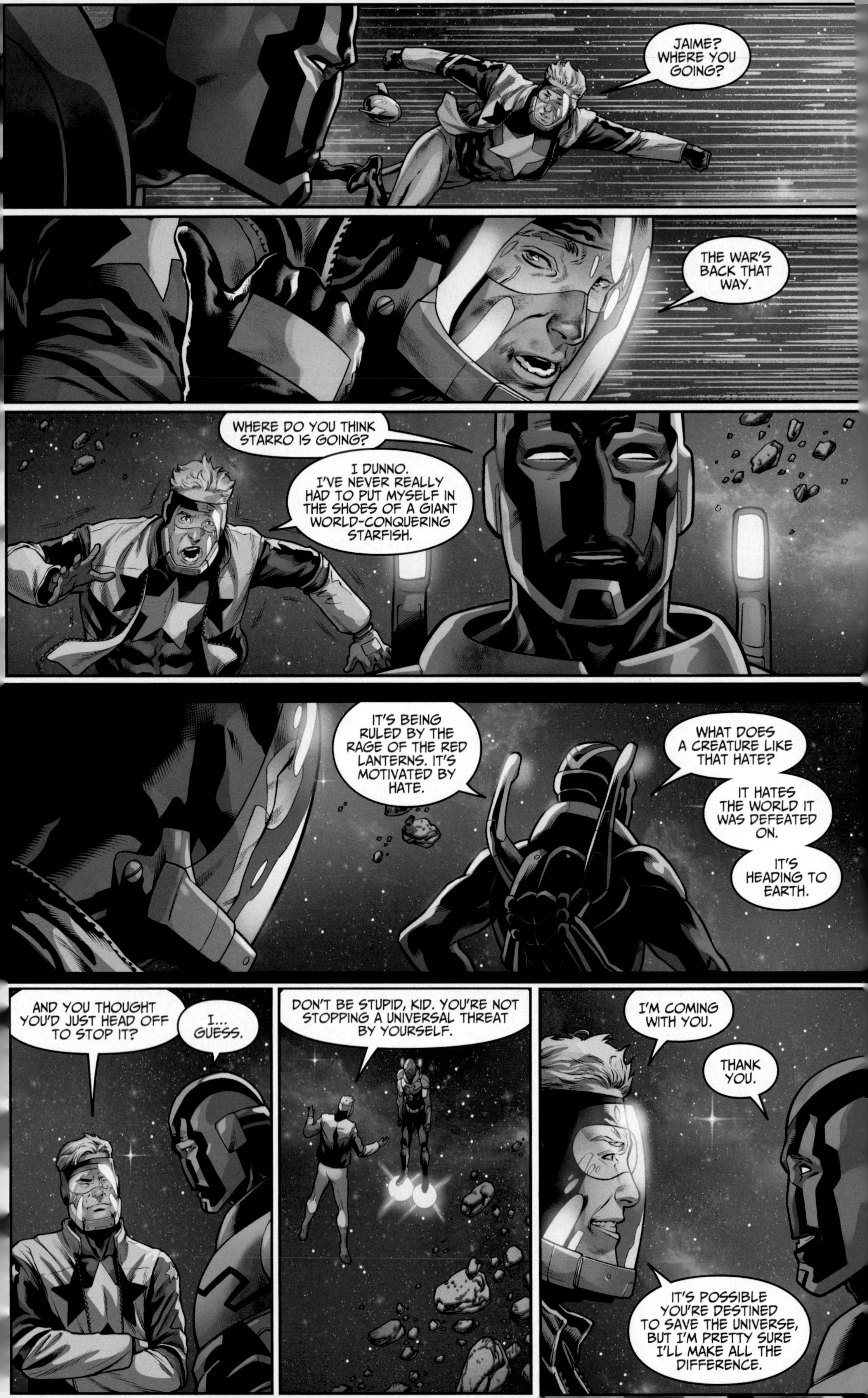
JAIME? WHERE YOU GOING?
THE WAR'S BACK THAT WAY.
WHERE DO YOU THINK STARRO IS GOING?
I DUNNO. I'VE NEVER REALLY HAD TO PUT MYSELF IN THE SHOES OF A GIANT WORLD-CONQUERING STARFISH.
IT'S BEING RULED BY THE RAGE OF THE RED LANTERNS. IT'S MOTIVATED BY HATE.
WHAT DOES A CREATURE LIKE THAT HATE?
IT HATES THE WORLD IT WAS DEFEATED ON.
IT'S HEADING TO EARTH.
AND YOU THOUGHT YOU'D JUST HEAD OFF TO STOP IT?
I... GUESS.
DON'T BE STUPID, KID. YOU'RE NOT STOPPING A UNIVERSAL THREAT BY YOURSELF.
I'M COMING WITH YOU.
THANK YOU.
IT'S POSSIBLE YOU'RE DESTINED TO SAVE THE UNIVERSE, BUT I'M PRETTY SURE I'LL MAKE ALL THE DIFFERENCE.

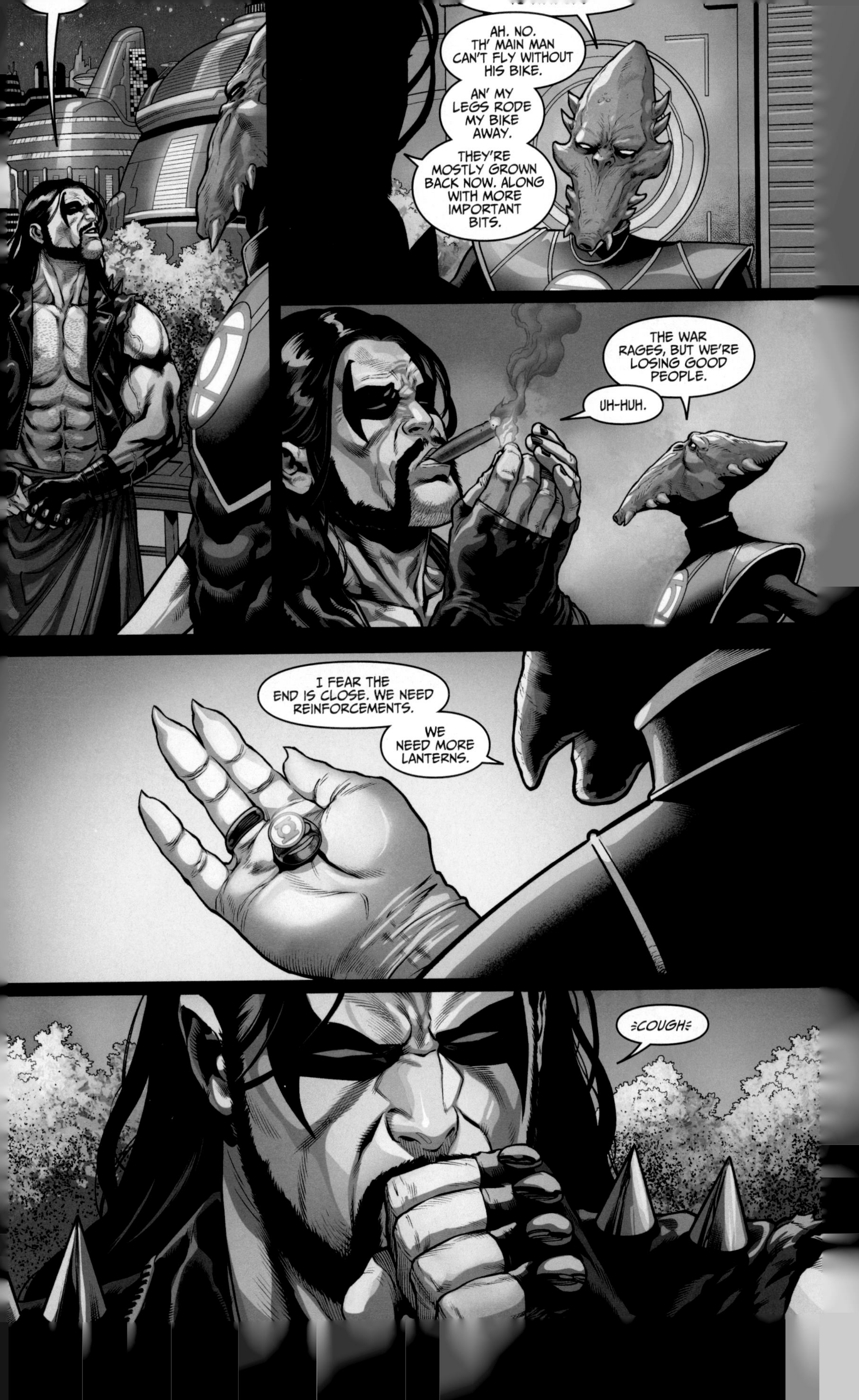
AH. NO. TH' MAIN MAN CAN'T FLY WITHOUT HIS BIKE.
AN' MY LEGS RODE MY BIKE AWAY.
THEY'RE MOSTLY GROWN BACK NOW. ALONG WITH MORE IMPORTANT BITS.
THE WAR RAGES, BUT WE'RE LOSING GOOD PEOPLE.
UH-HUH.
I FEAR THE END IS CLOSE. WE NEED REINFORCEMENTS.
WE NEED MORE LANTERNS.
COUGH

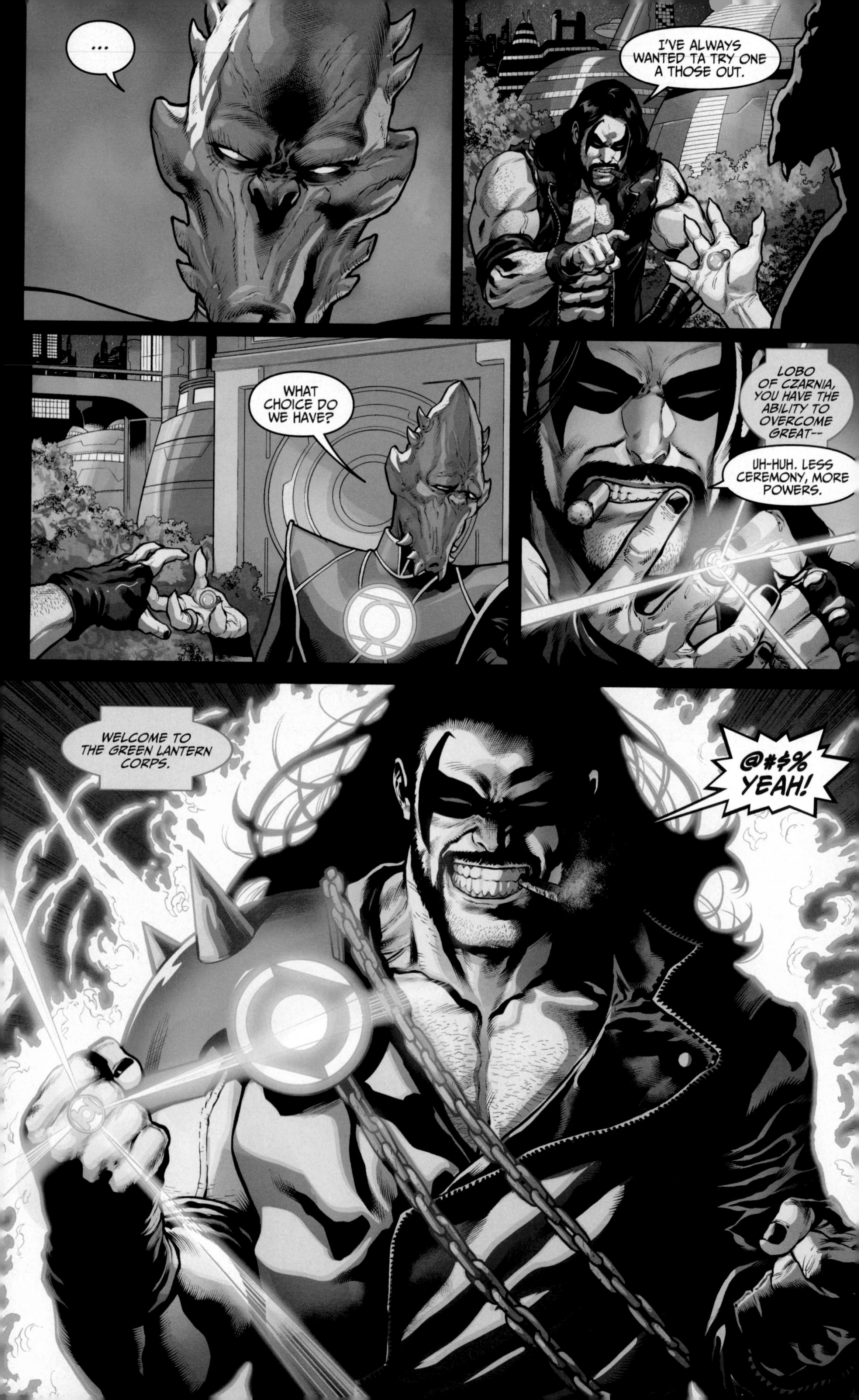
...
I'VE ALWAYS WANTED TA TRY ONE A THOSE OUT.
WHAT CHOICE DO WE HAVE?
LOBO OF CZARNIA, YOU HAVE THE ABILITY TO OVERCOME GREAT--
UH-HUH. LESS CEREMONY, MORE POWERS.
WELCOME TO THE GREEN LANTERN CORPS.
@#$% YEAH!

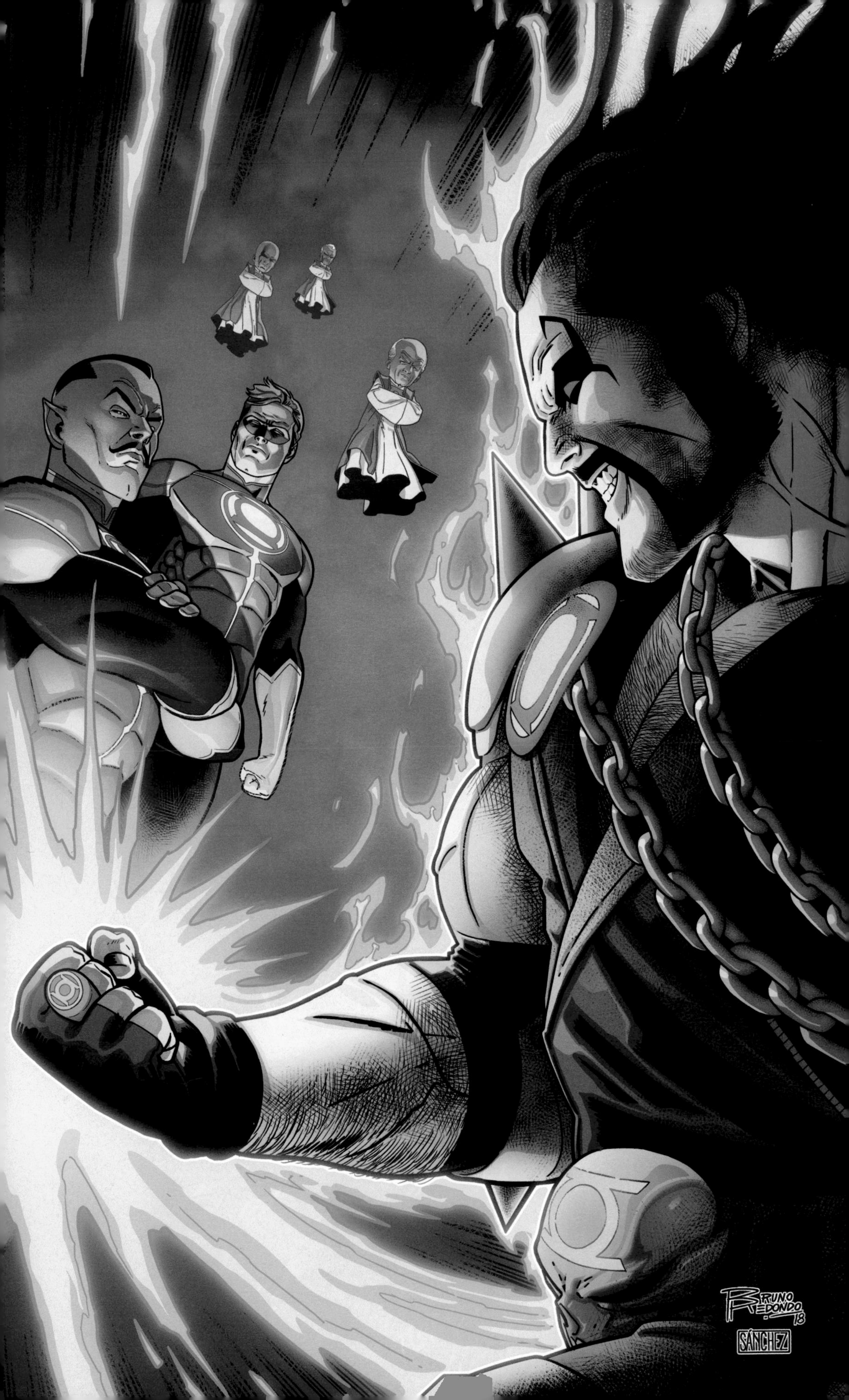
BRUNO REDONDO '18
SÁNCHEZ

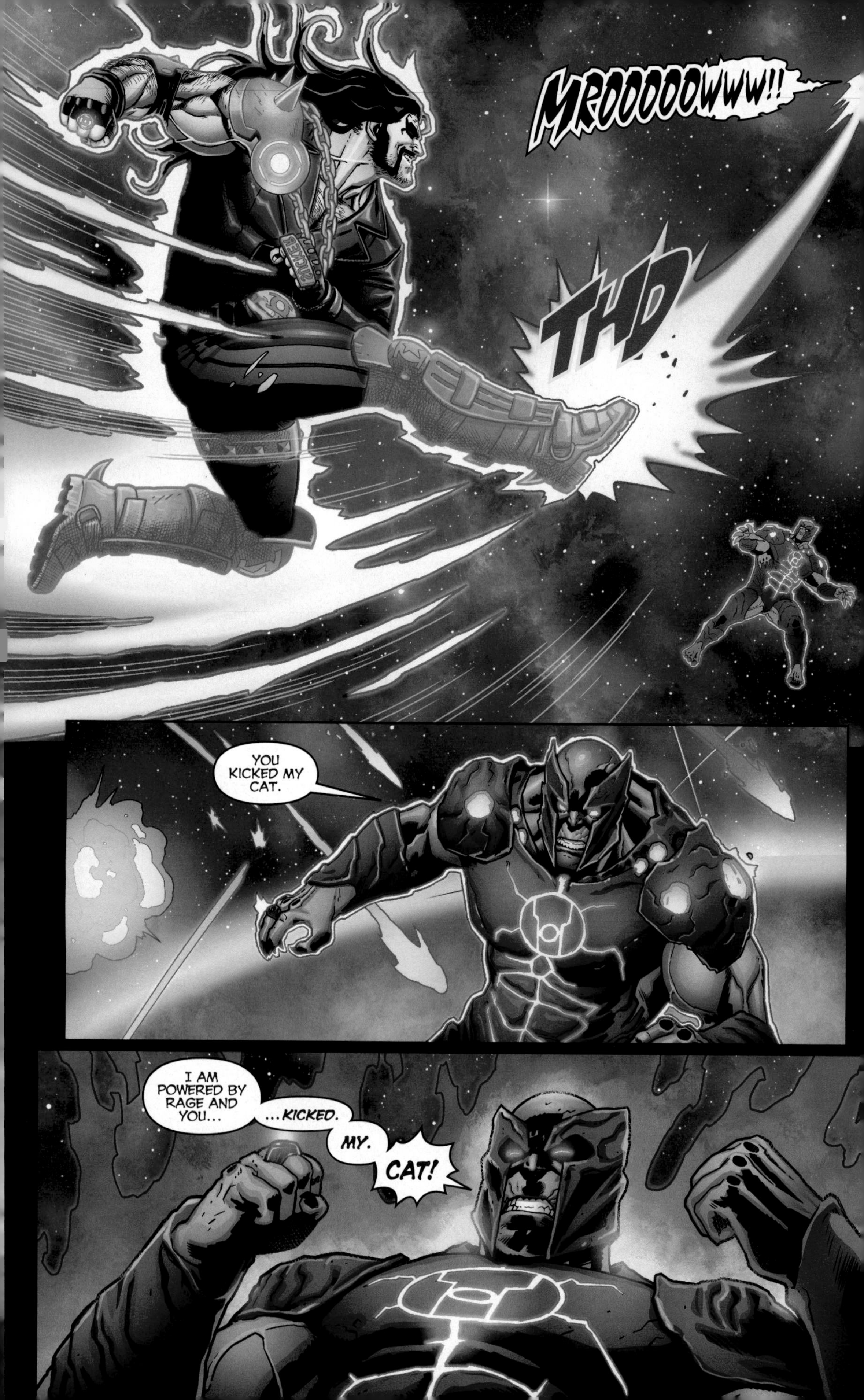
MROOOOOOWWW!!
THD
YOU KICKED MY CAT.
I AM POWERED BY RAGE AND YOU...
...KICKED.
MY.
CAT!

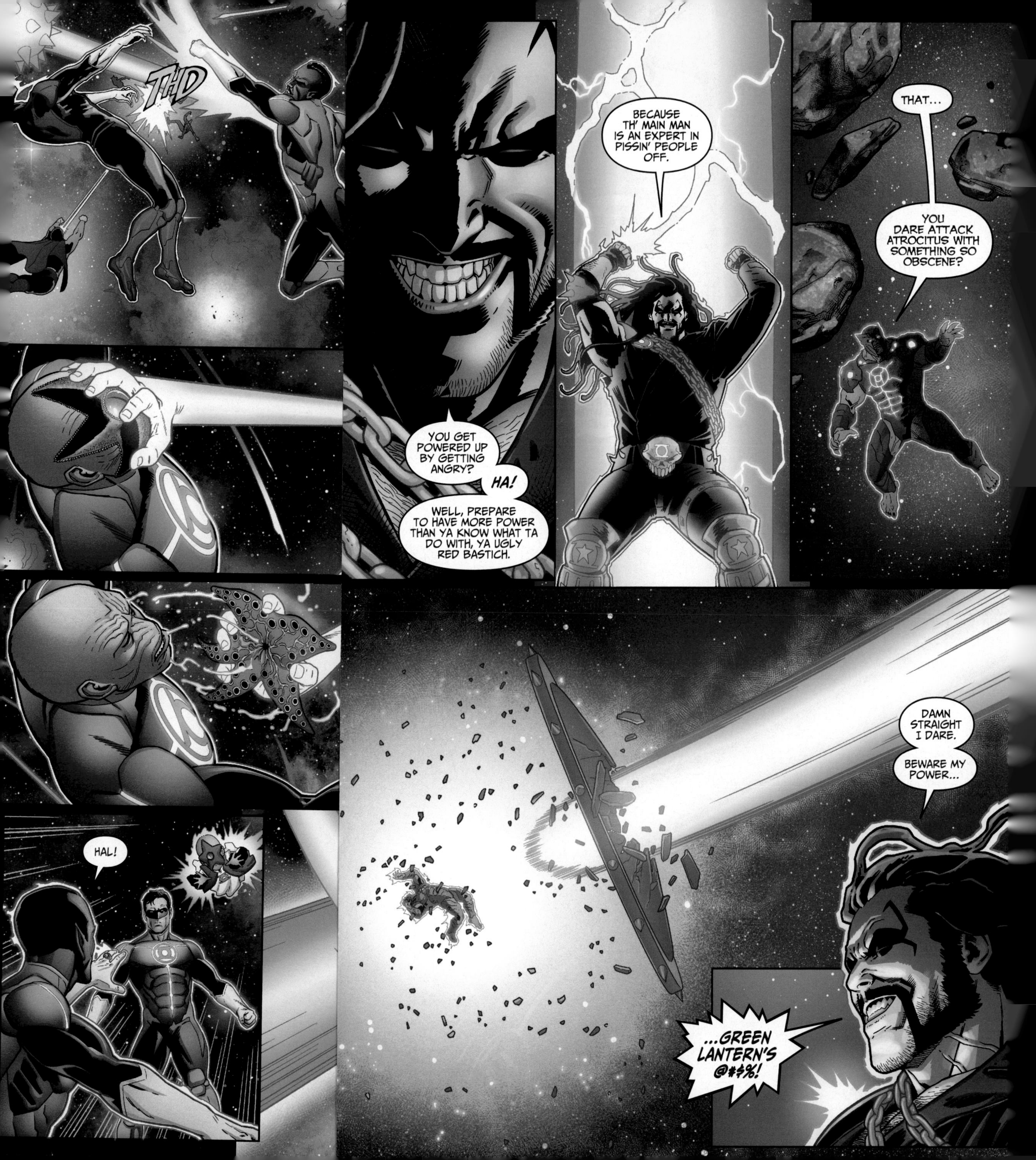
THD
YOU GET POWERED UP BY GETTING ANGRY?
HA!
WELL, PREPARE TO HAVE MORE POWER THAN YA KNOW WHAT TA DO WITH, YA UGLY RED BASTICH.
BECAUSE TH' MAIN MAN IS AN EXPERT IN PISSIN' PEOPLE OFF.
THAT...
YOU DARE ATTACK ATROCITUS WITH SOMETHING SO OBSCENE?
HAL!
DAMN STRAIGHT I DARE.
BEWARE MY POWER...
...GREEN LANTERN'S @#$%!

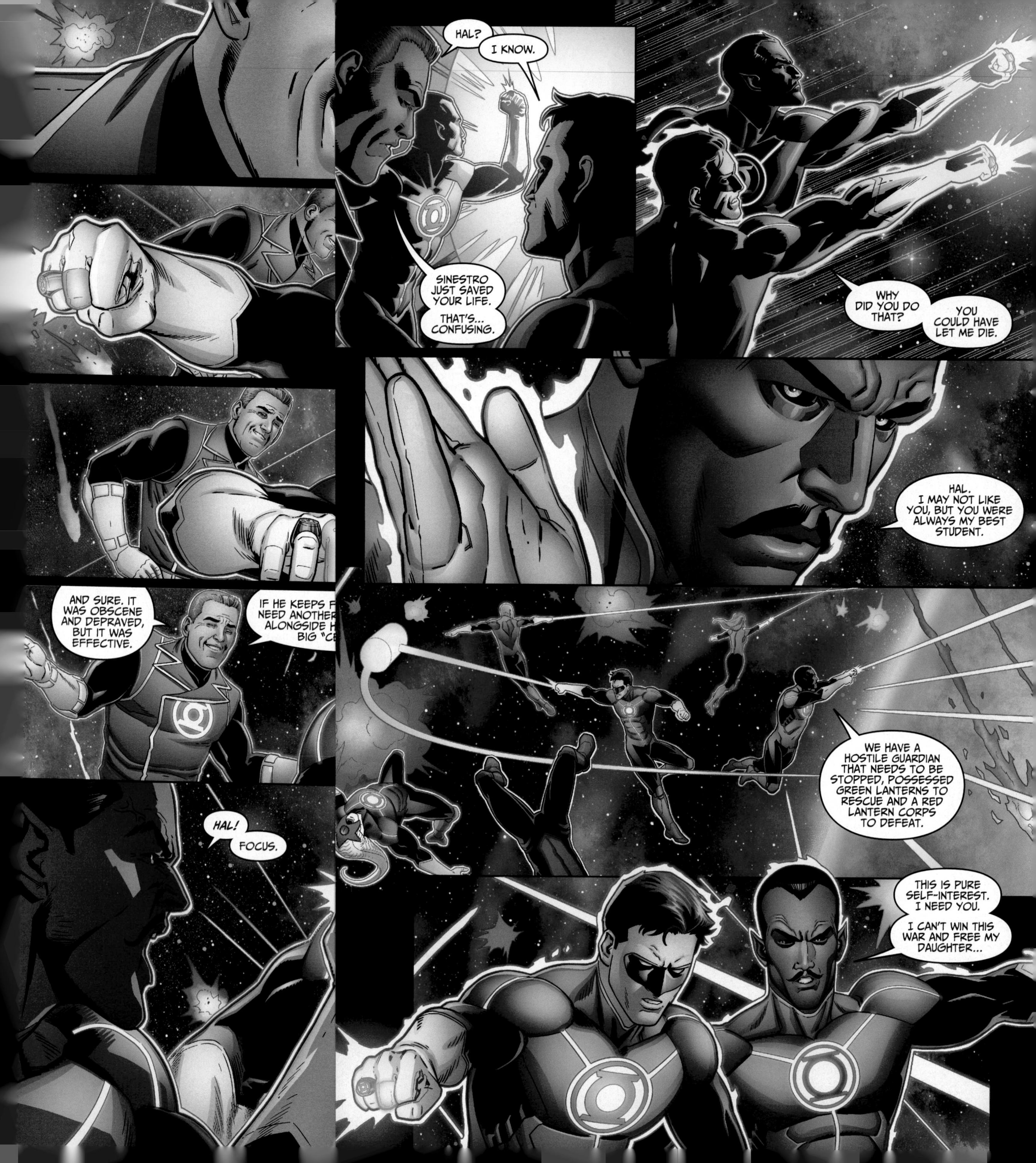
HAL?
I KNOW.
SINESTRO JUST SAVED YOUR LIFE.
THAT'S... CONFUSING.
WHY DID YOU DO THAT?
YOU COULD HAVE LET ME DIE.
HAL. I MAY NOT LIKE YOU, BUT YOU WERE ALWAYS MY BEST STUDENT.
WE HAVE A HOSTILE GUARDIAN THAT NEEDS TO BE STOPPED, POSSESSED GREEN LANTERNS TO RESCUE AND A RED LANTERN CORPS TO DEFEAT.
THIS IS PURE SELF-INTEREST. I NEED YOU.
I CAN'T WIN THIS WAR AND FREE MY DAUGHTER...
AND SURE. IT WAS OBSCENE AND DEPRAVED, BUT IT WAS EFFECTIVE.
HAL!
FOCUS.

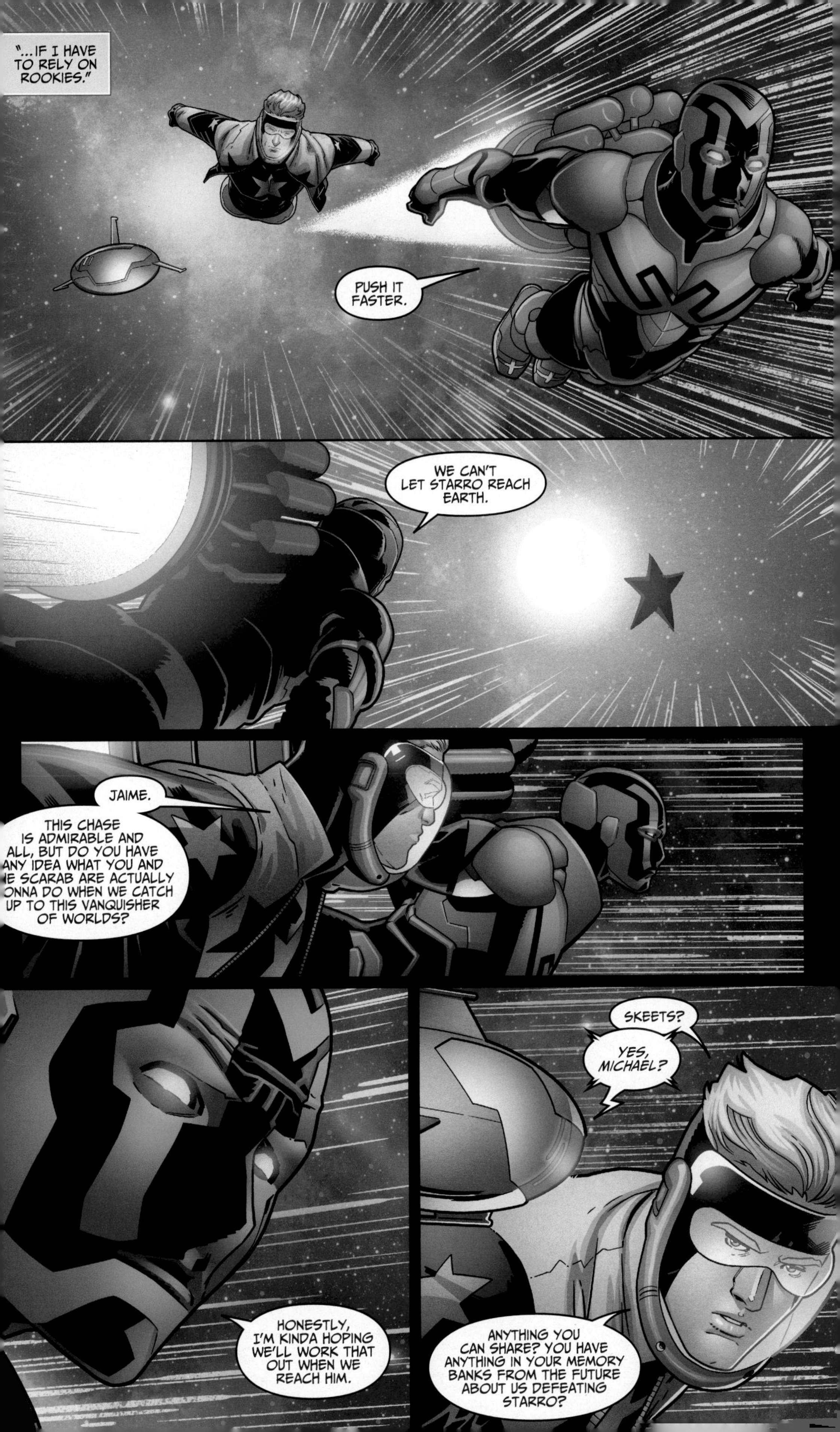
"...IF I HAVE TO RELY ON ROOKIES."
PUSH IT FASTER.
WE CAN'T LET STARRO REACH EARTH.
JAIME.
THIS CHASE IS ADMIRABLE AND ALL, BUT DO YOU HAVE ANY IDEA WHAT YOU AND E SCARAB ARE ACTUALLY ONNA DO WHEN WE CATCH UP TO THIS VANQUISHER OF WORLDS?
HONESTLY, I'M KINDA HOPING WE'LL WORK THAT OUT WHEN WE REACH HIM.
SKEETS?
YES, MICHAEL?
ANYTHING YOU CAN SHARE? YOU HAVE ANYTHING IN YOUR MEMORY BANKS FROM THE FUTURE ABOUT US DEFEATING STARRO?

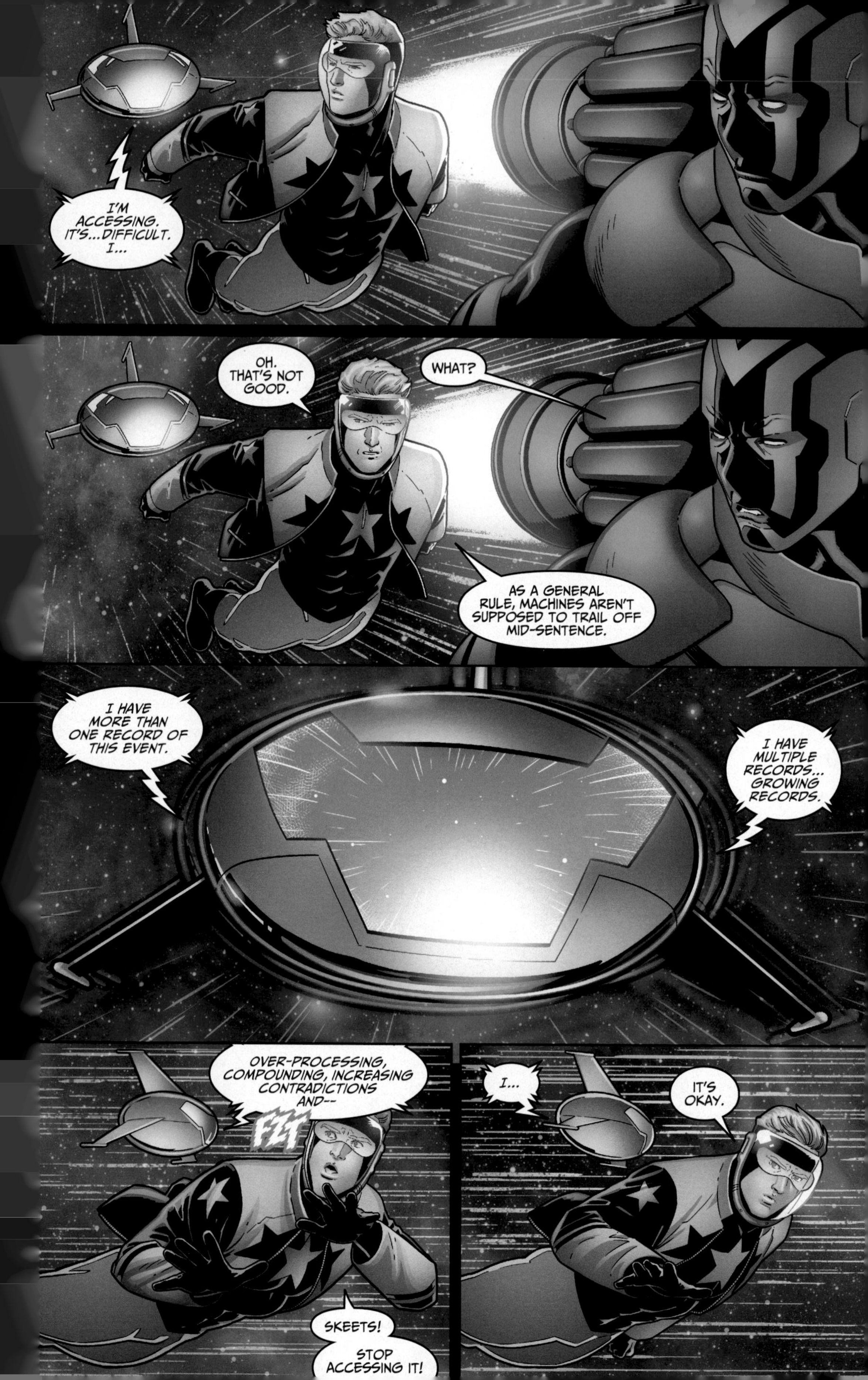
I'M ACCESSING. IT'S...DIFFICULT. I...
OH. THAT'S NOT GOOD.
WHAT?
AS A GENERAL RULE, MACHINES AREN'T SUPPOSED TO TRAIL OFF MID-SENTENCE.
I HAVE MORE THAN ONE RECORD OF THIS EVENT.
I HAVE MULTIPLE RECORDS... GROWING RECORDS.
OVER-PROCESSING, COMPOUNDING, INCREASING CONTRADICTIONS AND--
FZT
SKEETS!
STOP ACCESSING IT!
I...
IT'S OKAY.

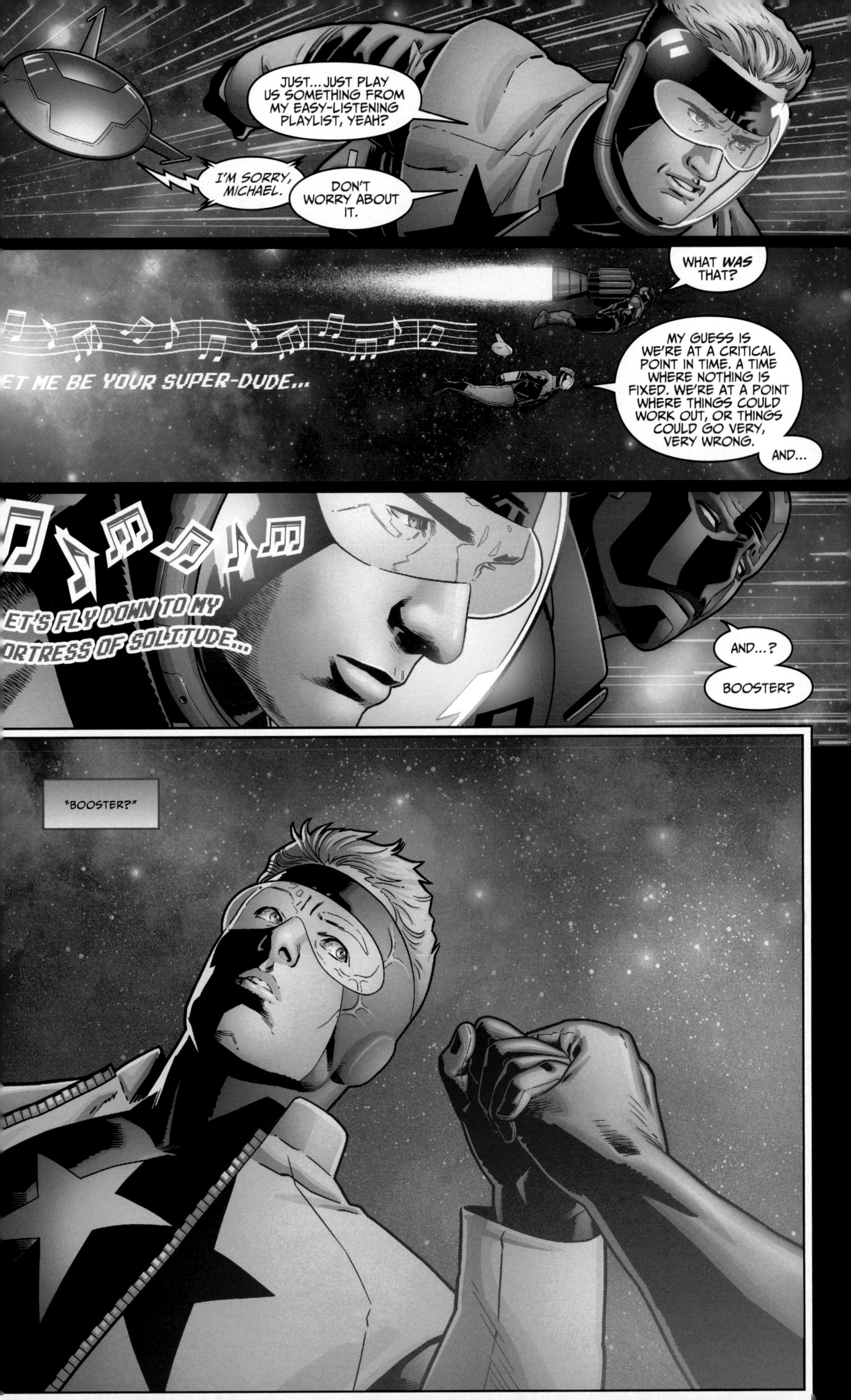

JUST... JUST PLAY US SOMETHING FROM MY EASY-LISTENING PLAYLIST, YEAH?
I'M SORRY, MICHAEL.
DON'T WORRY ABOUT IT.
WHAT *WAS* THAT?
ET ME BE YOUR SUPER-DUDE...
MY GUESS IS WE'RE AT A CRITICAL POINT IN TIME. A TIME WHERE NOTHING IS FIXED. WE'RE AT A POINT WHERE THINGS COULD WORK OUT, OR THINGS COULD GO VERY, VERY WRONG.
AND...
ET'S FLY DOWN TO MY
ORTRESS OF SOLITUDE...
AND...?
BOOSTER?
"BOOSTER?"

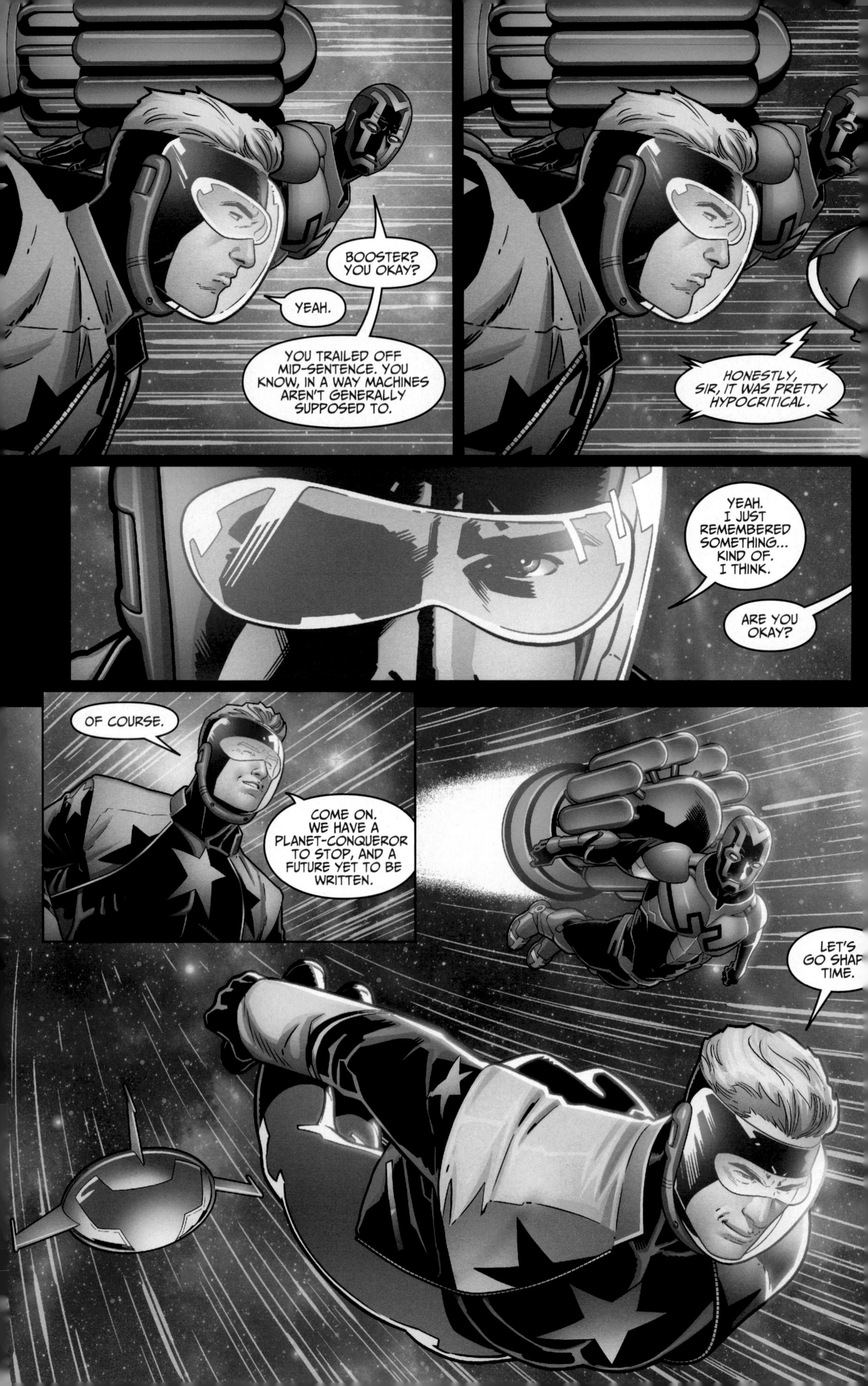
BOOSTER? YOU OKAY?
YEAH.
YOU TRAILED OFF MID-SENTENCE. YOU KNOW, IN A WAY MACHINES AREN'T GENERALLY SUPPOSED TO.
HONESTLY, SIR, IT WAS PRETTY HYPOCRITICAL.
YEAH. I JUST REMEMBERED SOMETHING... KIND OF. I THINK.
ARE YOU OKAY?
OF COURSE.
COME ON. WE HAVE A PLANET-CONQUEROR TO STOP, AND A FUTURE YET TO BE WRITTEN.
LET'S GO SHAP TIME.

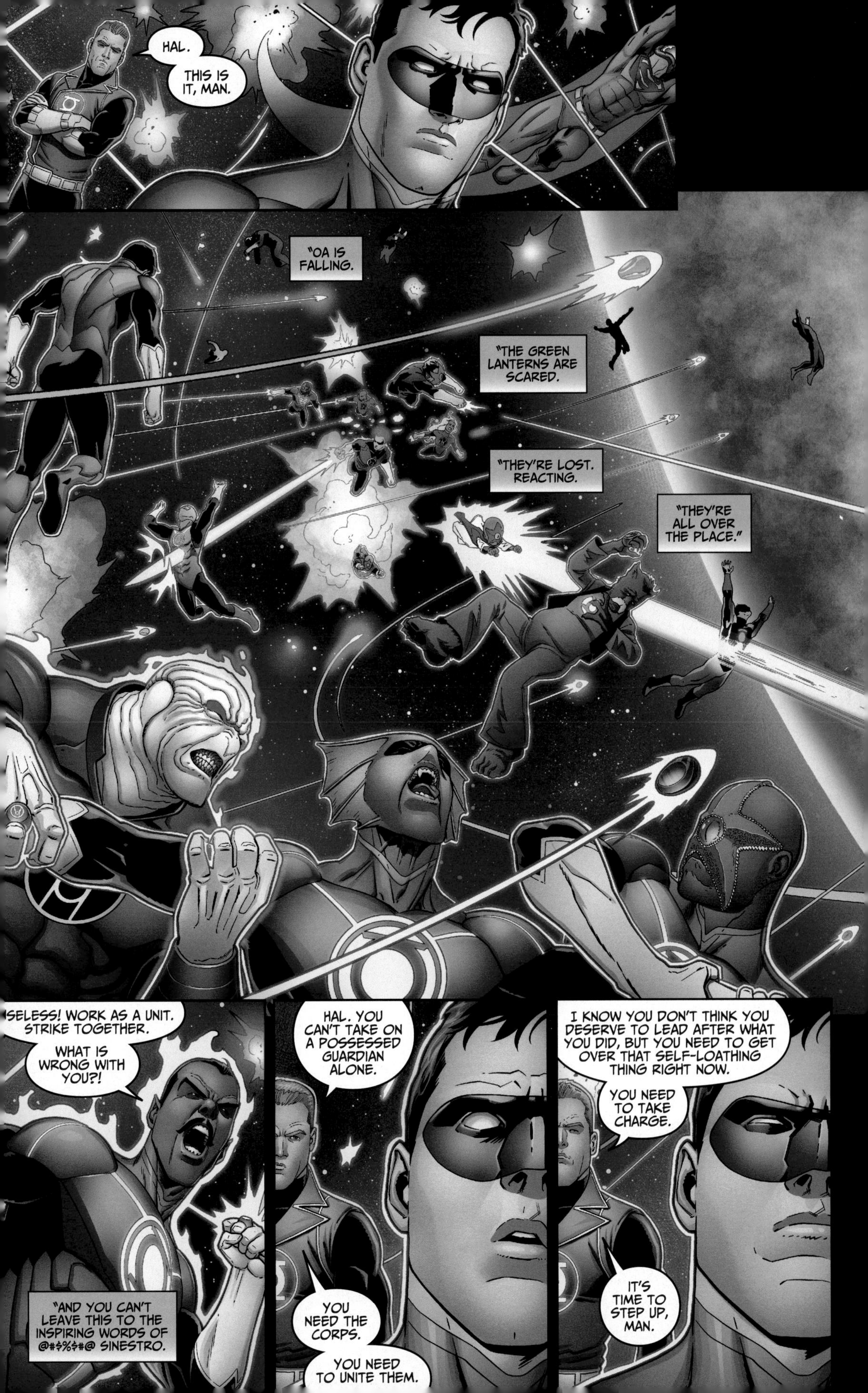
HAL.
THIS IS IT, MAN.
"OA IS FALLING.
"THE GREEN LANTERNS ARE SCARED.
"THEY'RE LOST. REACTING.
"THEY'RE ALL OVER THE PLACE."
SELESS! WORK AS A UNIT. STRIKE TOGETHER.
WHAT IS WRONG WITH YOU?!
"AND YOU CAN'T LEAVE THIS TO THE INSPIRING WORDS OF @#$%$#@ SINESTRO.
HAL. YOU CAN'T TAKE ON A POSSESSED GUARDIAN ALONE.
YOU NEED THE CORPS.
YOU NEED TO UNITE THEM.
I KNOW YOU DON'T THINK YOU DESERVE TO LEAD AFTER WHAT YOU DID, BUT YOU NEED TO GET OVER THAT SELF-LOATHING THING RIGHT NOW.
YOU NEED TO TAKE CHARGE.
IT'S TIME TO STEP UP, MAN.

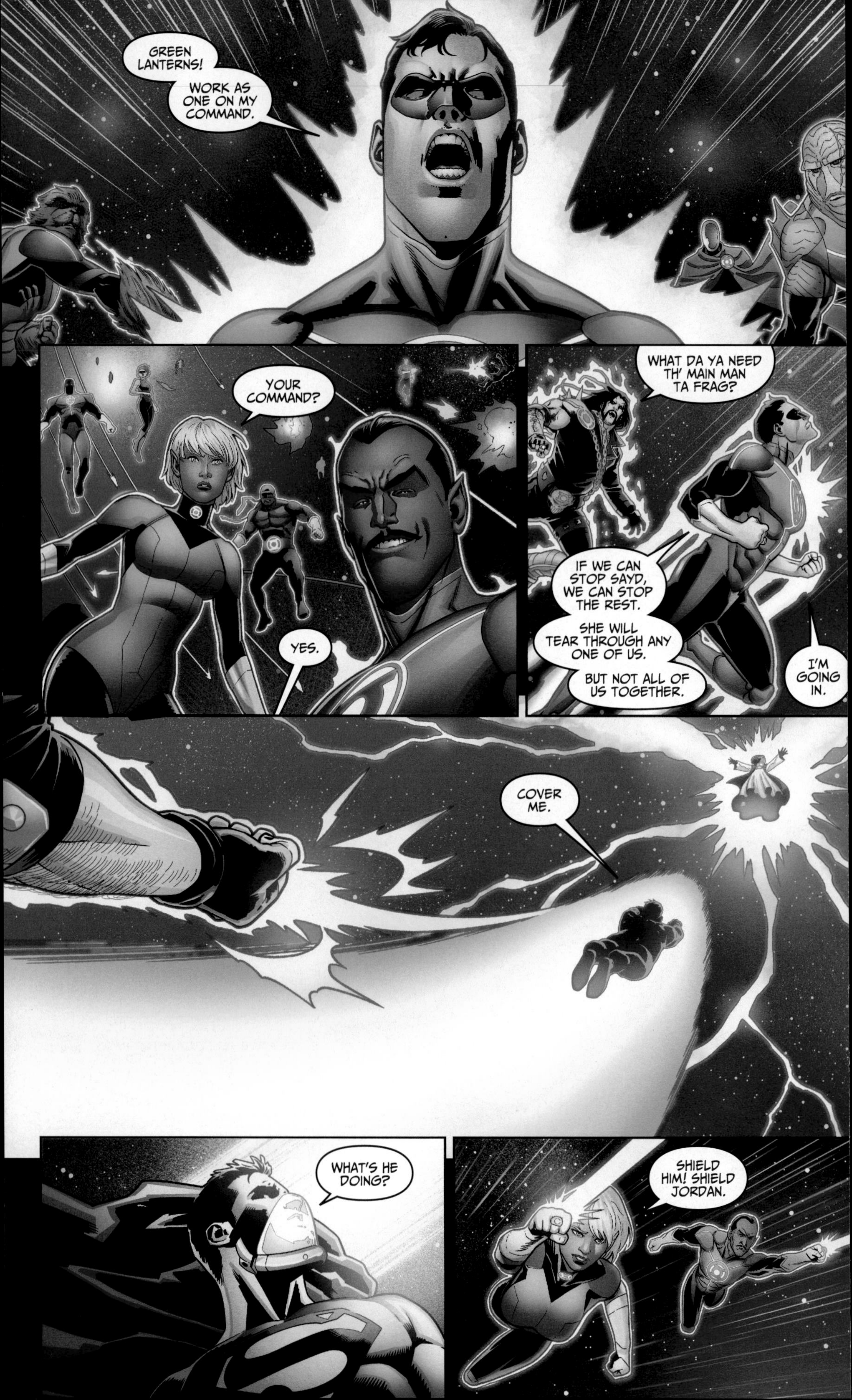
GREEN LANTERNS!
WORK AS ONE ON MY COMMAND.
YOUR COMMAND?
YES.
WHAT DA YA NEED TH' MAIN MAN TA FRAG?
IF WE CAN STOP SAYD, WE CAN STOP THE REST.
SHE WILL TEAR THROUGH ANY ONE OF US.
BUT NOT ALL OF US TOGETHER.
I'M GOING IN.
COVER ME.
WHAT'S HE DOING?
SHIELD HIM! SHIELD JORDAN.

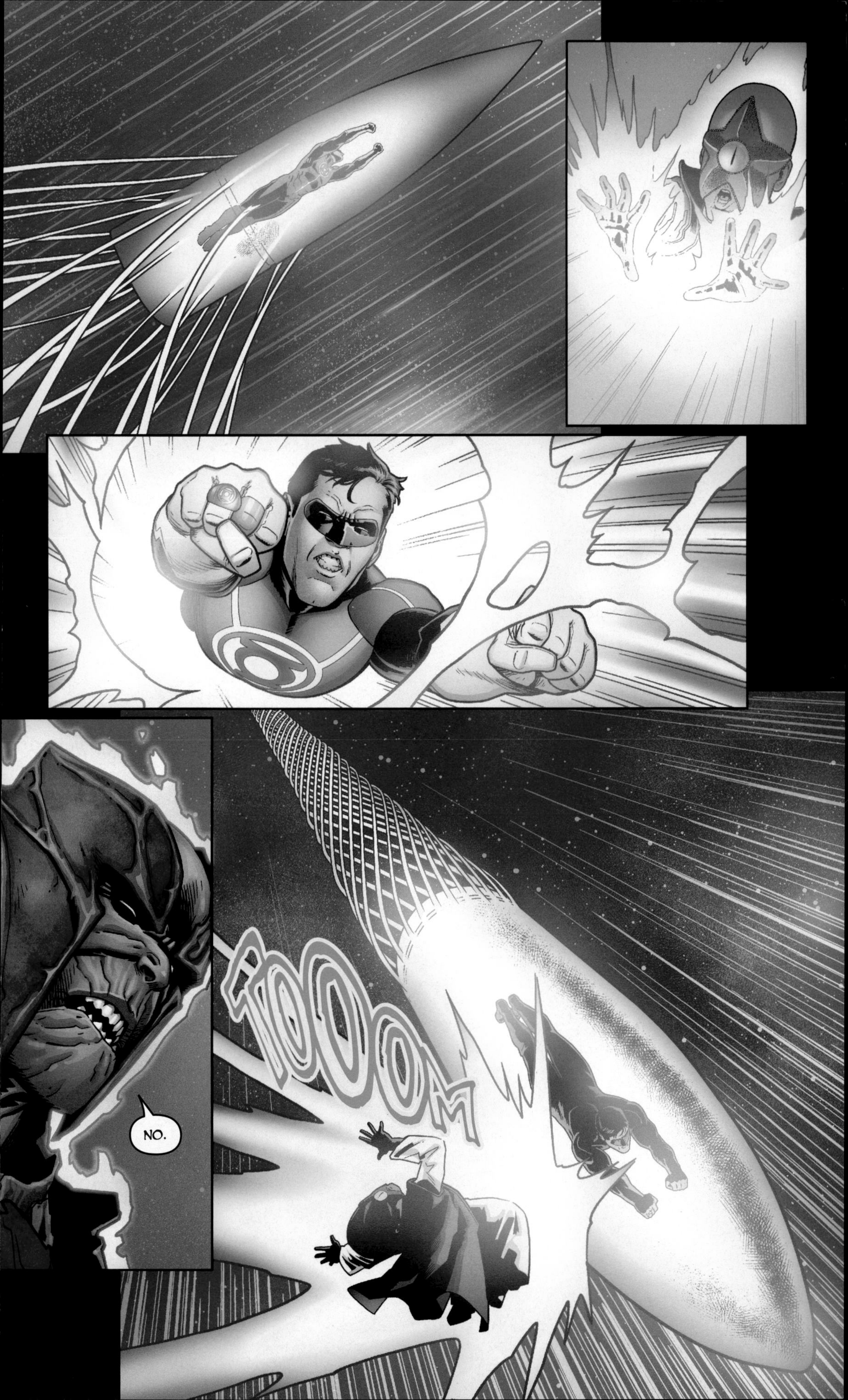
FOOOOM
NO.

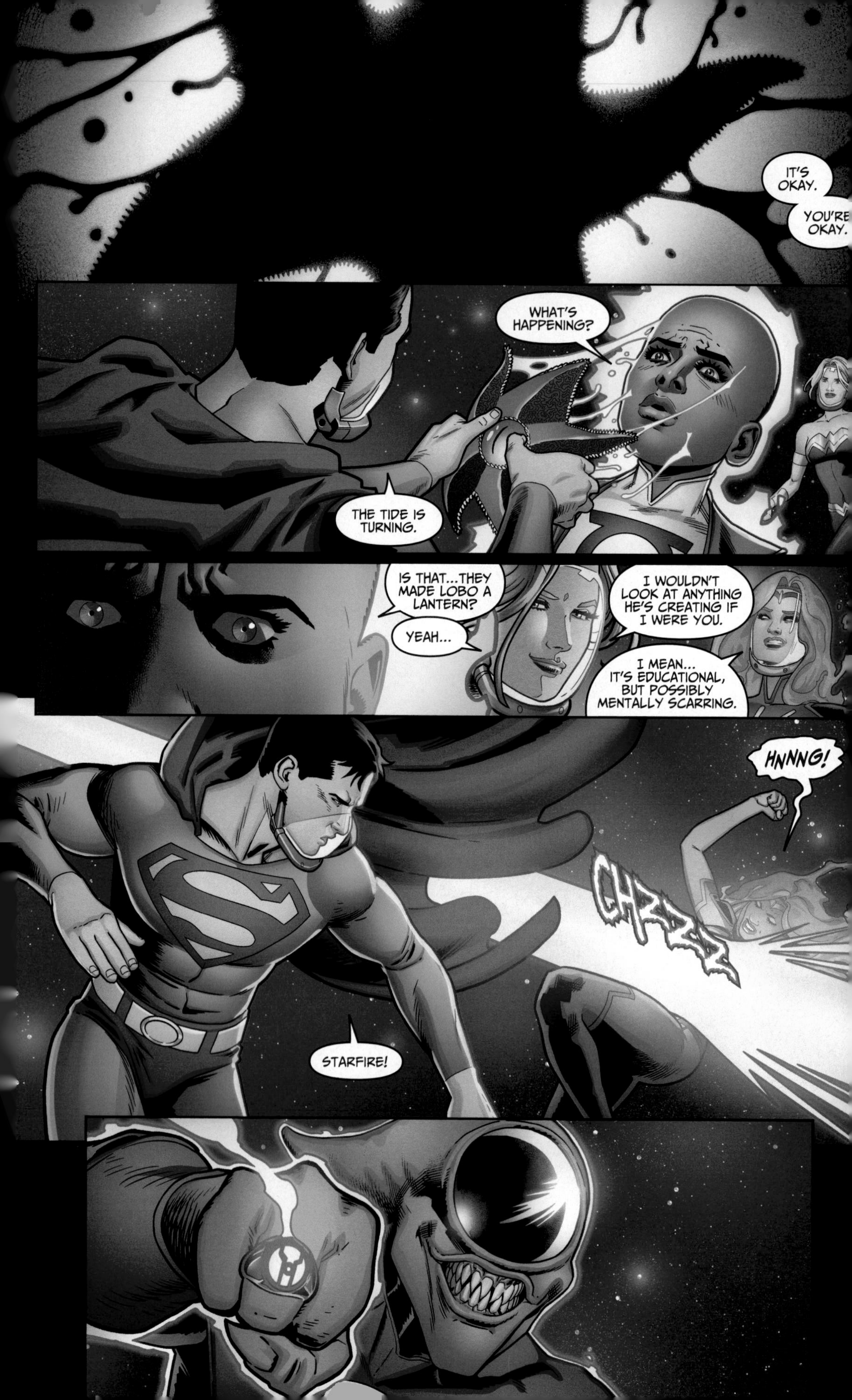
IT'S OKAY.
YOU'RE OKAY.
WHAT'S HAPPENING?
THE TIDE IS TURNING.
IS THAT...THEY MADE LOBO A LANTERN?
YEAH...
I WOULDN'T LOOK AT ANYTHING HE'S CREATING IF I WERE YOU.
I MEAN... IT'S EDUCATIONAL, BUT POSSIBLY MENTALLY SCARRING.
HNNNG!
CHZZZ
STARFIRE!

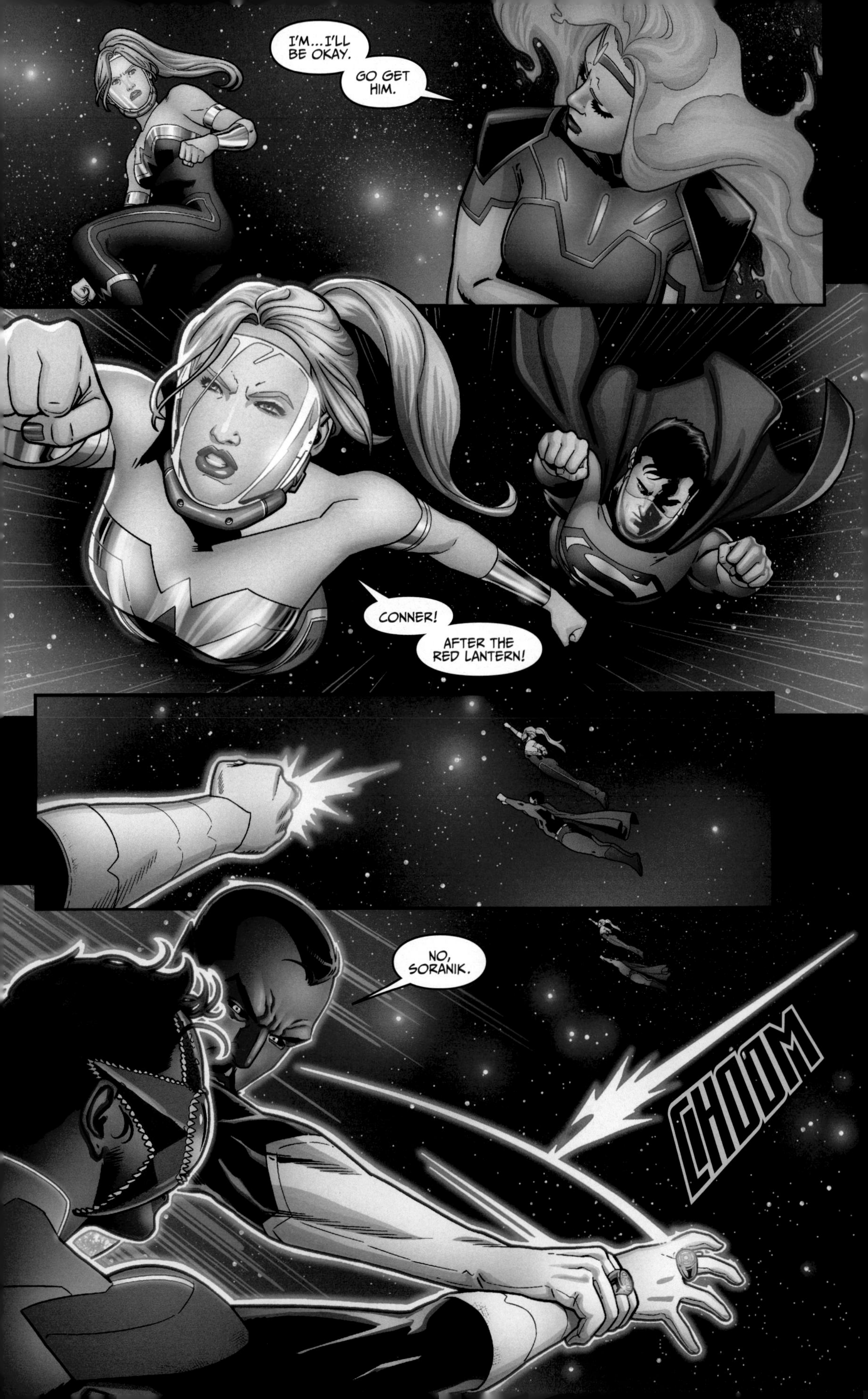
I'M...I'LL BE OKAY.
GO GET HIM.
CONNER!
AFTER THE RED LANTERN!
NO, SORANIK.
CHOOM

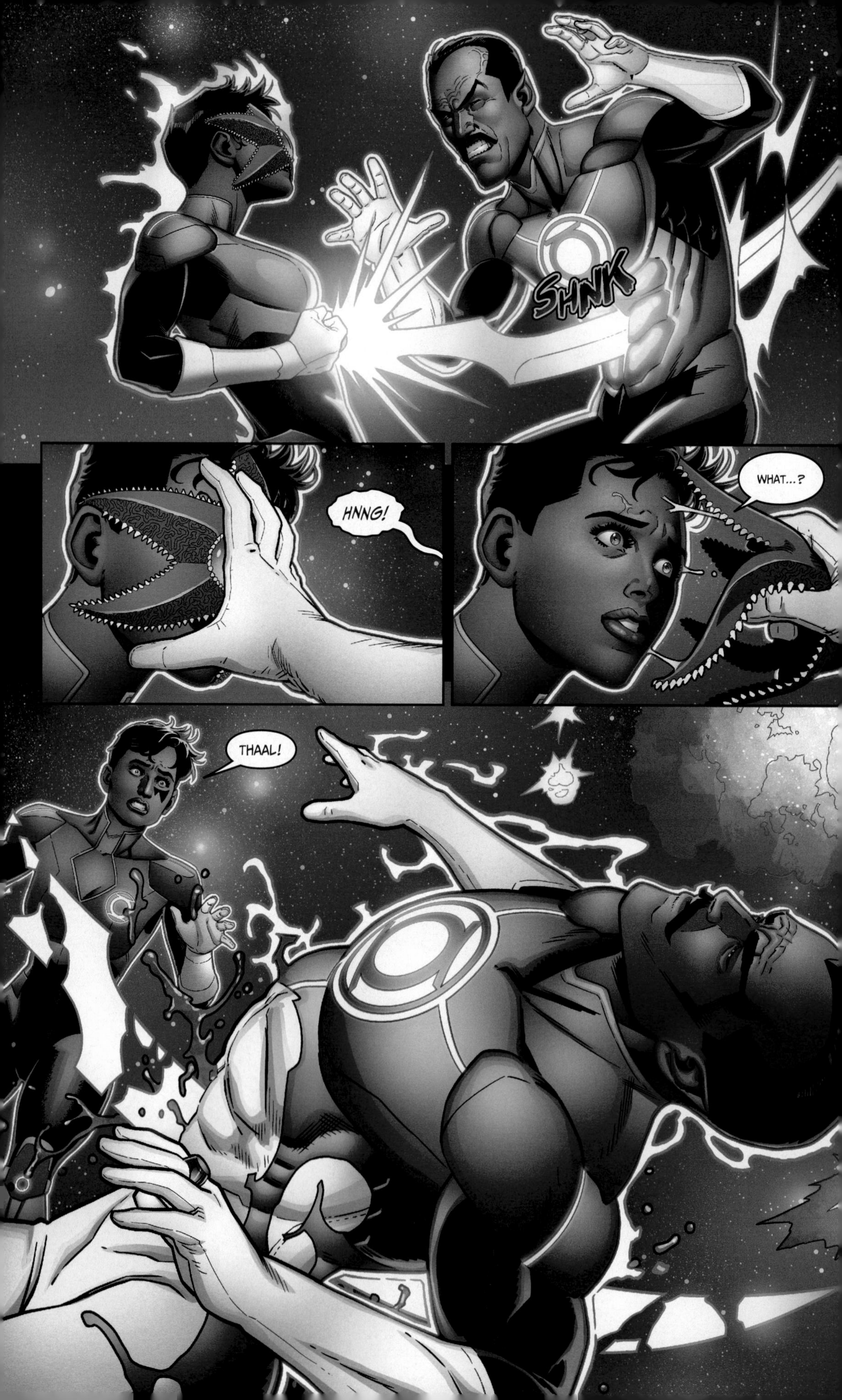
SHNK
HNNG!
WHAT...?
THAAL!

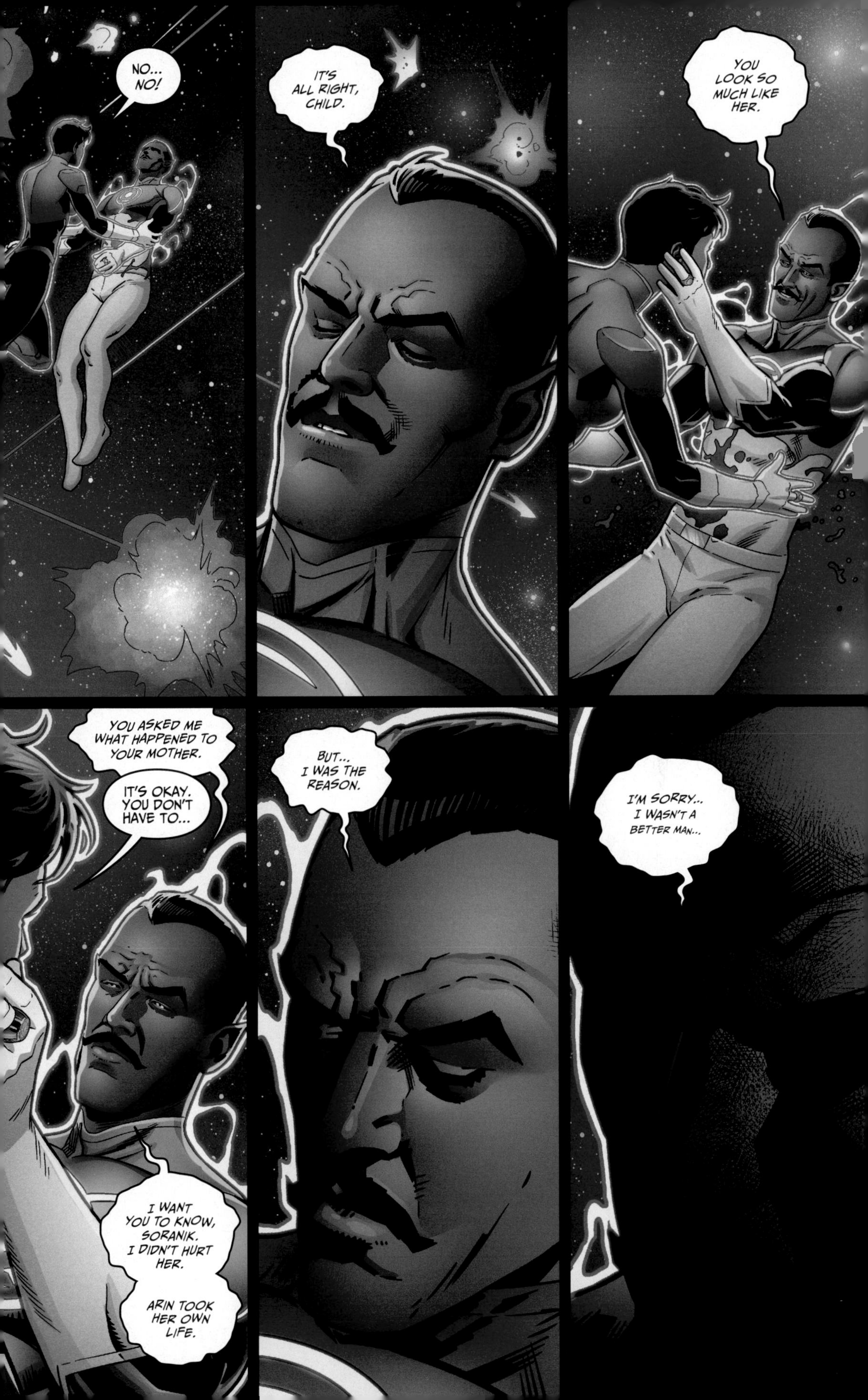
NO... NO!
IT'S ALL RIGHT, CHILD.
YOU LOOK SO MUCH LIKE HER.
YOU ASKED ME WHAT HAPPENED TO YOUR MOTHER.
IT'S OKAY. YOU DON'T HAVE TO...
I WANT YOU TO KNOW, SORANIK. I DIDN'T HURT HER.
ARIN TOOK HER OWN LIFE.
BUT... I WAS THE REASON.
I'M SORRY... I WASN'T A BETTER MAN...

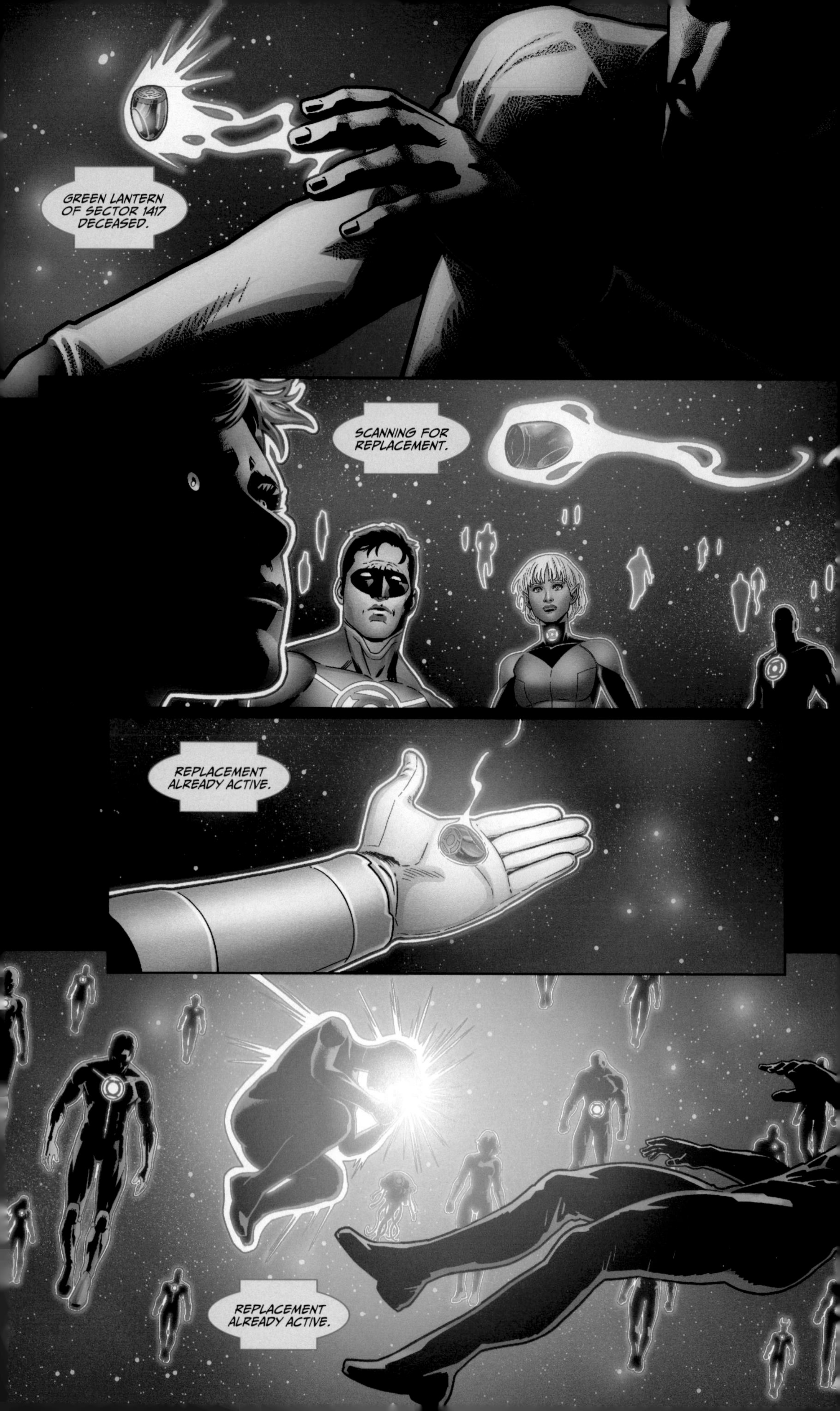

GREEN LANTERN OF SECTOR 1417 DECEASED.
SCANNING FOR REPLACEMENT.
REPLACEMENT ALREADY ACTIVE.
REPLACEMENT ALREADY ACTIVE.

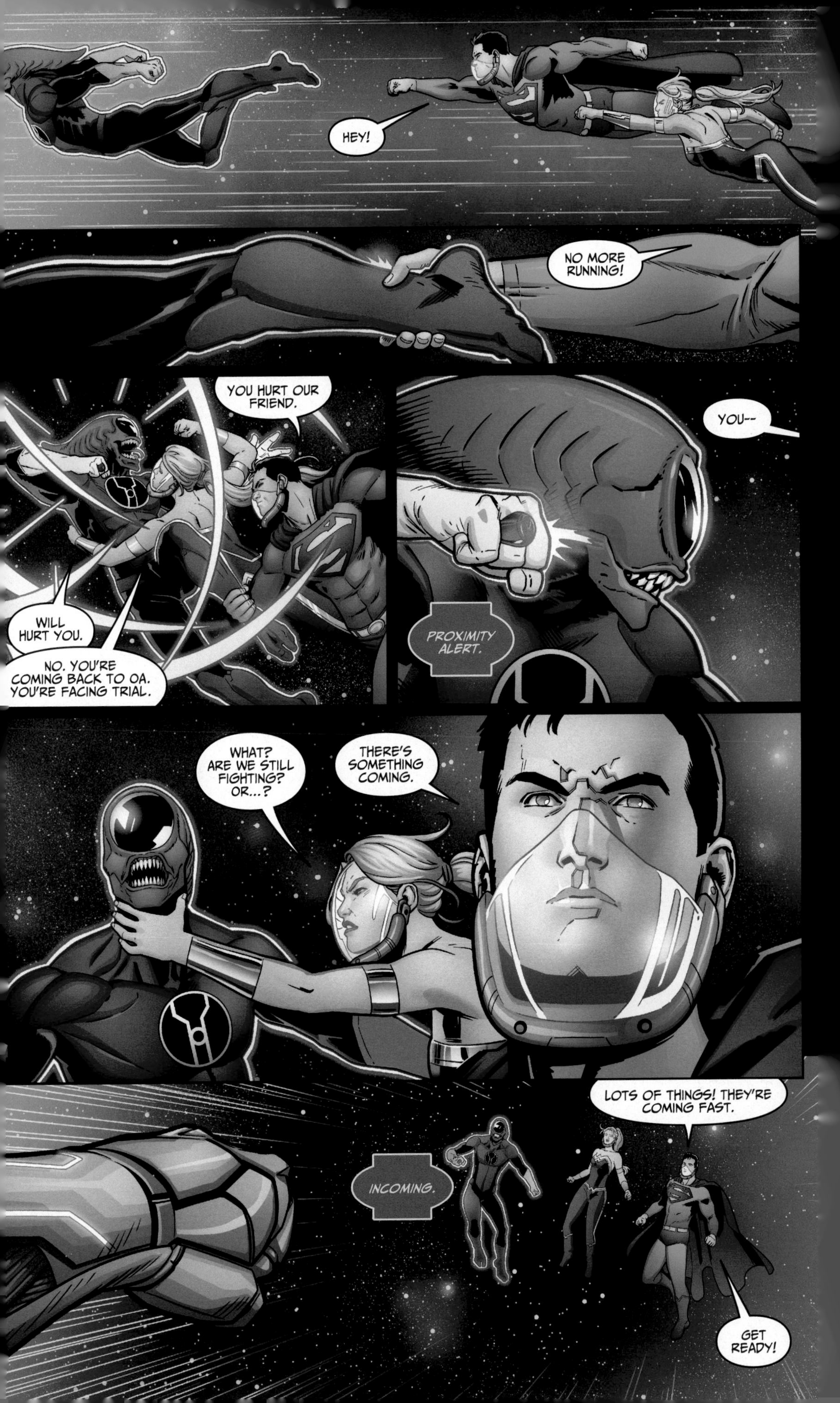
HEY!
NO MORE RUNNING!
YOU HURT OUR FRIEND.
WILL HURT YOU.
NO. YOU'RE COMING BACK TO OA. YOU'RE FACING TRIAL.
YOU--
PROXIMITY ALERT.
WHAT? ARE WE STILL FIGHTING? OR...?
THERE'S SOMETHING COMING.
INCOMING.
LOTS OF THINGS! THEY'RE COMING FAST.
GET READY!

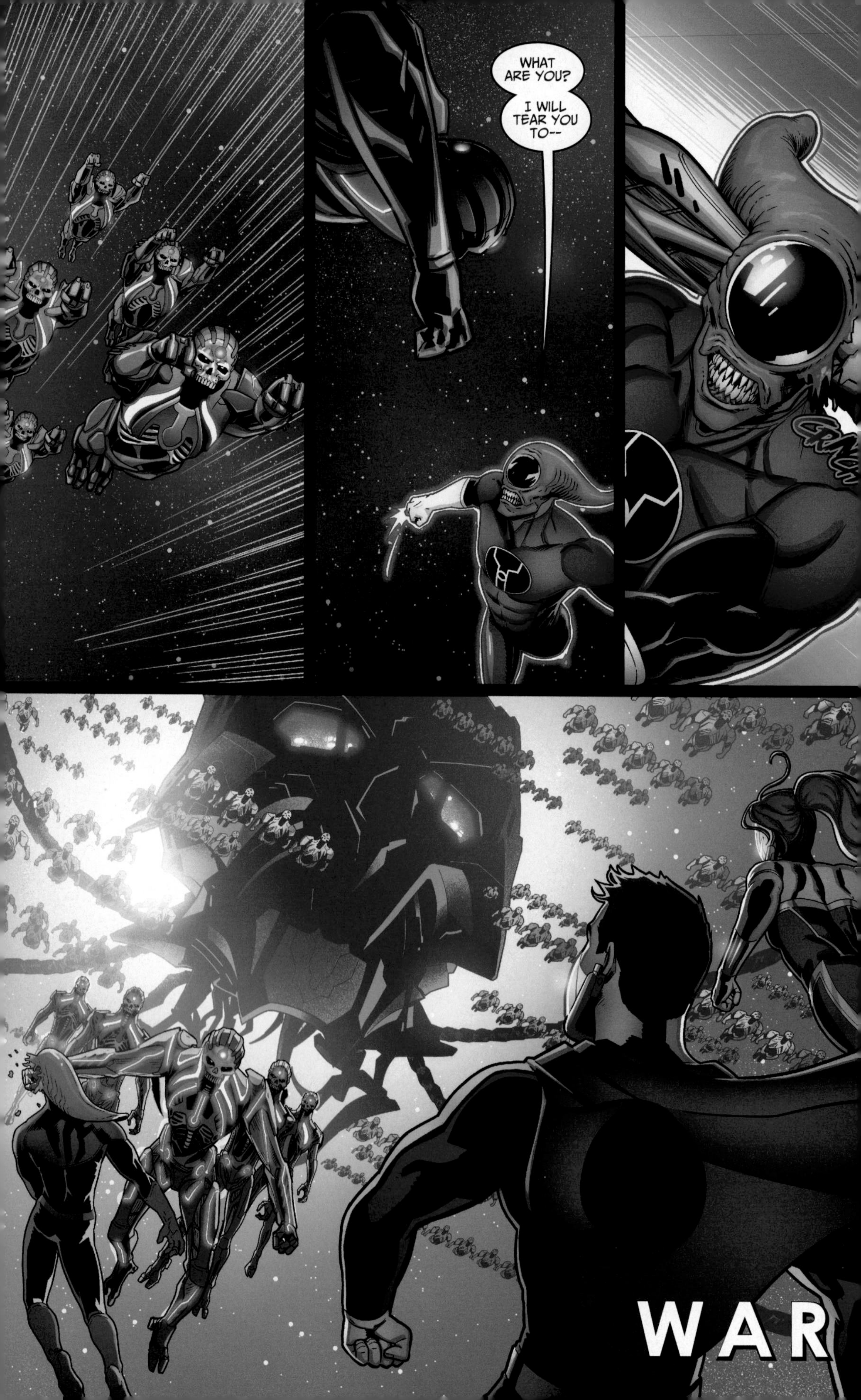

WHAT ARE YOU?
I WILL TEAR YOU TO--
WAR

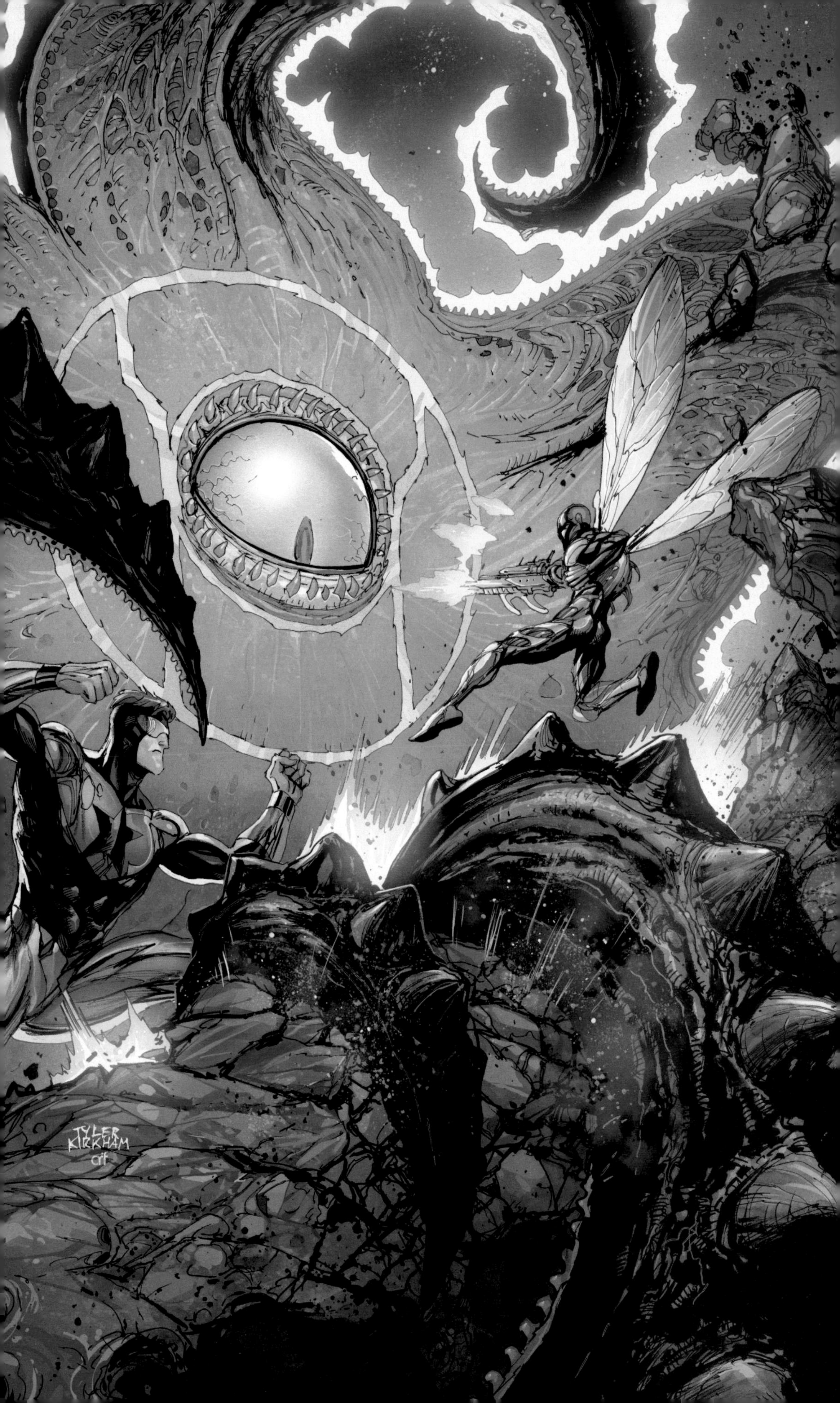
TYLER
KIRKHAM

"Last Stop"

Tom Taylor Writer **Xermanico** Artist **J. Nanjan** Colorist **Wes Abbott** Letterer

Cover art by **Tyler Kirkham** and **Arif Prianto**

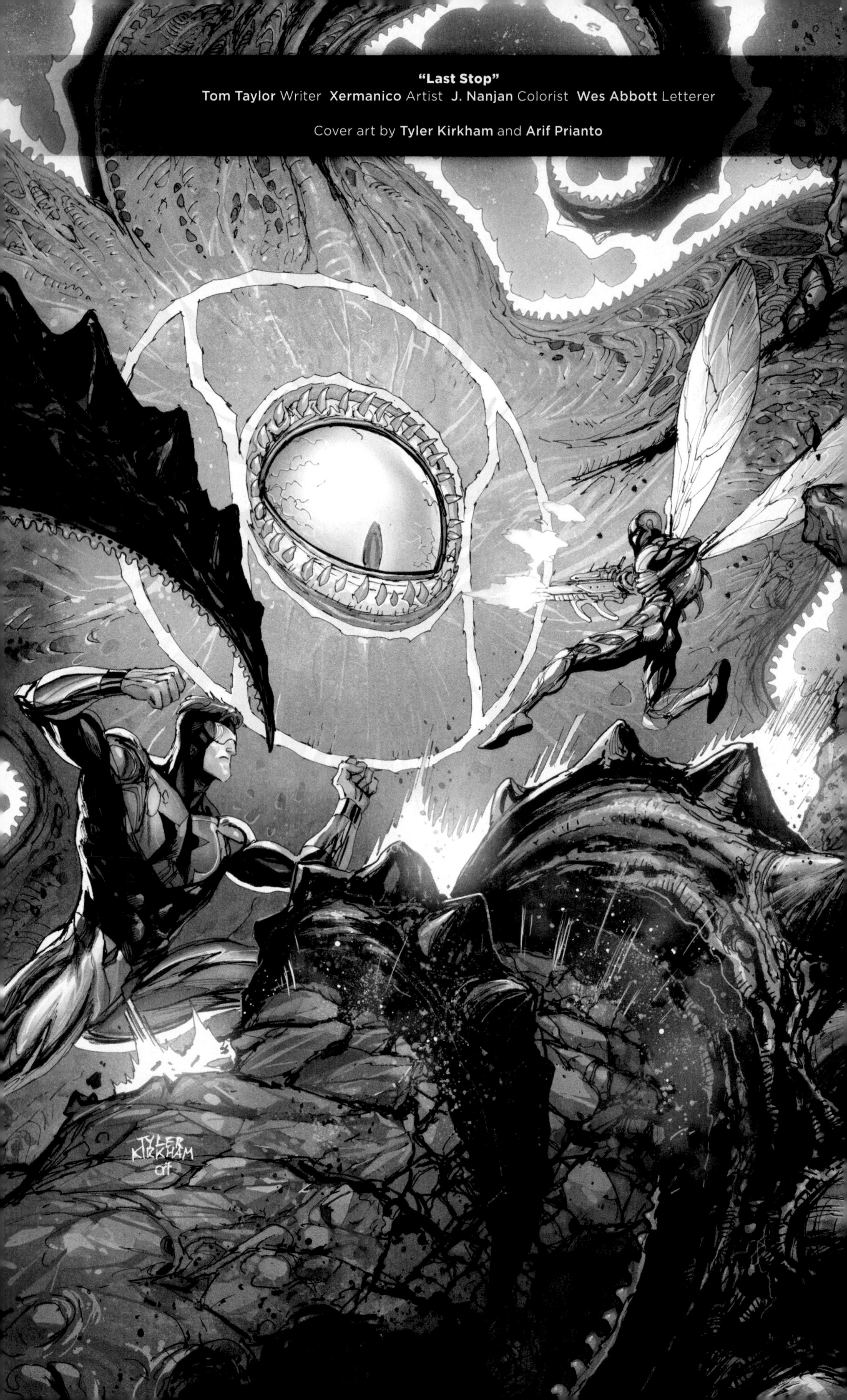

TYLER KIRKHAM
arif

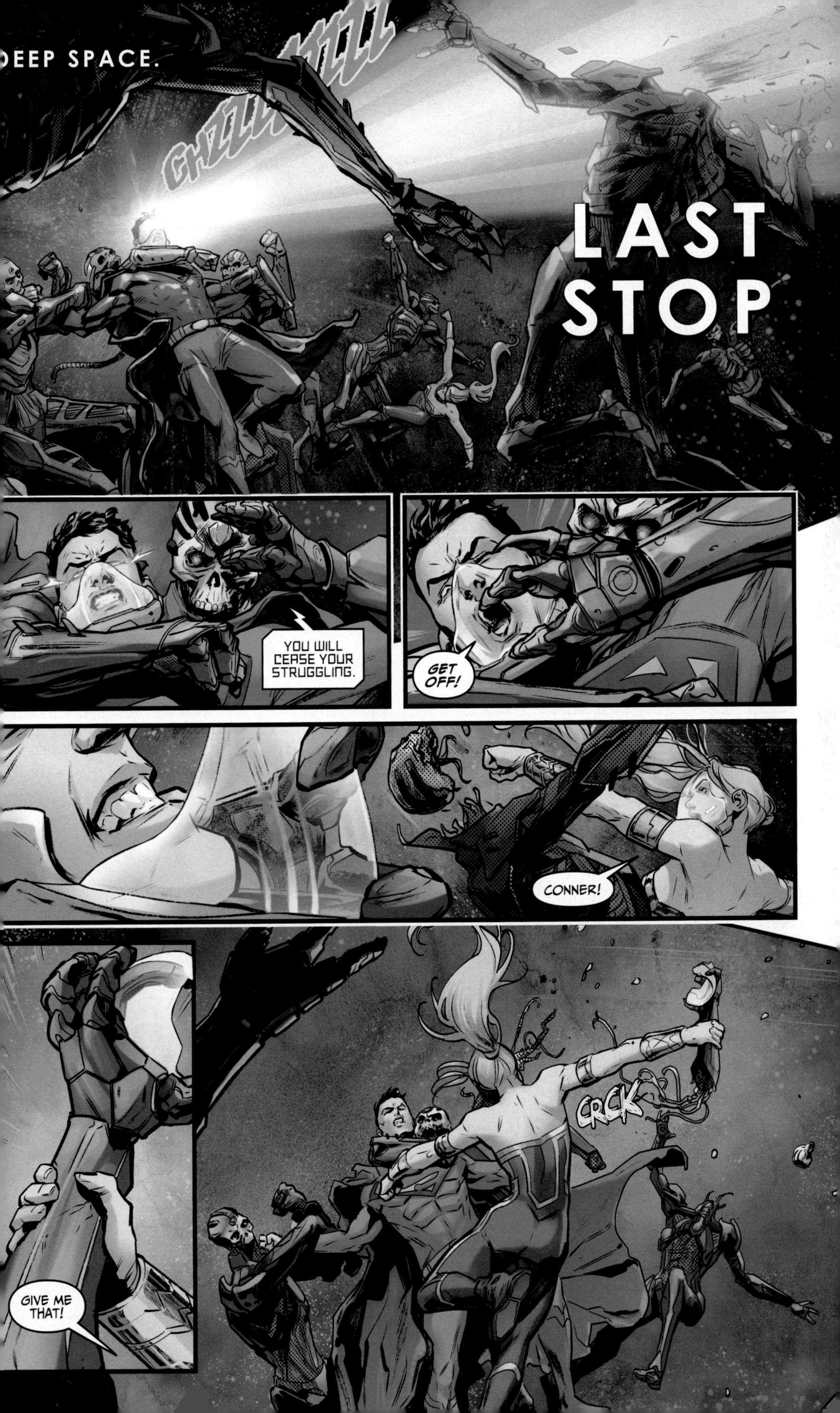
DEEP SPACE.
CHZZZZZZZZ
LAST STOP
YOU WILL CEASE YOUR STRUGGLING.
GET OFF!
CONNER!
CRCK
GIVE ME THAT!

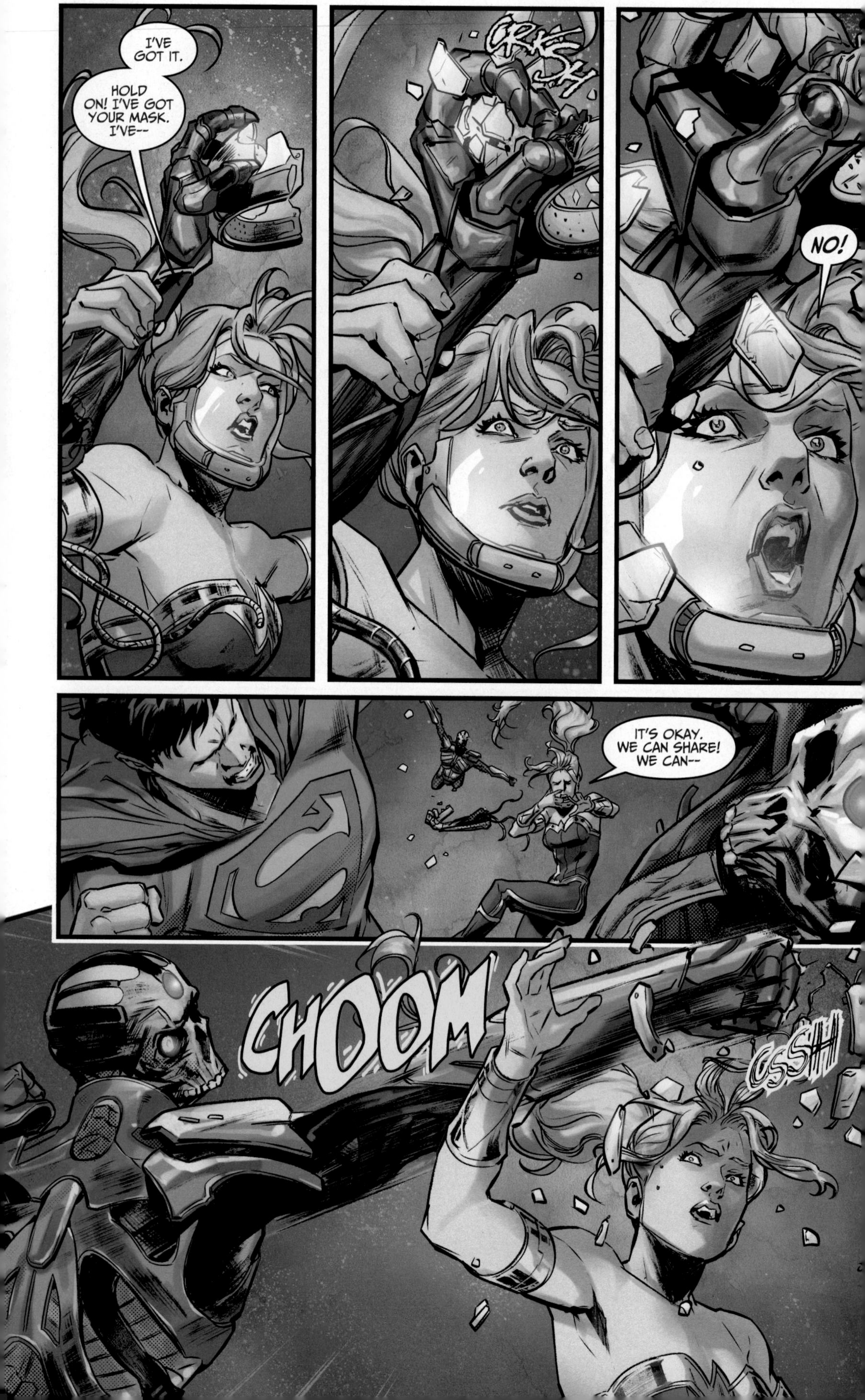
I'VE GOT IT.
HOLD ON! I'VE GOT YOUR MASK. I'VE--
NO!
IT'S OKAY. WE CAN SHARE! WE CAN--
CHOOM
GSSHH

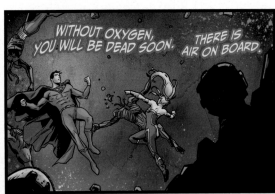

WITHOUT OXYGEN, YOU WILL BE DEAD SOON. THERE IS AIR ON BOARD.

COME.

COME.

AAAGHHHH

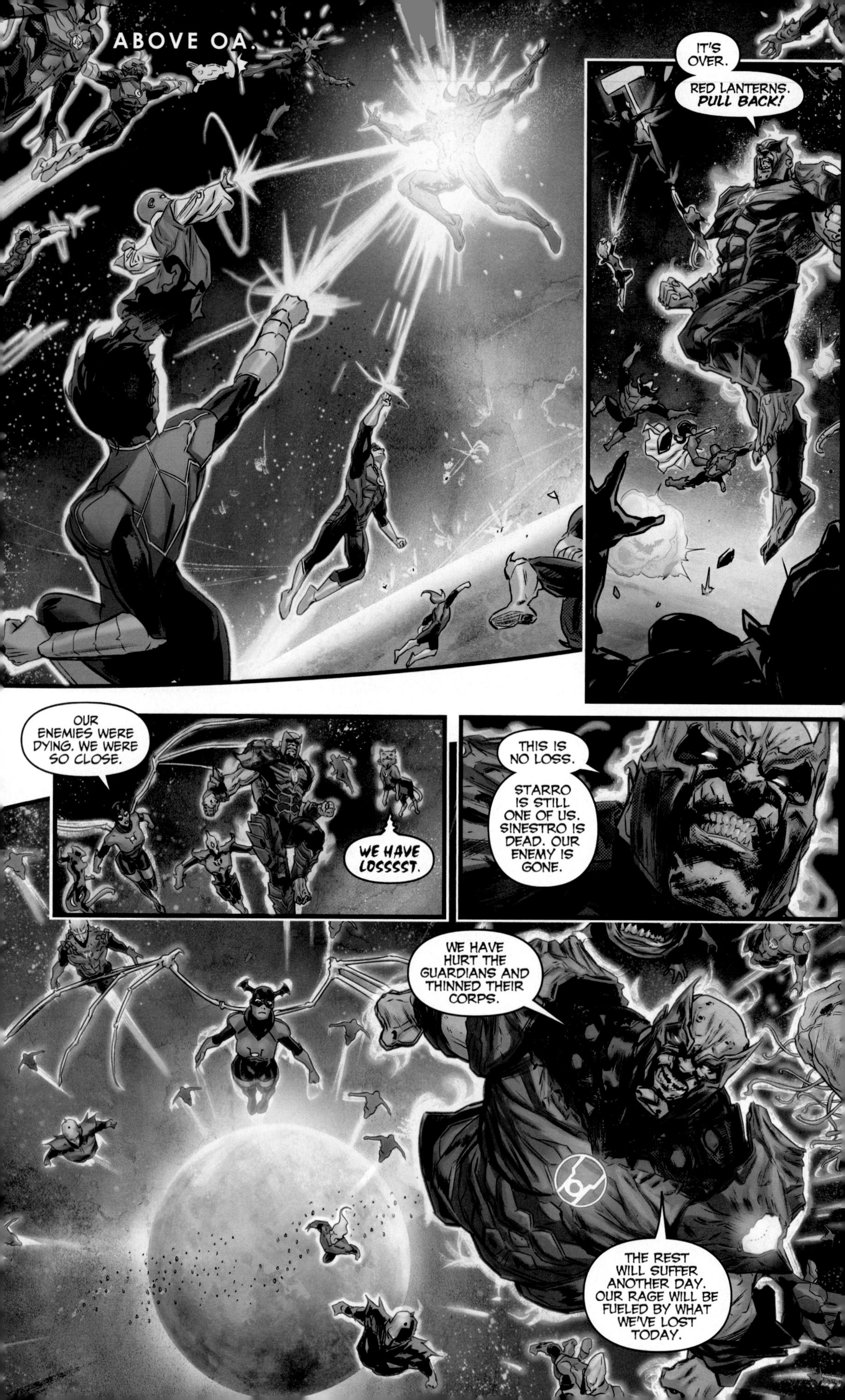
ABOVE OA.
IT'S OVER.
RED LANTERNS. PULL BACK!
OUR ENEMIES WERE DYING. WE WERE SO CLOSE.
WE HAVE LOSSSST.
THIS IS NO LOSS.
STARRO IS STILL ONE OF US. SINESTRO IS DEAD. OUR ENEMY IS GONE.
WE HAVE HURT THE GUARDIANS AND THINNED THEIR CORPS.
THE REST WILL SUFFER ANOTHER DAY. OUR RAGE WILL BE FUELED BY WHAT WE'VE LOST TODAY.

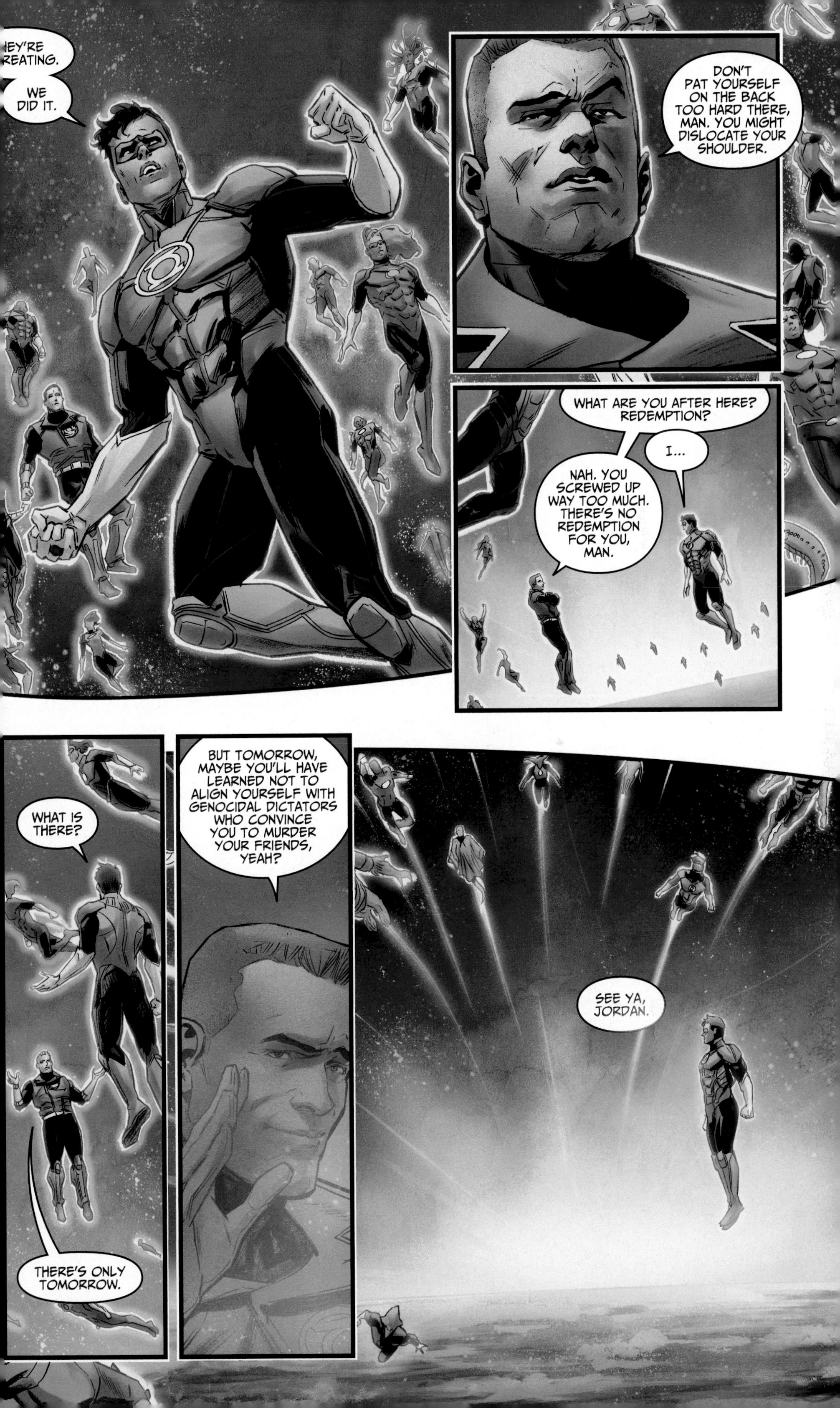

HEY'RE
REATING.
WE DID IT.
DON'T PAT YOURSELF ON THE BACK TOO HARD THERE, MAN. YOU MIGHT DISLOCATE YOUR SHOULDER.
WHAT ARE YOU AFTER HERE? REDEMPTION?
I...
NAH. YOU SCREWED UP WAY TOO MUCH. THERE'S NO REDEMPTION FOR YOU, MAN.
WHAT IS THERE?
THERE'S ONLY TOMORROW.
BUT TOMORROW, MAYBE YOU'LL HAVE LEARNED NOT TO ALIGN YOURSELF WITH GENOCIDAL DICTATORS WHO CONVINCE YOU TO MURDER YOUR FRIENDS, YEAH?
SEE YA, JORDAN.

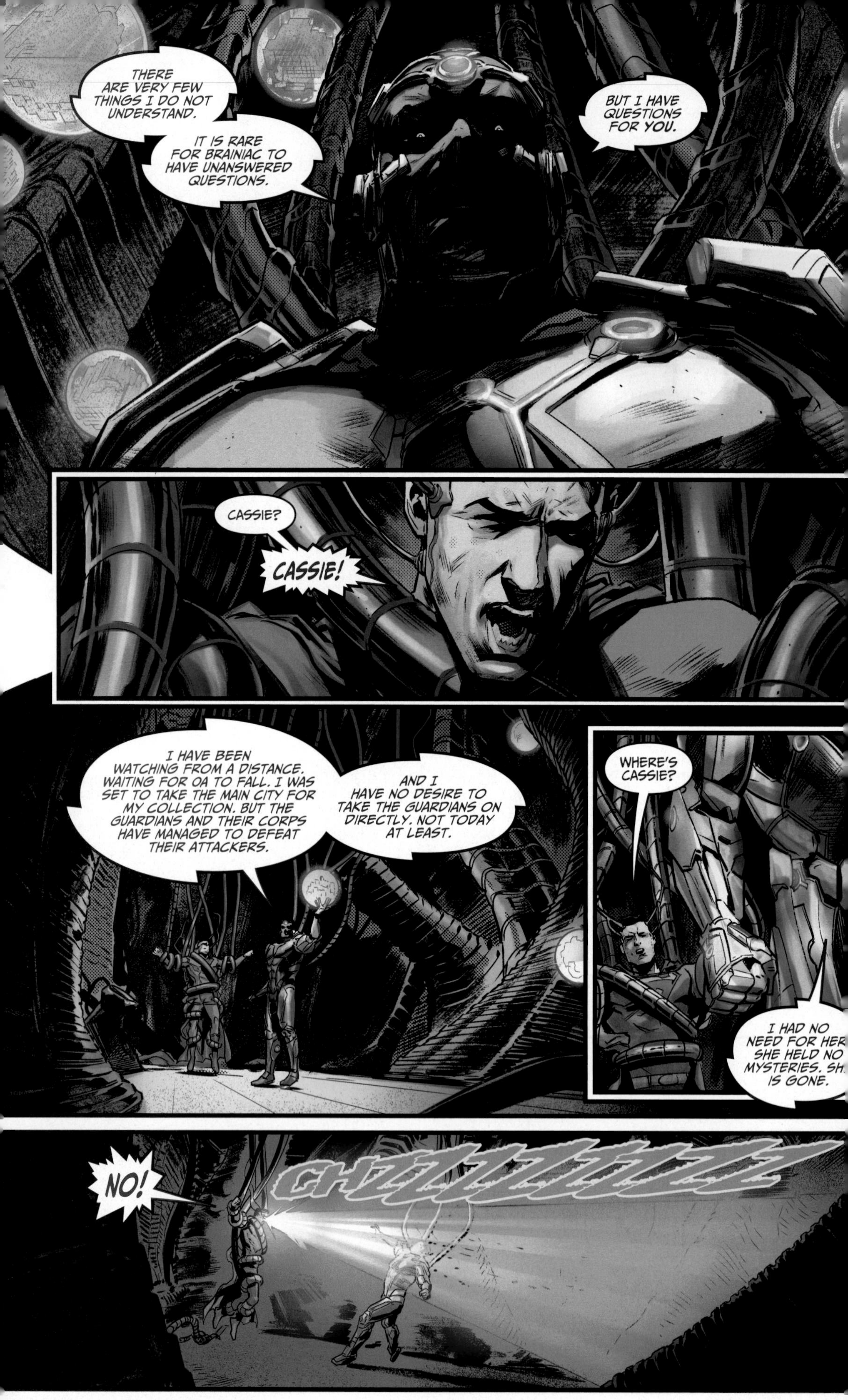
THERE ARE VERY FEW THINGS I DO NOT UNDERSTAND.
IT IS RARE FOR BRAINIAC TO HAVE UNANSWERED QUESTIONS.
BUT I HAVE QUESTIONS FOR YOU.
CASSIE?
CASSIE!
I HAVE BEEN WATCHING FROM A DISTANCE. WAITING FOR OA TO FALL. I WAS SET TO TAKE THE MAIN CITY FOR MY COLLECTION. BUT THE GUARDIANS AND THEIR CORPS HAVE MANAGED TO DEFEAT THEIR ATTACKERS.
AND I HAVE NO DESIRE TO TAKE THE GUARDIANS ON DIRECTLY. NOT TODAY AT LEAST.
WHERE'S CASSIE?
I HAD NO NEED FOR HER SHE HELD NO MYSTERIES. SH IS GONE.
NO!
CHZZZZZZZZZ

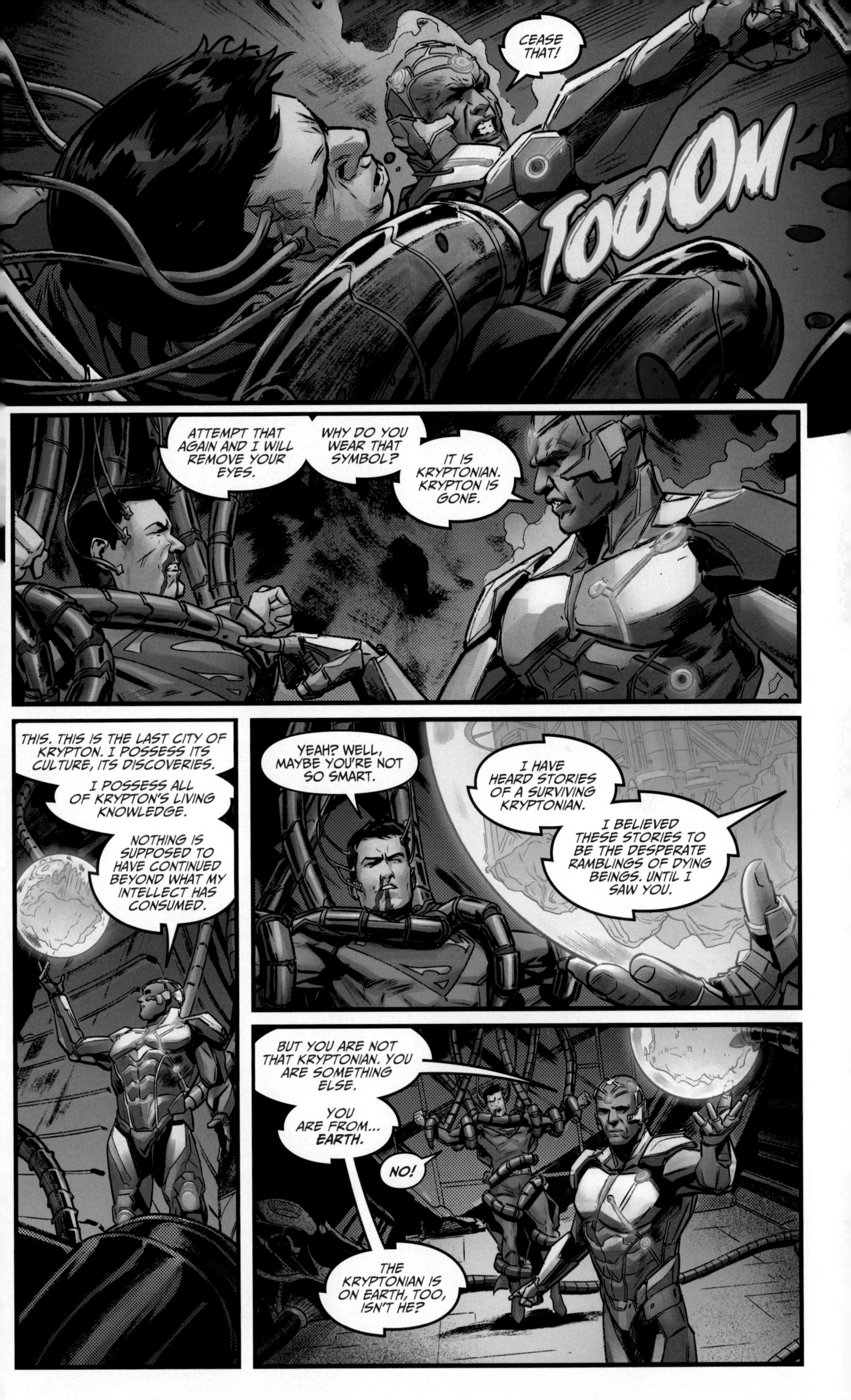
CEASE THAT!
TOOOM
ATTEMPT THAT AGAIN AND I WILL REMOVE YOUR EYES.
WHY DO YOU WEAR THAT SYMBOL?
IT IS KRYPTONIAN. KRYPTON IS GONE.
THIS. THIS IS THE LAST CITY OF KRYPTON. I POSSESS ITS CULTURE, ITS DISCOVERIES.
I POSSESS ALL OF KRYPTON'S LIVING KNOWLEDGE.
NOTHING IS SUPPOSED TO HAVE CONTINUED BEYOND WHAT MY INTELLECT HAS CONSUMED.
YEAH? WELL, MAYBE YOU'RE NOT SO SMART.
I HAVE HEARD STORIES OF A SURVIVING KRYPTONIAN.
I BELIEVED THESE STORIES TO BE THE DESPERATE RAMBLINGS OF DYING BEINGS. UNTIL I SAW YOU.
BUT YOU ARE NOT THAT KRYPTONIAN. YOU ARE SOMETHING ELSE.
YOU ARE FROM... EARTH.
NO!
THE KRYPTONIAN IS ON EARTH, TOO, ISN'T HE?

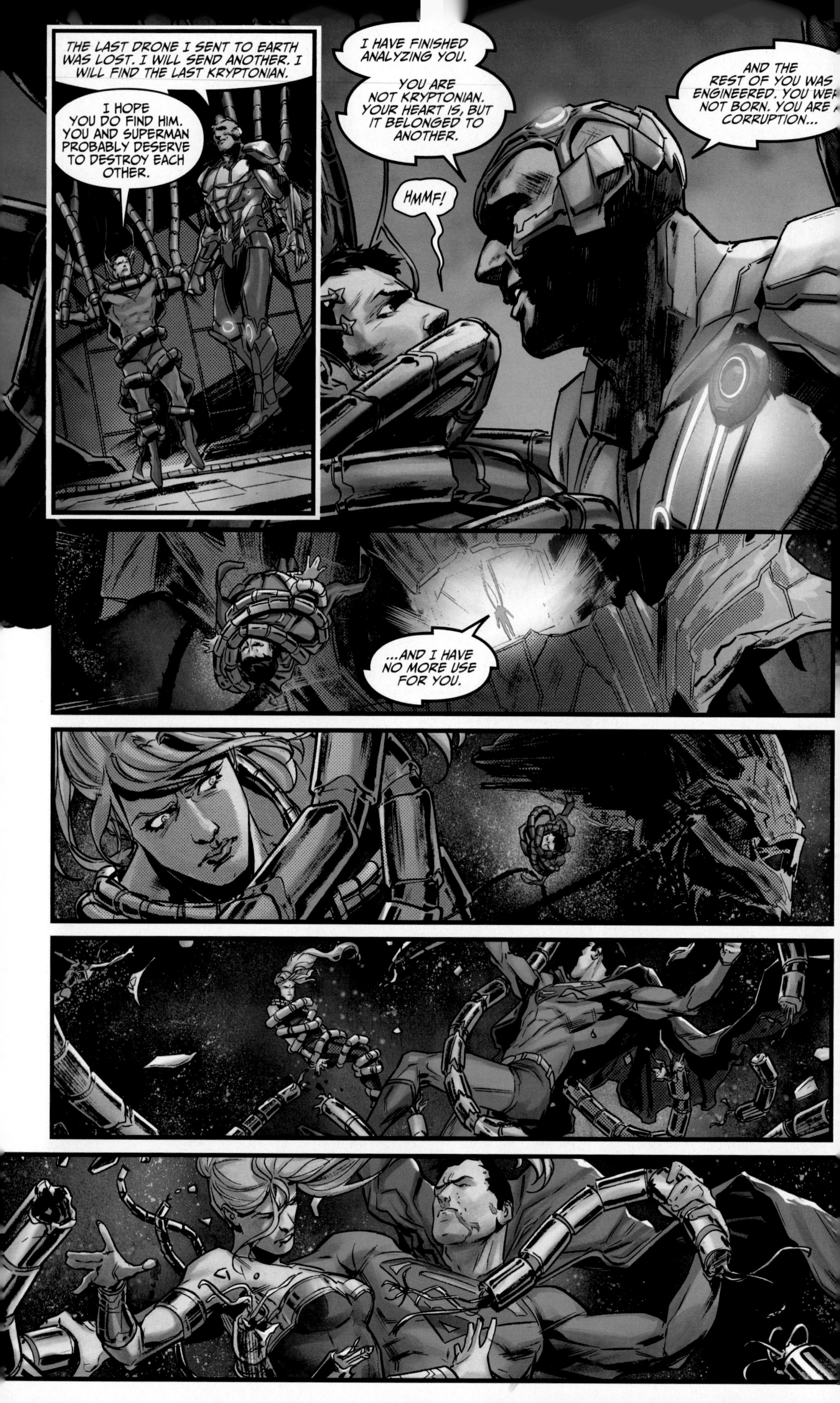
THE LAST DRONE I SENT TO EARTH WAS LOST. I WILL SEND ANOTHER. I WILL FIND THE LAST KRYPTONIAN.
I HOPE YOU DO FIND HIM. YOU AND SUPERMAN PROBABLY DESERVE TO DESTROY EACH OTHER.
I HAVE FINISHED ANALYZING YOU.
YOU ARE NOT KRYPTONIAN. YOUR HEART IS, BUT IT BELONGED TO ANOTHER.
HMMF!
AND THE REST OF YOU WAS ENGINEERED. YOU WER NOT BORN. YOU ARE A CORRUPTION...
...AND I HAVE NO MORE USE FOR YOU.

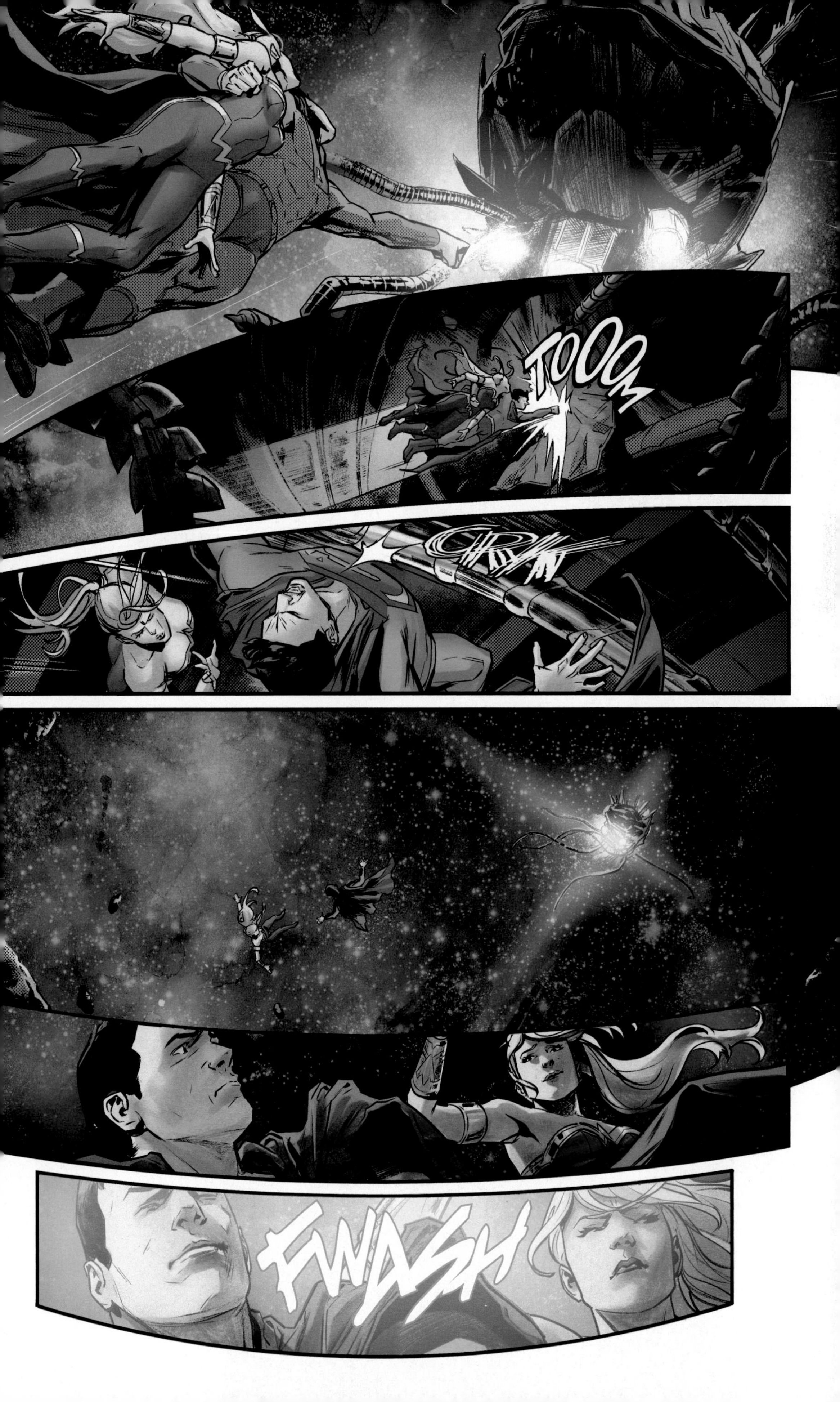
TOOOM
FWASH

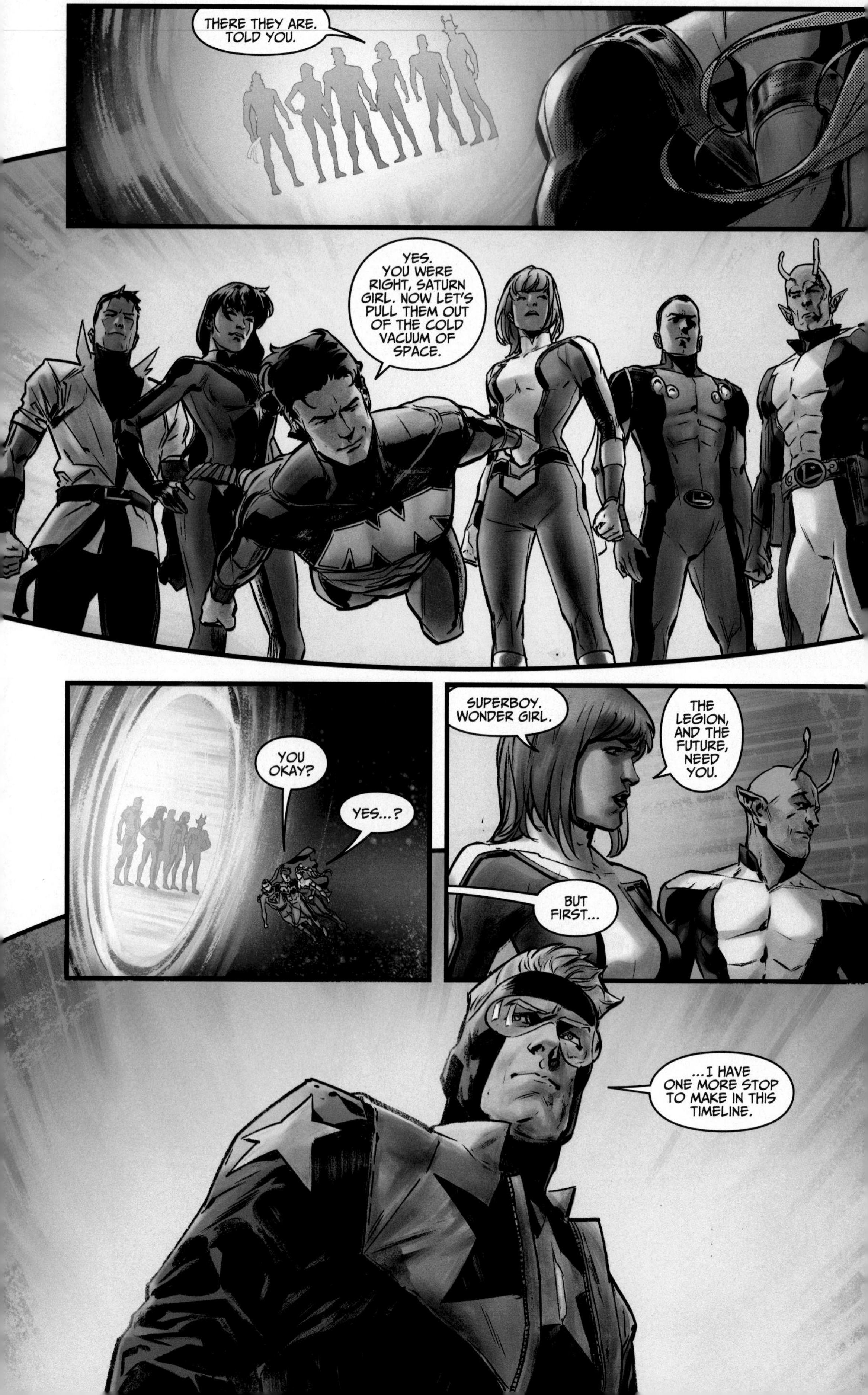
THERE THEY ARE. TOLD YOU.
YES. YOU WERE RIGHT, SATURN GIRL. NOW LET'S PULL THEM OUT OF THE COLD VACUUM OF SPACE.
YOU OKAY?
YES...?
SUPERBOY. WONDER GIRL.
THE LEGION, AND THE FUTURE, NEED YOU.
BUT FIRST...
...I HAVE ONE MORE STOP TO MAKE IN THIS TIMELINE.

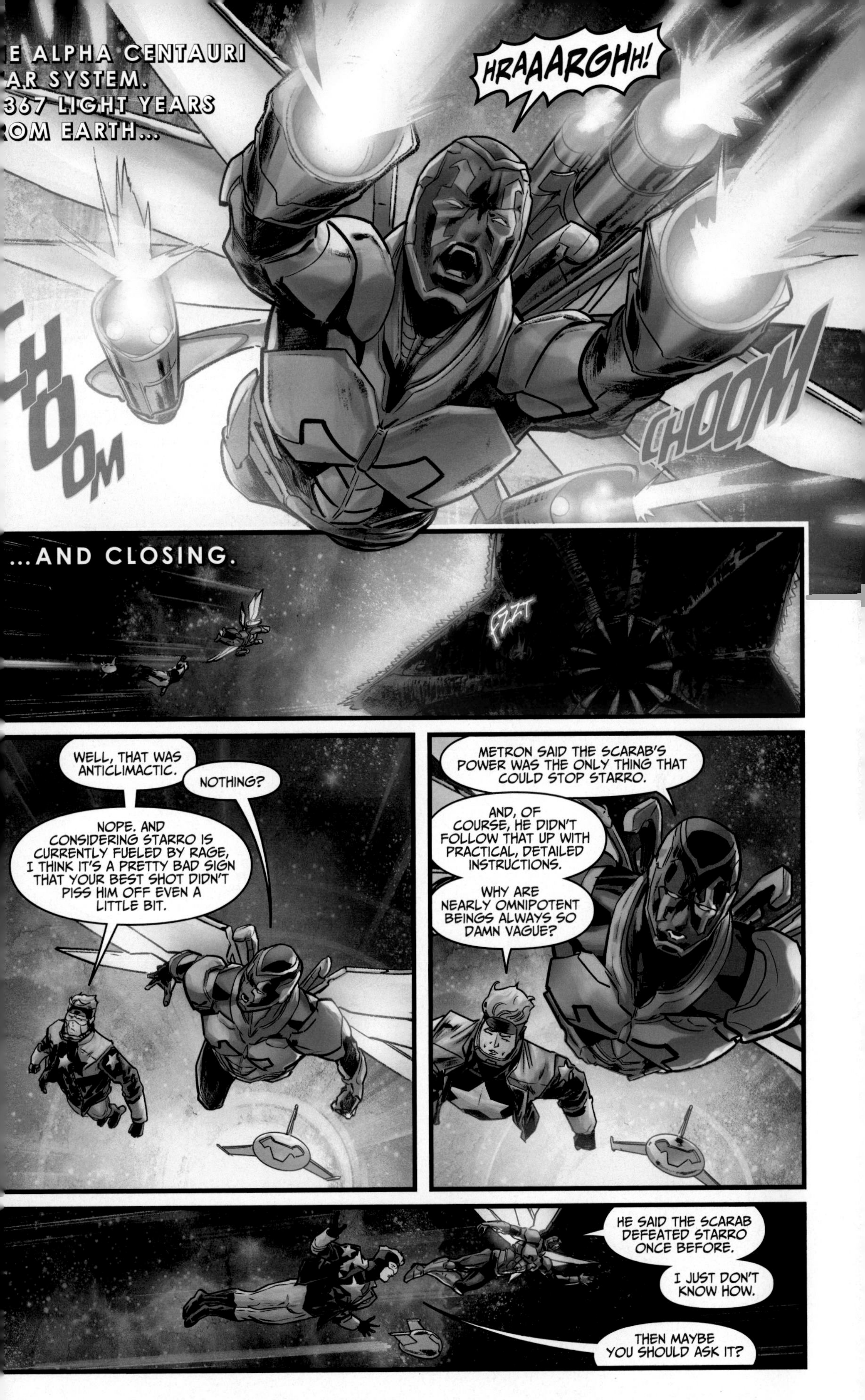
E ALPHA CENTAURI
AR SYSTEM.
367 LIGHT YEARS
OM EARTH...
HRAAARGHH!
CHOOM
CHOOM
...AND CLOSING.
FZZT
WELL, THAT WAS ANTICLIMACTIC.
NOTHING?
NOPE. AND CONSIDERING STARRO IS CURRENTLY FUELED BY RAGE, I THINK IT'S A PRETTY BAD SIGN THAT YOUR BEST SHOT DIDN'T PISS HIM OFF EVEN A LITTLE BIT.
METRON SAID THE SCARAB'S POWER WAS THE ONLY THING THAT COULD STOP STARRO.
AND, OF COURSE, HE DIDN'T FOLLOW THAT UP WITH PRACTICAL, DETAILED INSTRUCTIONS.
WHY ARE NEARLY OMNIPOTENT BEINGS ALWAYS SO DAMN VAGUE?
HE SAID THE SCARAB DEFEATED STARRO ONCE BEFORE.
I JUST DON'T KNOW HOW.
THEN MAYBE YOU SHOULD ASK IT?

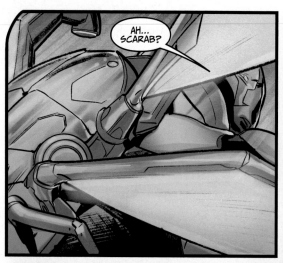

AH... SCARAB?

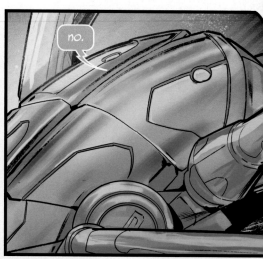

no.

WHAT DO YOU MEAN, "NO"?

I DO NOT WANT TO.

I DO NOT WANT OUR BOND BROKEN.

OKAY, BUT IF STARRO TAKES THE EARTH, IF MY WORLD DIES, I'LL PROBABLY END UP DYING TRYING TO PROTECT IT, AND OUR BOND WILL BE BROKEN ANYWAY. I NEED YOU TO SHOW ME.

PLEASE...

"...SHOW ME.

"HOW DO WE DEFEAT STARRO?"

WE CAN'T DEFEAT STARRO...

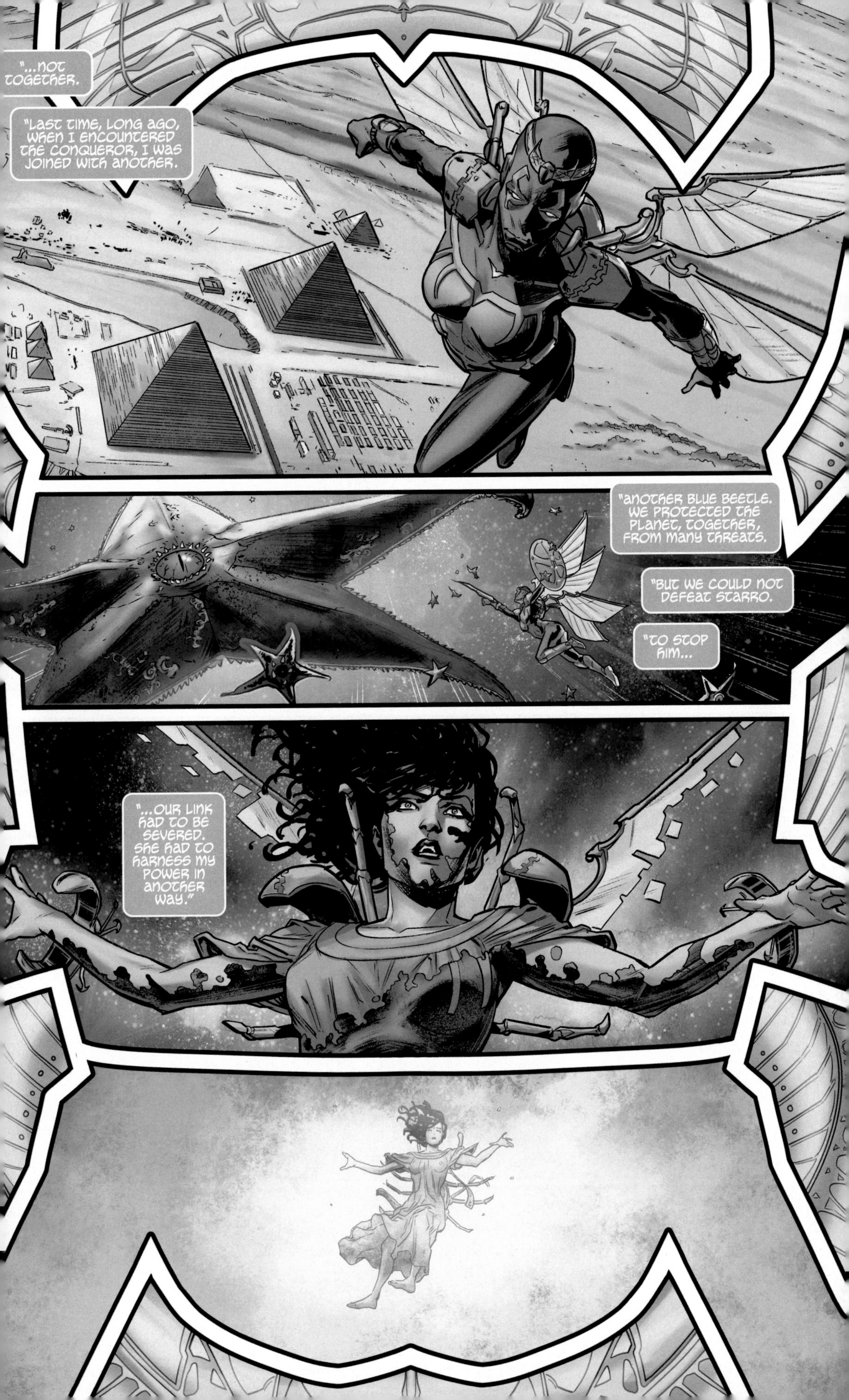
"...NOT TOGETHER.
"LAST TIME, LONG AGO, WHEN I ENCOUNTERED THE CONQUEROR, I WAS JOINED WITH ANOTHER.
"ANOTHER BLUE BEETLE. WE PROTECTED THE PLANET, TOGETHER, FROM MANY THREATS.
"BUT WE COULD NOT DEFEAT STARRO.
"TO STOP HIM...
"...OUR LINK HAD TO BE SEVERED. SHE HAD TO HARNESS MY POWER IN ANOTHER WAY."

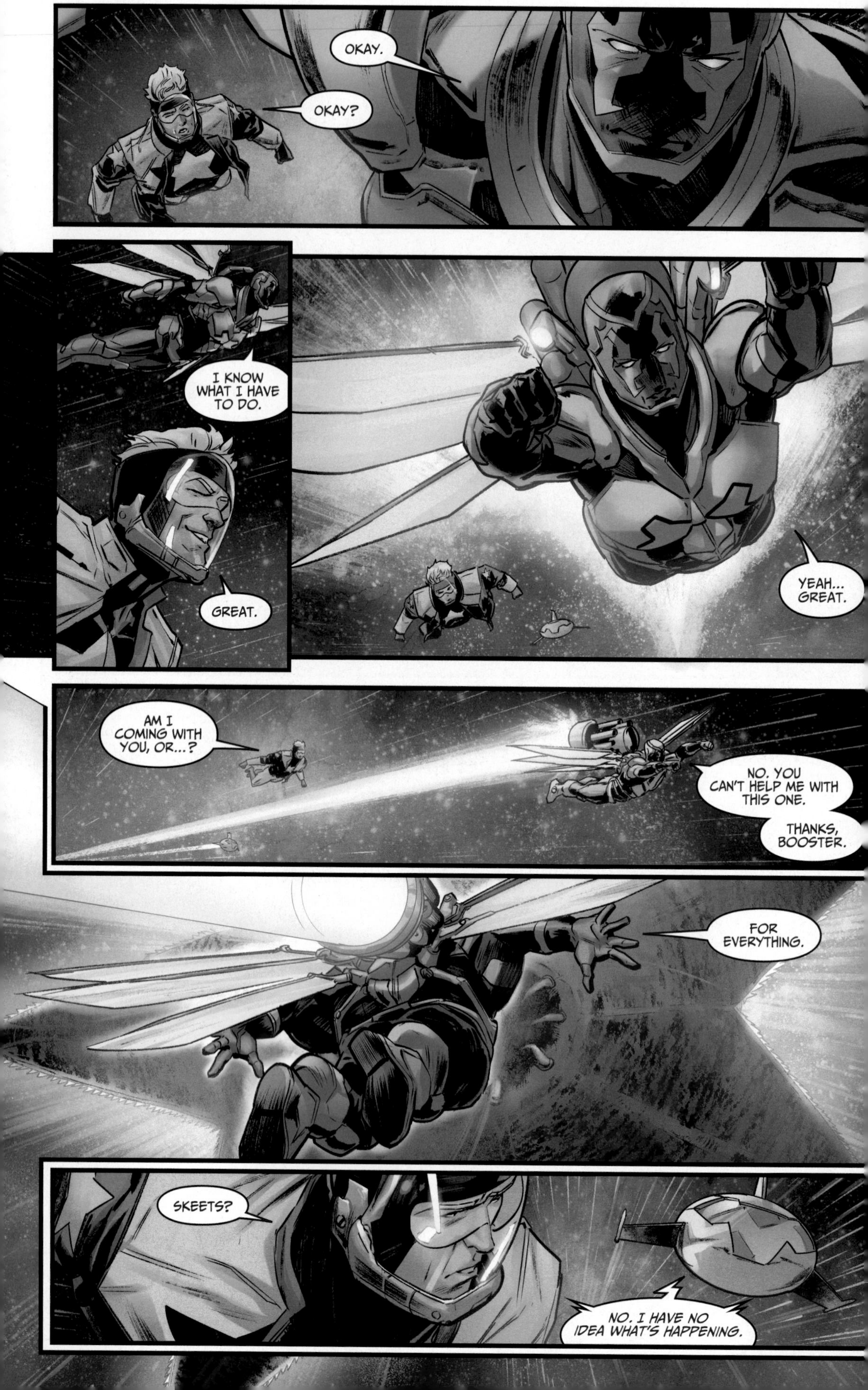
OKAY.
OKAY?
I KNOW WHAT I HAVE TO DO.
GREAT.
YEAH... GREAT.
AM I COMING WITH YOU, OR...?
NO. YOU CAN'T HELP ME WITH THIS ONE.
THANKS, BOOSTER.
FOR EVERYTHING.
SKEETS?
NO. I HAVE NO IDEA WHAT'S HAPPENING.

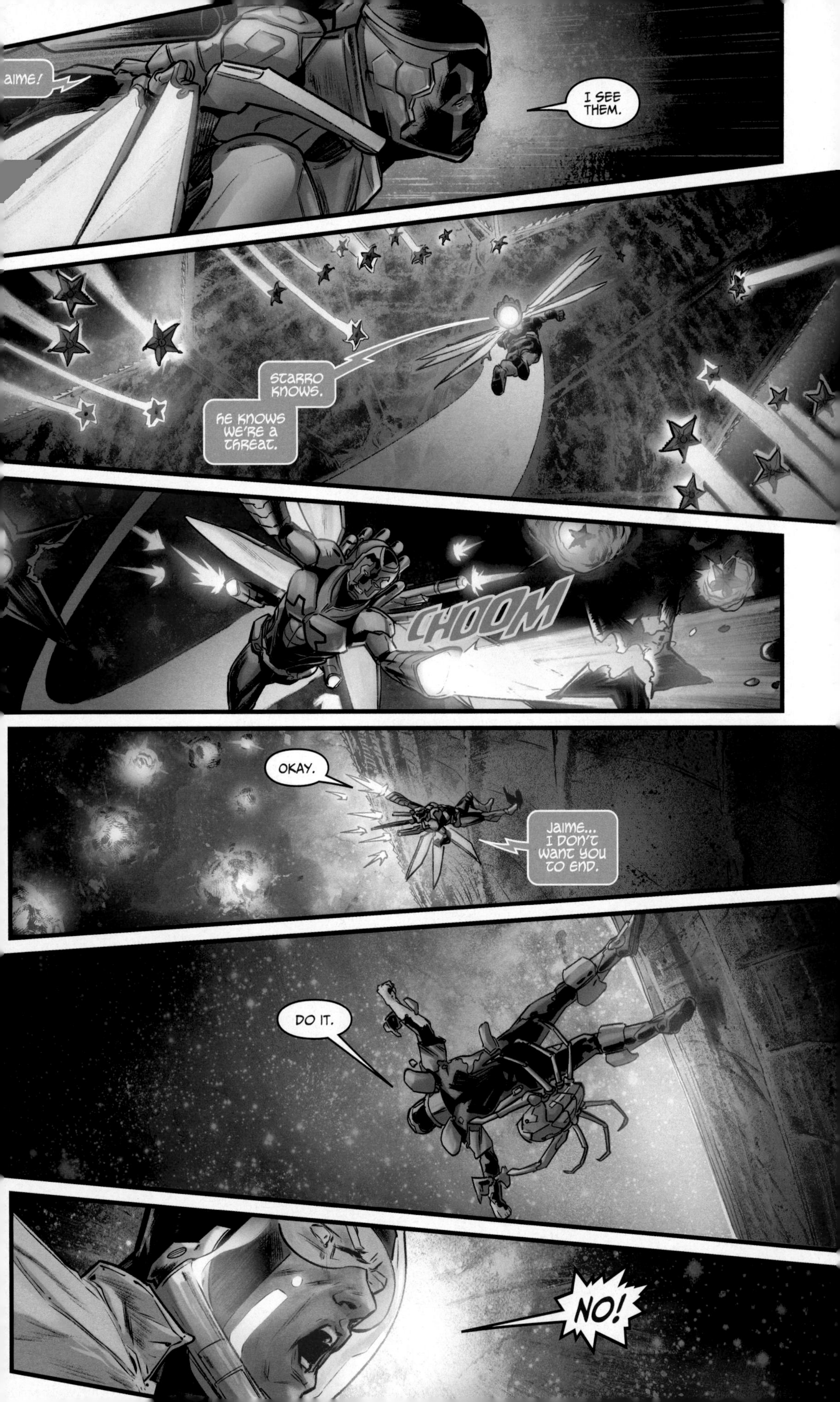
aime!
I SEE THEM.
STARRO KNOWS.
HE KNOWS WE'RE A THREAT.
CHOOM
OKAY.
JAIME... I DON'T WANT YOU TO END.
DO IT.
NO!

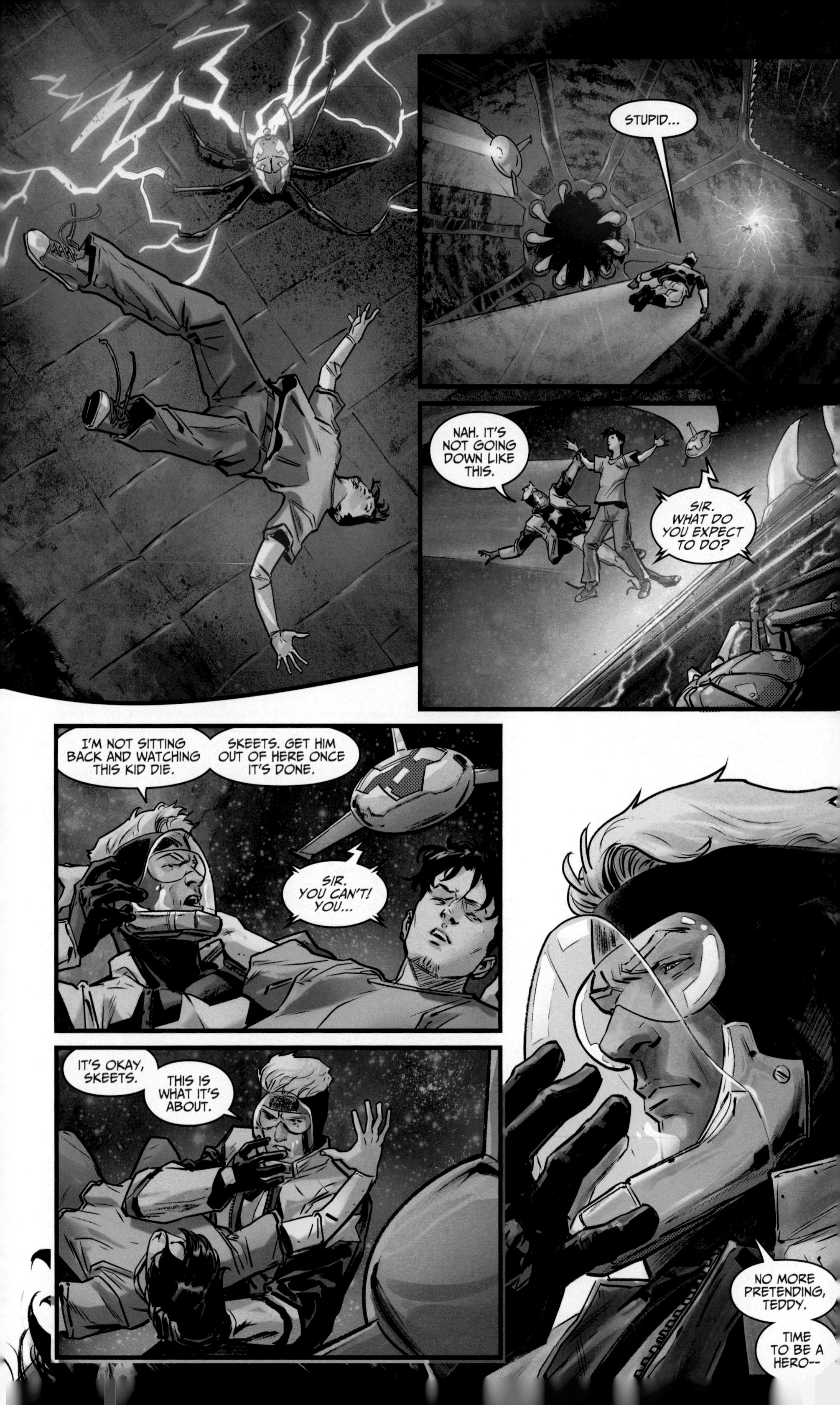
STUPID...
NAH. IT'S NOT GOING DOWN LIKE THIS.
SIR. WHAT DO YOU EXPECT TO DO?
I'M NOT SITTING BACK AND WATCHING THIS KID DIE.
SKEETS. GET HIM OUT OF HERE ONCE IT'S DONE.
SIR. YOU CAN'T! YOU...
IT'S OKAY, SKEETS.
THIS IS WHAT IT'S ABOUT.
NO MORE PRETENDING, TEDDY.
TIME TO BE A HERO--

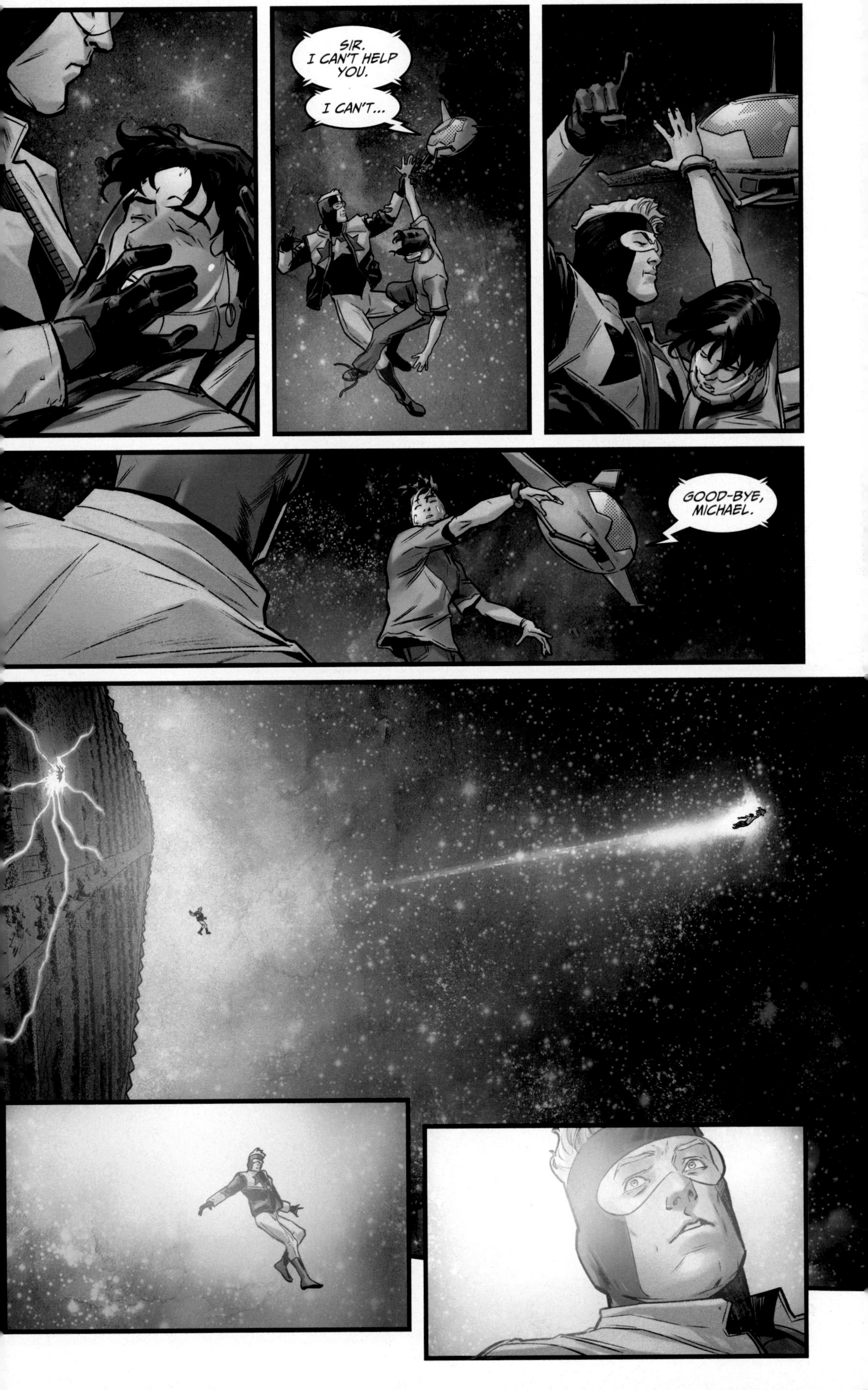
SIR. I CAN'T HELP YOU.
I CAN'T...
GOOD-BYE, MICHAEL.

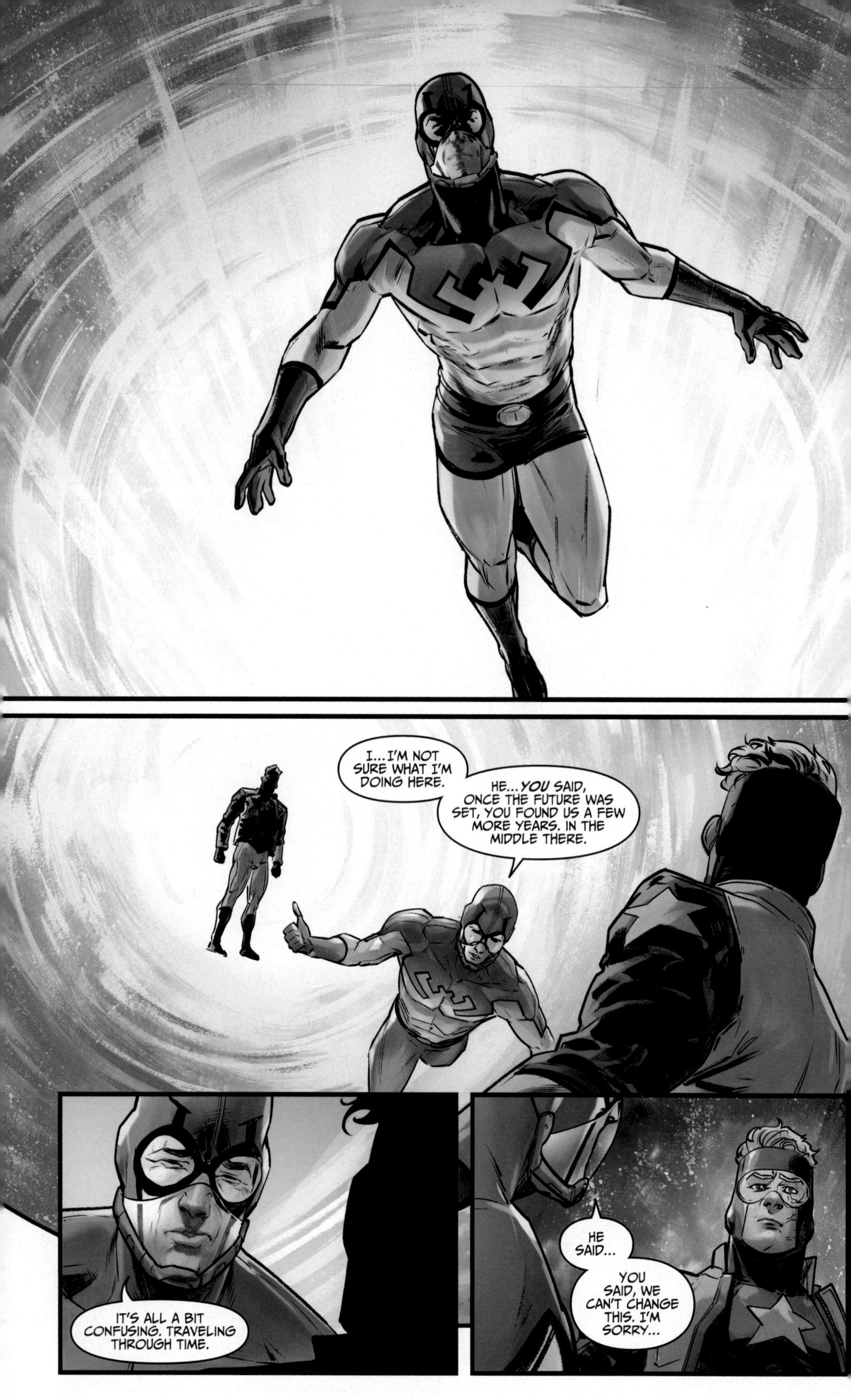
I...I'M NOT SURE WHAT I'M DOING HERE.
HE...*YOU* SAID, ONCE THE FUTURE WAS SET, YOU FOUND US A FEW MORE YEARS. IN THE MIDDLE THERE.
IT'S ALL A BIT CONFUSING. TRAVELING THROUGH TIME.
HE SAID...
YOU SAID, WE CAN'T CHANGE THIS. I'M SORRY...

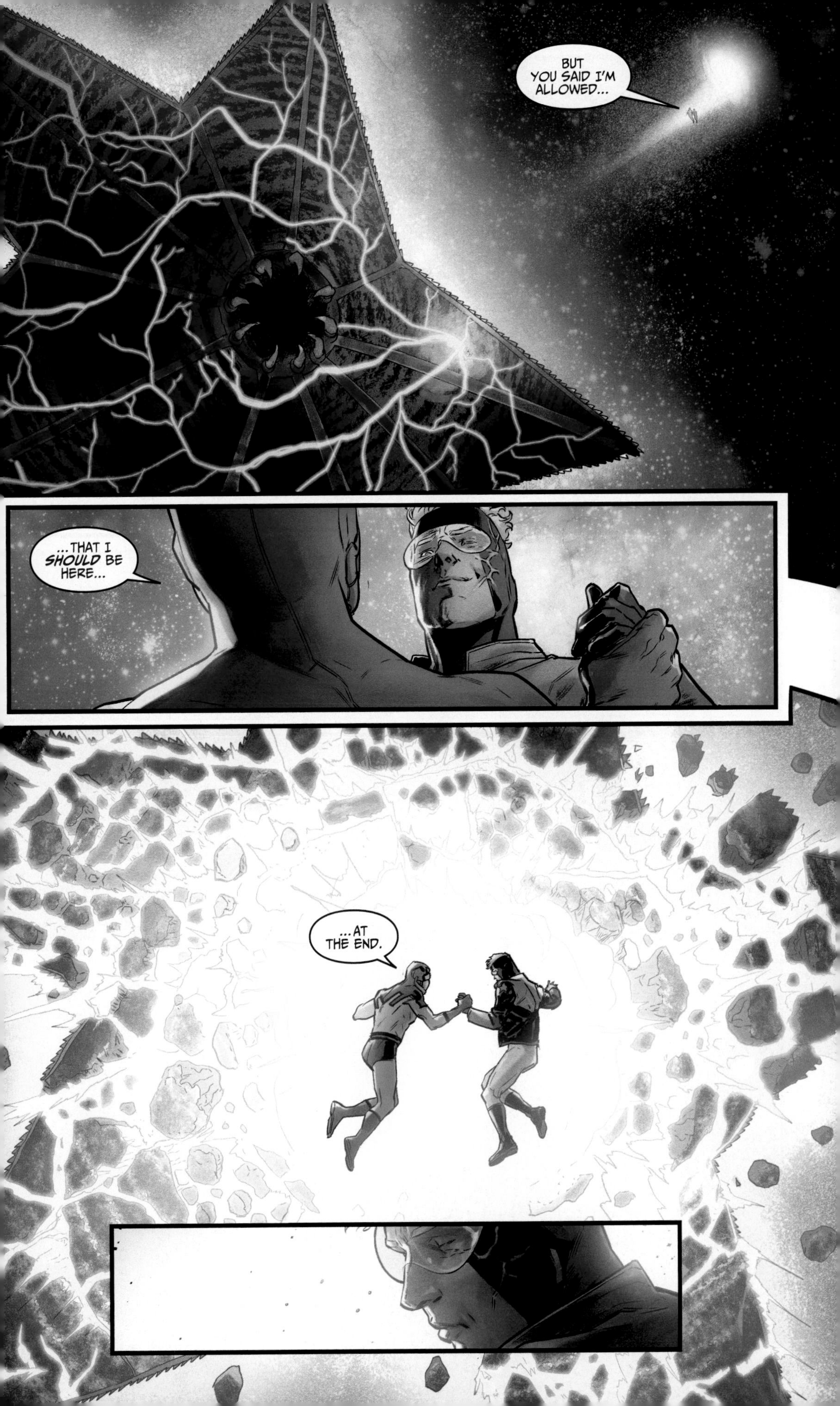
BUT YOU SAID I'M ALLOWED...
...THAT I *SHOULD* BE HERE...
...AT THE END.

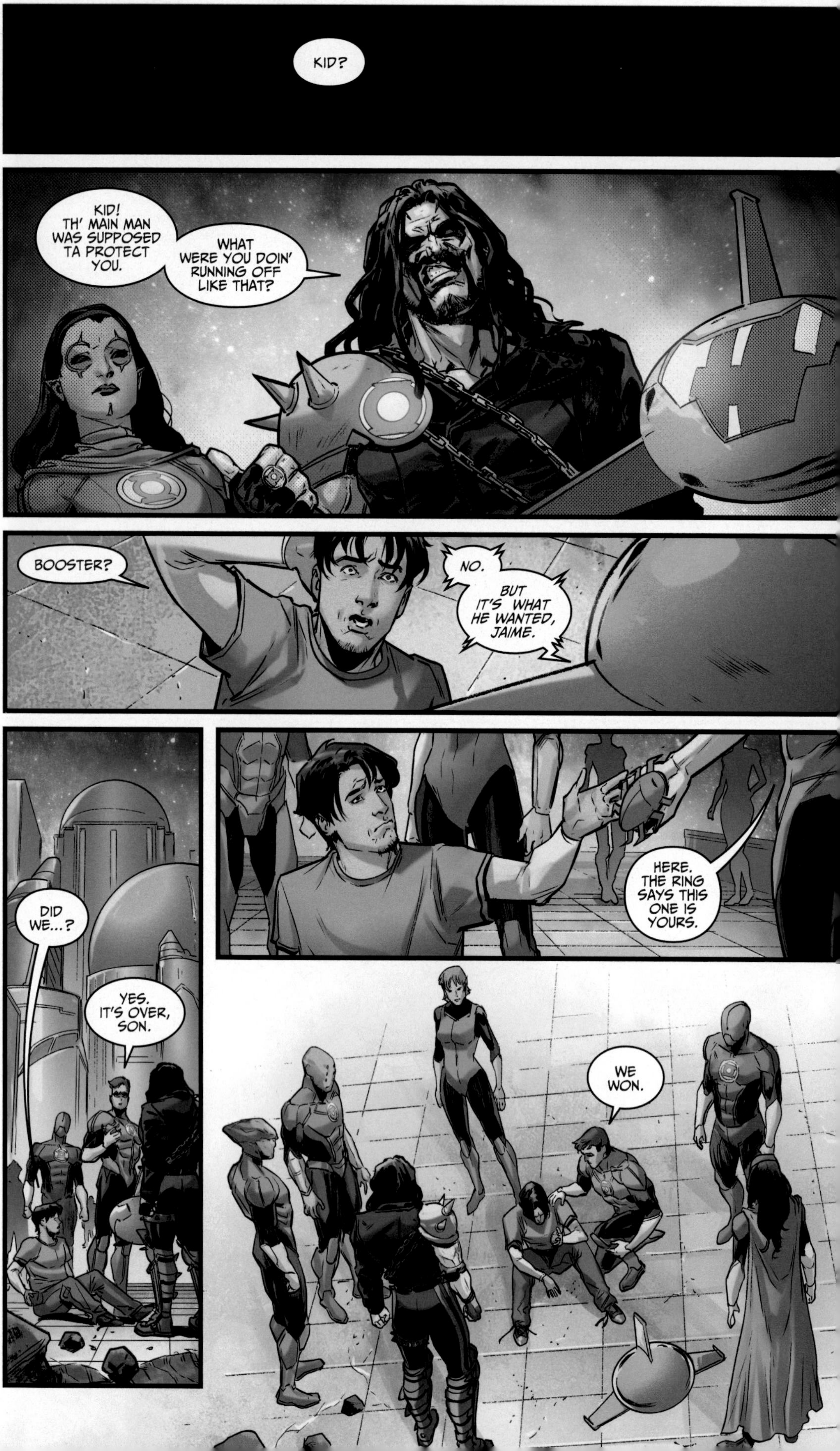
KID?
KID! TH' MAIN MAN WAS SUPPOSED TA PROTECT YOU.
WHAT WERE YOU DOIN' RUNNING OFF LIKE THAT?
BOOSTER?
NO.
BUT IT'S WHAT HE WANTED, JAIME.
HERE. THE RING SAYS THIS ONE IS YOURS.
DID WE...?
YES. IT'S OVER, SON.
WE WON.

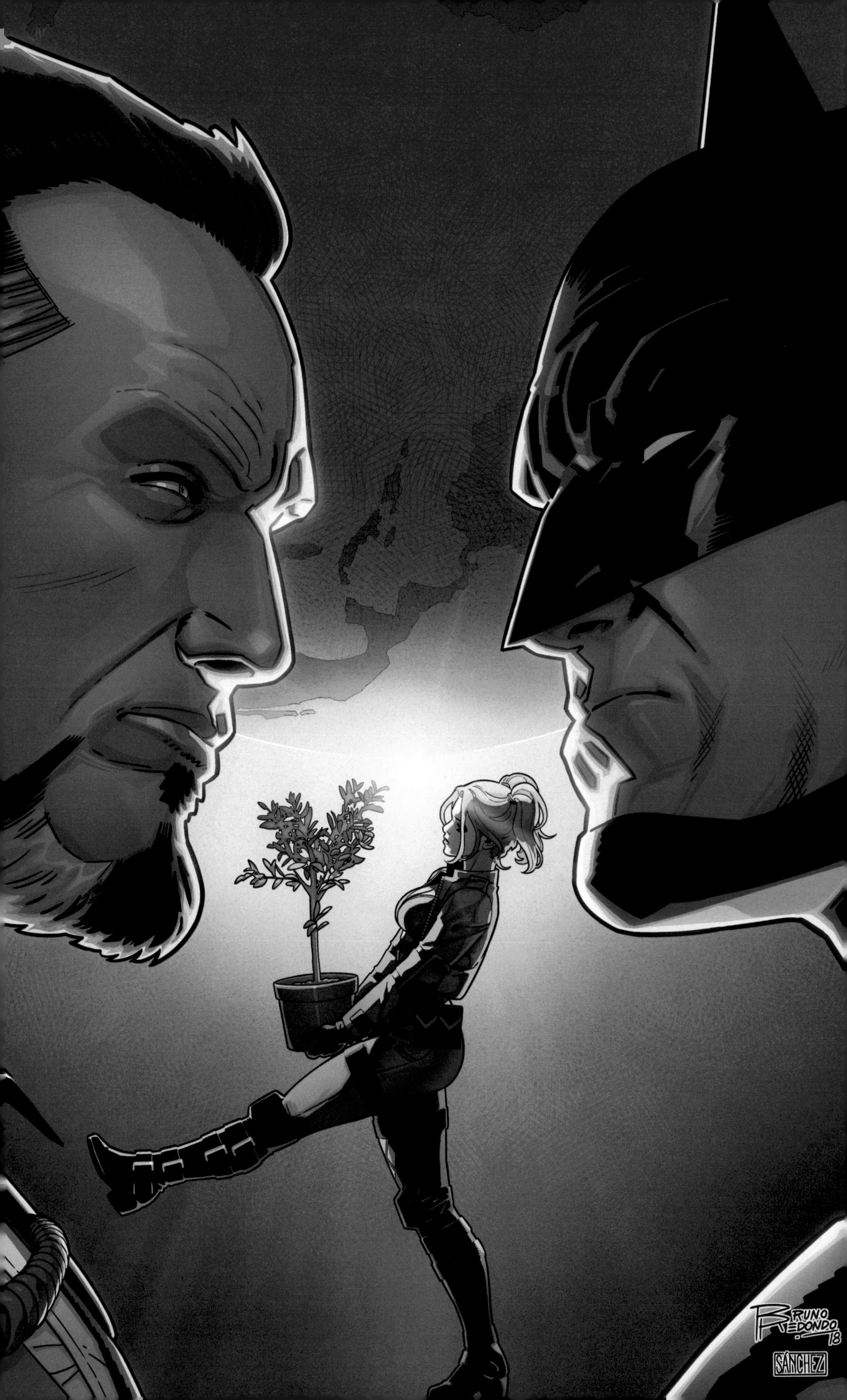
BRUNO REDONDO 18
SÁNCHEZ

Tom Taylor Writer Daniel Sampere Bruno Redondo Pencillers Juan Albarran Inker
Rex Lokus Colorist Wes Abbott Letterer

Cover art by Daniel Sampere and Alejandro Sanchez

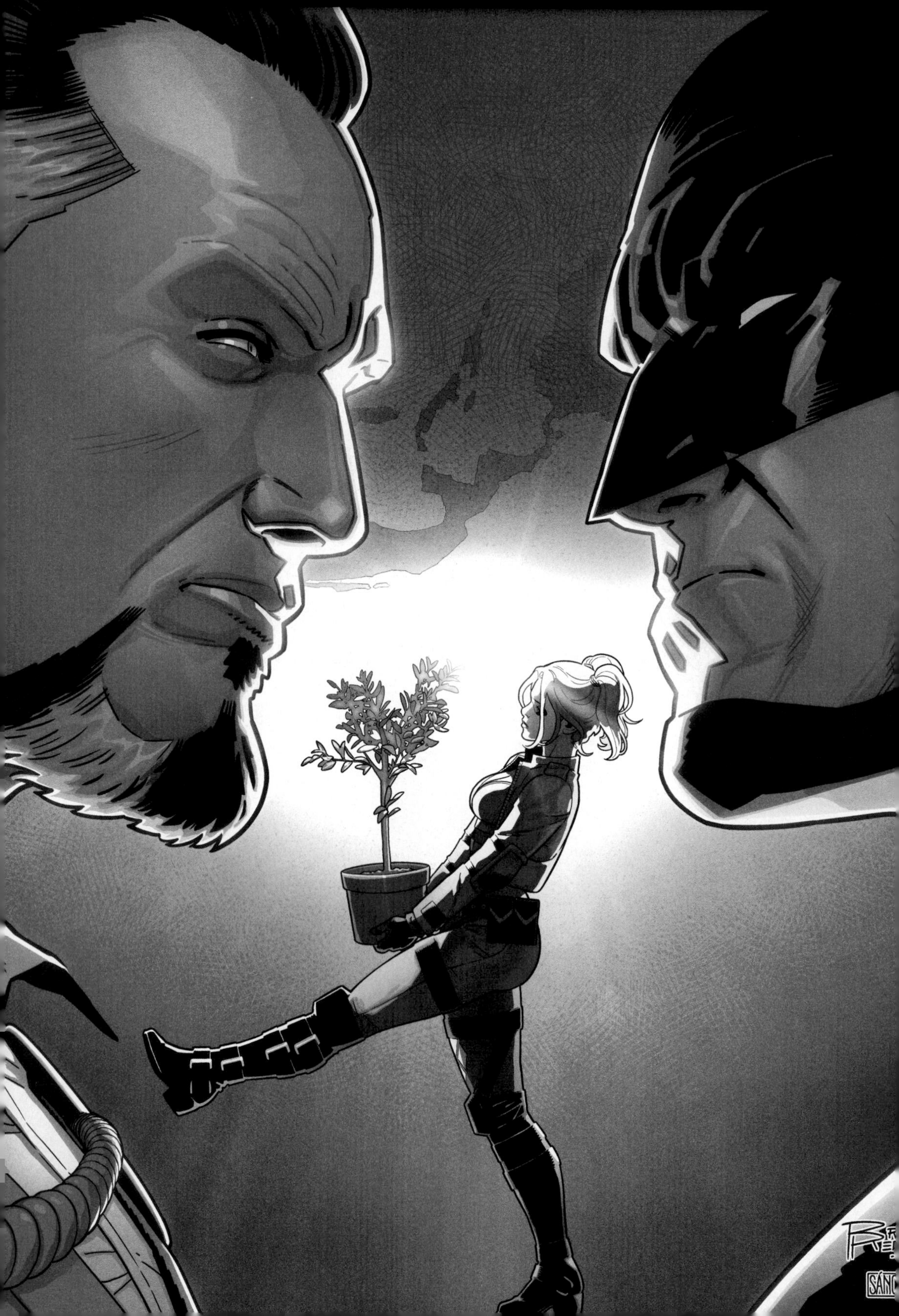

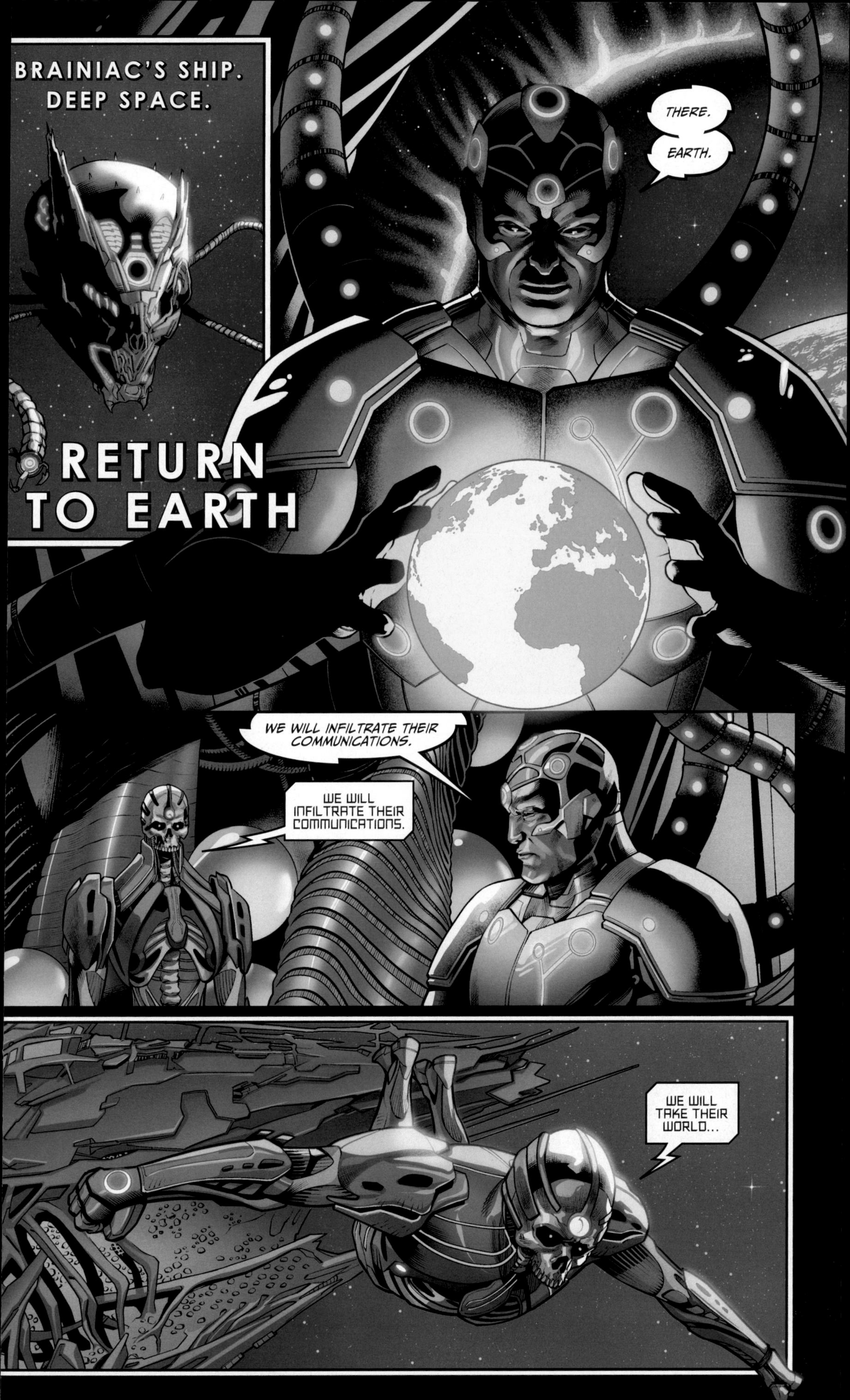
BRAINIAC'S SHIP. DEEP SPACE.
RETURN TO EARTH
THERE.
EARTH.
WE WILL INFILTRATE THEIR COMMUNICATIONS.
WE WILL INFILTRATE THEIR COMMUNICATIONS.
WE WILL TAKE THEIR WORLD...

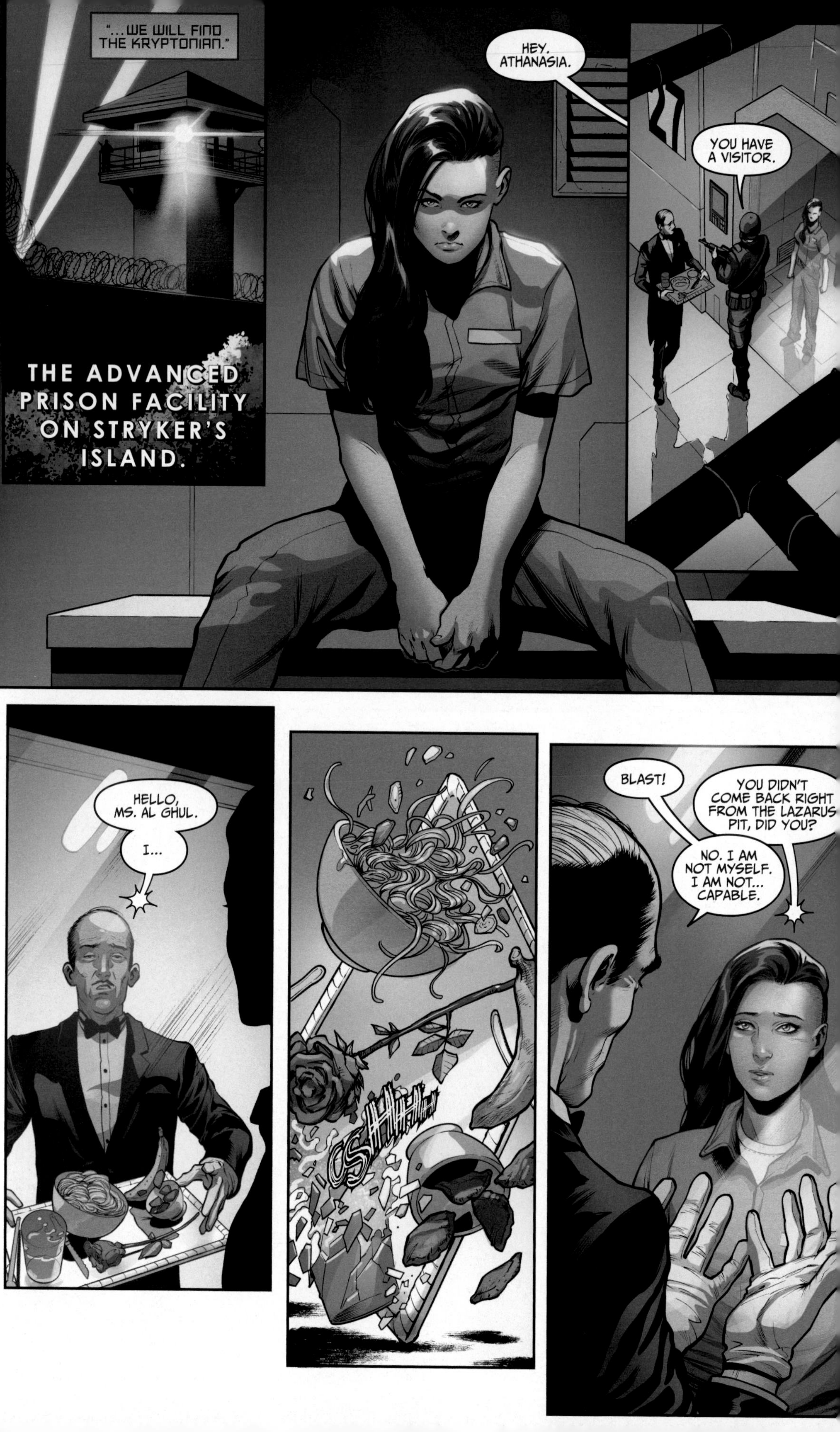
"...WE WILL FIND THE KRYPTONIAN."
THE ADVANCED PRISON FACILITY ON STRYKER'S ISLAND.
HEY. ATHANASIA.
YOU HAVE A VISITOR.
HELLO, MS. AL GHUL.
I...
BLAST!
YOU DIDN'T COME BACK RIGHT FROM THE LAZARUS PIT, DID YOU?
NO. I AM NOT MYSELF. I AM NOT... CAPABLE.

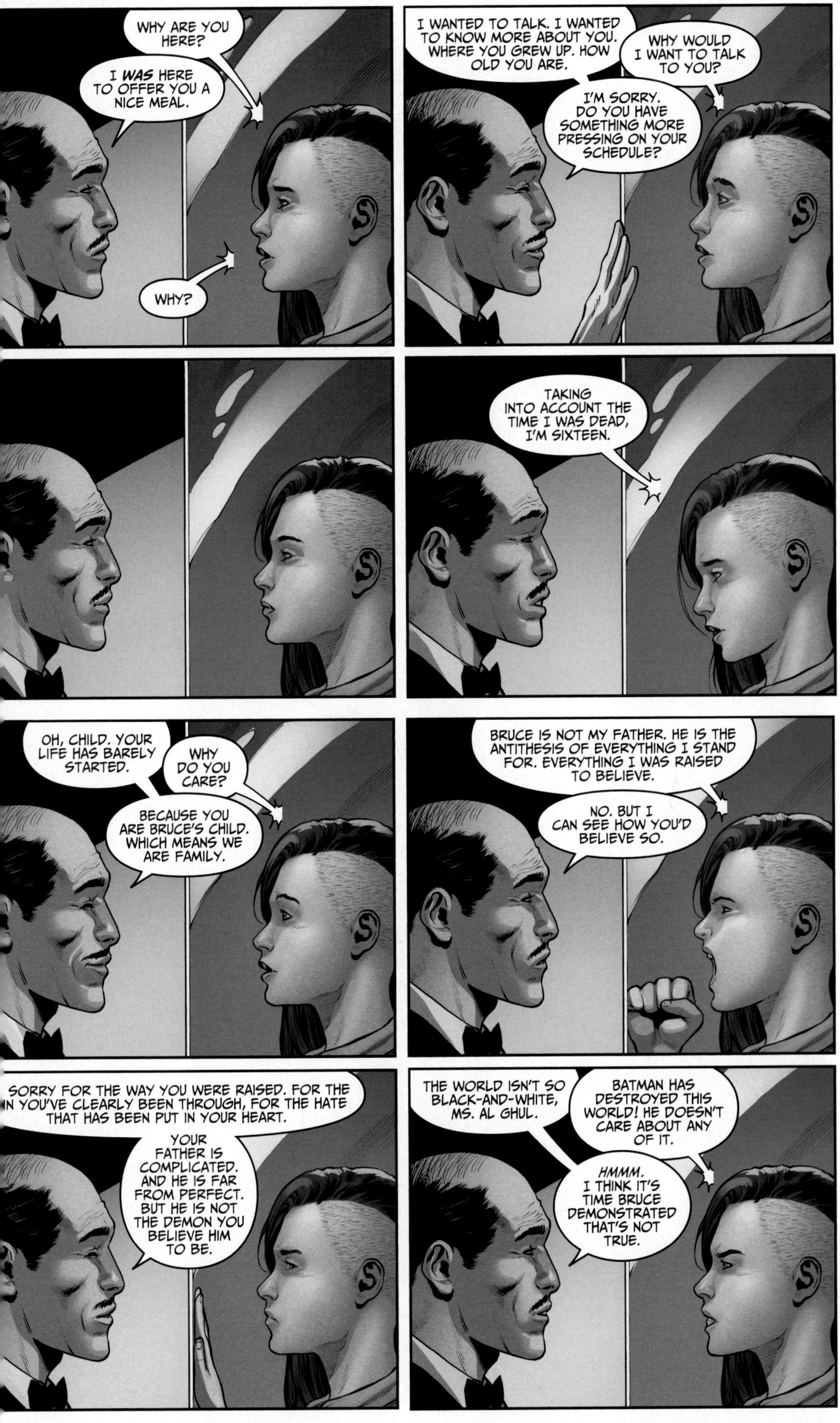
WHY ARE YOU HERE?
I *WAS* HERE TO OFFER YOU A NICE MEAL.
WHY?
I WANTED TO TALK. I WANTED TO KNOW MORE ABOUT YOU. WHERE YOU GREW UP. HOW OLD YOU ARE.
WHY WOULD I WANT TO TALK TO YOU?
I'M SORRY. DO YOU HAVE SOMETHING MORE PRESSING ON YOUR SCHEDULE?
TAKING INTO ACCOUNT THE TIME I WAS DEAD, I'M SIXTEEN.
OH, CHILD. YOUR LIFE HAS BARELY STARTED.
WHY DO YOU CARE?
BECAUSE YOU ARE BRUCE'S CHILD. WHICH MEANS WE ARE FAMILY.
BRUCE IS NOT MY FATHER. HE IS THE ANTITHESIS OF EVERYTHING I STAND FOR. EVERYTHING I WAS RAISED TO BELIEVE.
NO. BUT I CAN SEE HOW YOU'D BELIEVE SO.
SORRY FOR THE WAY YOU WERE RAISED. FOR THE N YOU'VE CLEARLY BEEN THROUGH, FOR THE HATE THAT HAS BEEN PUT IN YOUR HEART.
YOUR FATHER IS COMPLICATED. AND HE IS FAR FROM PERFECT. BUT HE IS NOT THE DEMON YOU BELIEVE HIM TO BE.
THE WORLD ISN'T SO BLACK-AND-WHITE, MS. AL GHUL.
BATMAN HAS DESTROYED THIS WORLD! HE DOESN'T CARE ABOUT ANY OF IT.
HMMM. I THINK IT'S TIME BRUCE DEMONSTRATED THAT'S NOT TRUE.

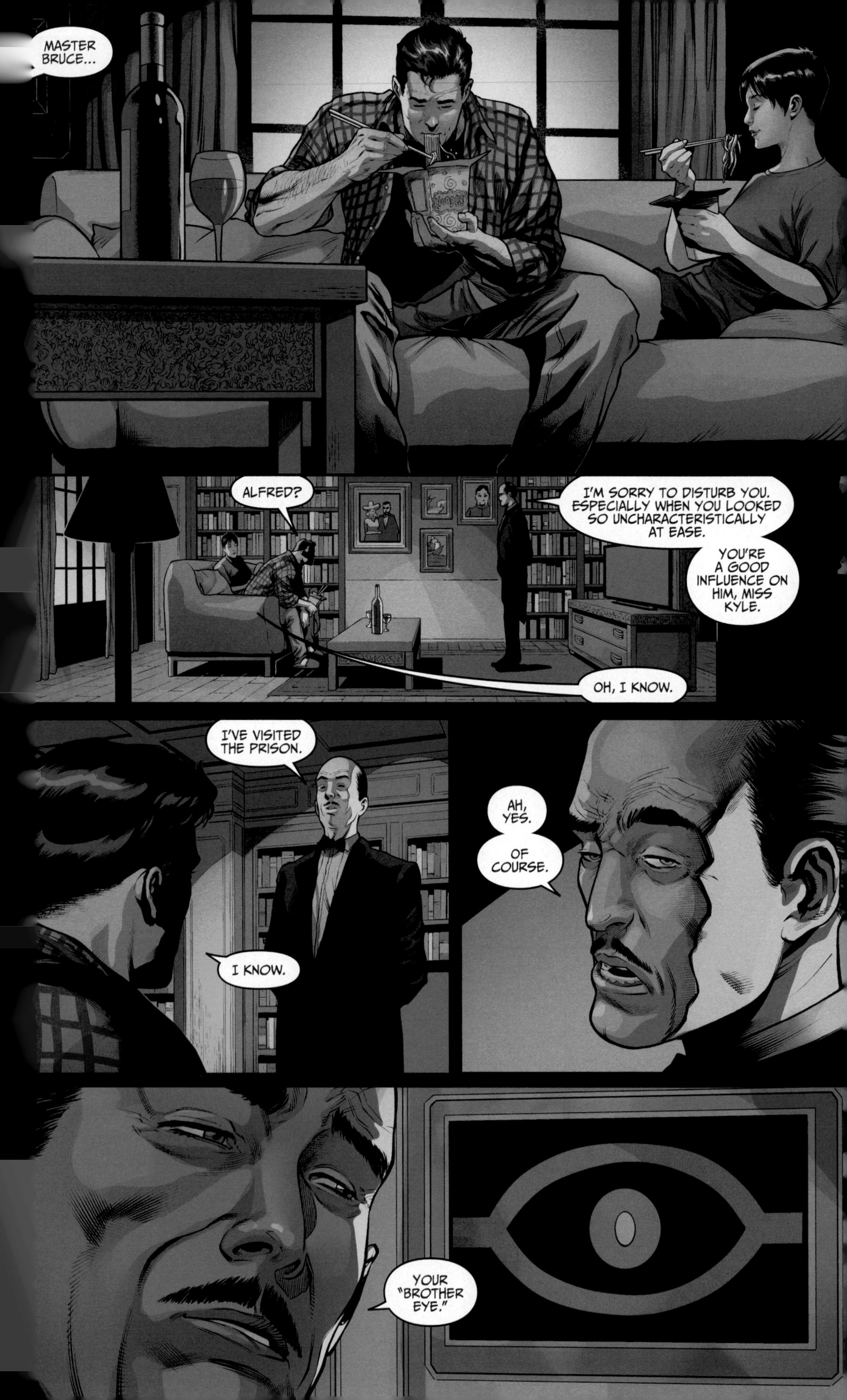
MASTER BRUCE...
ALFRED?
I'M SORRY TO DISTURB YOU. ESPECIALLY WHEN YOU LOOKED SO UNCHARACTERISTICALLY AT EASE.
YOU'RE A GOOD INFLUENCE ON HIM, MISS KYLE.
OH, I KNOW.
I'VE VISITED THE PRISON.
I KNOW.
AH, YES.
OF COURSE.
YOUR "BROTHER EYE."

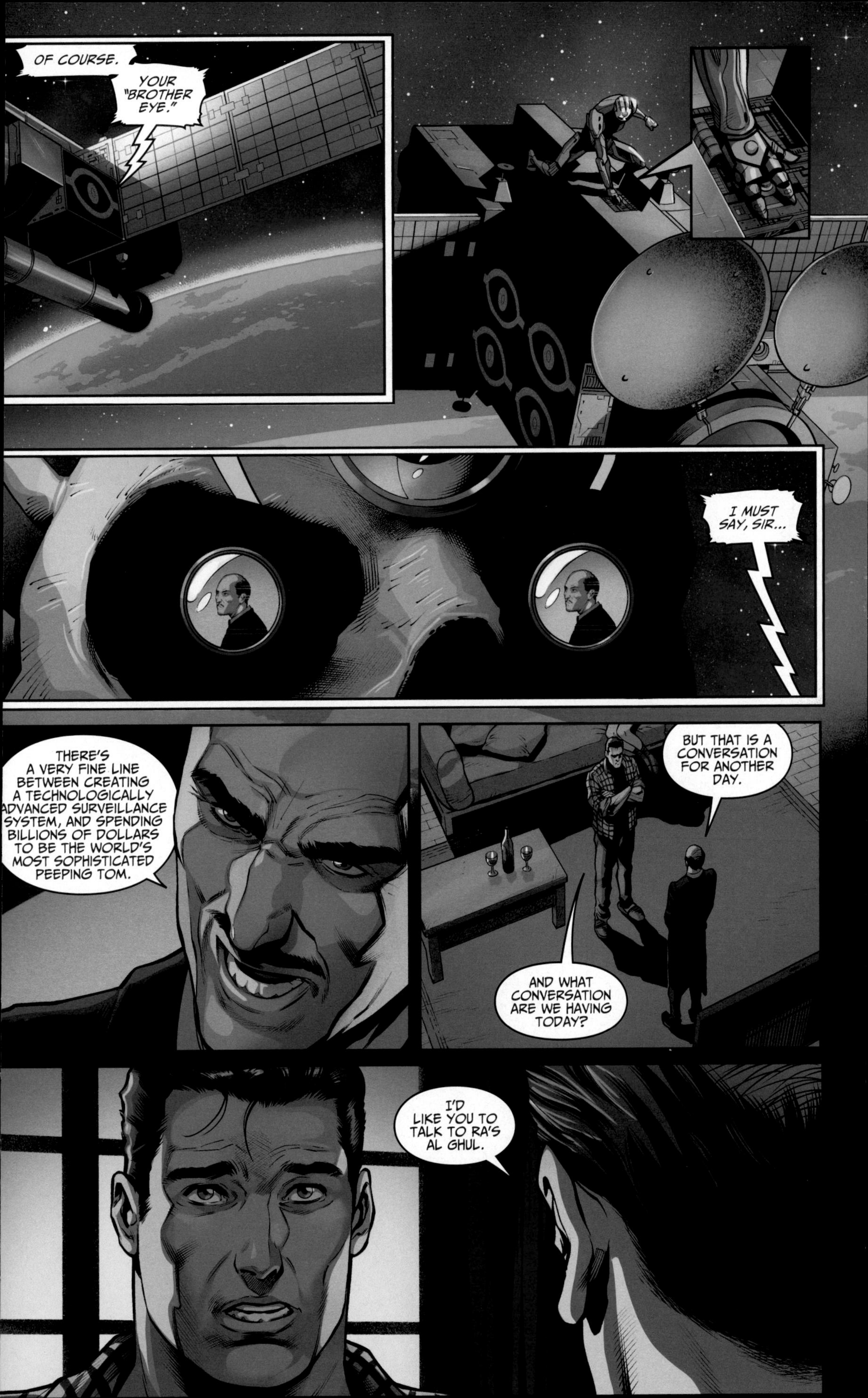
OF COURSE.
YOUR "BROTHER EYE."
I MUST SAY, SIR...
THERE'S A VERY FINE LINE BETWEEN CREATING A TECHNOLOGICALLY ADVANCED SURVEILLANCE SYSTEM, AND SPENDING BILLIONS OF DOLLARS TO BE THE WORLD'S MOST SOPHISTICATED PEEPING TOM.
BUT THAT IS A CONVERSATION FOR ANOTHER DAY.
AND WHAT CONVERSATION ARE WE HAVING TODAY?
I'D LIKE YOU TO TALK TO RA'S AL GHUL.

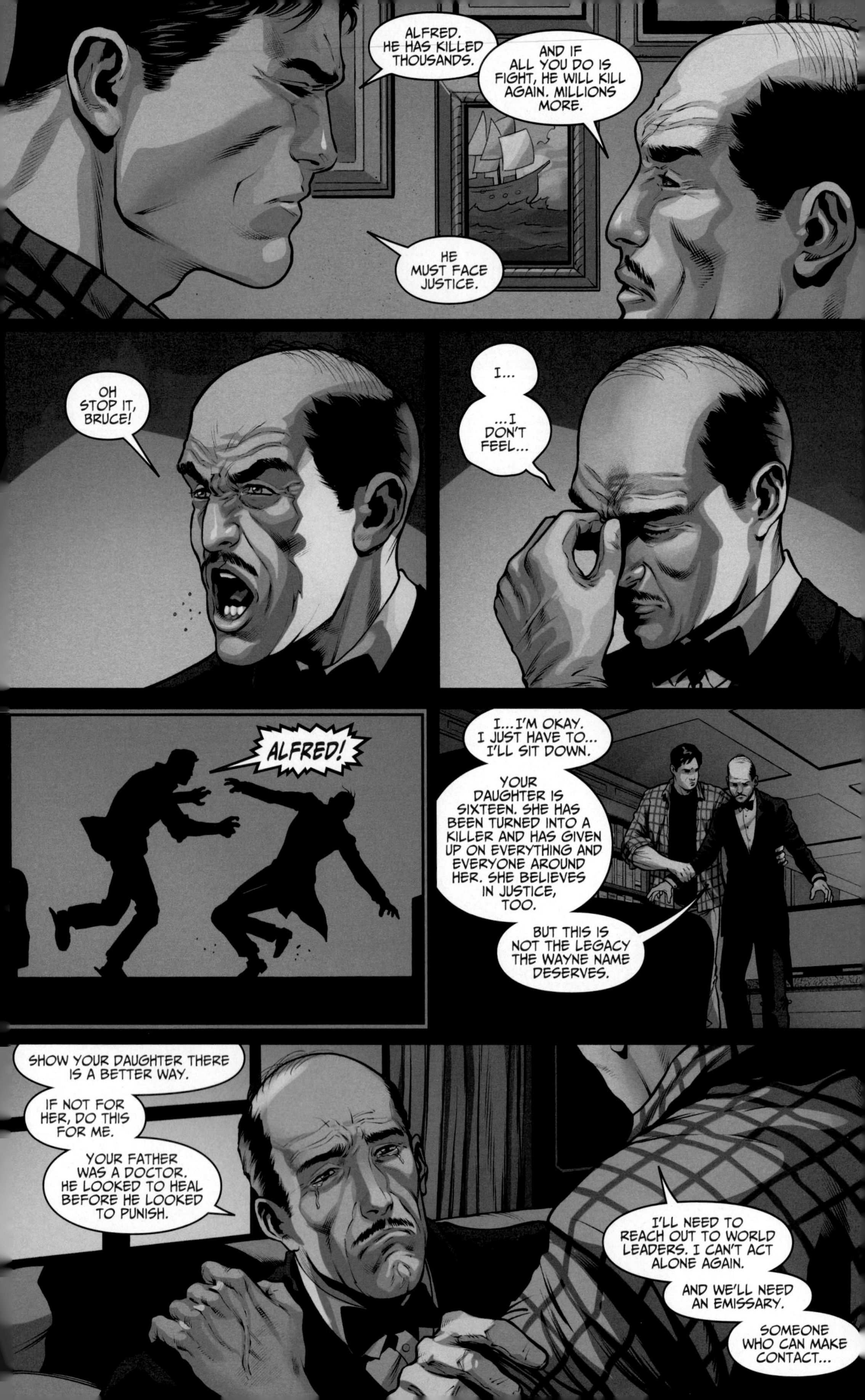

ALFRED. HE HAS KILLED THOUSANDS.
AND IF ALL YOU DO IS FIGHT, HE WILL KILL AGAIN. MILLIONS MORE.
HE MUST FACE JUSTICE.
OH STOP IT, BRUCE!
I...
...I DON'T FEEL...
ALFRED!
I...I'M OKAY. I JUST HAVE TO... I'LL SIT DOWN.
YOUR DAUGHTER IS SIXTEEN. SHE HAS BEEN TURNED INTO A KILLER AND HAS GIVEN UP ON EVERYTHING AND EVERYONE AROUND HER. SHE BELIEVES IN JUSTICE, TOO.
BUT THIS IS NOT THE LEGACY THE WAYNE NAME DESERVES.
SHOW YOUR DAUGHTER THERE IS A BETTER WAY.
IF NOT FOR HER, DO THIS FOR ME.
YOUR FATHER WAS A DOCTOR. HE LOOKED TO HEAL BEFORE HE LOOKED TO PUNISH.
I'LL NEED TO REACH OUT TO WORLD LEADERS. I CAN'T ACT ALONE AGAIN.
AND WE'LL NEED AN EMISSARY.
SOMEONE WHO CAN MAKE CONTACT...

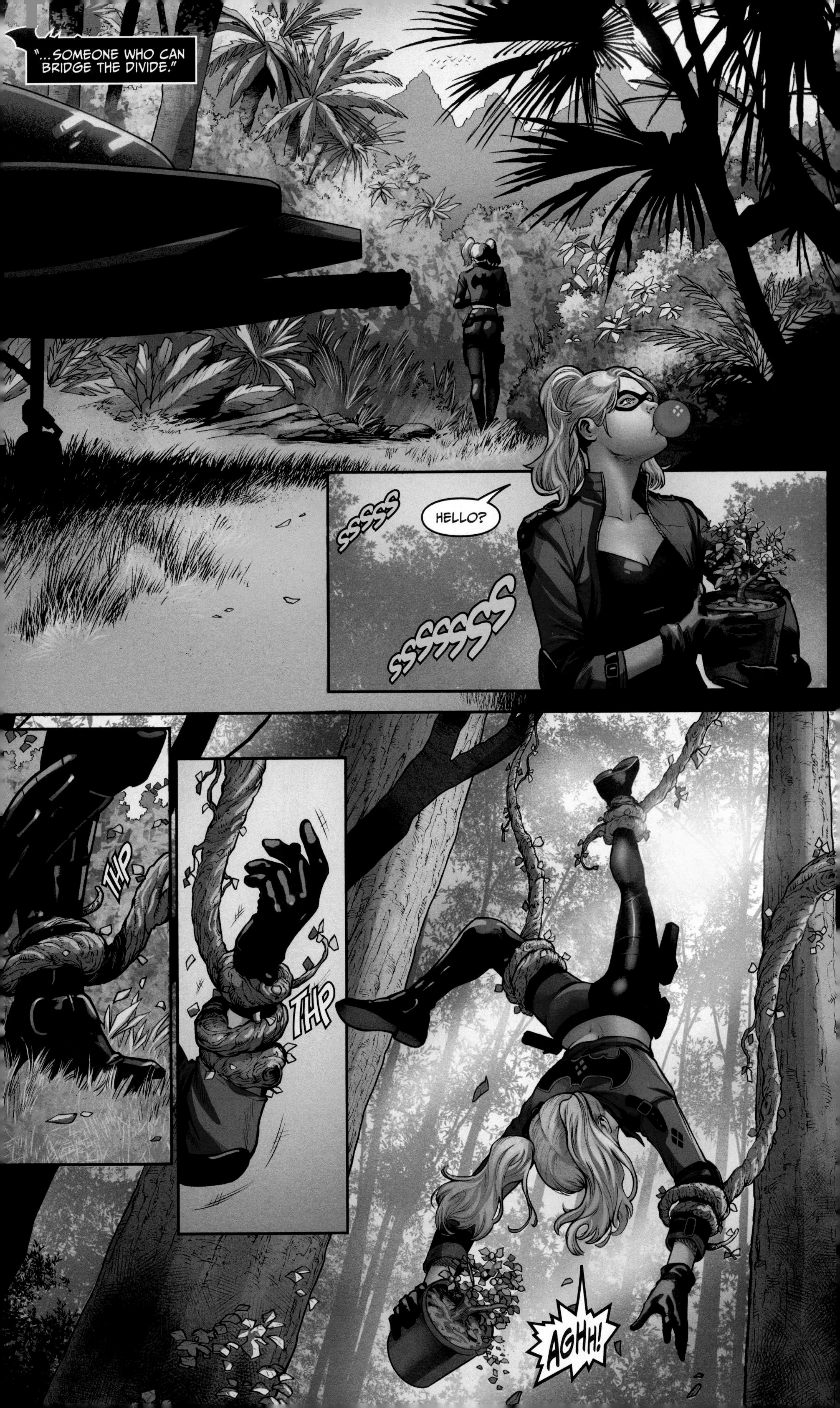
"...SOMEONE WHO CAN BRIDGE THE DIVIDE."
SSSSS
HELLO?
SSSSSS
THP
THP
AGHH!

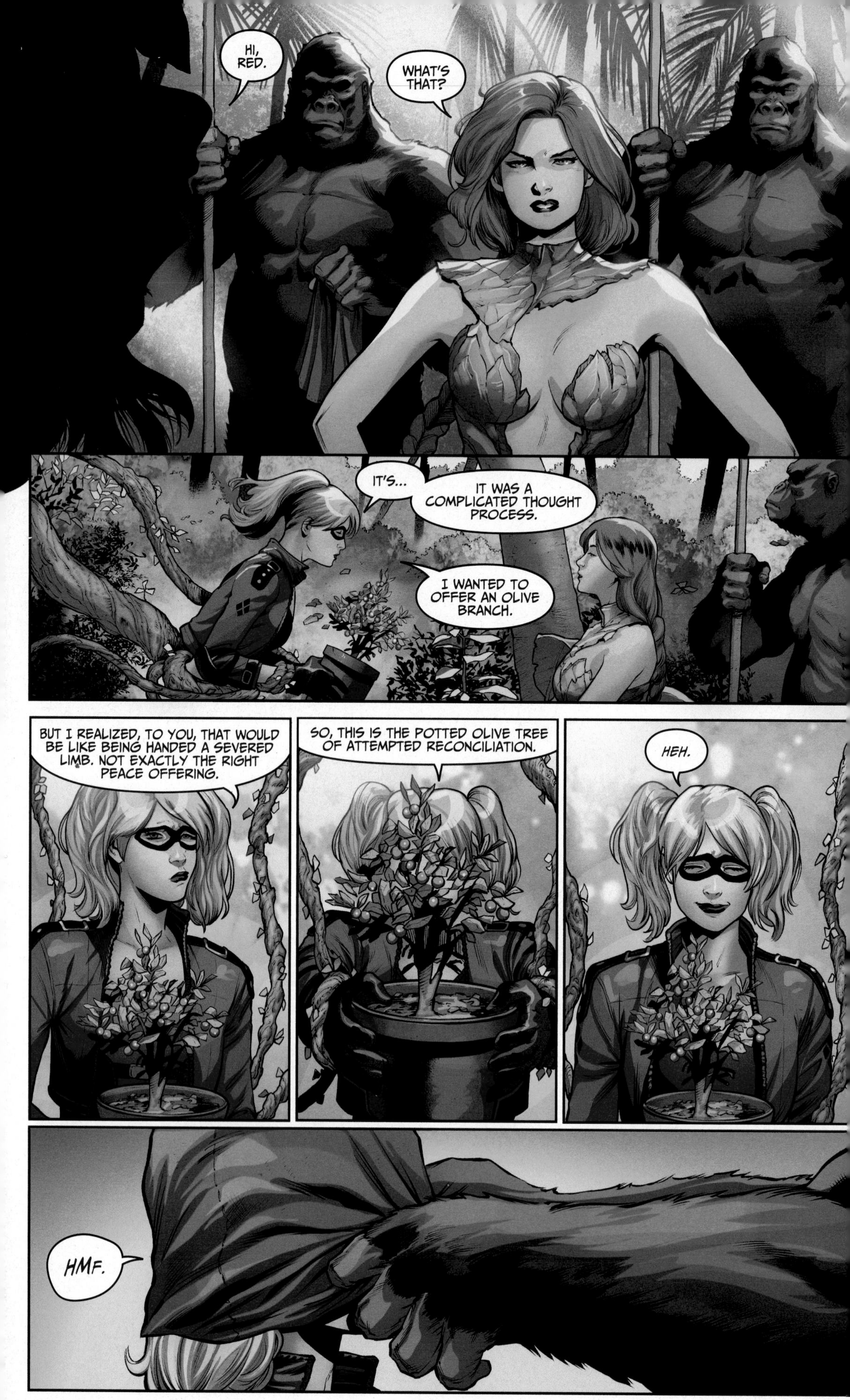
HI, RED.
WHAT'S THAT?
IT'S...
IT WAS A COMPLICATED THOUGHT PROCESS.
I WANTED TO OFFER AN OLIVE BRANCH.
BUT I REALIZED, TO YOU, THAT WOULD BE LIKE BEING HANDED A SEVERED LIMB. NOT EXACTLY THE RIGHT PEACE OFFERING.
SO, THIS IS THE POTTED OLIVE TREE OF ATTEMPTED RECONCILIATION.
HEH.
HMF.

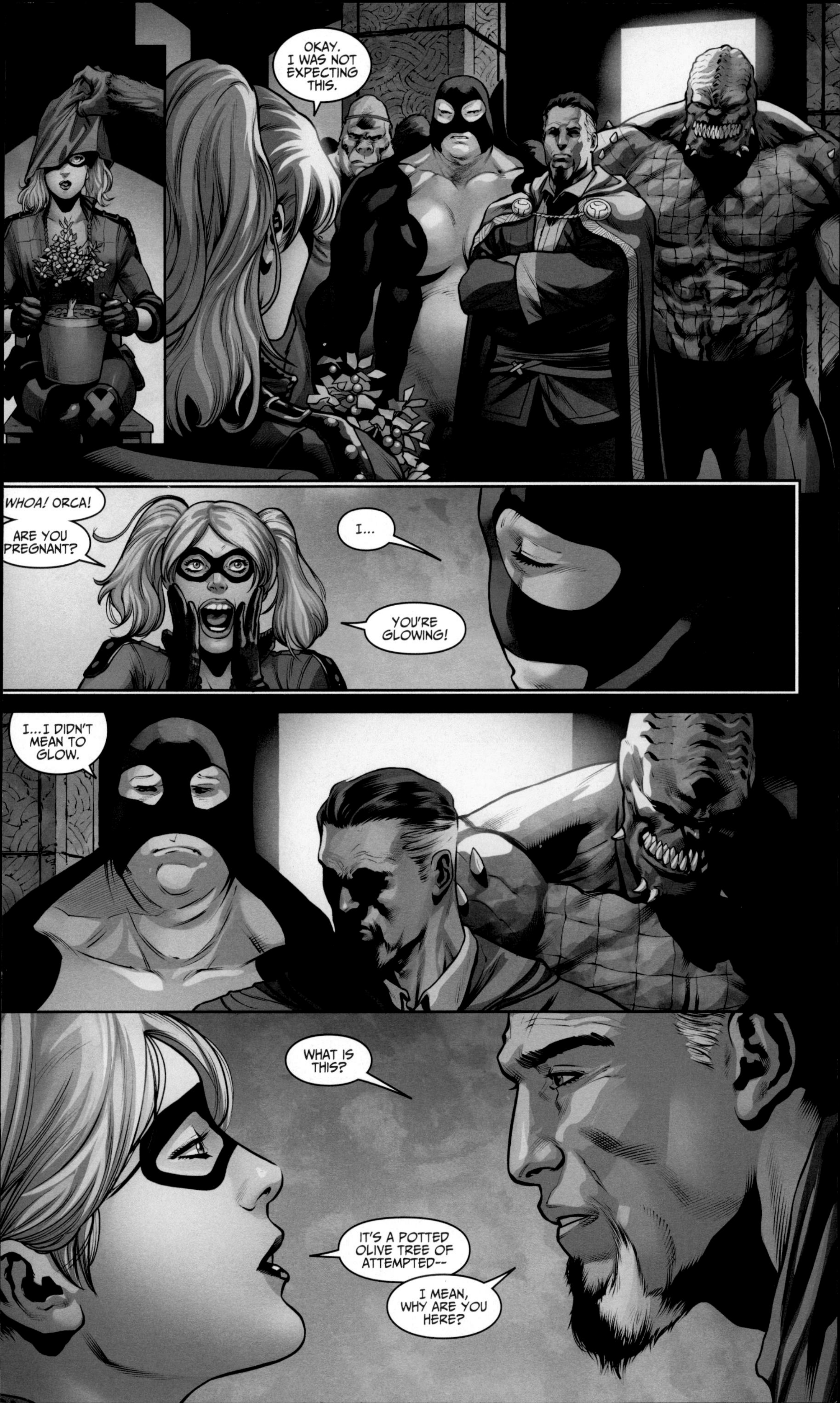
OKAY. I WAS NOT EXPECTING THIS.
WHOA! ORCA!
ARE YOU PREGNANT?
I...
YOU'RE GLOWING!
I...I DIDN'T MEAN TO GLOW.
WHAT IS THIS?
IT'S A POTTED OLIVE TREE OF ATTEMPTED--
I MEAN, WHY ARE YOU HERE?

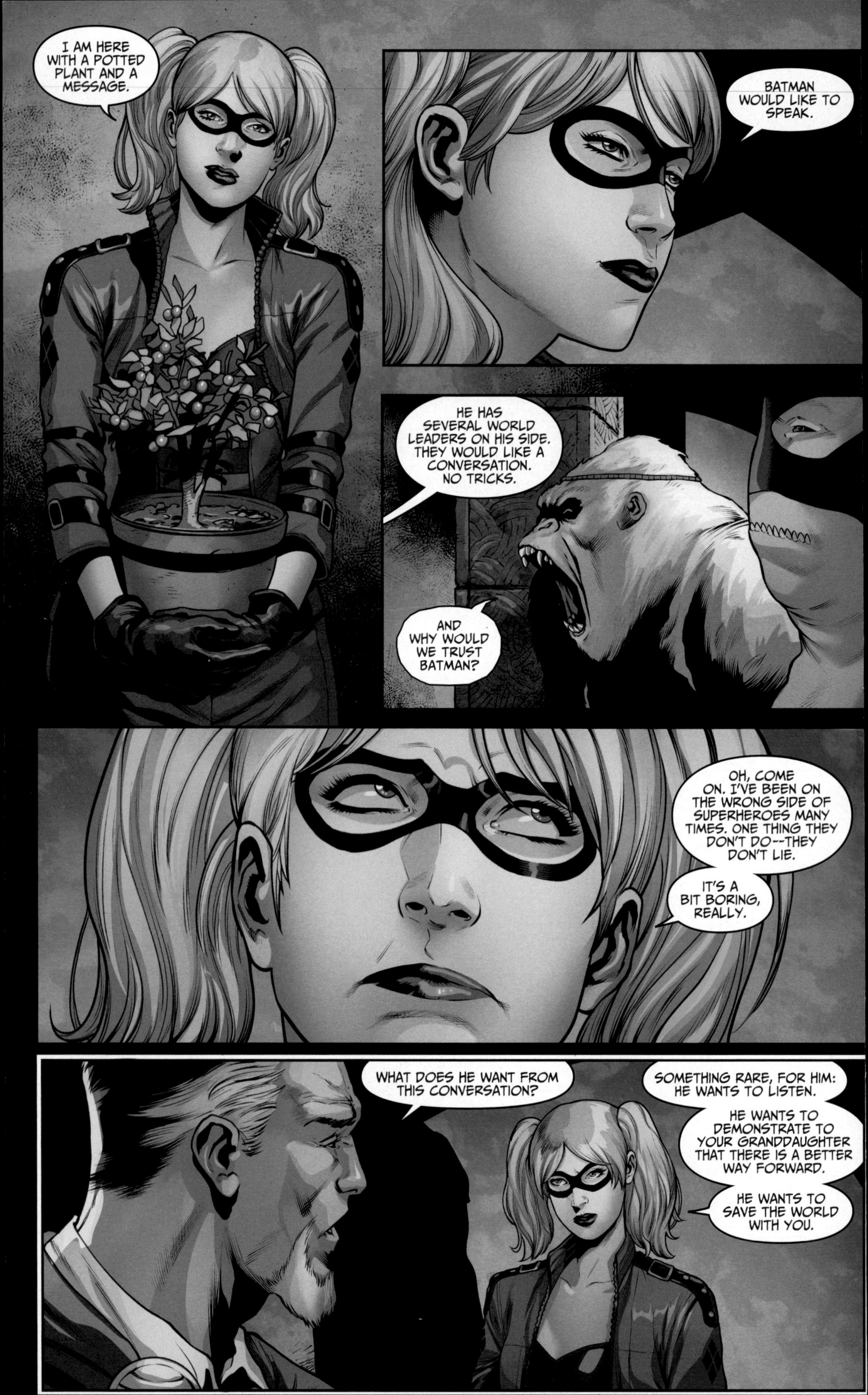
I AM HERE WITH A POTTED PLANT AND A MESSAGE.
BATMAN WOULD LIKE TO SPEAK.
HE HAS SEVERAL WORLD LEADERS ON HIS SIDE. THEY WOULD LIKE A CONVERSATION. NO TRICKS.
AND WHY WOULD WE TRUST BATMAN?
OH, COME ON. I'VE BEEN ON THE WRONG SIDE OF SUPERHEROES MANY TIMES. ONE THING THEY DON'T DO--THEY DON'T LIE.
IT'S A BIT BORING, REALLY.
WHAT DOES HE WANT FROM THIS CONVERSATION?
SOMETHING RARE, FOR HIM: HE WANTS TO LISTEN.
HE WANTS TO DEMONSTRATE TO YOUR GRANDDAUGHTER THAT THERE IS A BETTER WAY FORWARD.
HE WANTS TO SAVE THE WORLD WITH YOU.

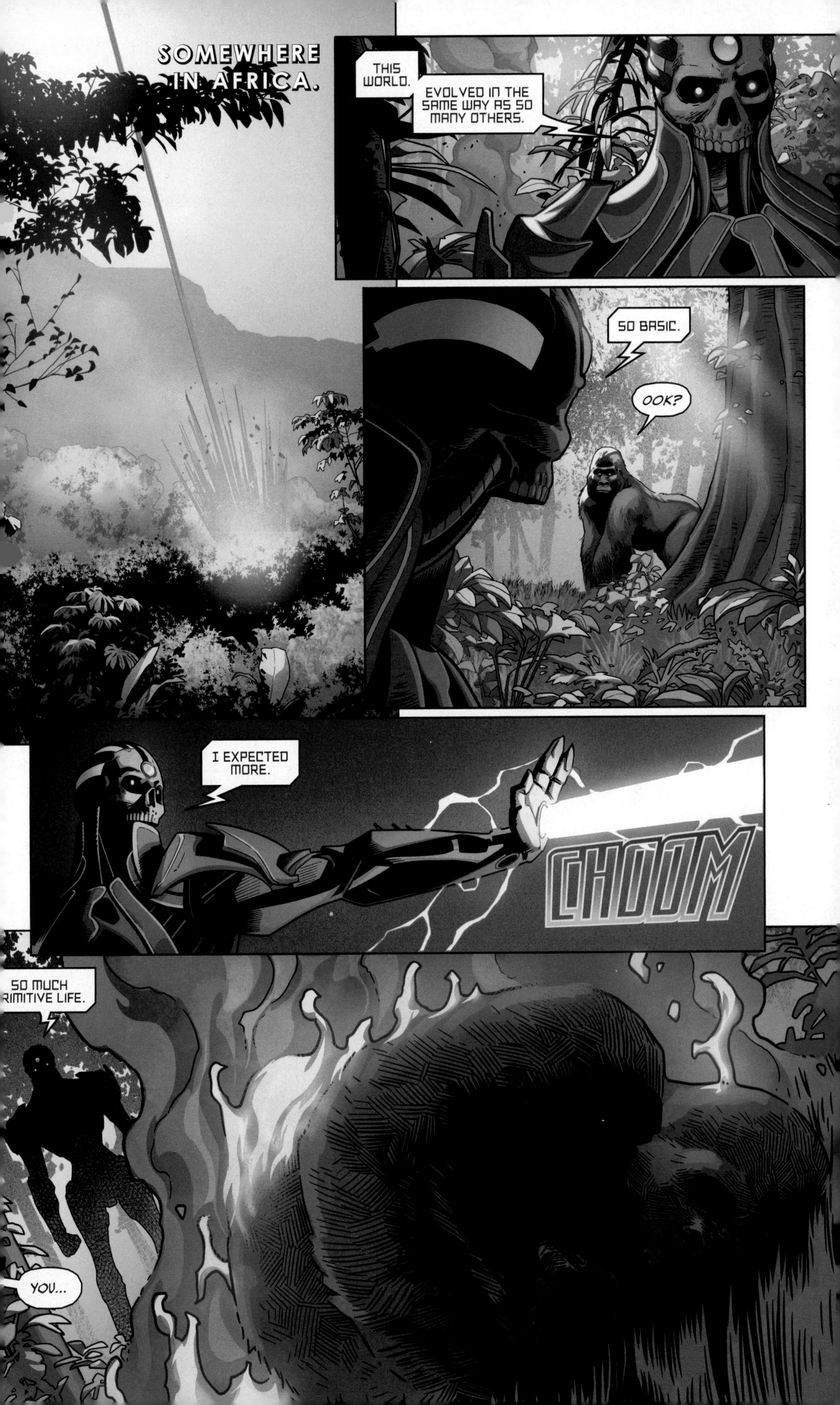
SOMEWHERE IN AFRICA.
THIS WORLD.
EVOLVED IN THE SAME WAY AS SO MANY OTHERS.
SO BASIC.
OOK?
I EXPECTED MORE.
CHOOM
SO MUCH RIMITIVE LIFE.
YOU...

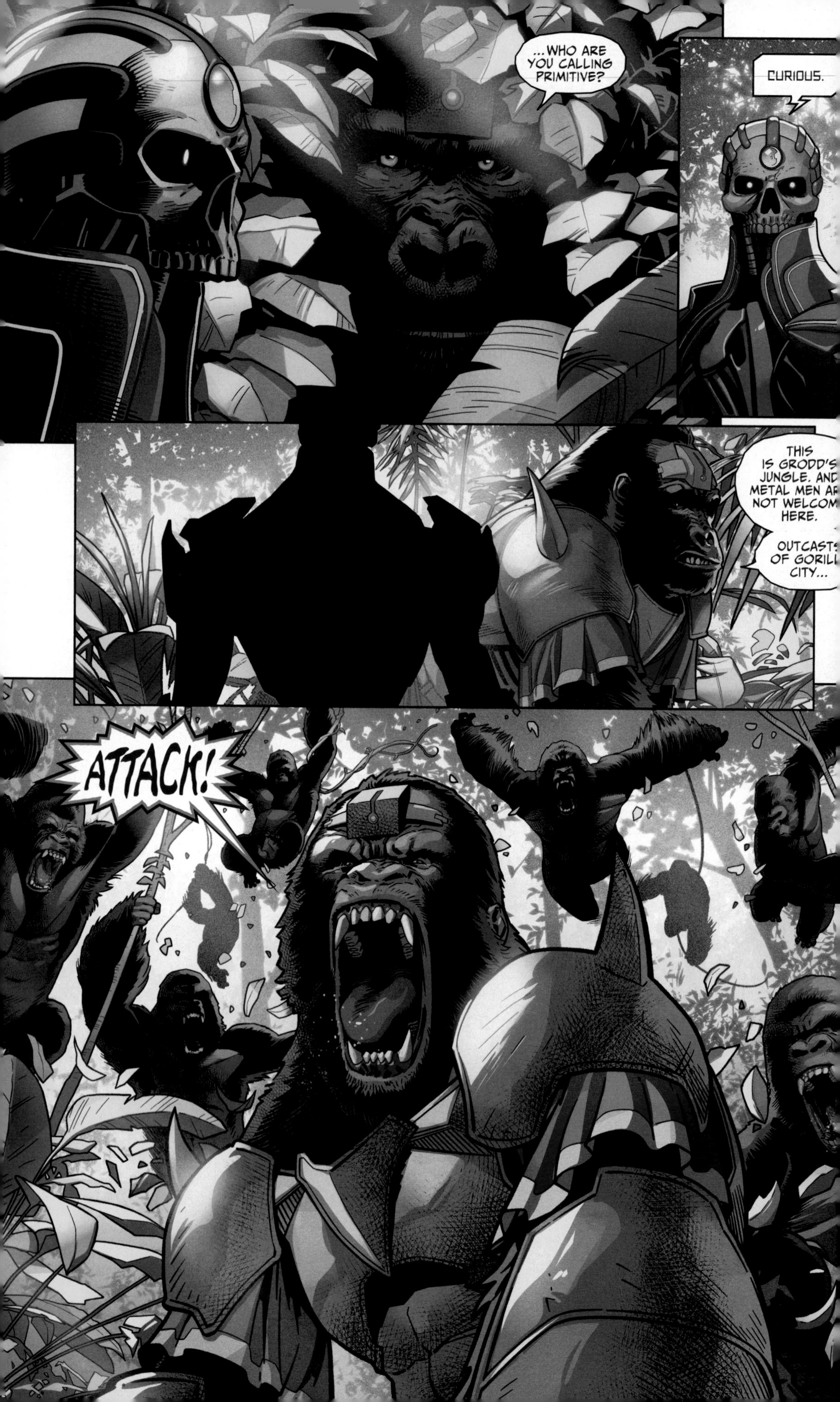
...WHO ARE YOU CALLING PRIMITIVE?
CURIOUS.
THIS IS GRODD'S JUNGLE. AND METAL MEN AR NOT WELCOM HERE.
OUTCASTS OF GORILL CITY...
ATTACK!

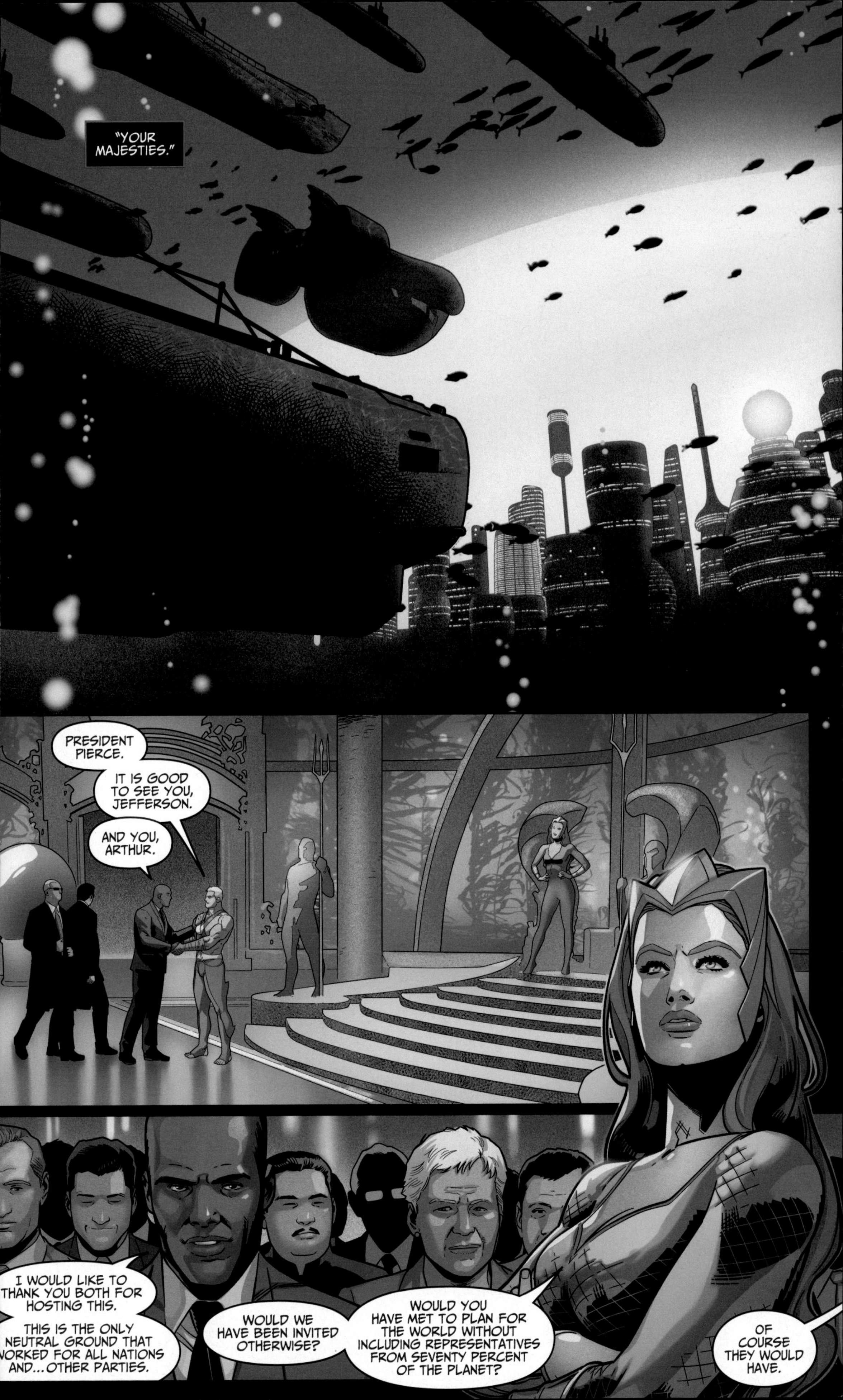
"YOUR MAJESTIES."
PRESIDENT PIERCE.
IT IS GOOD TO SEE YOU, JEFFERSON.
AND YOU, ARTHUR.
I WOULD LIKE TO THANK YOU BOTH FOR HOSTING THIS.
THIS IS THE ONLY NEUTRAL GROUND THAT WORKED FOR ALL NATIONS AND...OTHER PARTIES.
WOULD WE HAVE BEEN INVITED OTHERWISE?
WOULD YOU HAVE MET TO PLAN FOR THE WORLD WITHOUT INCLUDING REPRESENTATIVES FROM SEVENTY PERCENT OF THE PLANET?
OF COURSE THEY WOULD HAVE.

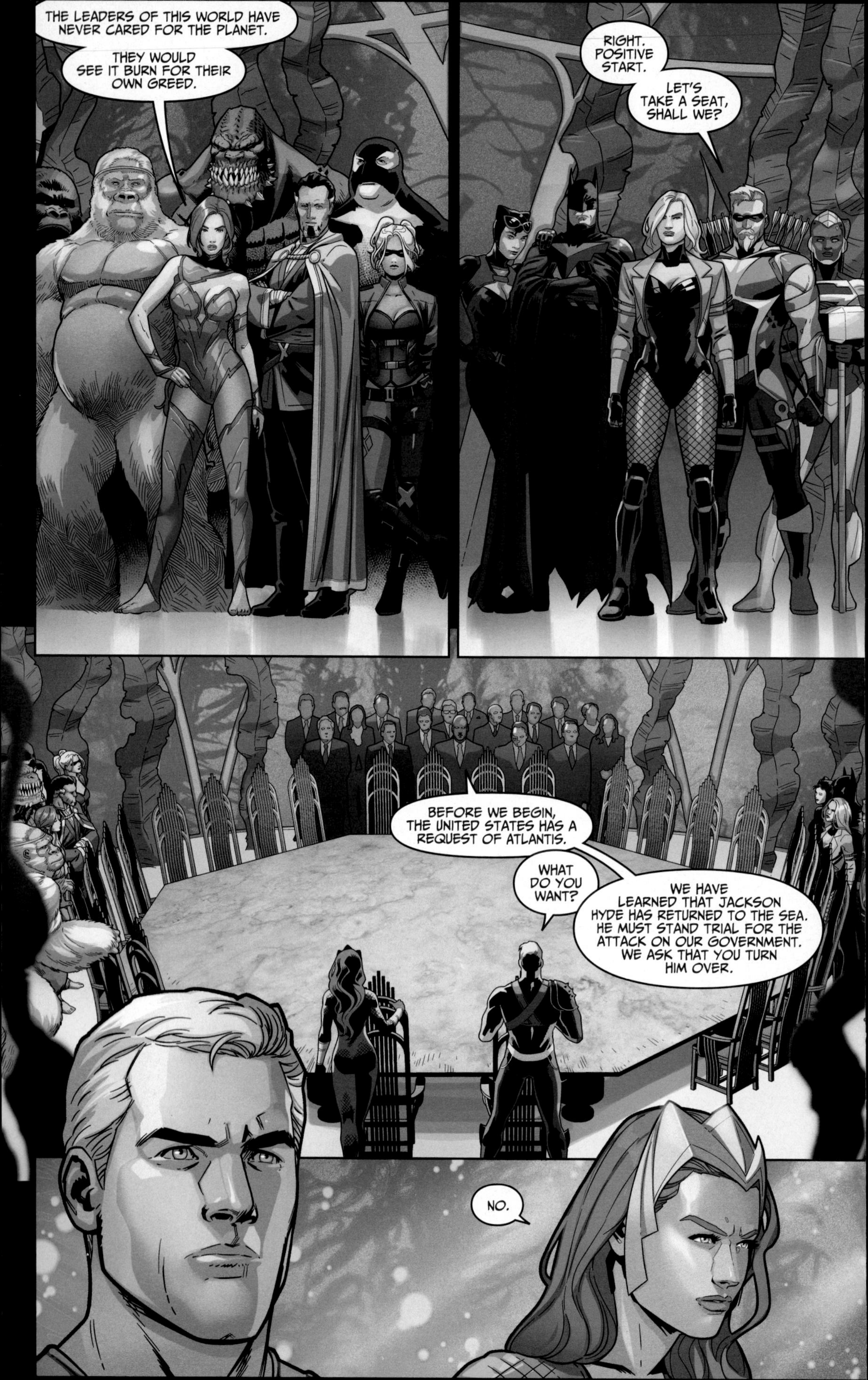
THE LEADERS OF THIS WORLD HAVE NEVER CARED FOR THE PLANET.
THEY WOULD SEE IT BURN FOR THEIR OWN GREED.
RIGHT. POSITIVE START.
LET'S TAKE A SEAT, SHALL WE?
BEFORE WE BEGIN, THE UNITED STATES HAS A REQUEST OF ATLANTIS.
WHAT DO YOU WANT?
WE HAVE LEARNED THAT JACKSON HYDE HAS RETURNED TO THE SEA. HE MUST STAND TRIAL FOR THE ATTACK ON OUR GOVERNMENT. WE ASK THAT YOU TURN HIM OVER.
NO.

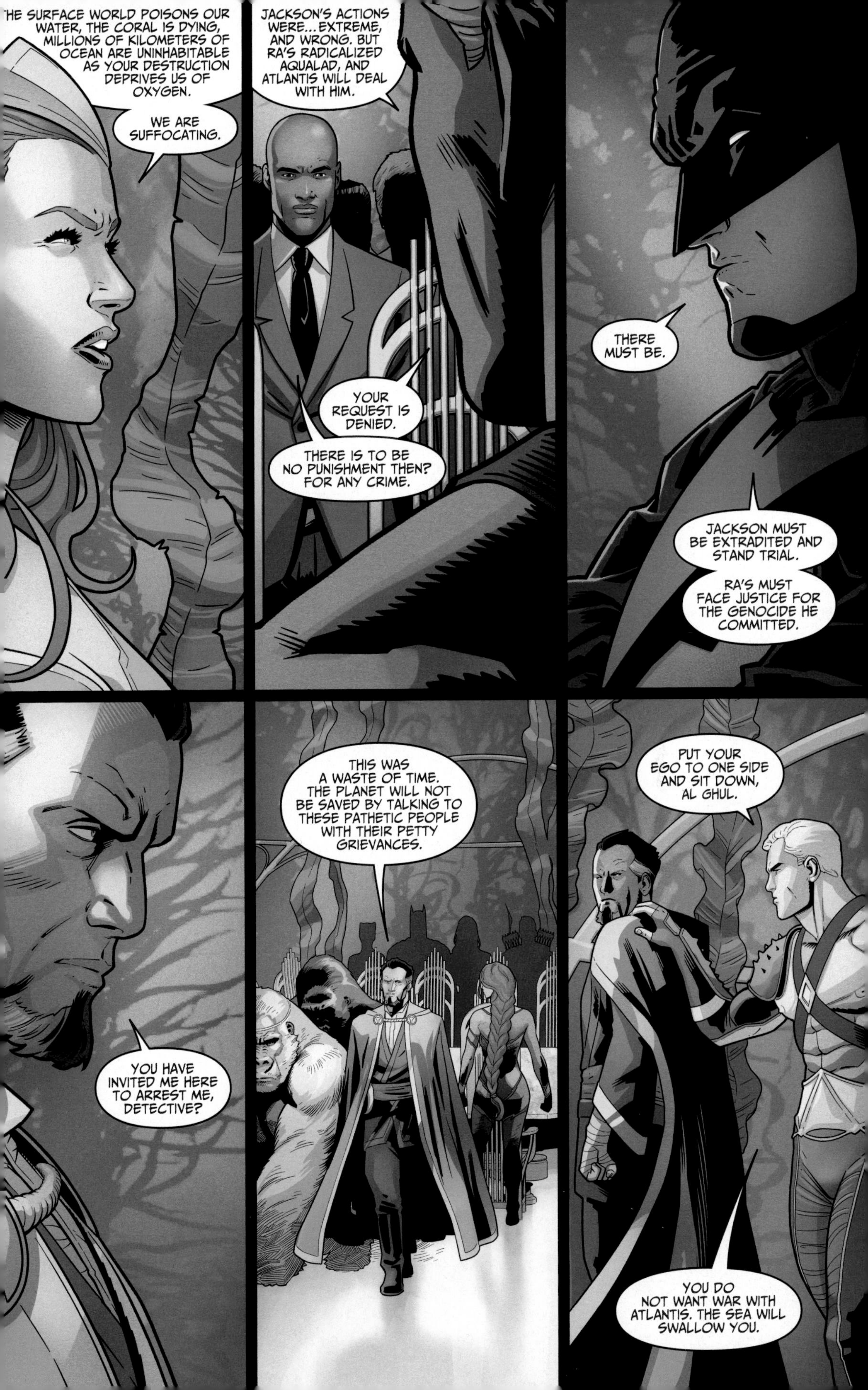
THE SURFACE WORLD POISONS OUR WATER, THE CORAL IS DYING, MILLIONS OF KILOMETERS OF OCEAN ARE UNINHABITABLE AS YOUR DESTRUCTION DEPRIVES US OF OXYGEN.
WE ARE SUFFOCATING.
JACKSON'S ACTIONS WERE...EXTREME, AND WRONG. BUT RA'S RADICALIZED AQUALAD, AND ATLANTIS WILL DEAL WITH HIM.
YOUR REQUEST IS DENIED.
THERE IS TO BE NO PUNISHMENT THEN? FOR ANY CRIME.
THERE MUST BE.
JACKSON MUST BE EXTRADITED AND STAND TRIAL.
RA'S MUST FACE JUSTICE FOR THE GENOCIDE HE COMMITTED.
YOU HAVE INVITED ME HERE TO ARREST ME, DETECTIVE?
THIS WAS A WASTE OF TIME. THE PLANET WILL NOT BE SAVED BY TALKING TO THESE PATHETIC PEOPLE WITH THEIR PETTY GRIEVANCES.
PUT YOUR EGO TO ONE SIDE AND SIT DOWN, AL GHUL.
YOU DO NOT WANT WAR WITH ATLANTIS. THE SEA WILL SWALLOW YOU.

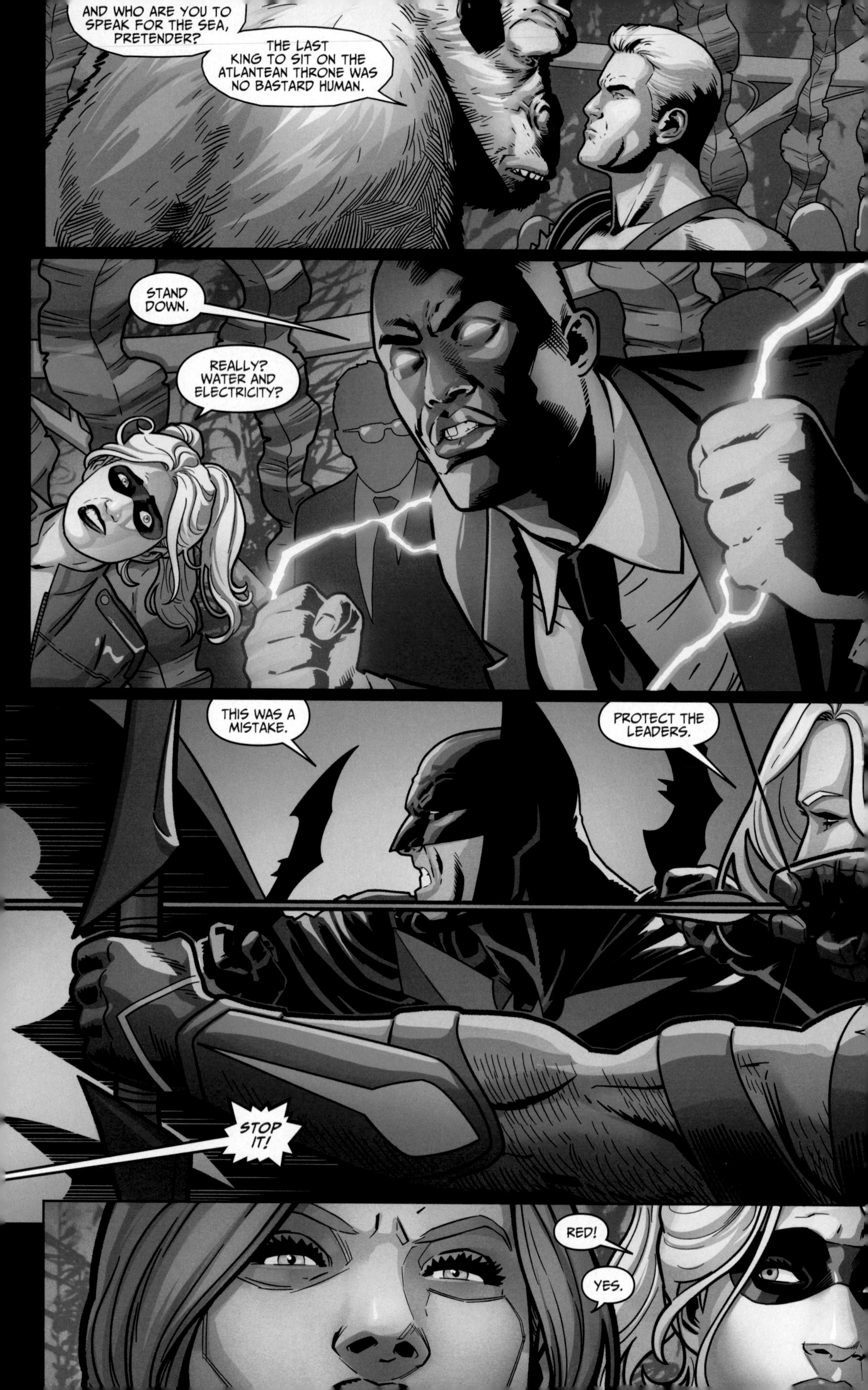
AND WHO ARE YOU TO SPEAK FOR THE SEA, PRETENDER?
THE LAST KING TO SIT ON THE ATLANTEAN THRONE WAS NO BASTARD HUMAN.
STAND DOWN.
REALLY? WATER AND ELECTRICITY?
THIS WAS A MISTAKE.
PROTECT THE LEADERS.
STOP IT!
RED!
YES.

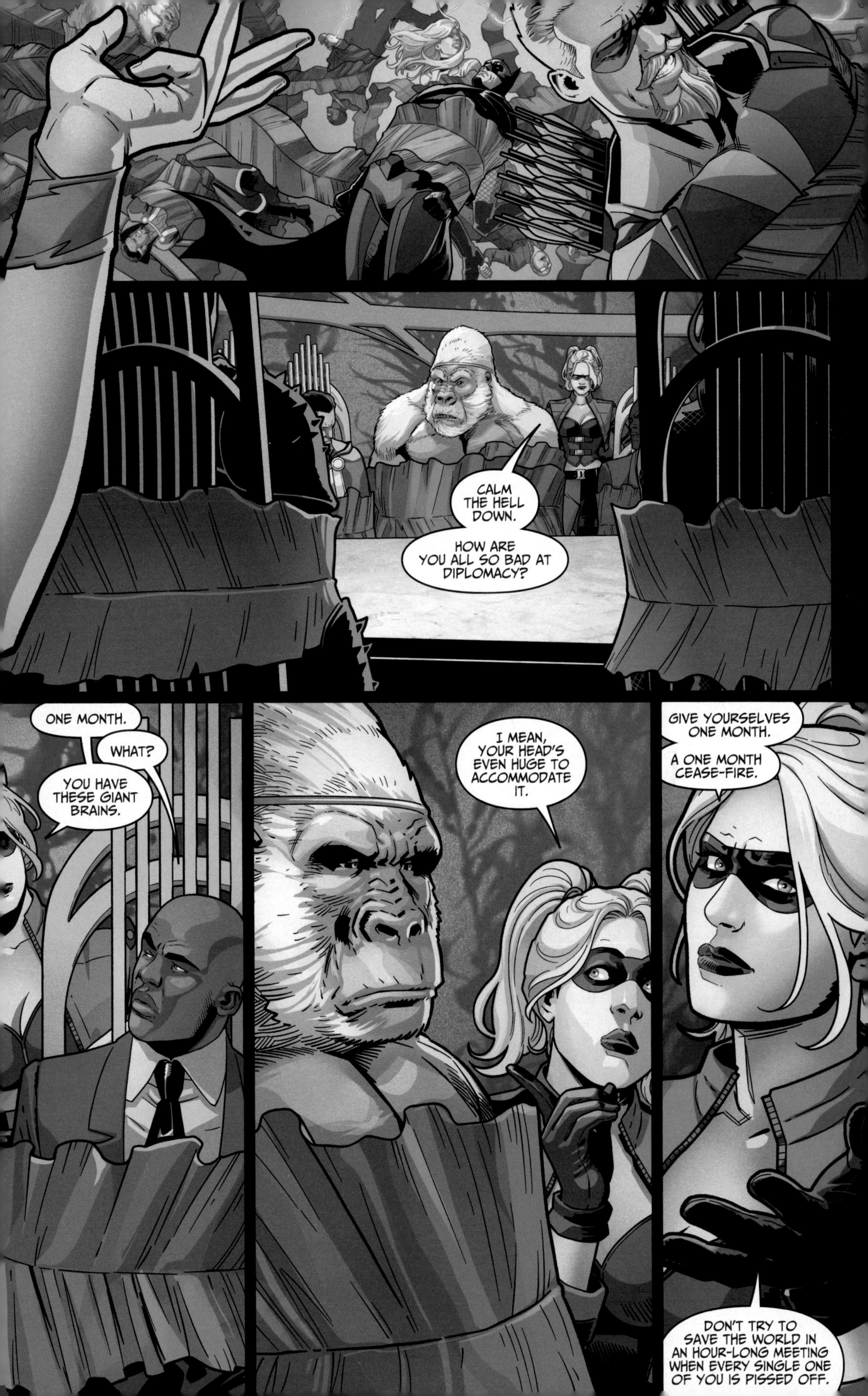
CALM THE HELL DOWN.
HOW ARE YOU ALL SO BAD AT DIPLOMACY?
ONE MONTH.
WHAT?
YOU HAVE THESE GIANT BRAINS.
I MEAN, YOUR HEAD'S EVEN HUGE TO ACCOMMODATE IT.
GIVE YOURSELVES ONE MONTH.
A ONE MONTH CEASE-FIRE.
DON'T TRY TO SAVE THE WORLD IN AN HOUR-LONG MEETING WHEN EVERY SINGLE ONE OF YOU IS PISSED OFF.

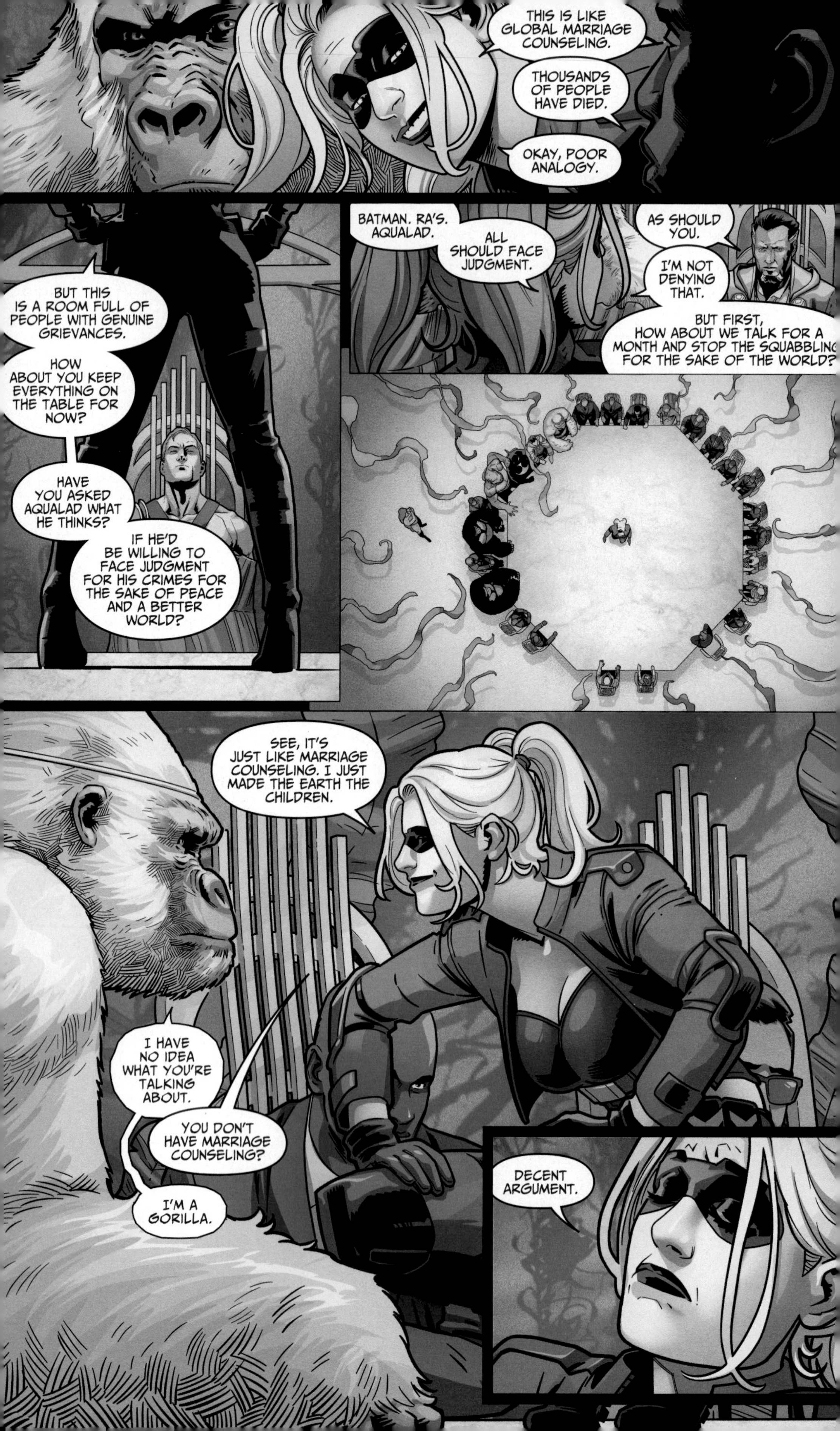
THIS IS LIKE GLOBAL MARRIAGE COUNSELING.
THOUSANDS OF PEOPLE HAVE DIED.
OKAY, POOR ANALOGY.
BUT THIS IS A ROOM FULL OF PEOPLE WITH GENUINE GRIEVANCES.
HOW ABOUT YOU KEEP EVERYTHING ON THE TABLE FOR NOW?
HAVE YOU ASKED AQUALAD WHAT HE THINKS?
IF HE'D BE WILLING TO FACE JUDGMENT FOR HIS CRIMES FOR THE SAKE OF PEACE AND A BETTER WORLD?
BATMAN. RA'S. AQUALAD.
ALL SHOULD FACE JUDGMENT.
AS SHOULD YOU.
I'M NOT DENYING THAT.
BUT FIRST, HOW ABOUT WE TALK FOR A MONTH AND STOP THE SQUABBLING FOR THE SAKE OF THE WORLD?
SEE, IT'S JUST LIKE MARRIAGE COUNSELING. I JUST MADE THE EARTH THE CHILDREN.
I HAVE NO IDEA WHAT YOU'RE TALKING ABOUT.
YOU DON'T HAVE MARRIAGE COUNSELING?
I'M A GORILLA.
DECENT ARGUMENT.

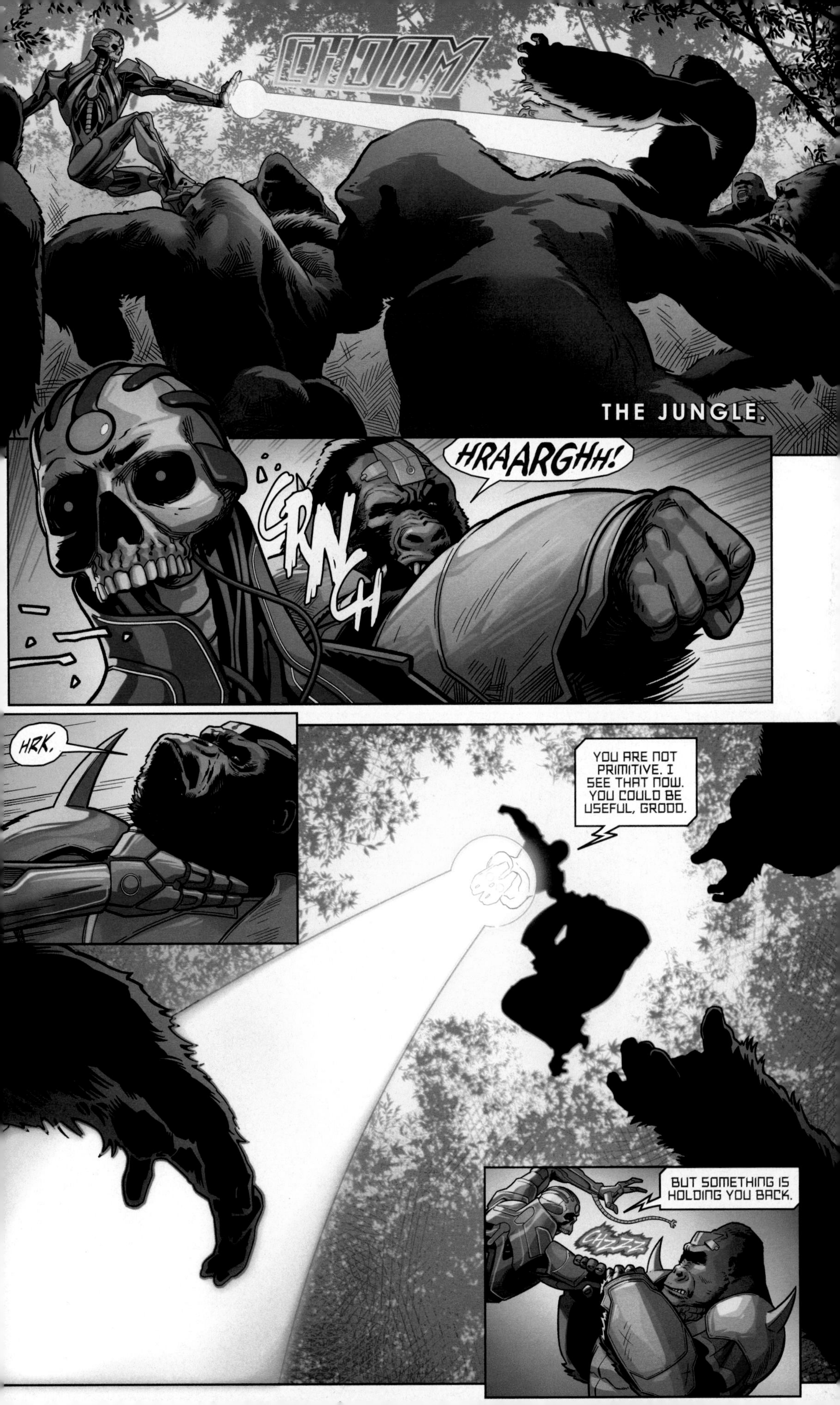
CHOOM
THE JUNGLE.
HRAARGHH!
CRNCH
HRK.
YOU ARE NOT PRIMITIVE. I SEE THAT NOW. YOU COULD BE USEFUL, GRODD.
BUT SOMETHING IS HOLDING YOU BACK.
CHZZZ

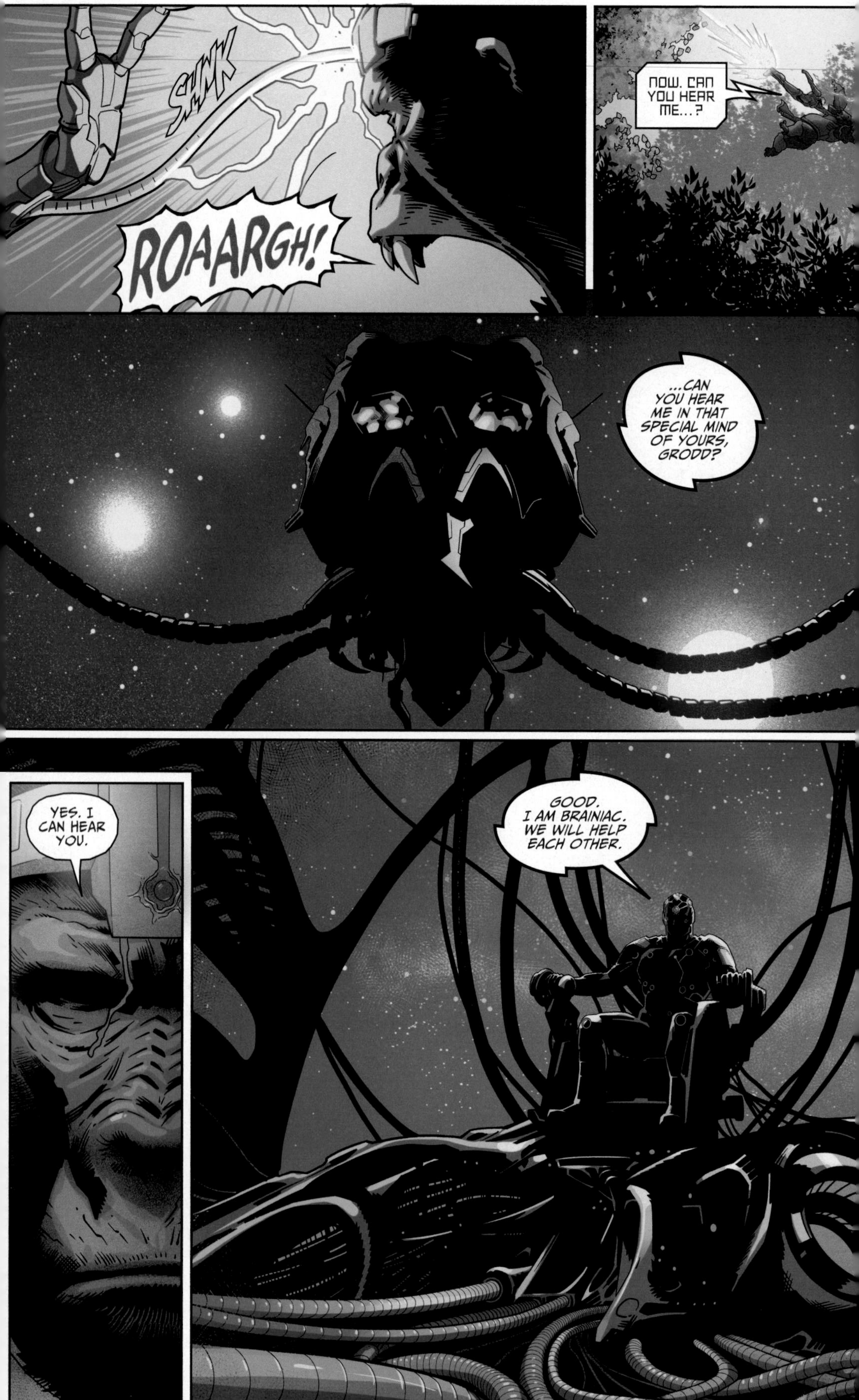
SHNK
ROAARGH!
NOW. CAN YOU HEAR ME...?
...CAN YOU HEAR ME IN THAT SPECIAL MIND OF YOURS, GRODD?
YES. I CAN HEAR YOU.
GOOD. I AM BRAINIAC. WE WILL HELP EACH OTHER.

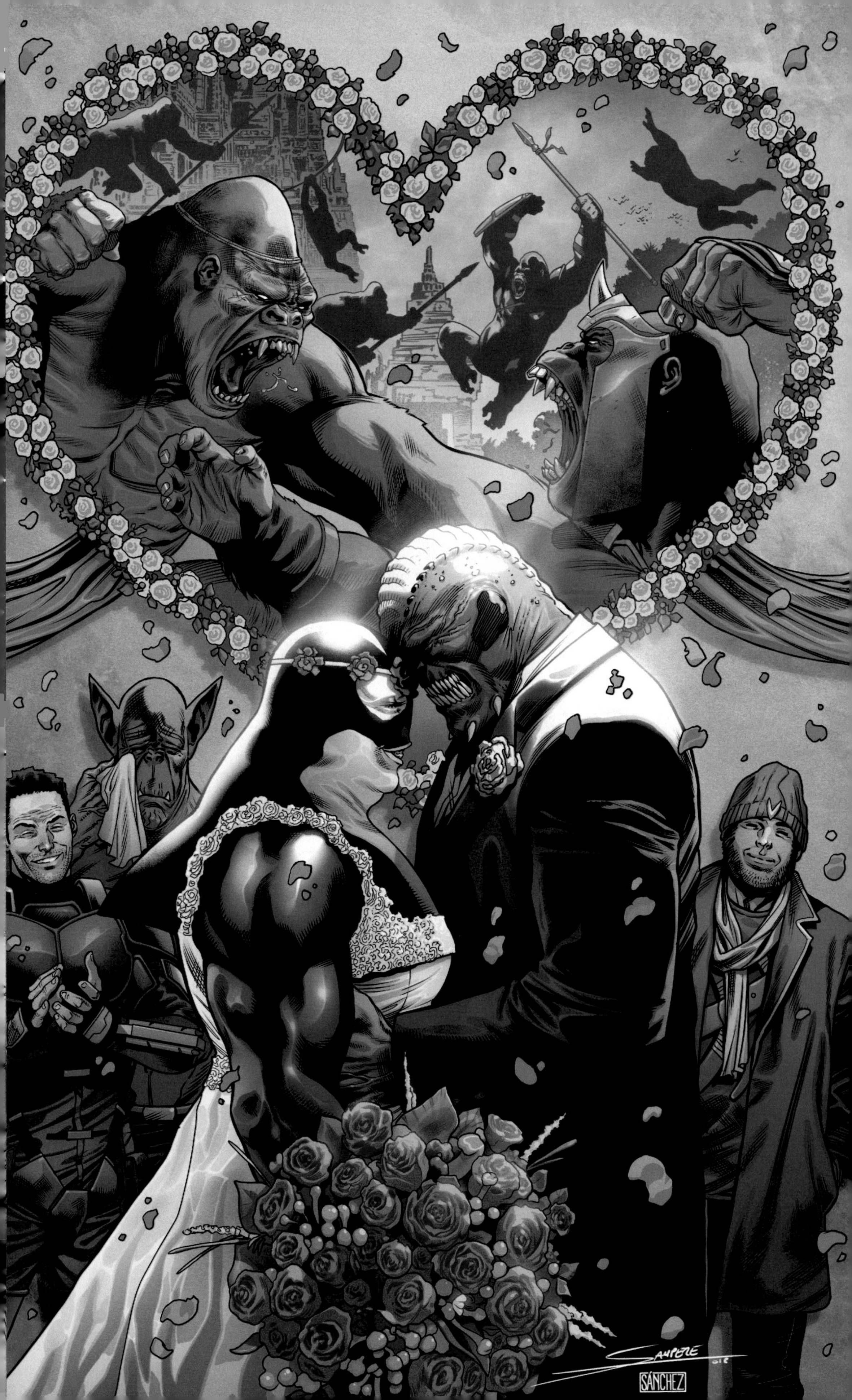
SÁNCHEZ

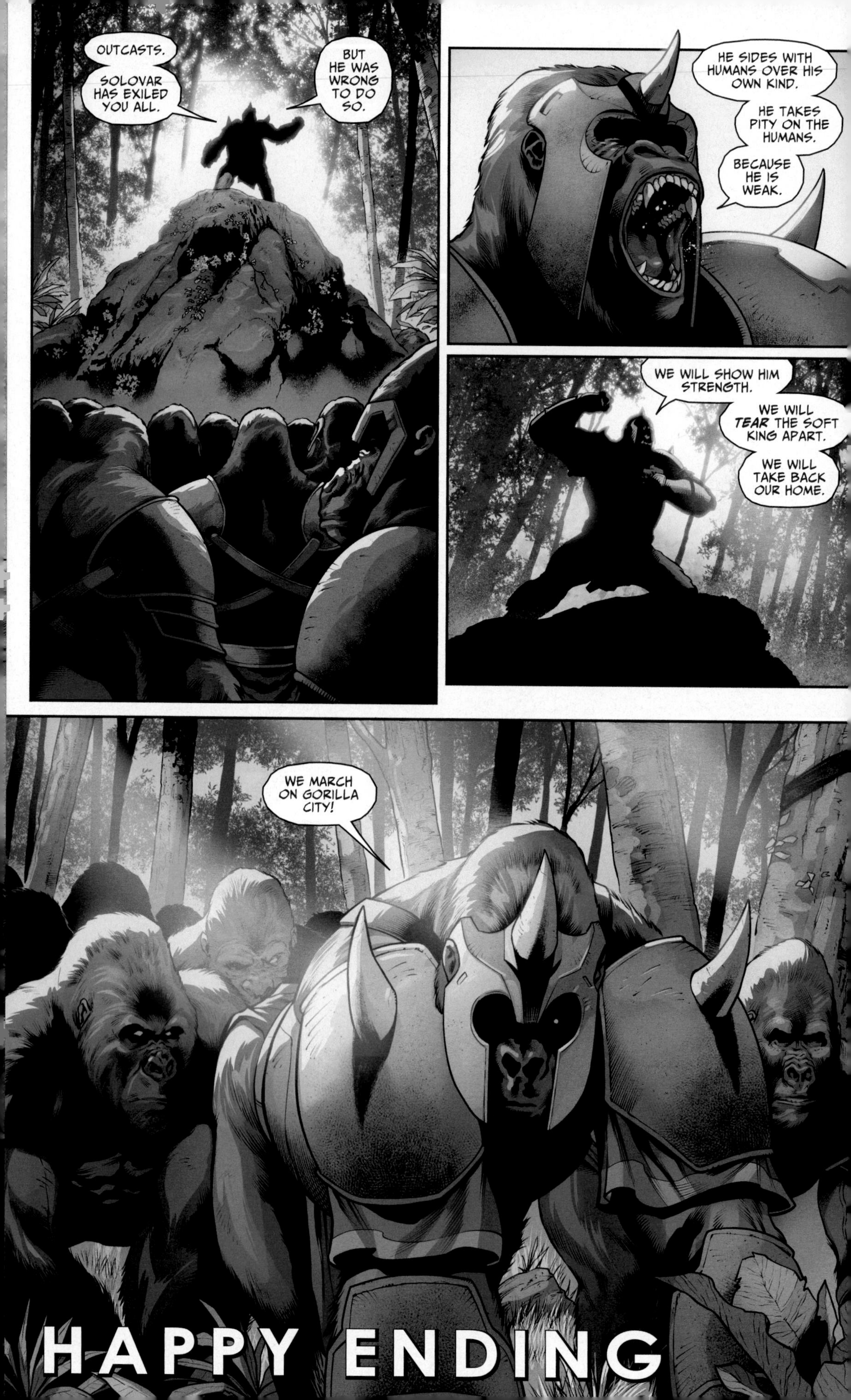
OUTCASTS.
SOLOVAR HAS EXILED YOU ALL.
BUT HE WAS WRONG TO DO SO.
HE SIDES WITH HUMANS OVER HIS OWN KIND.
HE TAKES PITY ON THE HUMANS.
BECAUSE HE IS WEAK.
WE WILL SHOW HIM STRENGTH.
WE WILL *TEAR* THE SOFT KING APART.
WE WILL TAKE BACK OUR HOME.
WE MARCH ON GORILLA CITY!
HAPPY ENDING

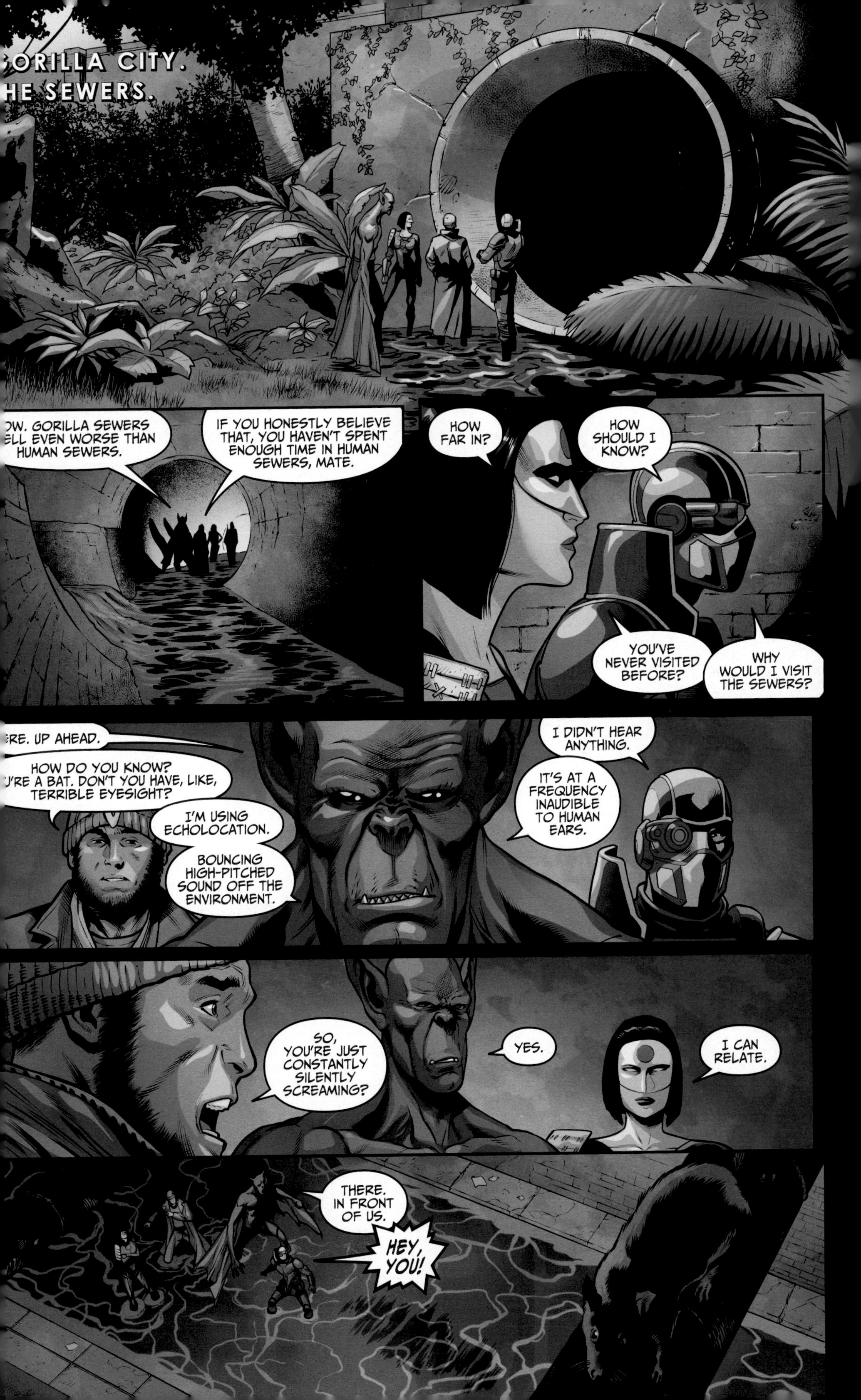

ORILLA CITY.
HE SEWERS.
OW. GORILLA SEWERS
ELL EVEN WORSE THAN
HUMAN SEWERS.
IF YOU HONESTLY BELIEVE THAT, YOU HAVEN'T SPENT ENOUGH TIME IN HUMAN SEWERS, MATE.
HOW FAR IN?
HOW SHOULD I KNOW?
YOU'VE NEVER VISITED BEFORE?
WHY WOULD I VISIT THE SEWERS?
RE. UP AHEAD.
HOW DO YOU KNOW?
'RE A BAT. DON'T YOU HAVE, LIKE, TERRIBLE EYESIGHT?
I'M USING ECHOLOCATION.
BOUNCING HIGH-PITCHED SOUND OFF THE ENVIRONMENT.
I DIDN'T HEAR ANYTHING.
IT'S AT A FREQUENCY INAUDIBLE TO HUMAN EARS.
SO, YOU'RE JUST CONSTANTLY SILENTLY SCREAMING?
YES.
I CAN RELATE.
THERE. IN FRONT OF US.
HEY, YOU!

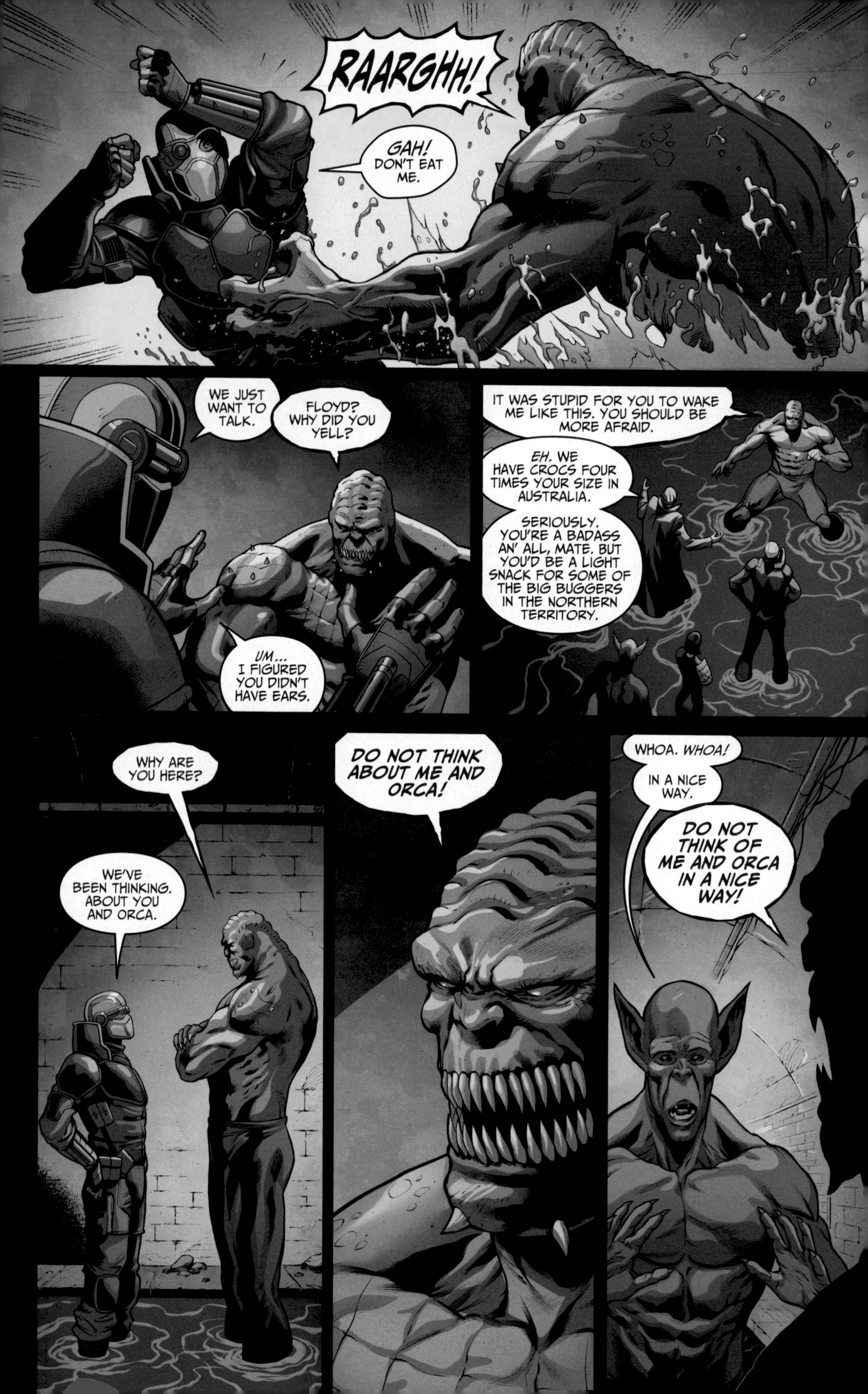
RAARGHH!
GAH! DON'T EAT ME.
WE JUST WANT TO TALK.
FLOYD? WHY DID YOU YELL?
UM... I FIGURED YOU DIDN'T HAVE EARS.
IT WAS STUPID FOR YOU TO WAKE ME LIKE THIS. YOU SHOULD BE MORE AFRAID.
EH. WE HAVE CROCS FOUR TIMES YOUR SIZE IN AUSTRALIA.
SERIOUSLY. YOU'RE A BADASS AN' ALL, MATE. BUT YOU'D BE A LIGHT SNACK FOR SOME OF THE BIG BUGGERS IN THE NORTHERN TERRITORY.
WHY ARE YOU HERE?
WE'VE BEEN THINKING. ABOUT YOU AND ORCA.
DO NOT THINK ABOUT ME AND ORCA!
WHOA. WHOA!
IN A NICE WAY.
DO NOT THINK OF ME AND ORCA IN A NICE WAY!

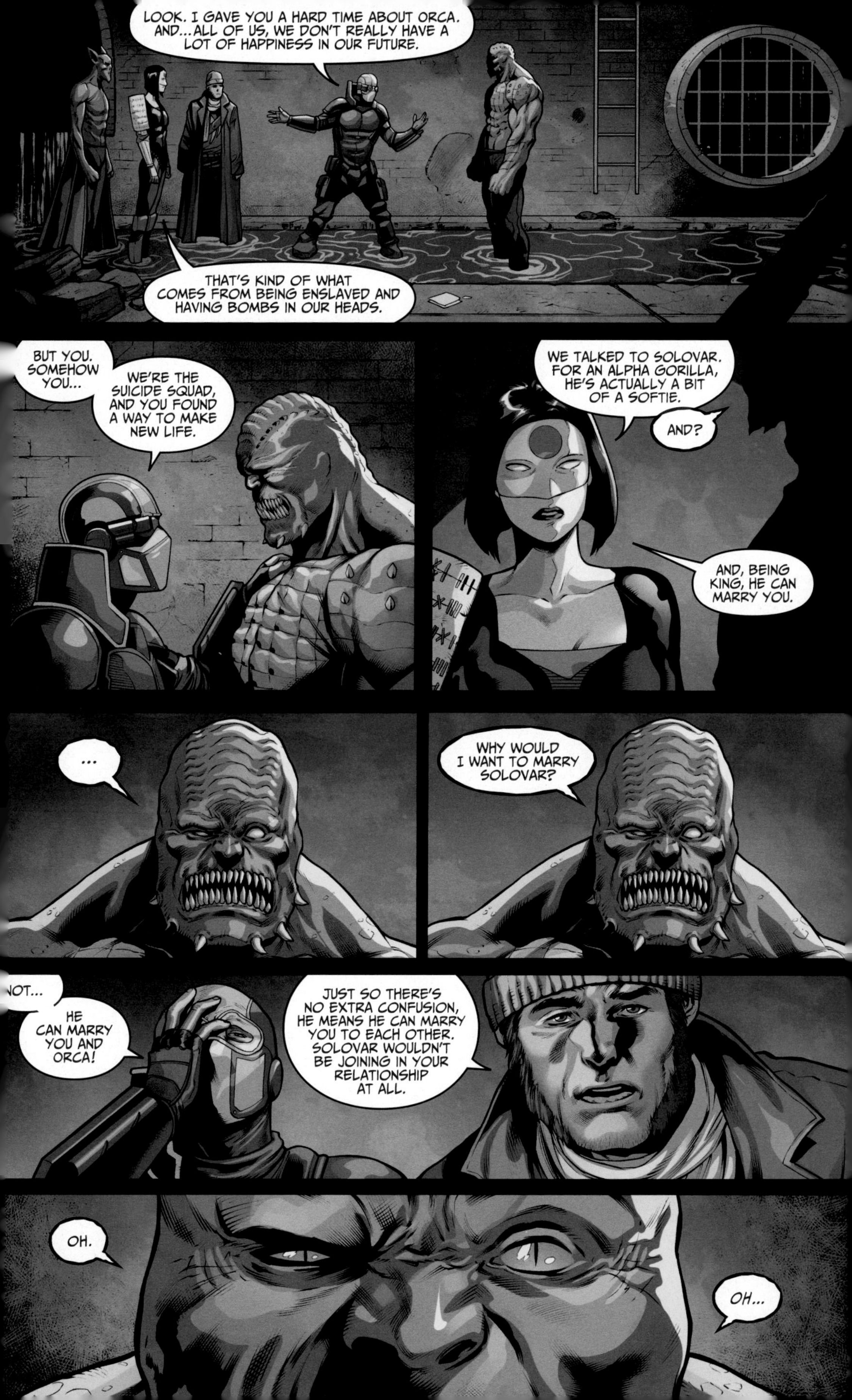
LOOK. I GAVE YOU A HARD TIME ABOUT ORCA. AND...ALL OF US, WE DON'T REALLY HAVE A LOT OF HAPPINESS IN OUR FUTURE.
THAT'S KIND OF WHAT COMES FROM BEING ENSLAVED AND HAVING BOMBS IN OUR HEADS.
BUT YOU. SOMEHOW YOU...
WE'RE THE SUICIDE SQUAD, AND YOU FOUND A WAY TO MAKE NEW LIFE.
WE TALKED TO SOLOVAR. FOR AN ALPHA GORILLA, HE'S ACTUALLY A BIT OF A SOFTIE.
AND?
AND, BEING KING, HE CAN MARRY YOU.
...
WHY WOULD I WANT TO MARRY SOLOVAR?
NOT...
HE CAN MARRY YOU AND ORCA!
JUST SO THERE'S NO EXTRA CONFUSION, HE MEANS HE CAN MARRY YOU TO EACH OTHER. SOLOVAR WOULDN'T BE JOINING IN YOUR RELATIONSHIP AT ALL.
OH.
OH...

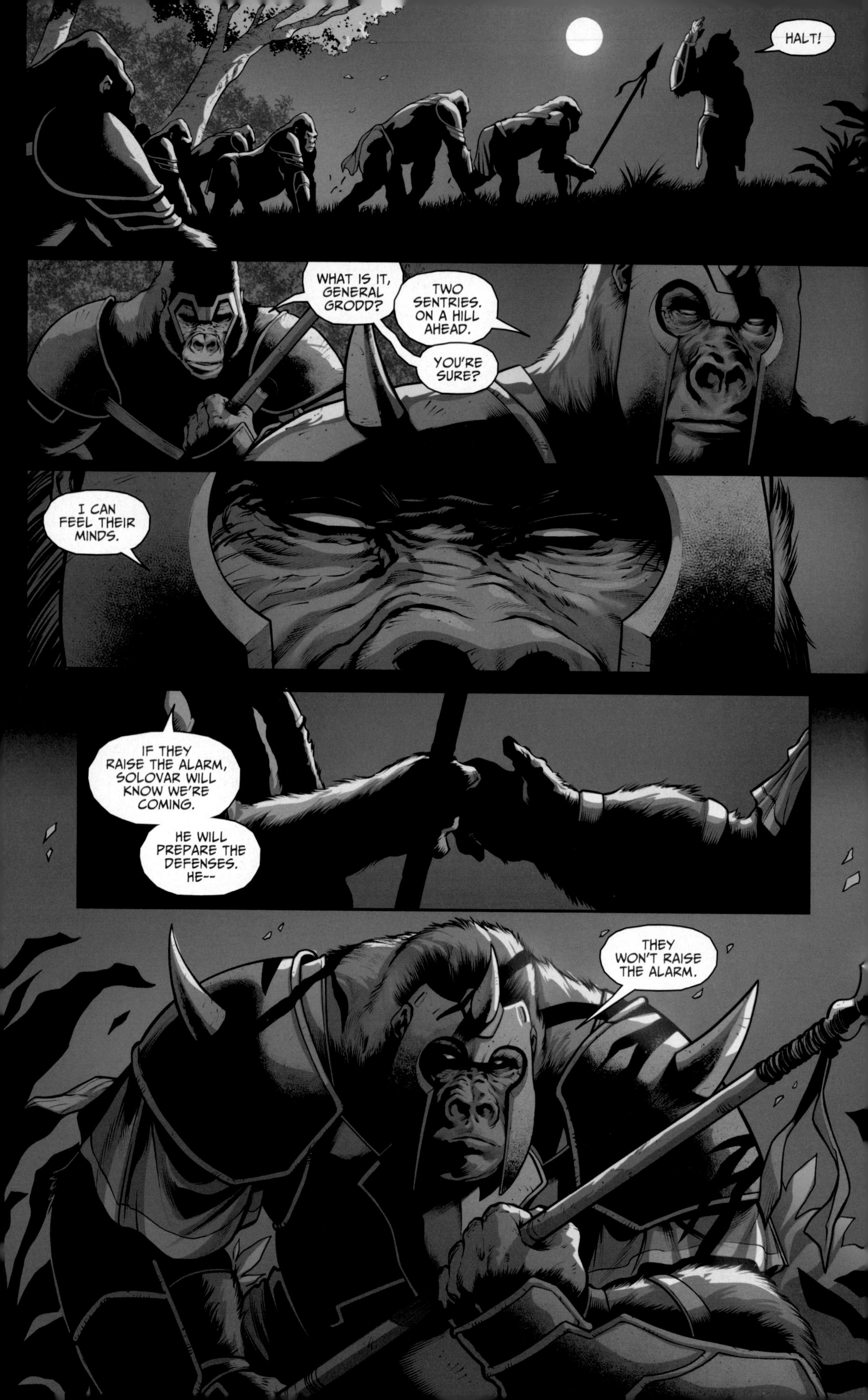
HALT!
WHAT IS IT, GENERAL GRODD?
TWO SENTRIES. ON A HILL AHEAD.
YOU'RE SURE?
I CAN FEEL THEIR MINDS.
IF THEY RAISE THE ALARM, SOLOVAR WILL KNOW WE'RE COMING.
HE WILL PREPARE THE DEFENSES. HE--
THEY WON'T RAISE THE ALARM.

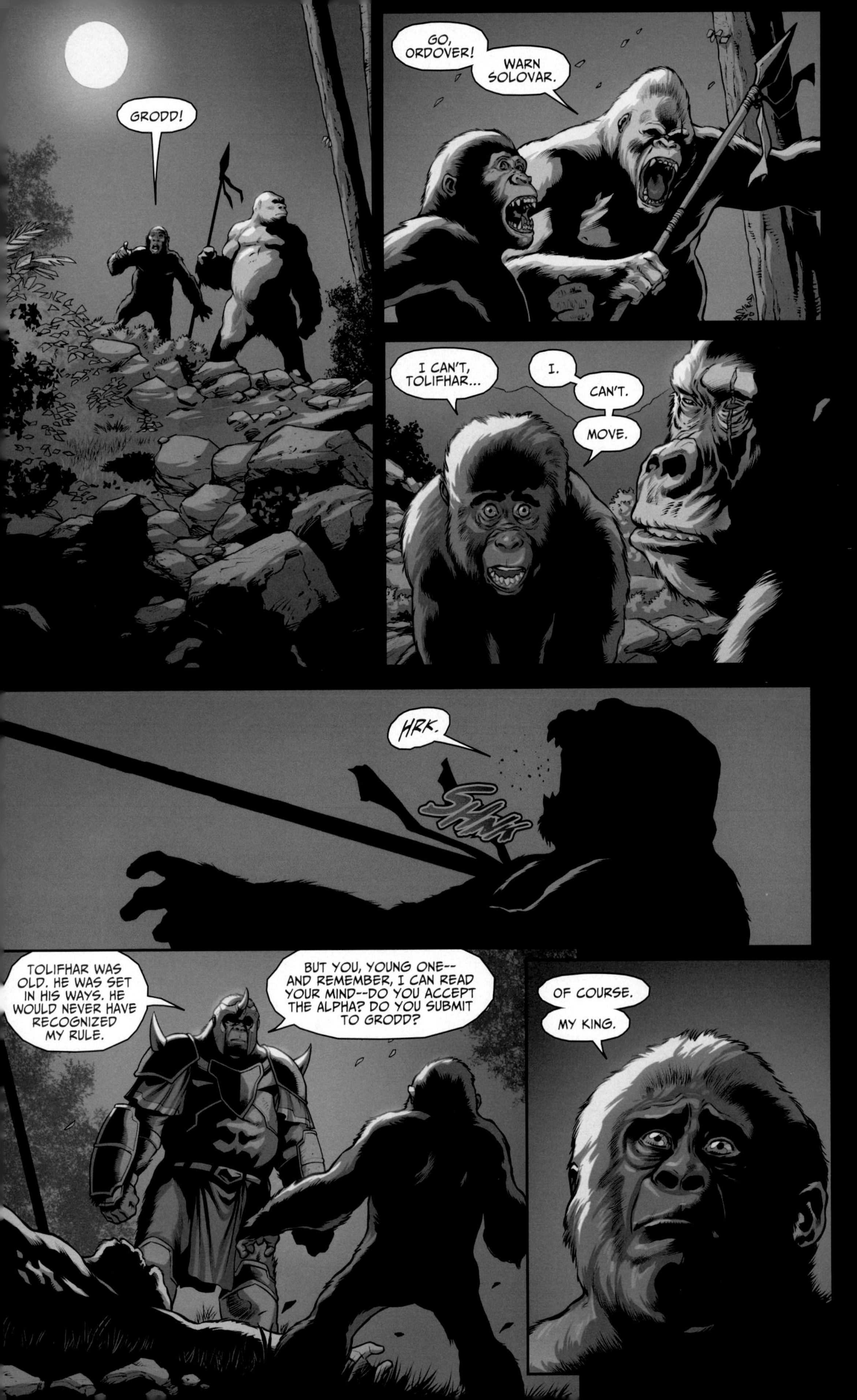
GRODD!
GO, ORDOVER!
WARN SOLOVAR.
I CAN'T, TOLIFHAR...
I.
CAN'T.
MOVE.
HRK.
SHNK
TOLIFHAR WAS OLD. HE WAS SET IN HIS WAYS. HE WOULD NEVER HAVE RECOGNIZED MY RULE.
BUT YOU, YOUNG ONE-- AND REMEMBER, I CAN READ YOUR MIND--DO YOU ACCEPT THE ALPHA? DO YOU SUBMIT TO GRODD?
OF COURSE.
MY KING.

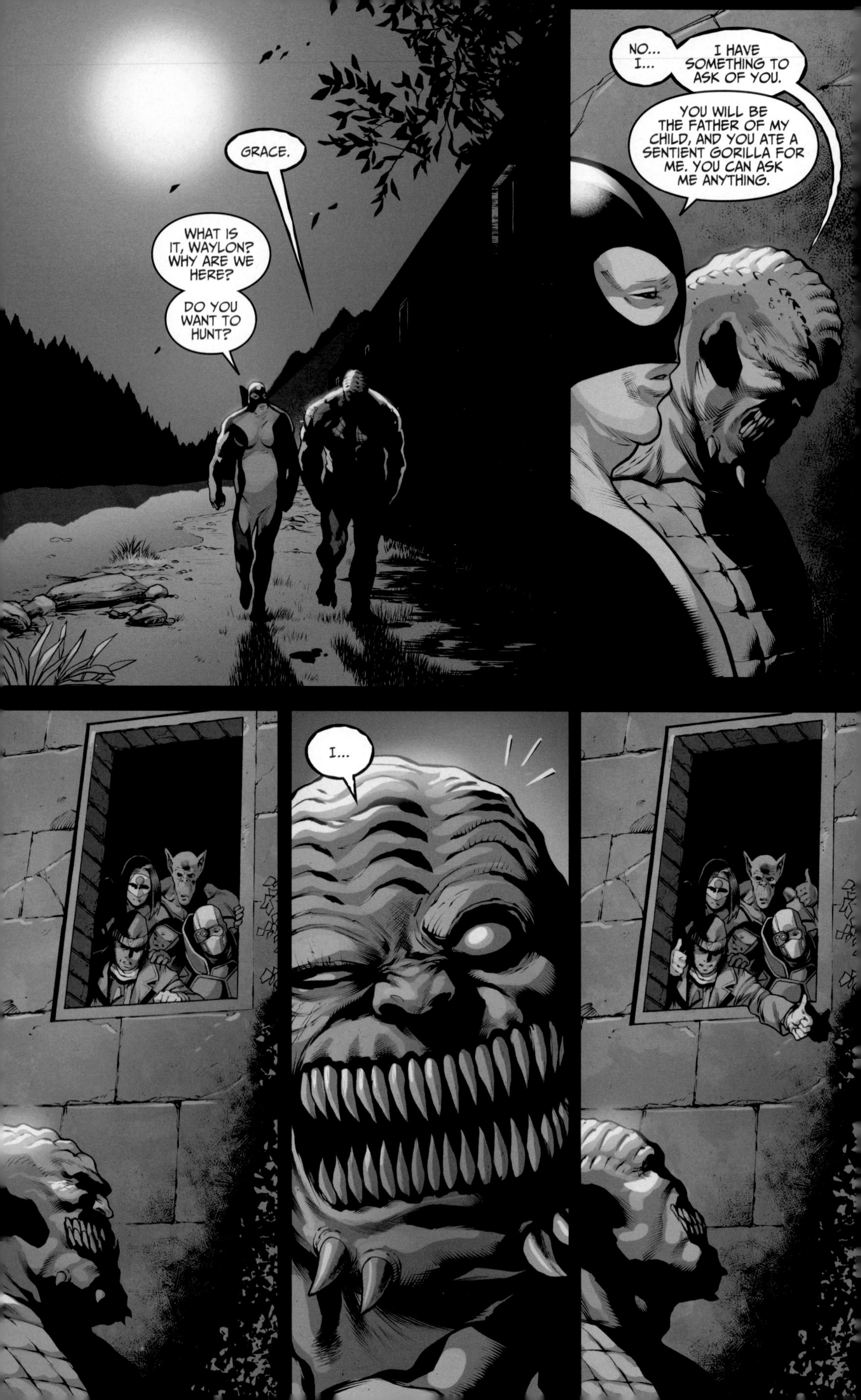
GRACE.
WHAT IS IT, WAYLON? WHY ARE WE HERE?
DO YOU WANT TO HUNT?
NO... I...
I HAVE SOMETHING TO ASK OF YOU.
YOU WILL BE THE FATHER OF MY CHILD, AND YOU ATE A SENTIENT GORILLA FOR ME. YOU CAN ASK ME ANYTHING.
I...

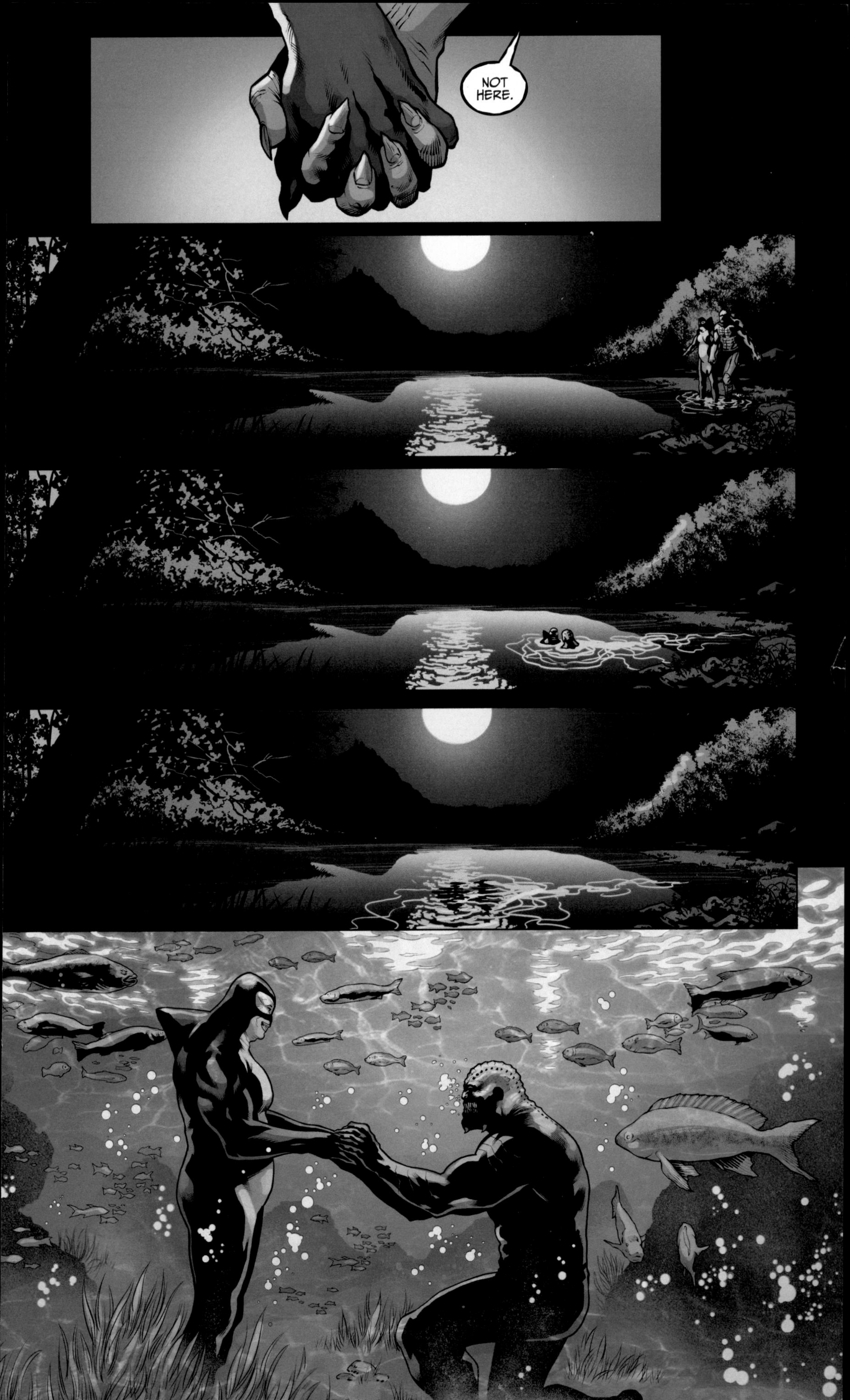
NOT HERE.

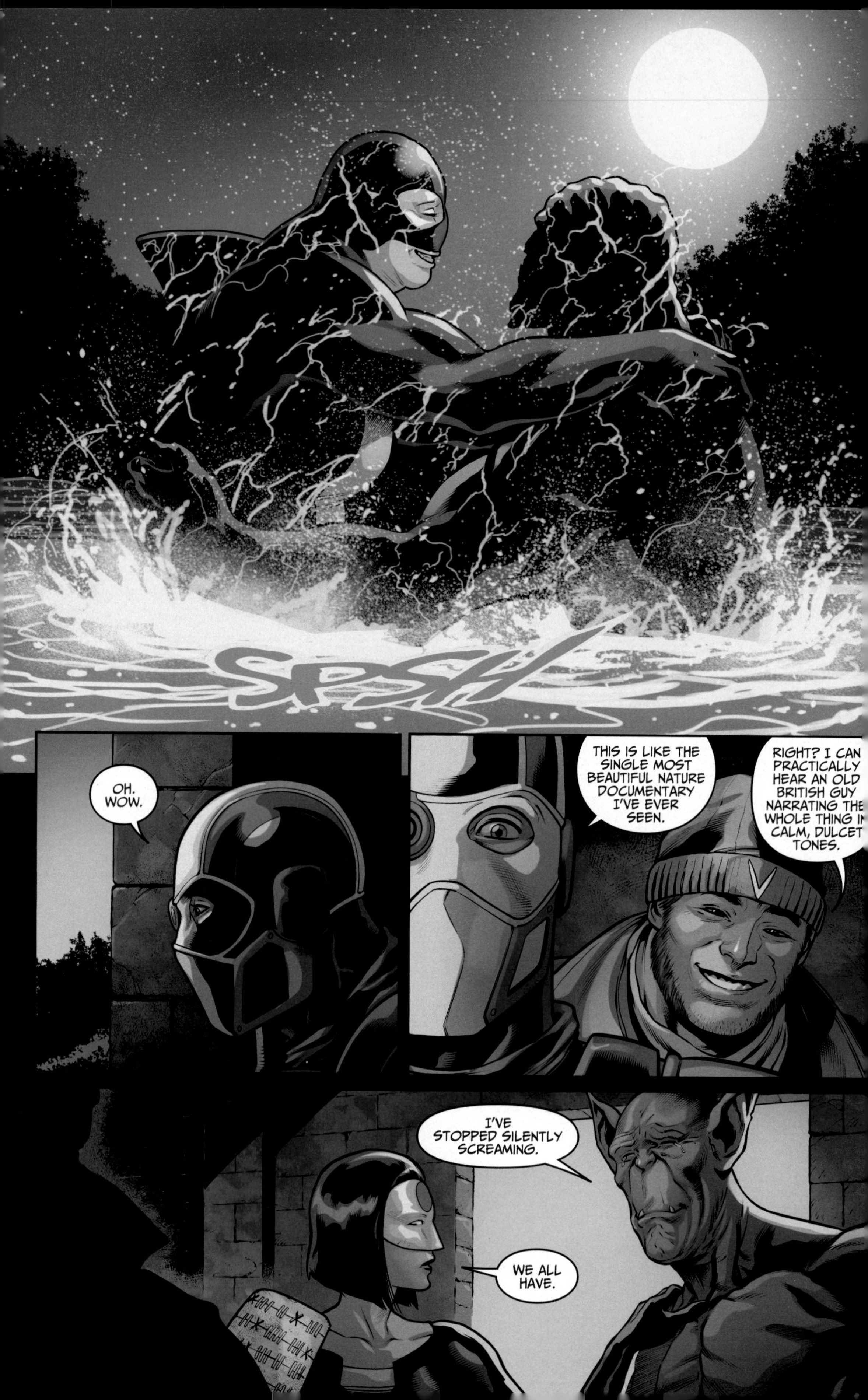
SPSH
OH. WOW.
THIS IS LIKE THE SINGLE MOST BEAUTIFUL NATURE DOCUMENTARY I'VE EVER SEEN.
RIGHT? I CAN PRACTICALLY HEAR AN OLD BRITISH GUY NARRATING THE WHOLE THING IN CALM, DULCET TONES.
I'VE STOPPED SILENTLY SCREAMING.
WE ALL HAVE.

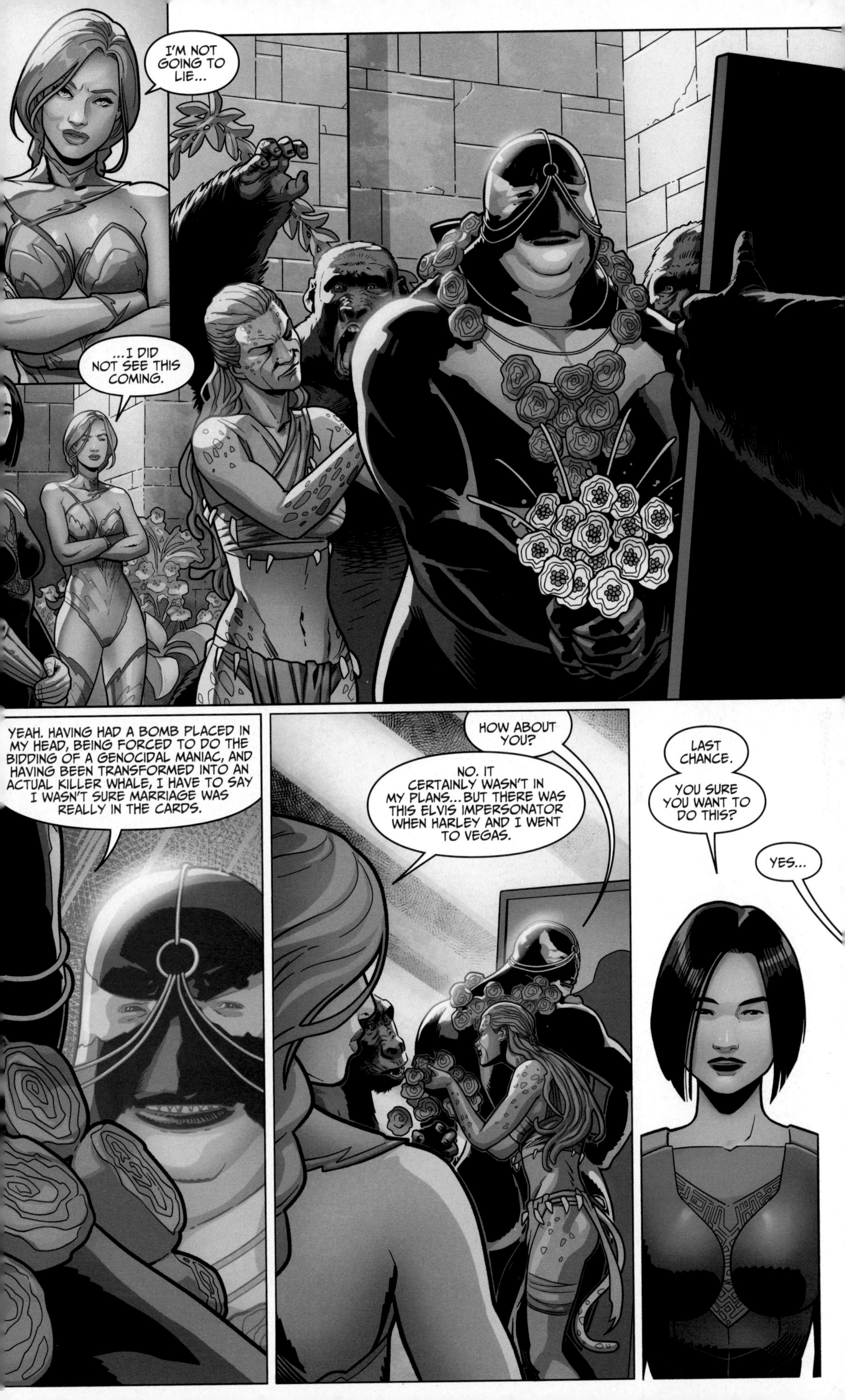
I'M NOT GOING TO LIE...
...I DID NOT SEE THIS COMING.
YEAH. HAVING HAD A BOMB PLACED IN MY HEAD, BEING FORCED TO DO THE BIDDING OF A GENOCIDAL MANIAC, AND HAVING BEEN TRANSFORMED INTO AN ACTUAL KILLER WHALE, I HAVE TO SAY I WASN'T SURE MARRIAGE WAS REALLY IN THE CARDS.
HOW ABOUT YOU?
NO. IT CERTAINLY WASN'T IN MY PLANS...BUT THERE WAS THIS ELVIS IMPERSONATOR WHEN HARLEY AND I WENT TO VEGAS.
LAST CHANCE.
YOU SURE YOU WANT TO DO THIS?
YES...

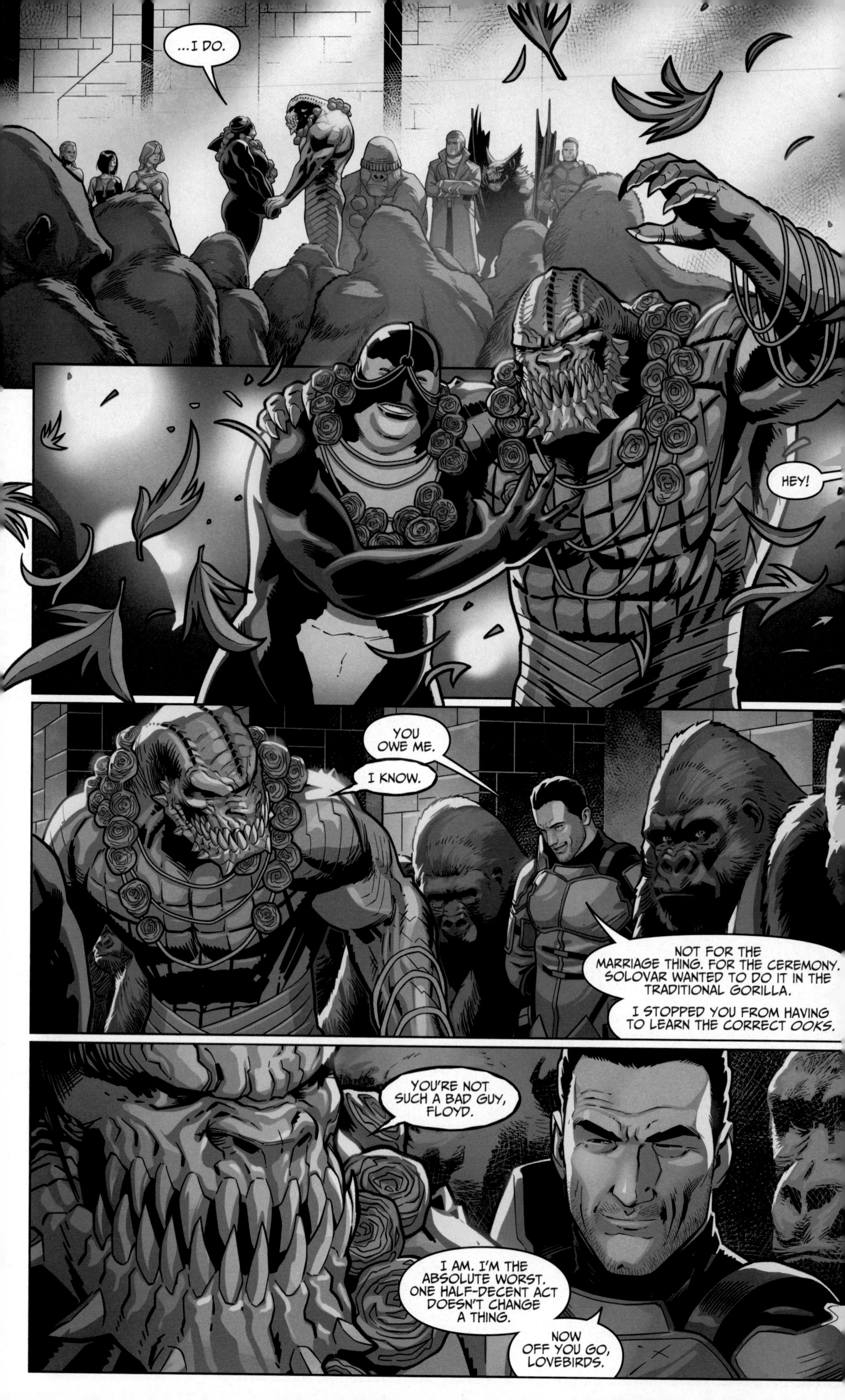
...I DO.
HEY!
YOU OWE ME.
I KNOW.
NOT FOR THE MARRIAGE THING. FOR THE CEREMONY. SOLOVAR WANTED TO DO IT IN THE TRADITIONAL GORILLA.
I STOPPED YOU FROM HAVING TO LEARN THE CORRECT OOKS.
YOU'RE NOT SUCH A BAD GUY, FLOYD.
I AM. I'M THE ABSOLUTE WORST. ONE HALF-DECENT ACT DOESN'T CHANGE A THING.
NOW OFF YOU GO, LOVEBIRDS.

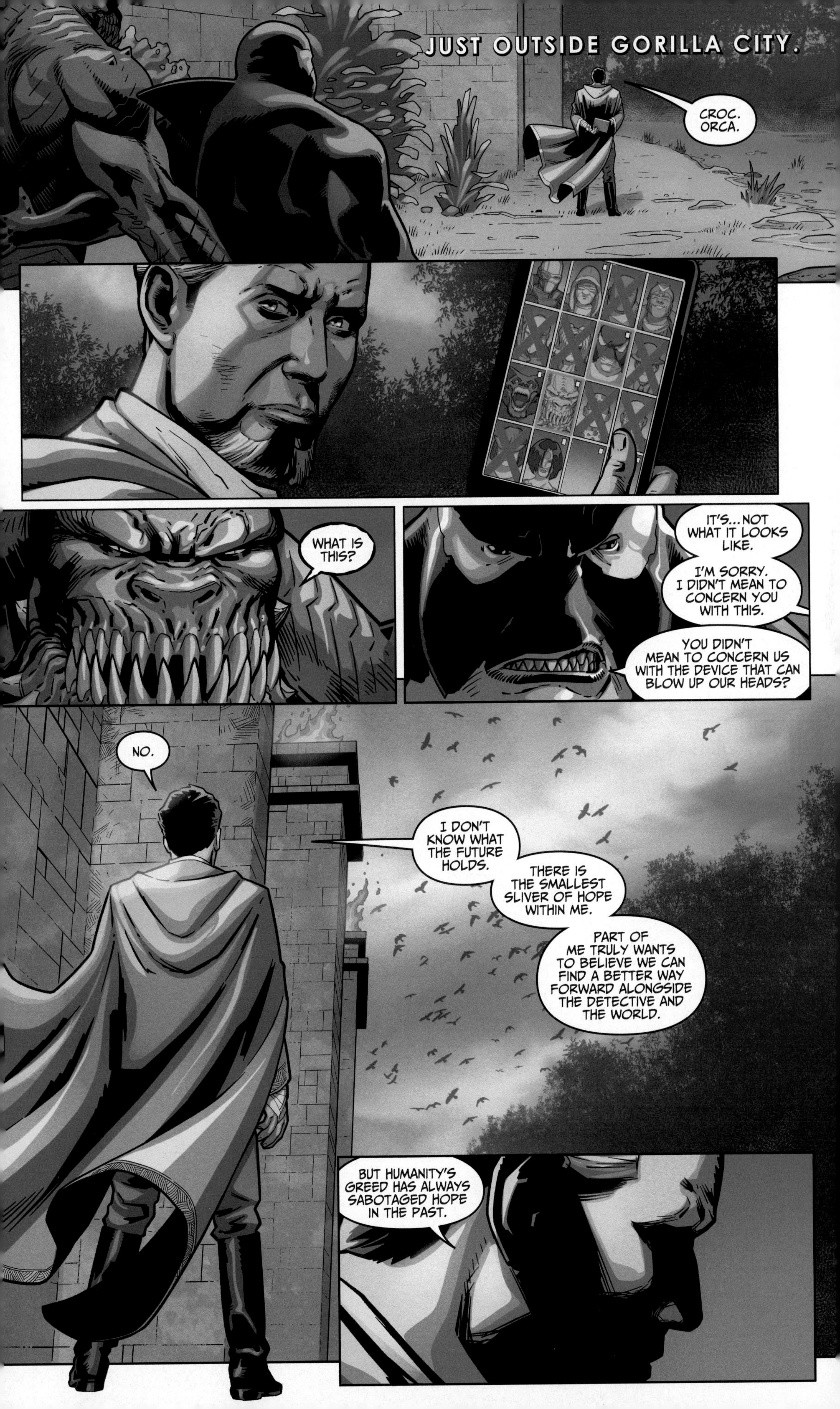
JUST OUTSIDE GORILLA CITY.
CROC. ORCA.
WHAT IS THIS?
IT'S...NOT WHAT IT LOOKS LIKE.
I'M SORRY. I DIDN'T MEAN TO CONCERN YOU WITH THIS.
YOU DIDN'T MEAN TO CONCERN US WITH THE DEVICE THAT CAN BLOW UP OUR HEADS?
NO.
I DON'T KNOW WHAT THE FUTURE HOLDS.
THERE IS THE SMALLEST SLIVER OF HOPE WITHIN ME.
PART OF ME TRULY WANTS TO BELIEVE WE CAN FIND A BETTER WAY FORWARD ALONGSIDE THE DETECTIVE AND THE WORLD.
BUT HUMANITY'S GREED HAS ALWAYS SABOTAGED HOPE IN THE PAST.

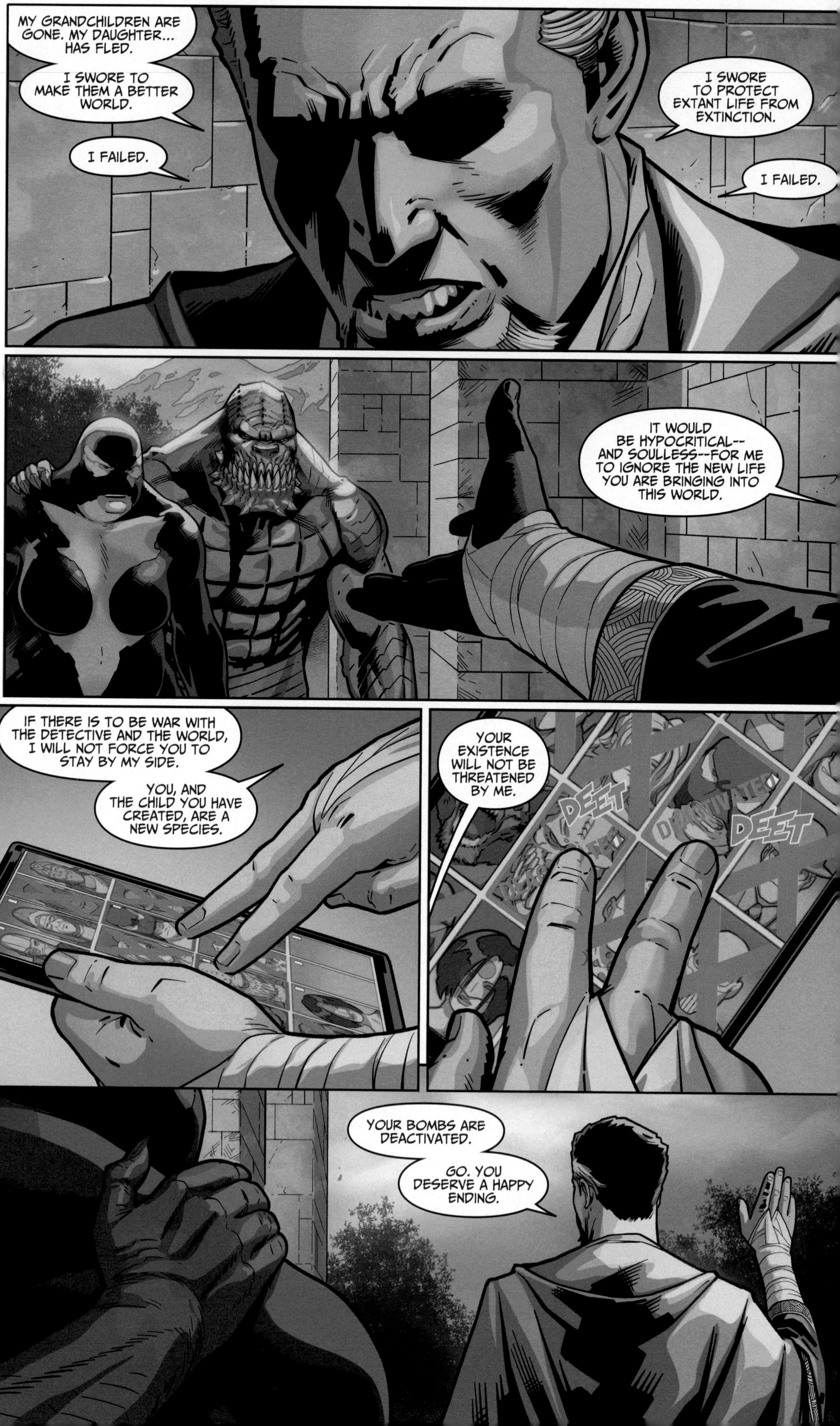
MY GRANDCHILDREN ARE GONE. MY DAUGHTER... HAS FLED.
I SWORE TO MAKE THEM A BETTER WORLD.
I FAILED.
I SWORE TO PROTECT EXTANT LIFE FROM EXTINCTION.
I FAILED.
IT WOULD BE HYPOCRITICAL--AND SOULLESS--FOR ME TO IGNORE THE NEW LIFE YOU ARE BRINGING INTO THIS WORLD.
IF THERE IS TO BE WAR WITH THE DETECTIVE AND THE WORLD, I WILL NOT FORCE YOU TO STAY BY MY SIDE.
YOU, AND THE CHILD YOU HAVE CREATED, ARE A NEW SPECIES.
YOUR EXISTENCE WILL NOT BE THREATENED BY ME.
DEET
DEACTIVATED
DEET
YOUR BOMBS ARE DEACTIVATED.
GO. YOU DESERVE A HAPPY ENDING.

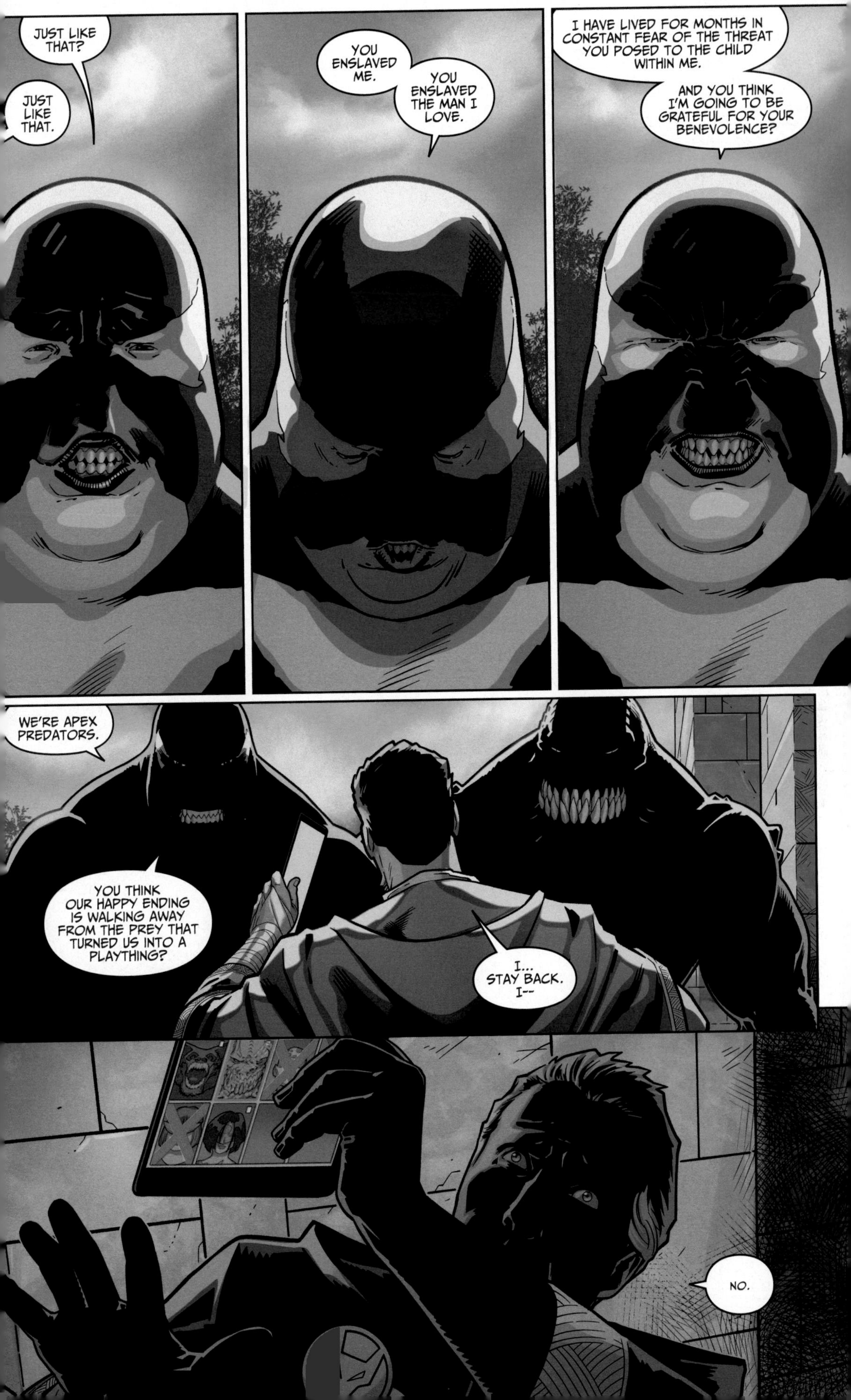
JUST LIKE THAT?
JUST LIKE THAT.
YOU ENSLAVED ME.
YOU ENSLAVED THE MAN I LOVE.
I HAVE LIVED FOR MONTHS IN CONSTANT FEAR OF THE THREAT YOU POSED TO THE CHILD WITHIN ME.
AND YOU THINK I'M GOING TO BE GRATEFUL FOR YOUR BENEVOLENCE?
WE'RE APEX PREDATORS.
YOU THINK OUR HAPPY ENDING IS WALKING AWAY FROM THE PREY THAT TURNED US INTO A PLAYTHING?
I... STAY BACK. I--
NO.

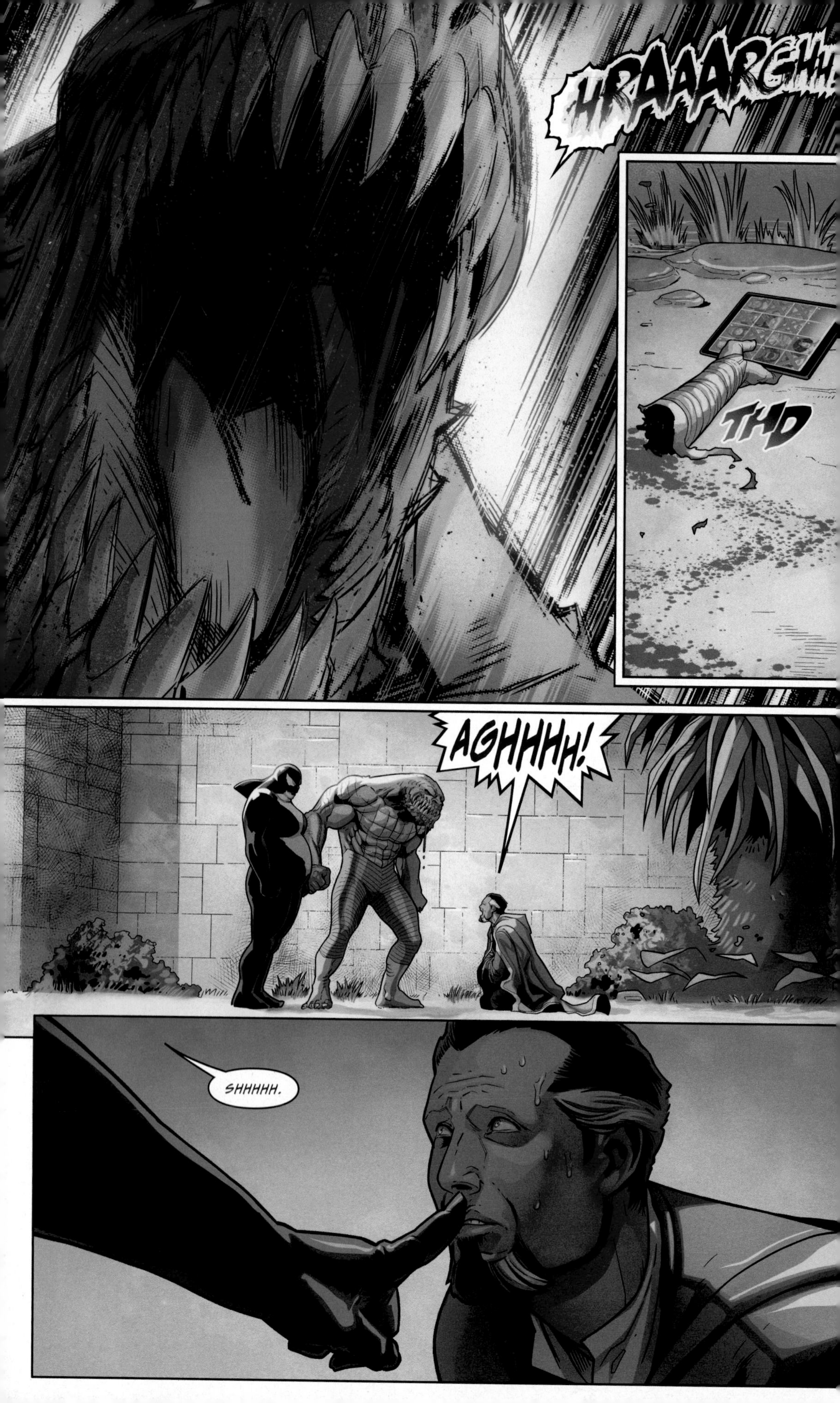
HRAAARGHH
THD
AGHHHH!
SHHHHH.

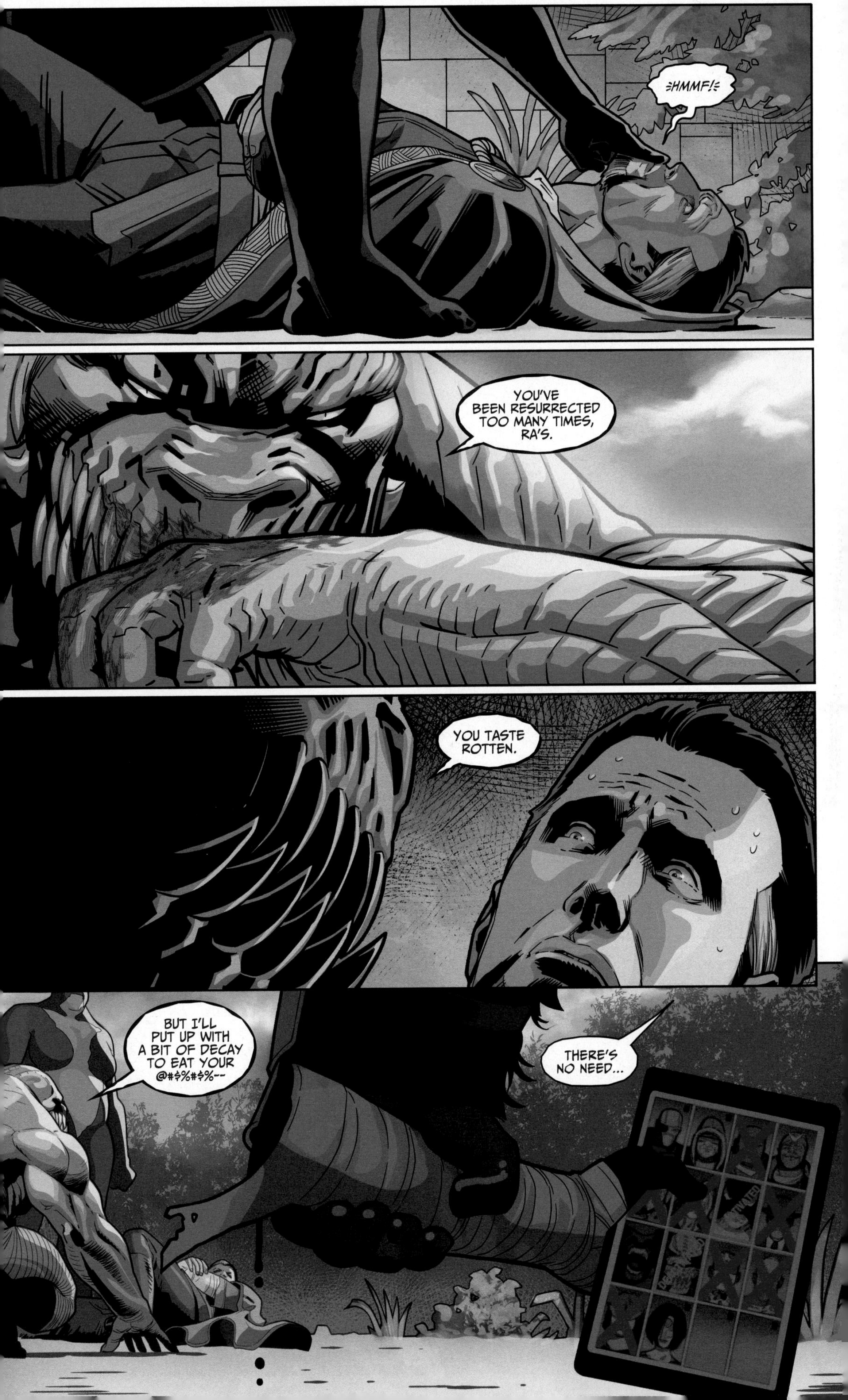

HMMF!
YOU'VE BEEN RESURRECTED TOO MANY TIMES, RA'S.
YOU TASTE ROTTEN.
BUT I'LL PUT UP WITH A BIT OF DECAY TO EAT YOUR @#$%#$%--
THERE'S NO NEED...

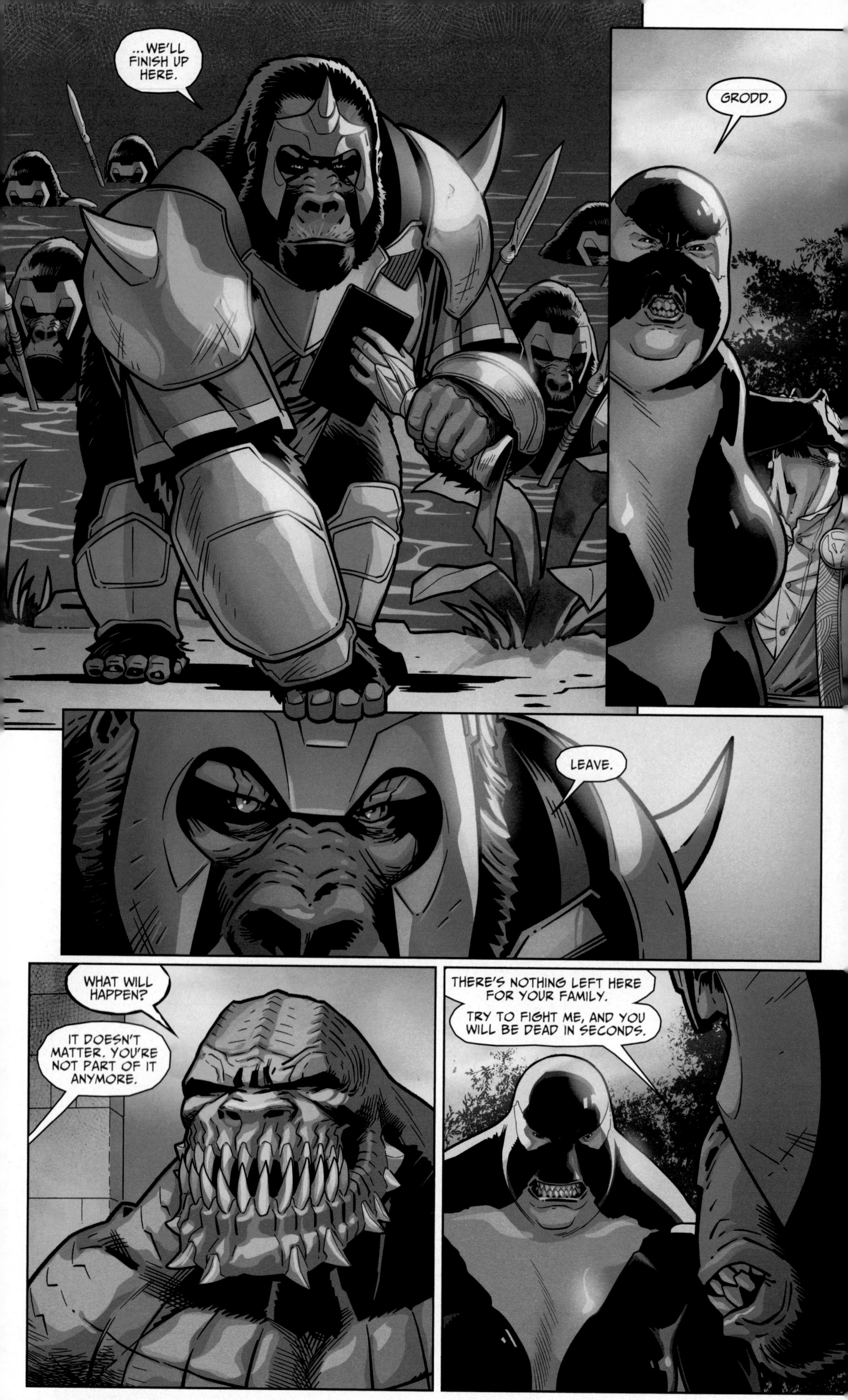
...WE'LL FINISH UP HERE.
GRODD.
LEAVE.
WHAT WILL HAPPEN?
IT DOESN'T MATTER. YOU'RE NOT PART OF IT ANYMORE.
THERE'S NOTHING LEFT HERE FOR YOUR FAMILY.
TRY TO FIGHT ME, AND YOU WILL BE DEAD IN SECONDS.

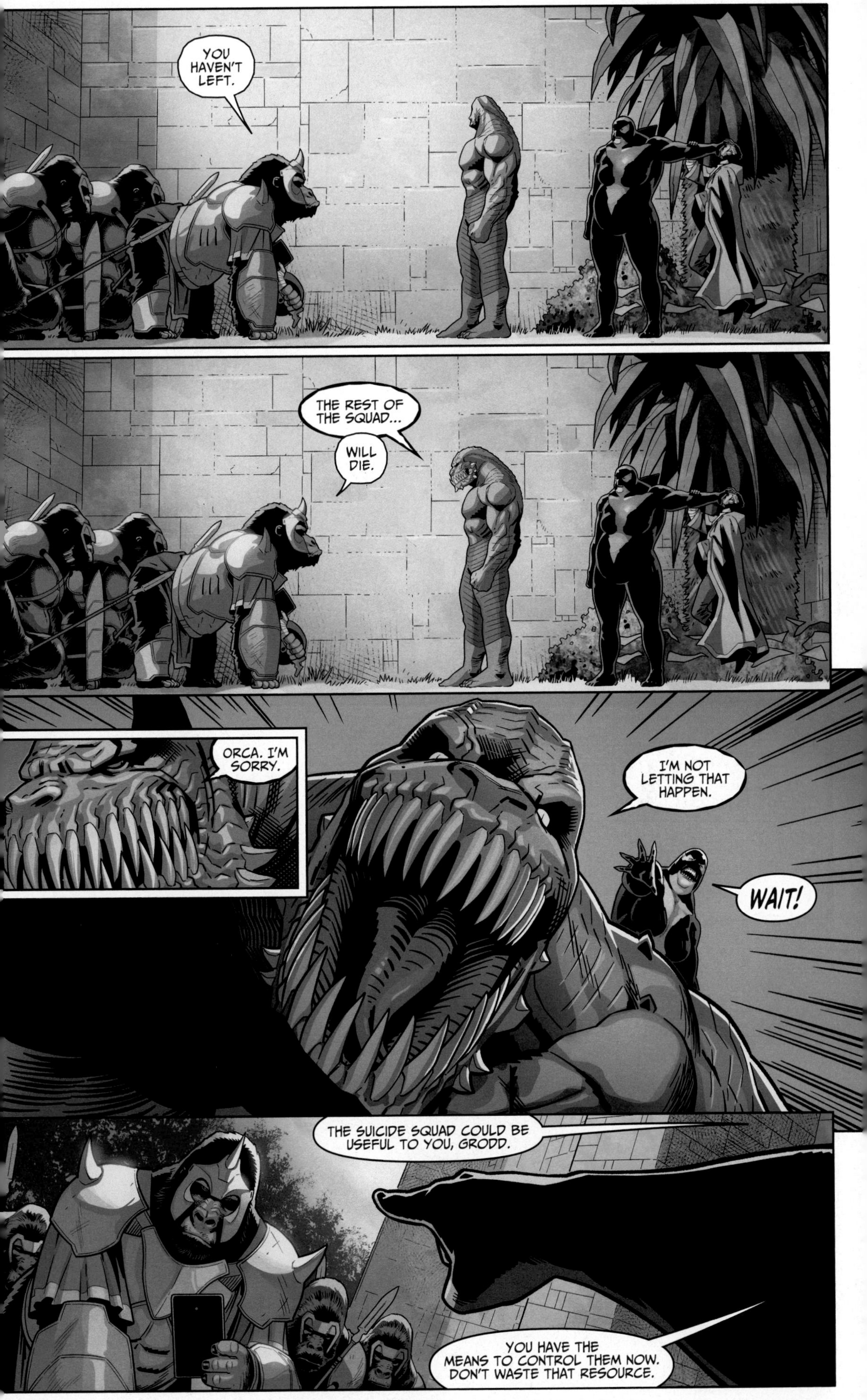
YOU HAVEN'T LEFT.
THE REST OF THE SQUAD...
WILL DIE.
ORCA. I'M SORRY.
I'M NOT LETTING THAT HAPPEN.
WAIT!
THE SUICIDE SQUAD COULD BE USEFUL TO YOU, GRODD.
YOU HAVE THE MEANS TO CONTROL THEM NOW. DON'T WASTE THAT RESOURCE.

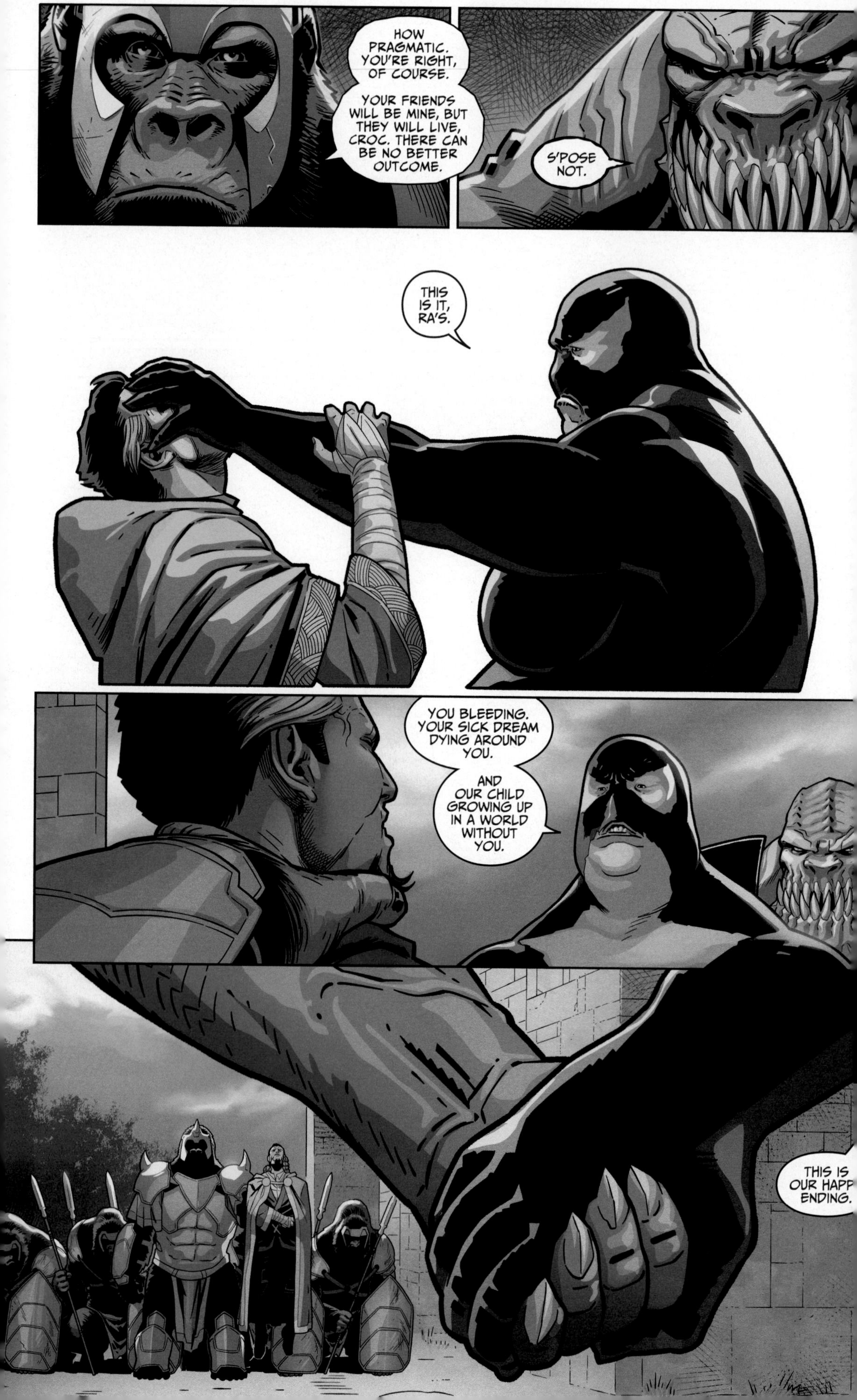
HOW PRAGMATIC. YOU'RE RIGHT, OF COURSE.
YOUR FRIENDS WILL BE MINE, BUT THEY WILL LIVE, CROC. THERE CAN BE NO BETTER OUTCOME.
S'POSE NOT.
THIS IS IT, RA'S.
YOU BLEEDING. YOUR SICK DREAM DYING AROUND YOU.
AND OUR CHILD GROWING UP IN A WORLD WITHOUT YOU.
THIS IS OUR HAPP
ENDING.

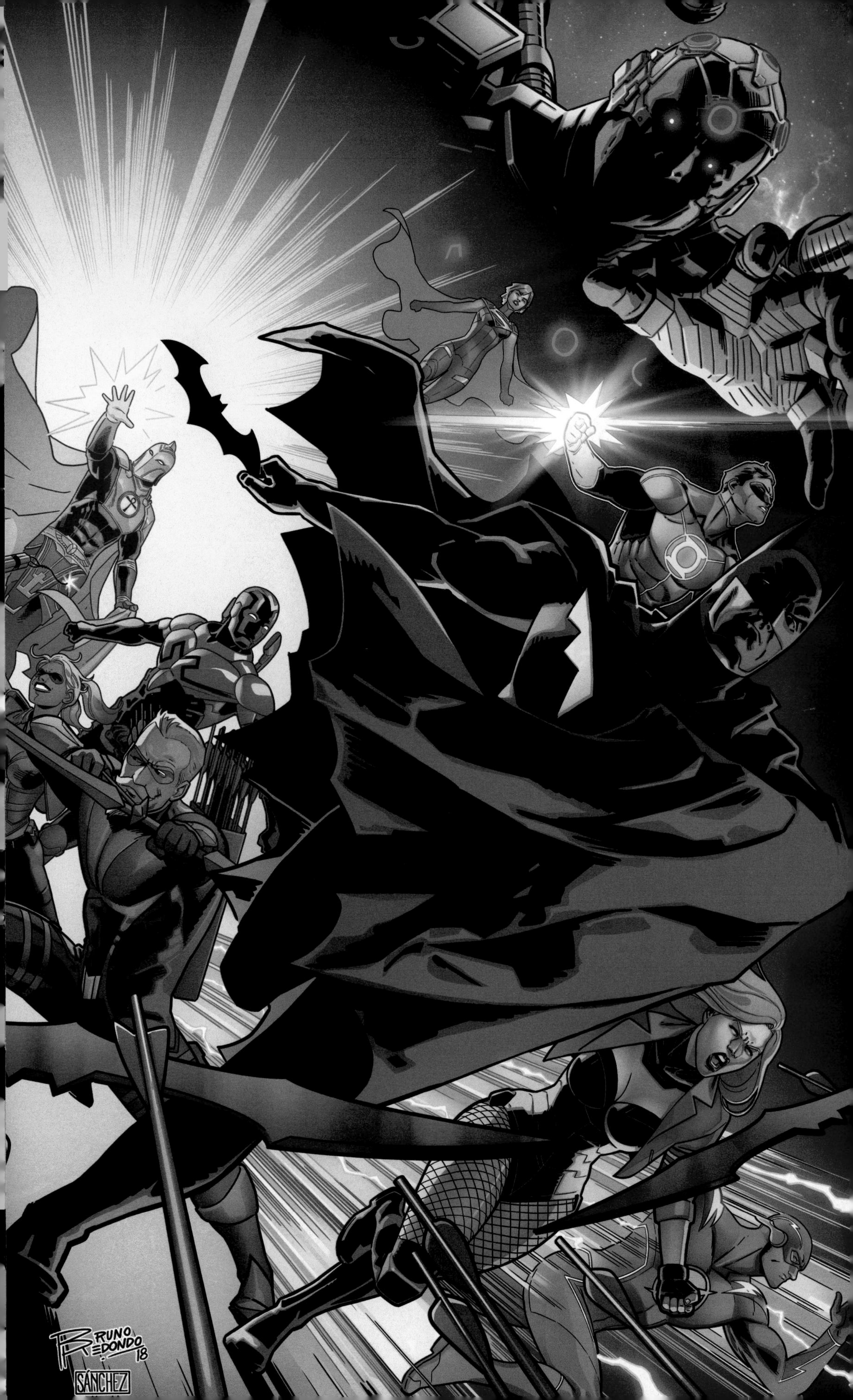
BRUNO REDONDO 18
SÁNCHEZ

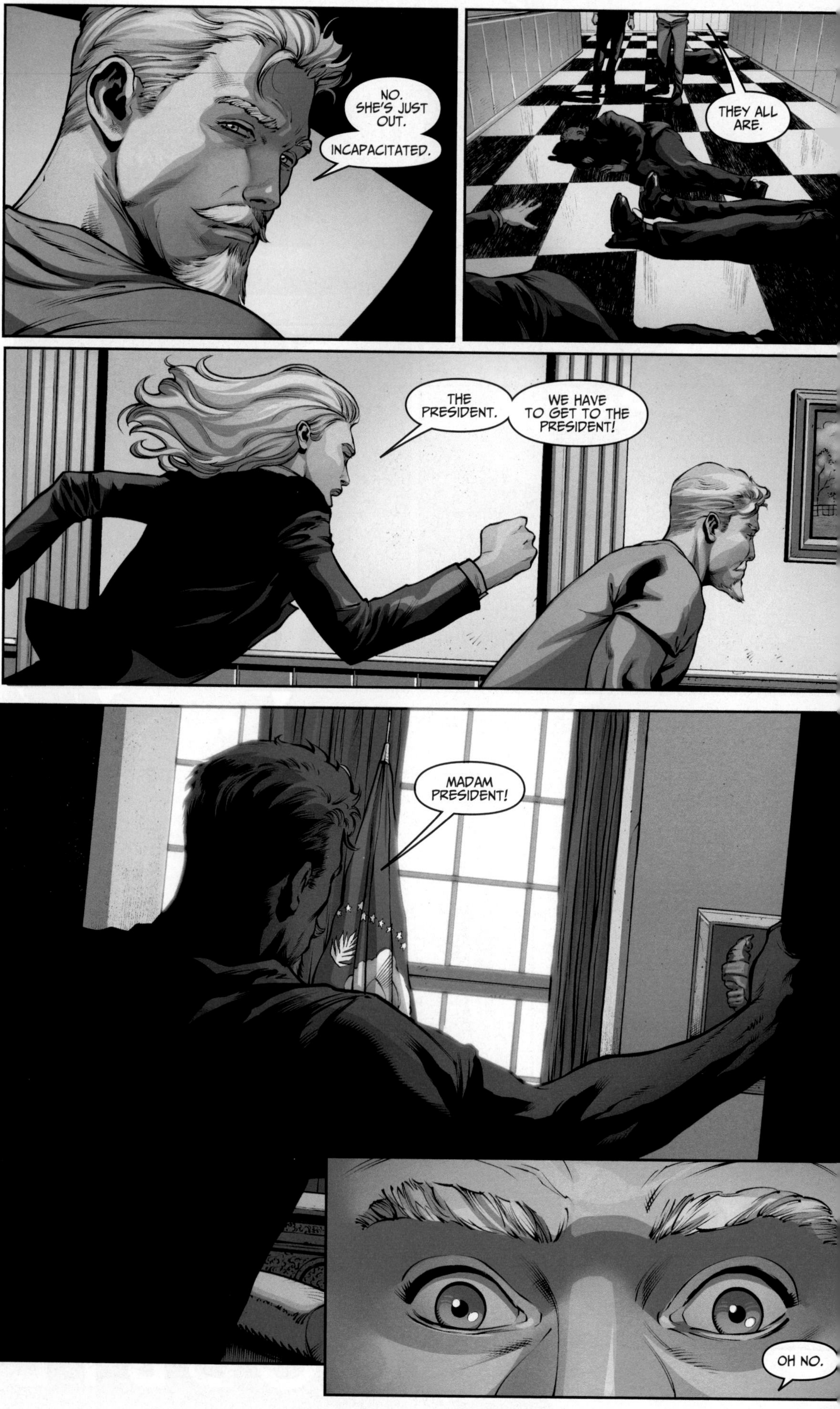
NO. SHE'S JUST OUT.
INCAPACITATED.
THEY ALL ARE.
THE PRESIDENT.
WE HAVE TO GET TO THE PRESIDENT!
MADAM PRESIDENT!
OH NO.

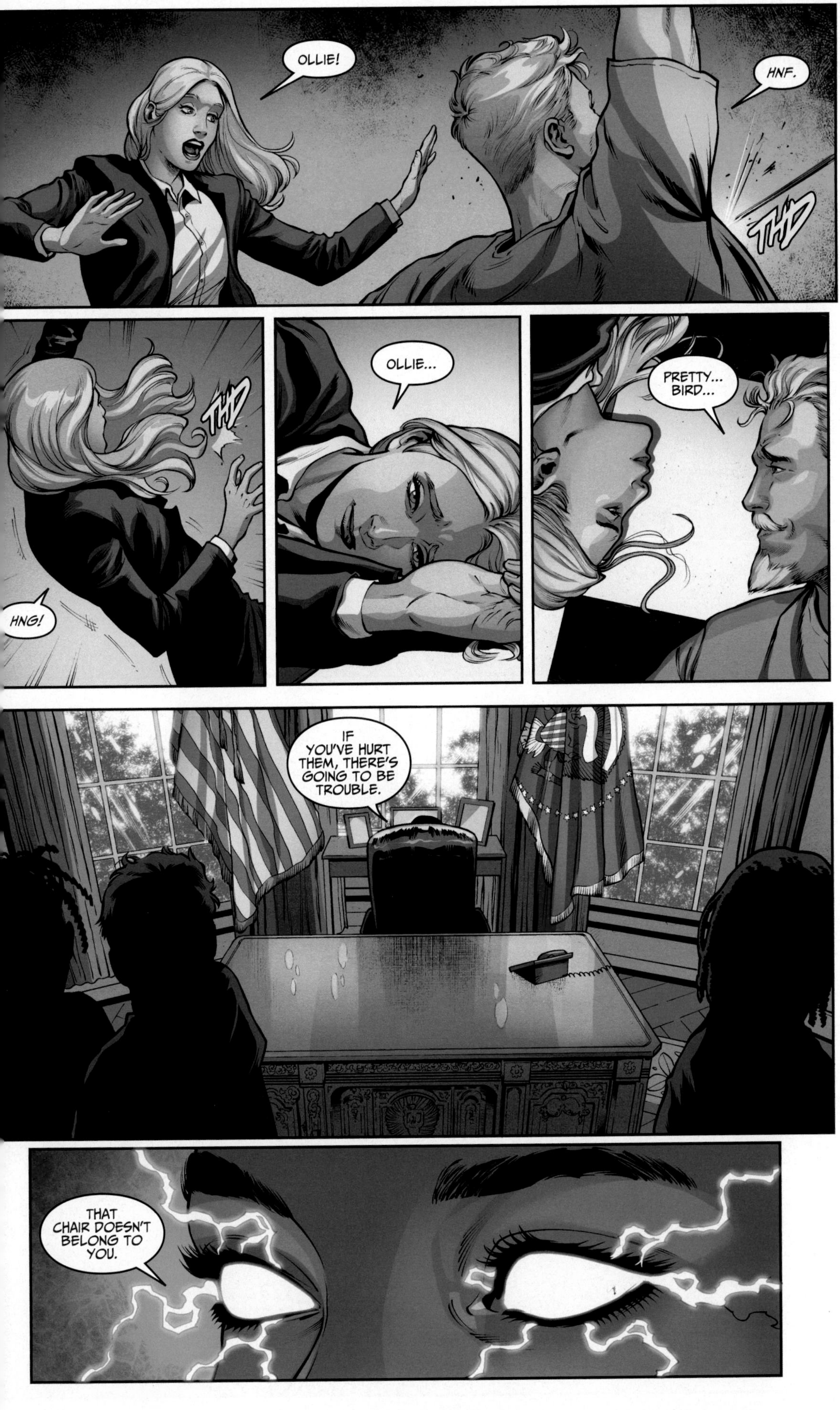
OLLIE!
HNF.
THD
THD
HNG!
OLLIE...
PRETTY... BIRD...
IF YOU'VE HURT THEM, THERE'S GOING TO BE TROUBLE.
THAT CHAIR DOESN'T BELONG TO YOU.

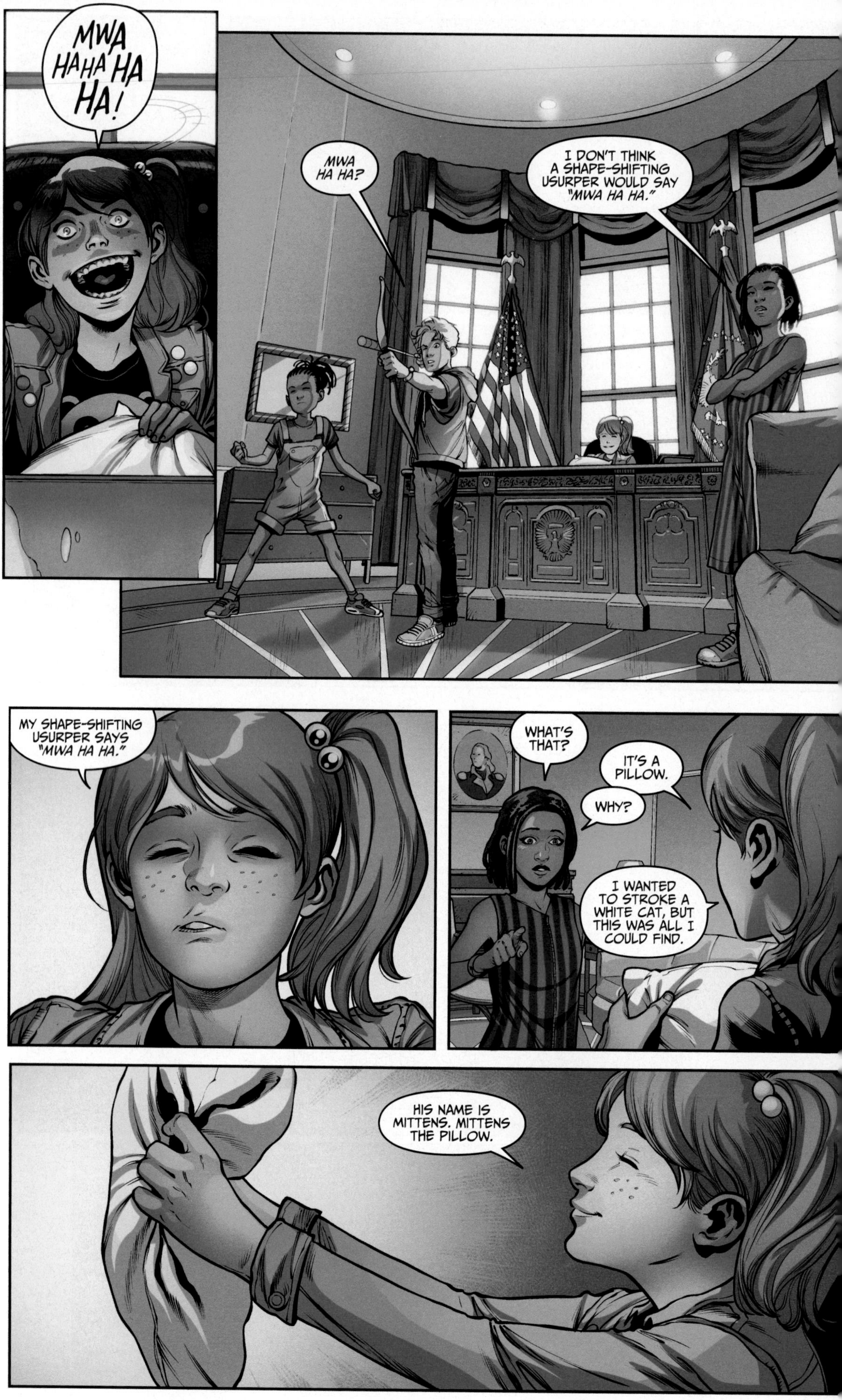
MWA HAHA HA HA!
MWA HA HA?
I DON'T THINK A SHAPE-SHIFTING USURPER WOULD SAY "MWA HA HA."
MY SHAPE-SHIFTING USURPER SAYS "MWA HA HA."
WHAT'S THAT?
IT'S A PILLOW.
WHY?
I WANTED TO STROKE A WHITE CAT, BUT THIS WAS ALL I COULD FIND.
HIS NAME IS MITTENS. MITTENS THE PILLOW.

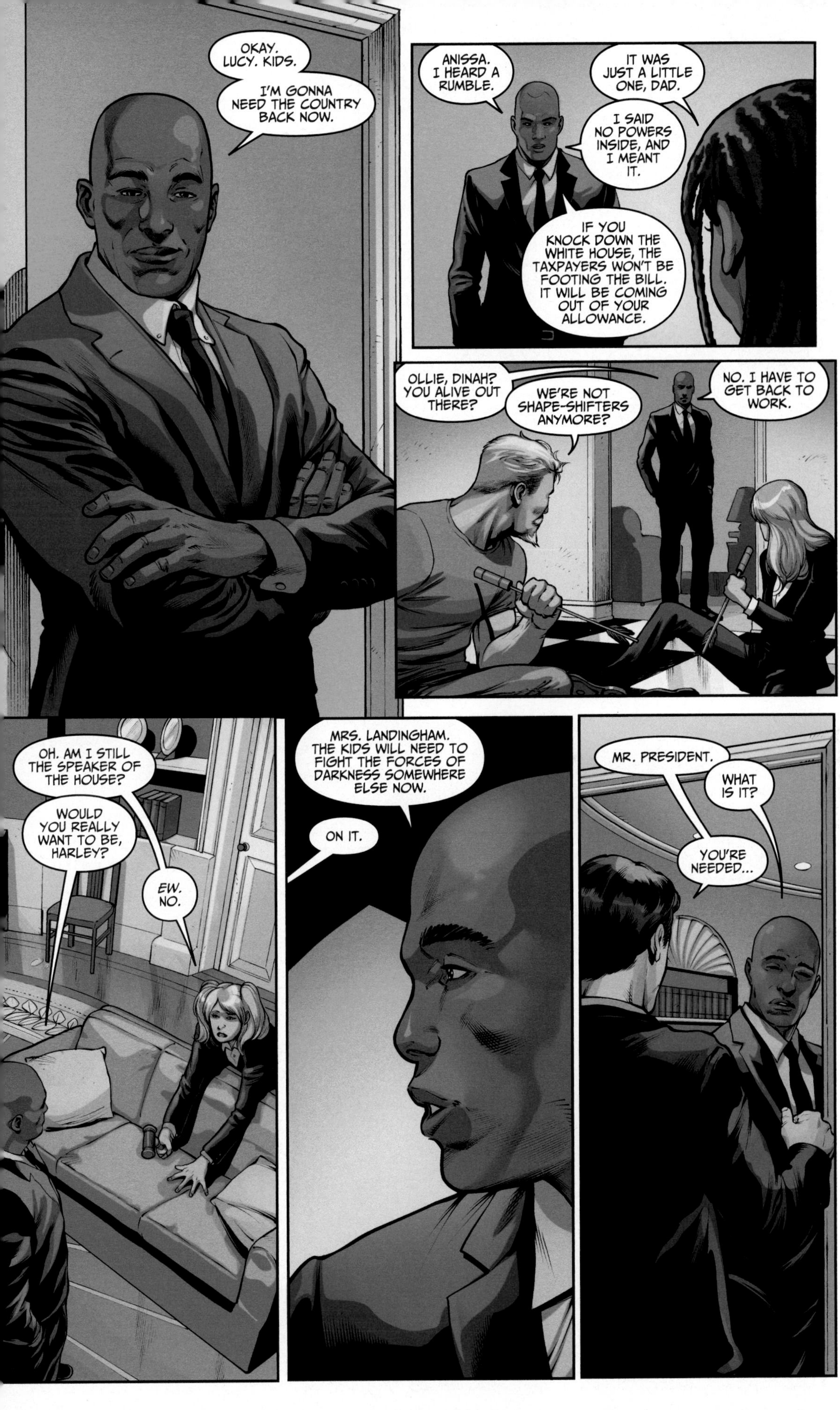

OKAY. LUCY. KIDS.
I'M GONNA NEED THE COUNTRY BACK NOW.
ANISSA. I HEARD A RUMBLE.
IT WAS JUST A LITTLE ONE, DAD.
I SAID NO POWERS INSIDE, AND I MEANT IT.
IF YOU KNOCK DOWN THE WHITE HOUSE, THE TAXPAYERS WON'T BE FOOTING THE BILL. IT WILL BE COMING OUT OF YOUR ALLOWANCE.
OLLIE, DINAH? YOU ALIVE OUT THERE?
WE'RE NOT SHAPE-SHIFTERS ANYMORE?
NO. I HAVE TO GET BACK TO WORK.
OH. AM I STILL THE SPEAKER OF THE HOUSE?
WOULD YOU REALLY WANT TO BE, HARLEY?
EW. NO.
MRS. LANDINGHAM. THE KIDS WILL NEED TO FIGHT THE FORCES OF DARKNESS SOMEWHERE ELSE NOW.
ON IT.
MR. PRESIDENT.
WHAT IS IT?
YOU'RE NEEDED...

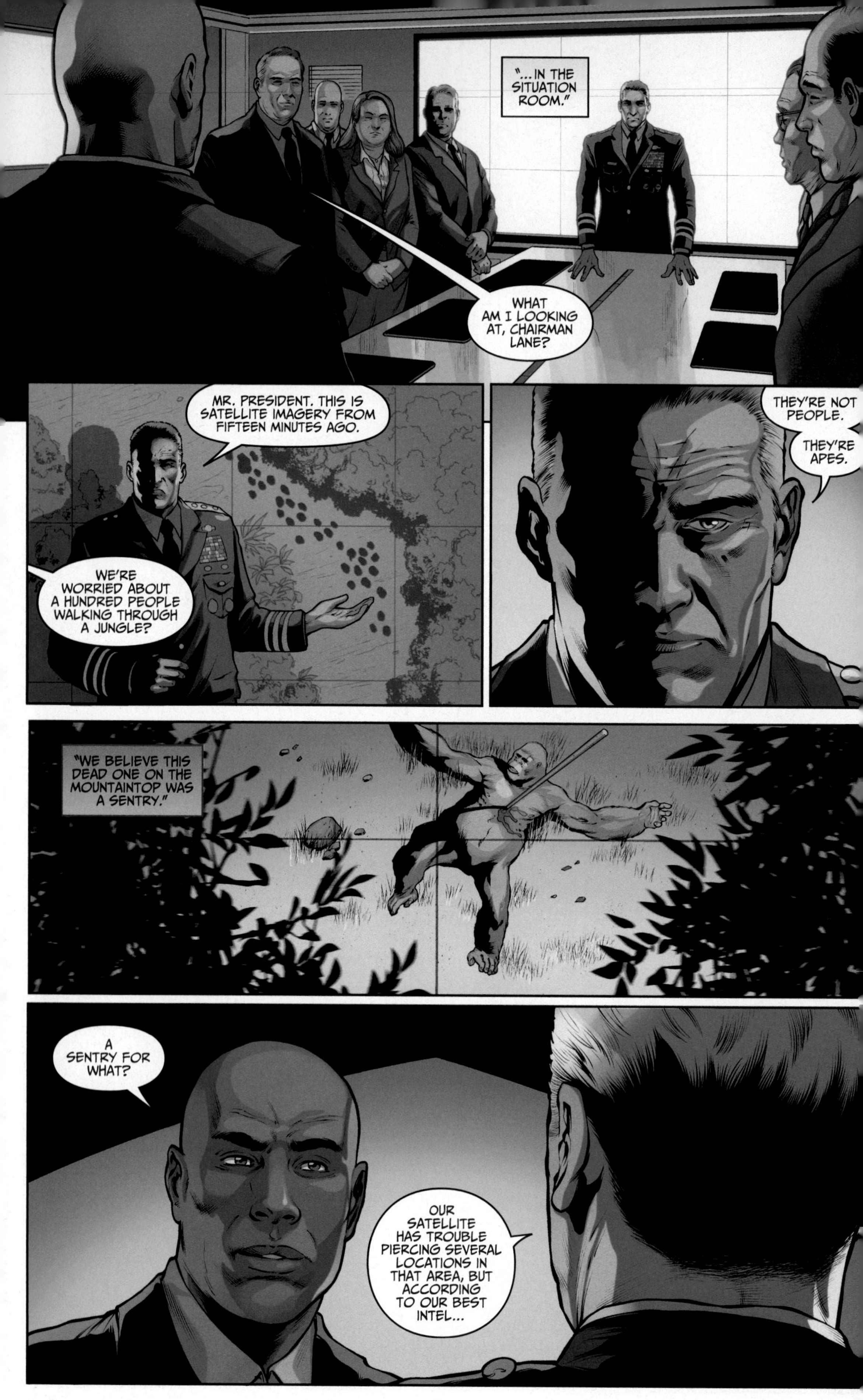
"...IN THE SITUATION ROOM."
WHAT AM I LOOKING AT, CHAIRMAN LANE?
MR. PRESIDENT. THIS IS SATELLITE IMAGERY FROM FIFTEEN MINUTES AGO.
WE'RE WORRIED ABOUT A HUNDRED PEOPLE WALKING THROUGH A JUNGLE?
THEY'RE NOT PEOPLE.
THEY'RE APES.
"WE BELIEVE THIS DEAD ONE ON THE MOUNTAINTOP WAS A SENTRY."
A SENTRY FOR WHAT?
OUR SATELLITE HAS TROUBLE PIERCING SEVERAL LOCATIONS IN THAT AREA, BUT ACCORDING TO OUR BEST INTEL...

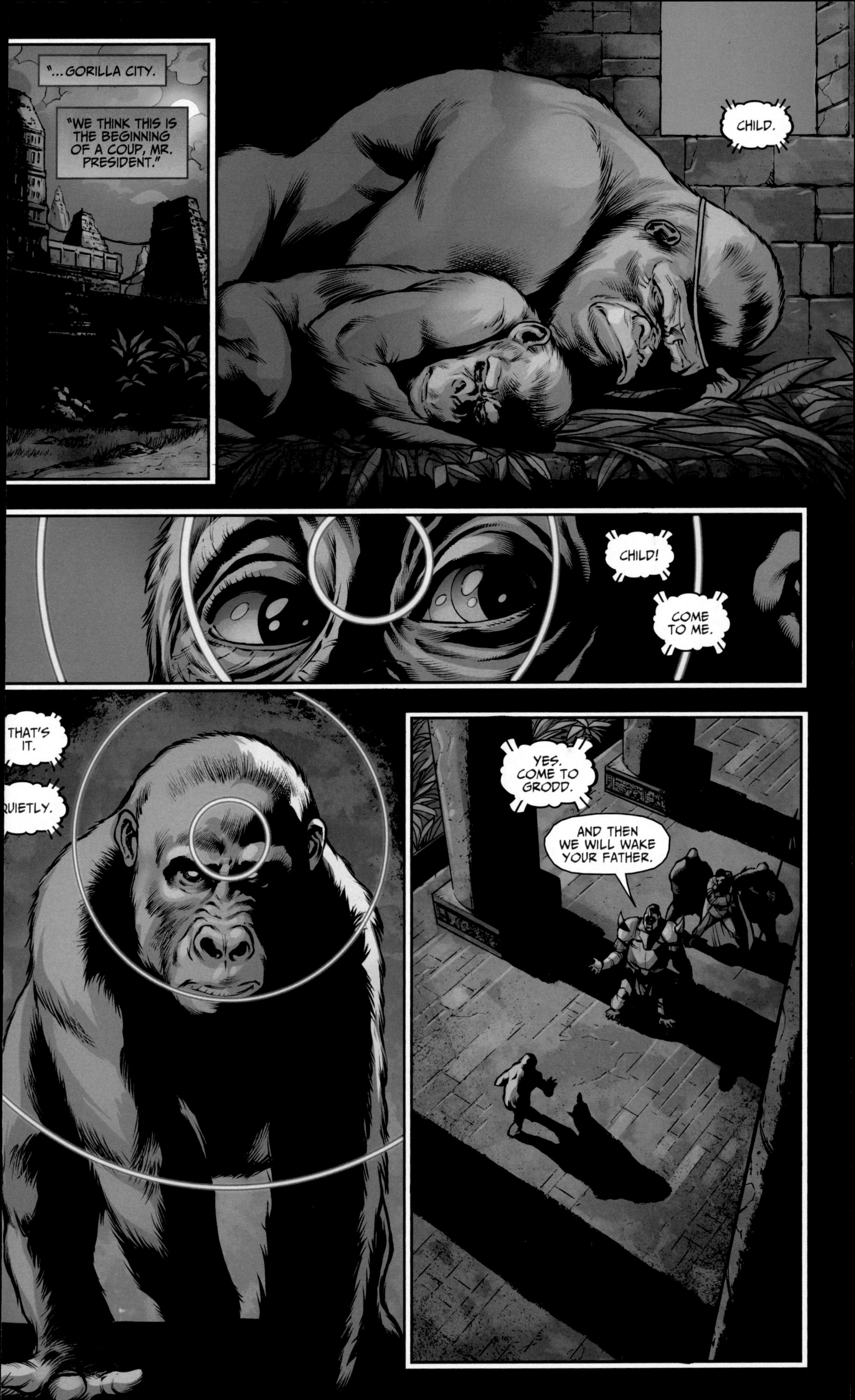
"...GORILLA CITY.
"WE THINK THIS IS THE BEGINNING OF A COUP, MR. PRESIDENT."
CHILD.
CHILD!
COME TO ME.
THAT'S IT.
QUIETLY.
YES. COME TO GRODD.
AND THEN WE WILL WAKE YOUR FATHER.

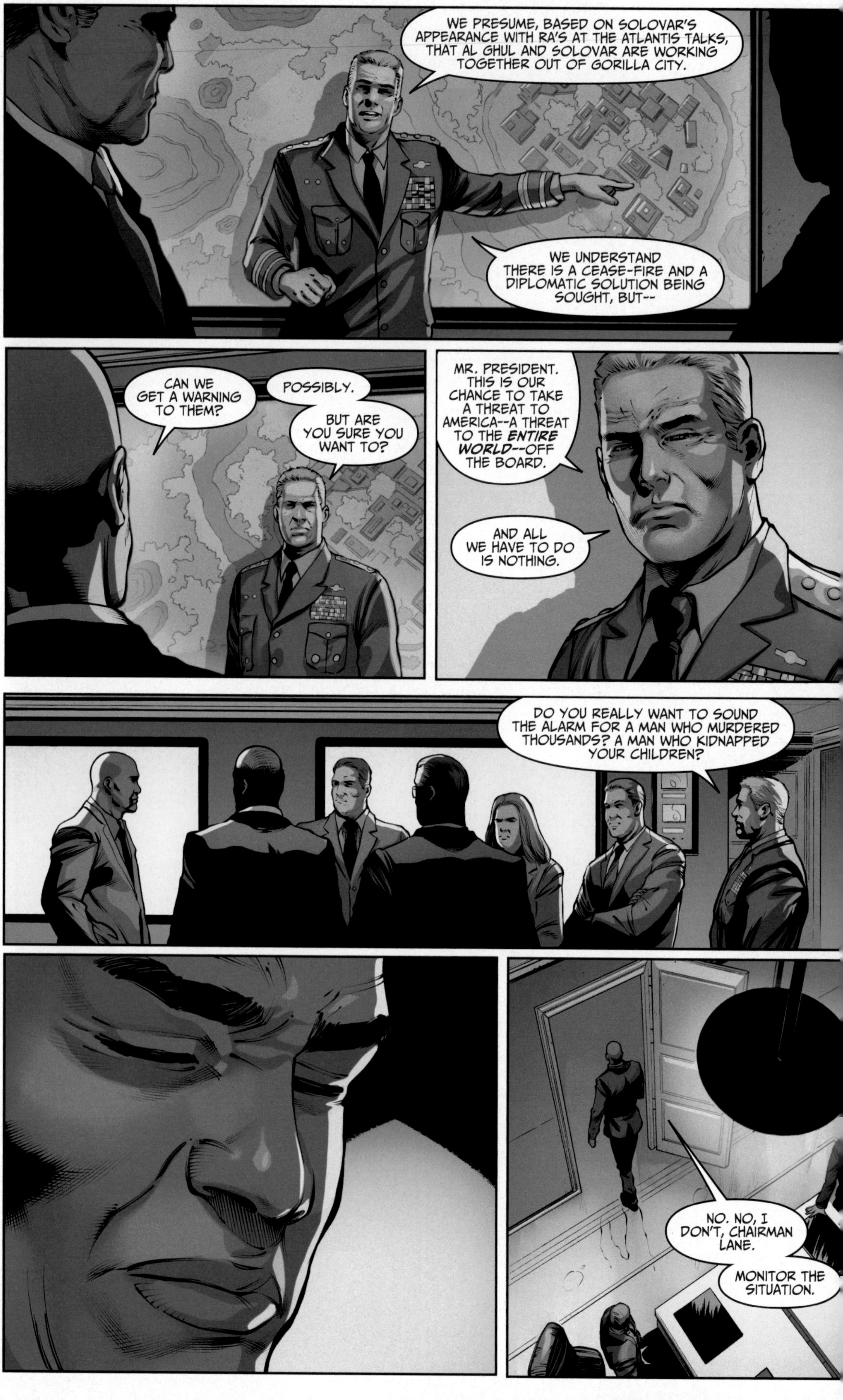
WE PRESUME, BASED ON SOLOVAR'S APPEARANCE WITH RA'S AT THE ATLANTIS TALKS, THAT AL GHUL AND SOLOVAR ARE WORKING TOGETHER OUT OF GORILLA CITY.
WE UNDERSTAND THERE IS A CEASE-FIRE AND A DIPLOMATIC SOLUTION BEING SOUGHT, BUT--
CAN WE GET A WARNING TO THEM?
POSSIBLY.
BUT ARE YOU SURE YOU WANT TO?
MR. PRESIDENT. THIS IS OUR CHANCE TO TAKE A THREAT TO AMERICA--A THREAT TO THE ENTIRE WORLD--OFF THE BOARD.
AND ALL WE HAVE TO DO IS NOTHING.
DO YOU REALLY WANT TO SOUND THE ALARM FOR A MAN WHO MURDERED THOUSANDS? A MAN WHO KIDNAPPED YOUR CHILDREN?
NO. NO, I DON'T, CHAIRMAN LANE.
MONITOR THE SITUATION.

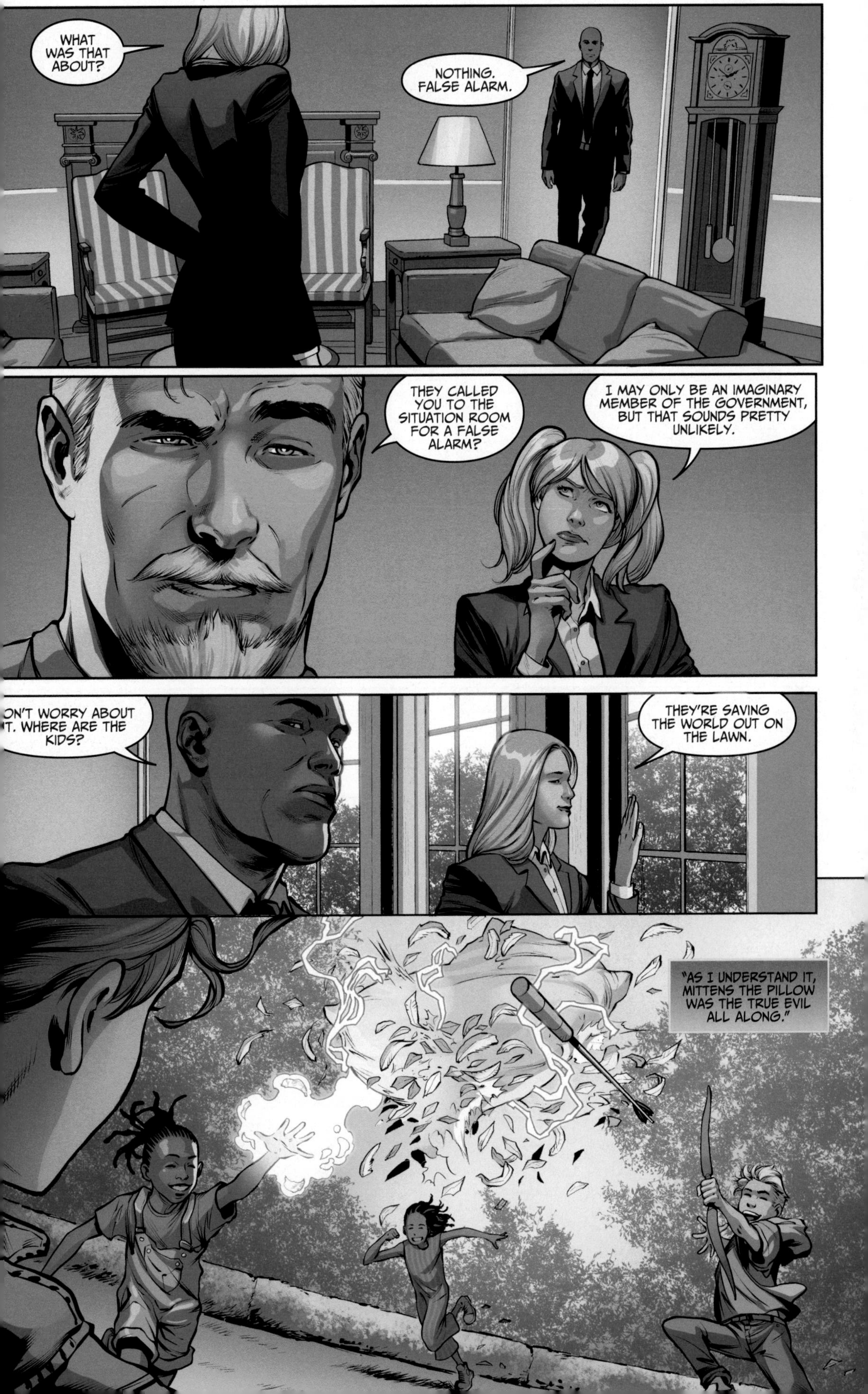
WHAT WAS THAT ABOUT?
NOTHING. FALSE ALARM.
THEY CALLED YOU TO THE SITUATION ROOM FOR A FALSE ALARM?
I MAY ONLY BE AN IMAGINARY MEMBER OF THE GOVERNMENT, BUT THAT SOUNDS PRETTY UNLIKELY.
ON'T WORRY ABOUT T. WHERE ARE THE KIDS?
THEY'RE SAVING THE WORLD OUT ON THE LAWN.
"AS I UNDERSTAND IT, MITTENS THE PILLOW WAS THE TRUE EVIL ALL ALONG."

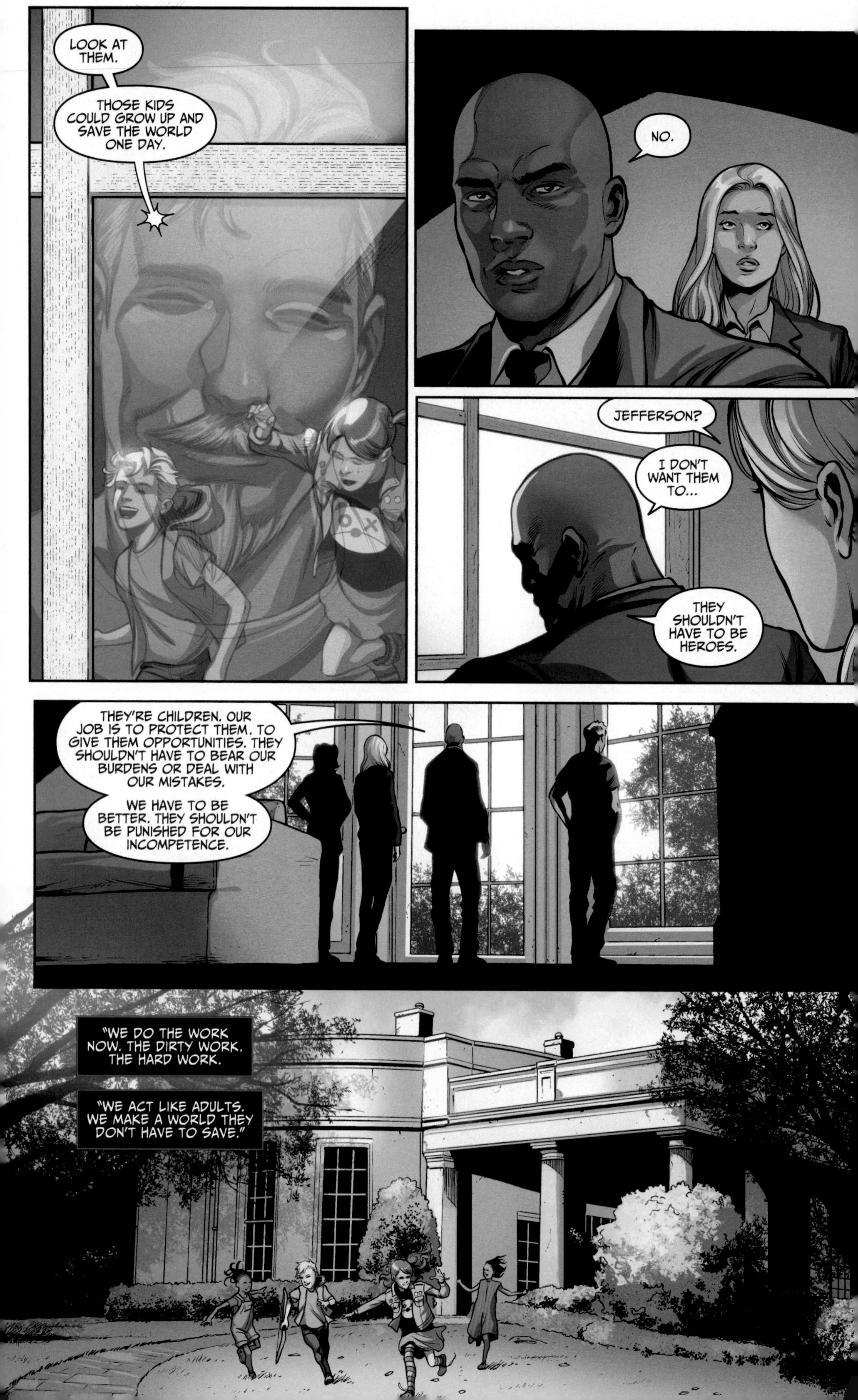
LOOK AT THEM.
THOSE KIDS COULD GROW UP AND SAVE THE WORLD ONE DAY.
NO.
JEFFERSON?
I DON'T WANT THEM TO...
THEY SHOULDN'T HAVE TO BE HEROES.
THEY'RE CHILDREN. OUR JOB IS TO PROTECT THEM. TO GIVE THEM OPPORTUNITIES. THEY SHOULDN'T HAVE TO BEAR OUR BURDENS OR DEAL WITH OUR MISTAKES.
WE HAVE TO BE BETTER. THEY SHOULDN'T BE PUNISHED FOR OUR INCOMPETENCE.
"WE DO THE WORK NOW. THE DIRTY WORK. THE HARD WORK.
"WE ACT LIKE ADULTS. WE MAKE A WORLD THEY DON'T HAVE TO SAVE."

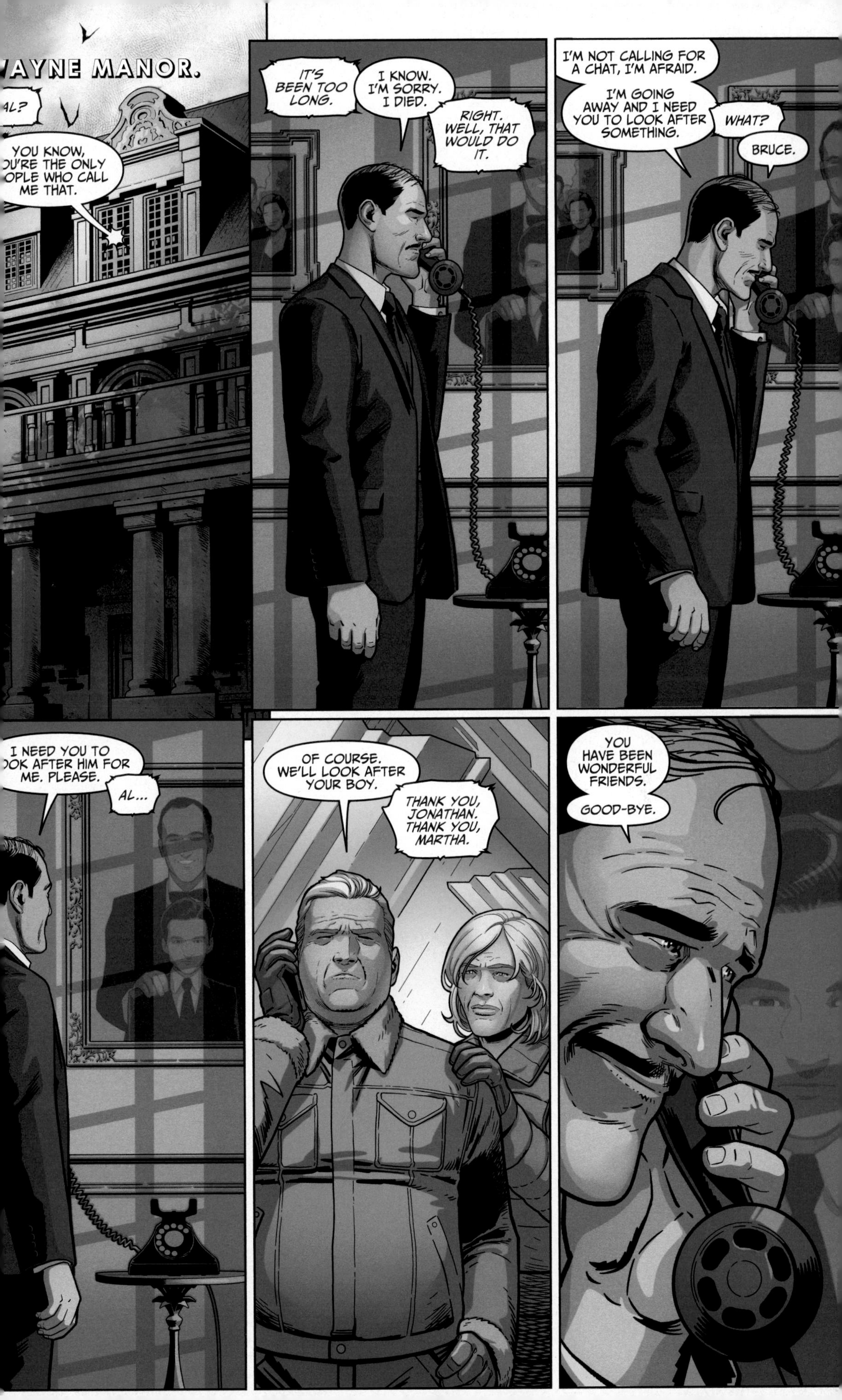

AYNE MANOR.
AL?
YOU KNOW, OU'RE THE ONLY OPLE WHO CALL ME THAT.
IT'S BEEN TOO LONG.
I KNOW. I'M SORRY. I DIED.
RIGHT. WELL, THAT WOULD DO IT.
I'M NOT CALLING FOR A CHAT, I'M AFRAID.
I'M GOING AWAY AND I NEED YOU TO LOOK AFTER SOMETHING.
WHAT?
BRUCE.
I NEED YOU TO OOK AFTER HIM FOR ME. PLEASE.
AL...
OF COURSE. WE'LL LOOK AFTER YOUR BOY.
THANK YOU, JONATHAN. THANK YOU, MARTHA.
YOU HAVE BEEN WONDERFUL FRIENDS.
GOOD-BYE.

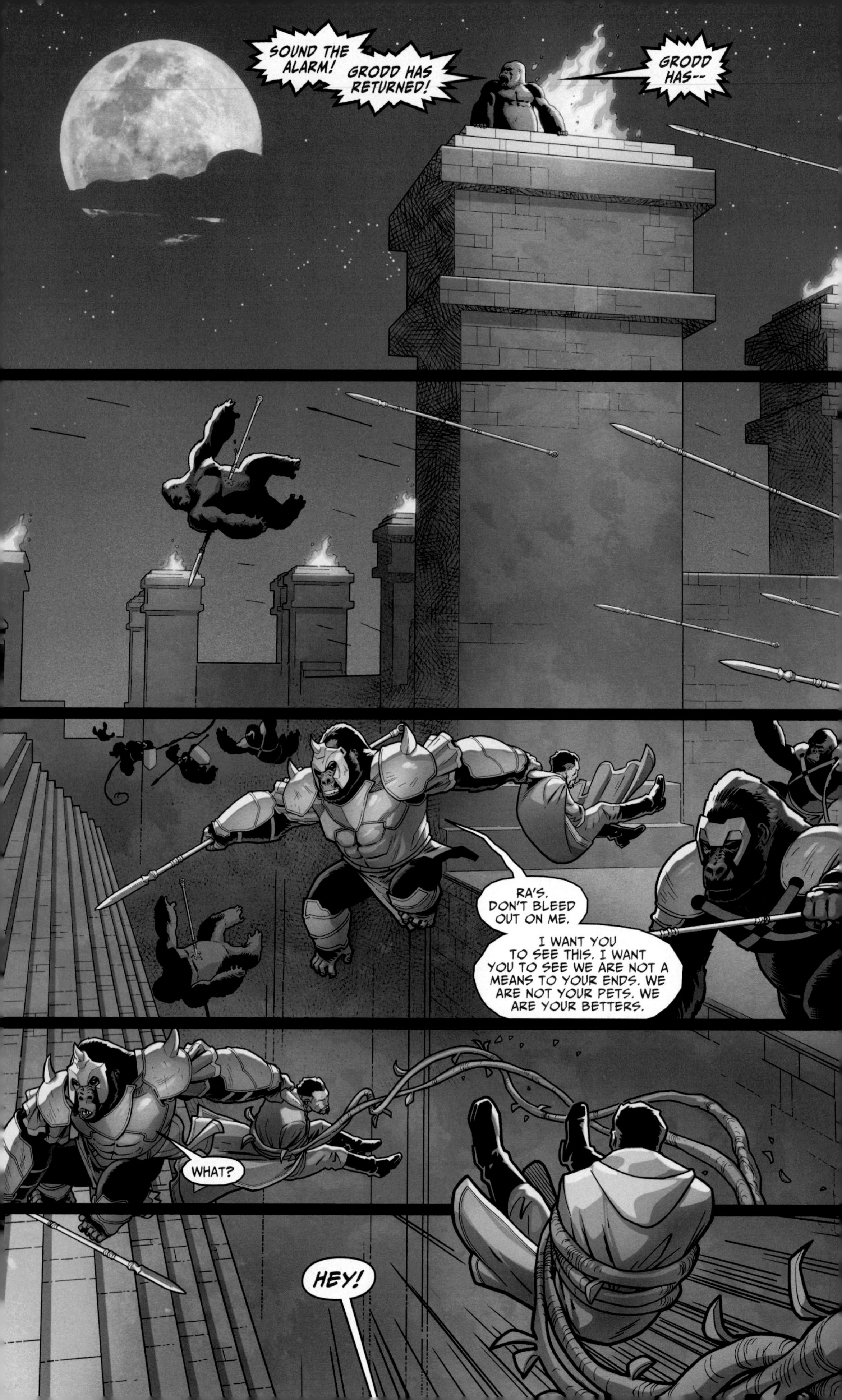
SOUND THE ALARM!
GRODD HAS RETURNED!
GRODD HAS--
RA'S. DON'T BLEED OUT ON ME.
I WANT YOU TO SEE THIS. I WANT YOU TO SEE WE ARE NOT A MEANS TO YOUR ENDS. WE ARE NOT YOUR PETS. WE ARE YOUR BETTERS.
WHAT?
HEY!

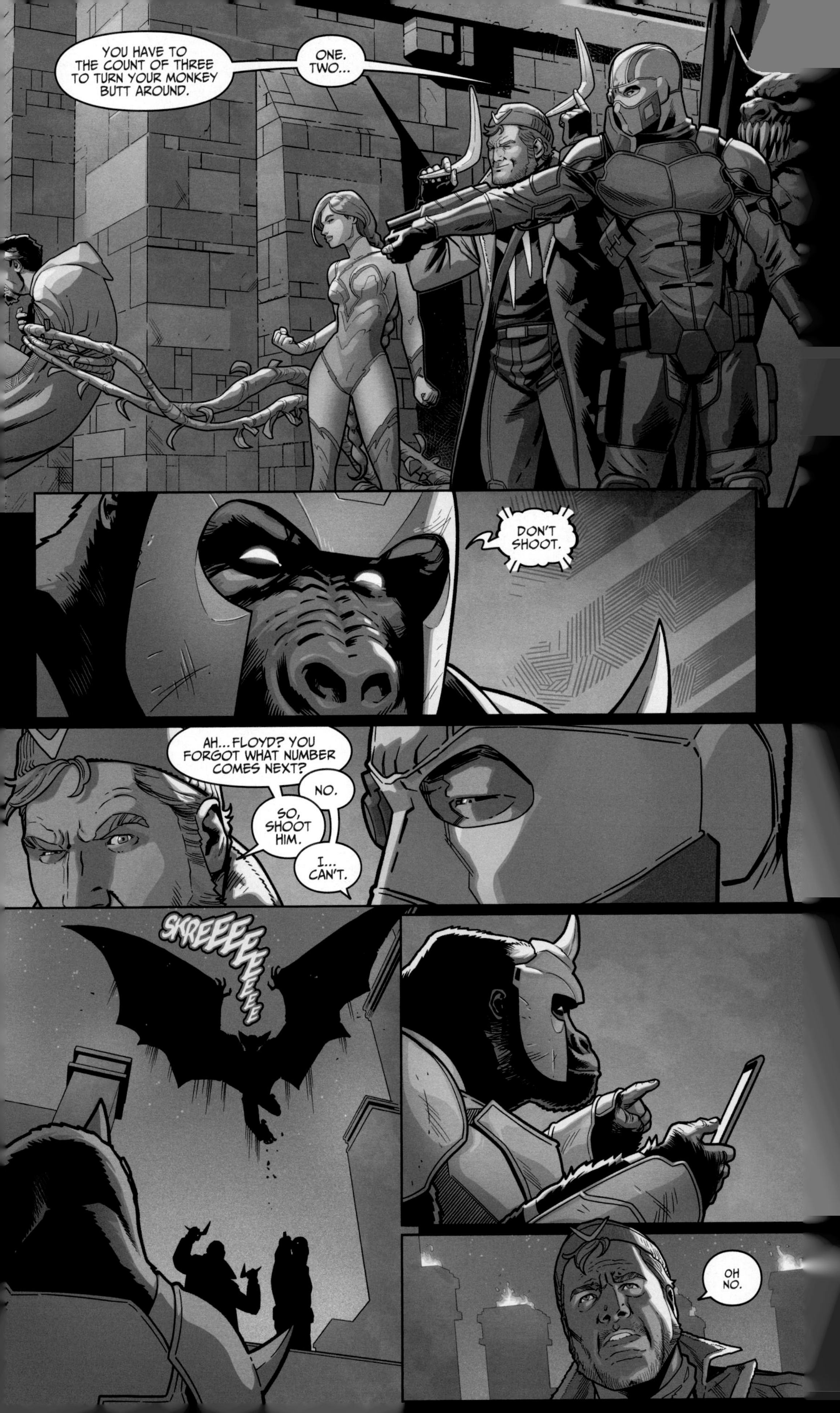
YOU HAVE TO THE COUNT OF THREE TO TURN YOUR MONKEY BUTT AROUND.
ONE. TWO...
DON'T SHOOT.
AH...FLOYD? YOU FORGOT WHAT NUMBER COMES NEXT?
NO.
SO, SHOOT HIM.
I... CAN'T.
SKREEEEEEEEEE
OH NO.

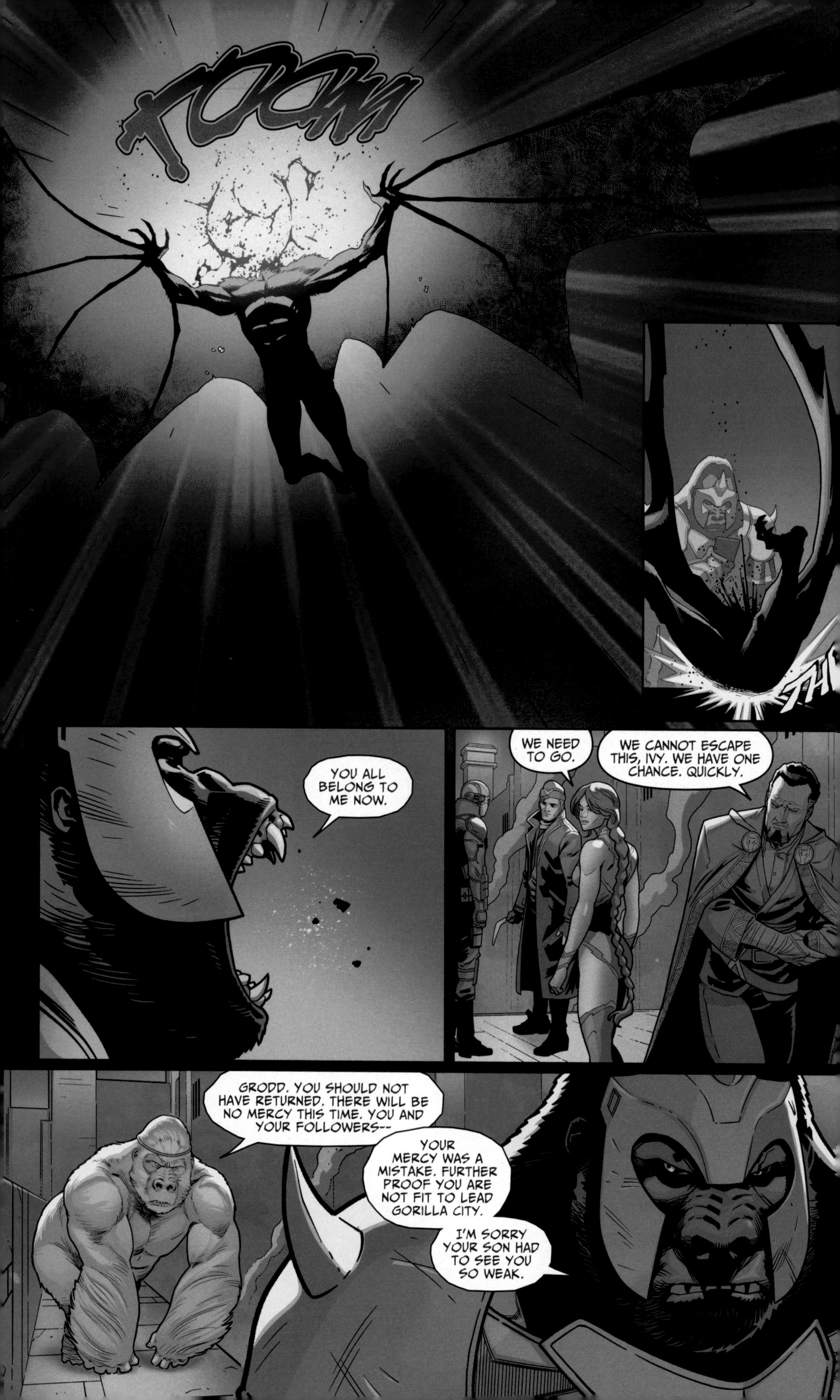
FOOM
TH
YOU ALL BELONG TO ME NOW.
WE NEED TO GO.
WE CANNOT ESCAPE THIS, IVY. WE HAVE ONE CHANCE. QUICKLY.
GRODD. YOU SHOULD NOT HAVE RETURNED. THERE WILL BE NO MERCY THIS TIME. YOU AND YOUR FOLLOWERS--
YOUR MERCY WAS A MISTAKE. FURTHER PROOF YOU ARE NOT FIT TO LEAD GORILLA CITY.
I'M SORRY YOUR SON HAD TO SEE YOU SO WEAK.

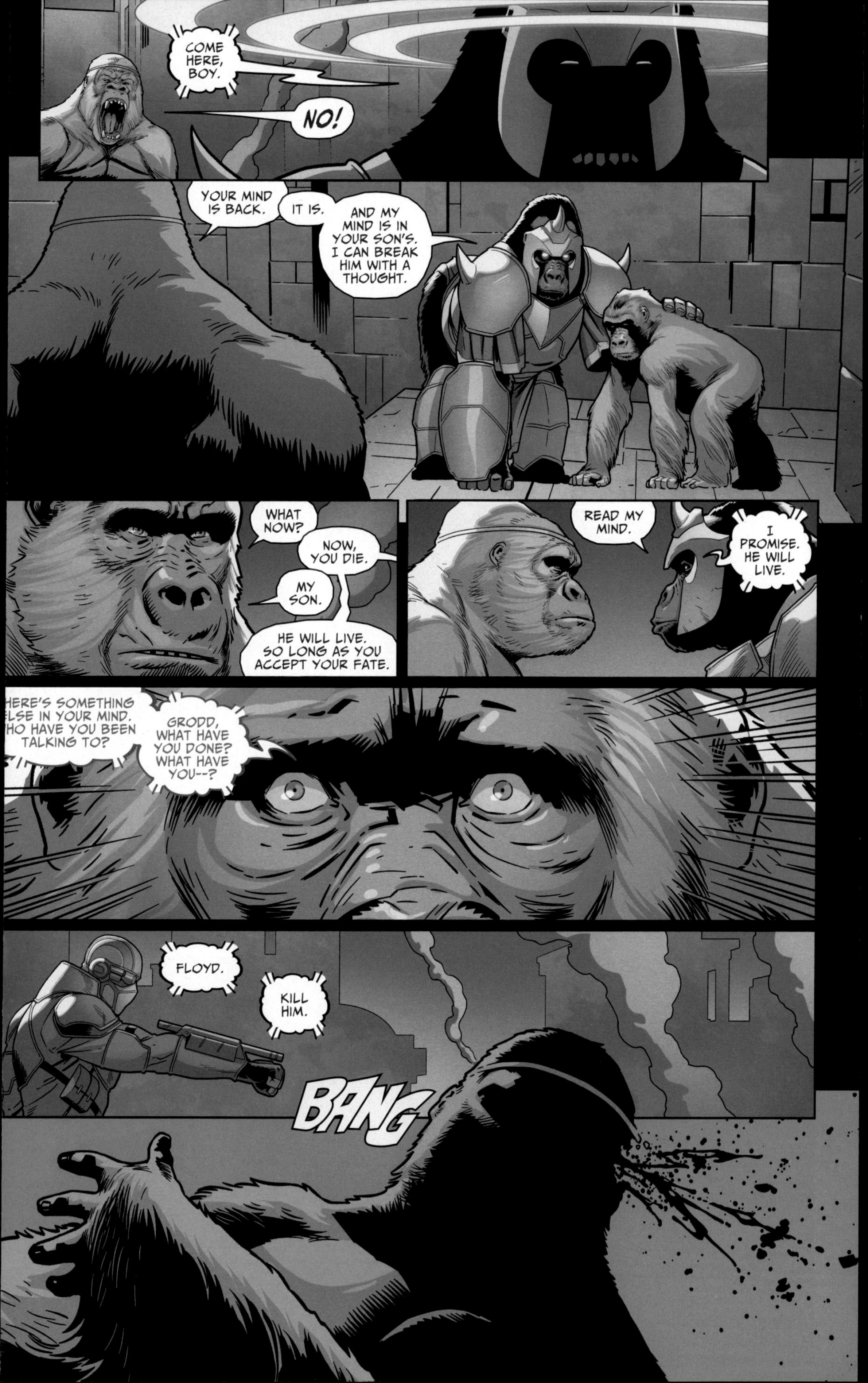
COME HERE, BOY.
NO!
YOUR MIND IS BACK.
IT IS.
AND MY MIND IS IN YOUR SON'S. I CAN BREAK HIM WITH A THOUGHT.
WHAT NOW?
NOW, YOU DIE.
MY SON.
HE WILL LIVE. SO LONG AS YOU ACCEPT YOUR FATE.
READ MY MIND.
I PROMISE. HE WILL LIVE.
HERE'S SOMETHING ELSE IN YOUR MIND. WHO HAVE YOU BEEN TALKING TO?
GRODD, WHAT HAVE YOU DONE? WHAT HAVE YOU--?
FLOYD.
KILL HIM.
BANG

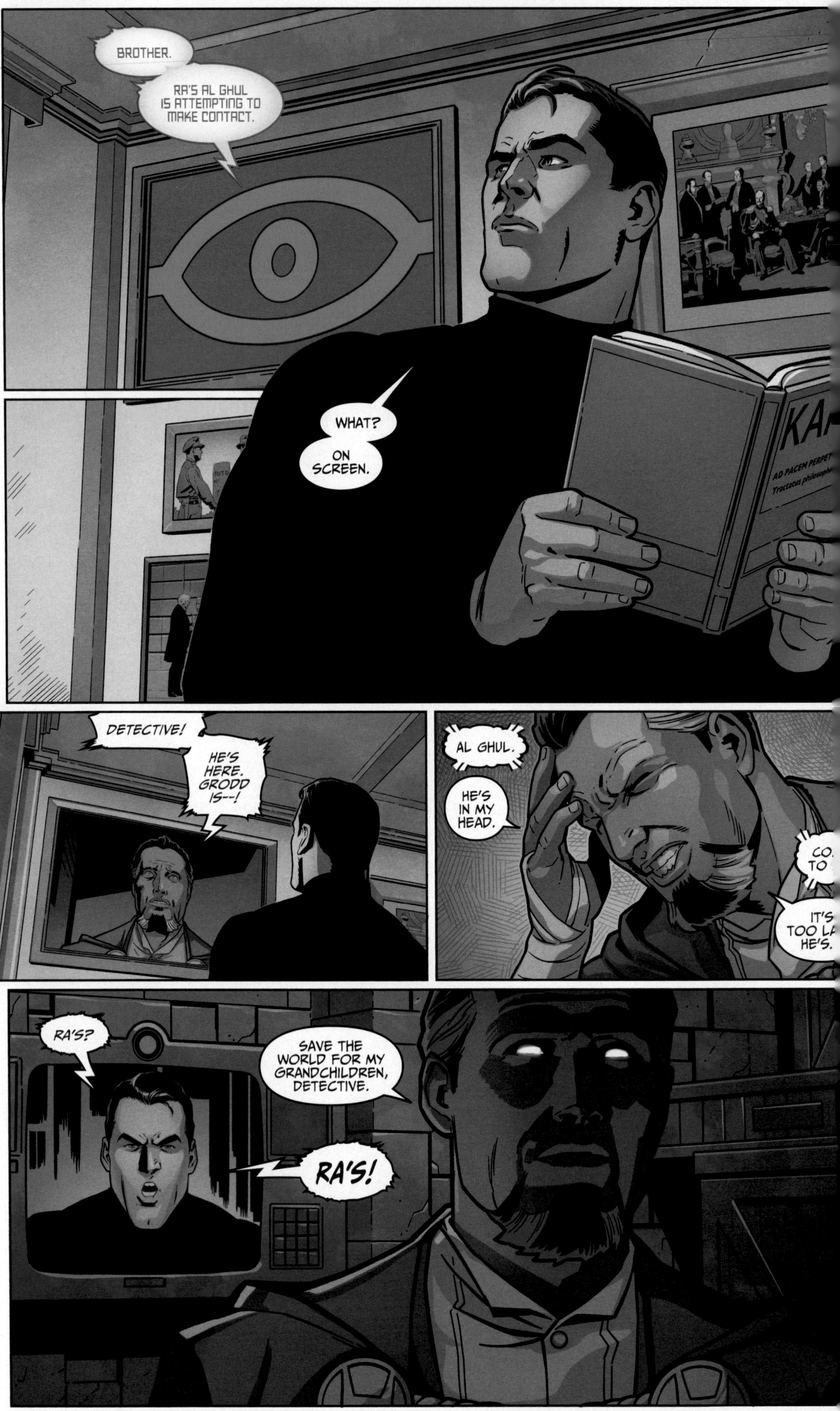
BROTHER.
RA'S AL GHUL IS ATTEMPTING TO MAKE CONTACT.
WHAT?
ON SCREEN.
DETECTIVE!
HE'S HERE. GRODD IS--!
AL GHUL.
HE'S IN MY HEAD.
CO TO
IT'S TOO LA HE'S.
RA'S?
SAVE THE WORLD FOR MY GRANDCHILDREN, DETECTIVE.
RA'S!

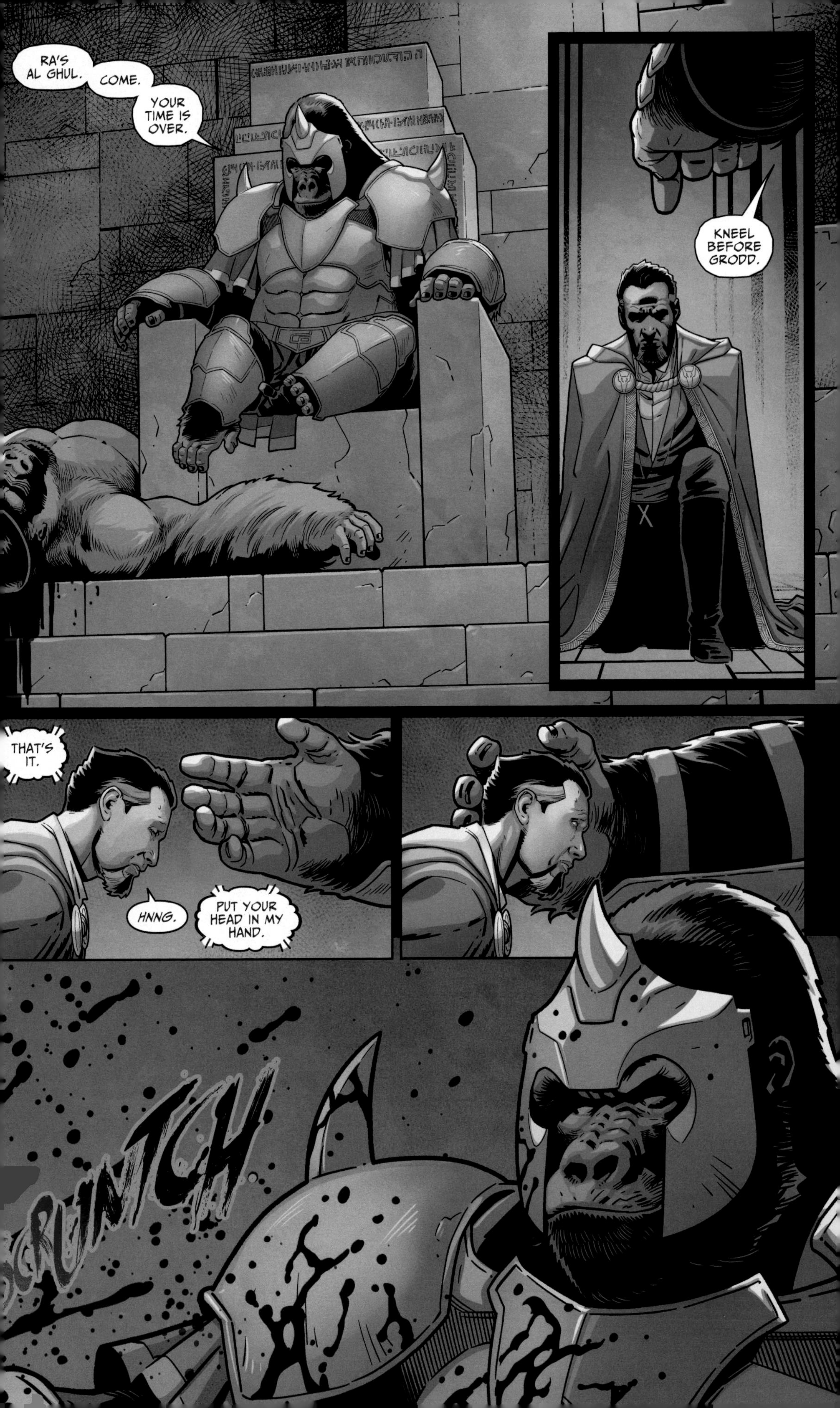
RA'S AL GHUL.
COME.
YOUR TIME IS OVER.
KNEEL BEFORE GRODD.
THAT'S IT.
HNNG.
PUT YOUR HEAD IN MY HAND.
SCRUNTCH

ALFRED!

SOMETHING HAPPENED. I THINK--

ALFRED?

DON'T WORRY.

I WASN'T GOING TO LEAVE WITHOUT SAYING GOOD-BYE.

WHERE ARE YOU GOING?

I CAN'T TELL YOU. BUT I'M GOING AWAY.

I KNOW YOU CAN FIND ME. BUT I'M ASKING YOU, PLEASE, DON'T.

WHY?

WHY? BECAUSE I CAN'T HELP YOU.

I'M NOT... RIGHT. NOT SINCE THE LAZARUS PIT. THERE ARE PARTS MISSING.

I'M STRUGGLING EVERY DAY. THESE WORDS ARE SO MUCH EFFORT.

BRUCE. I DIED.

I NEVE[R] REALLY C[AME] BACK.

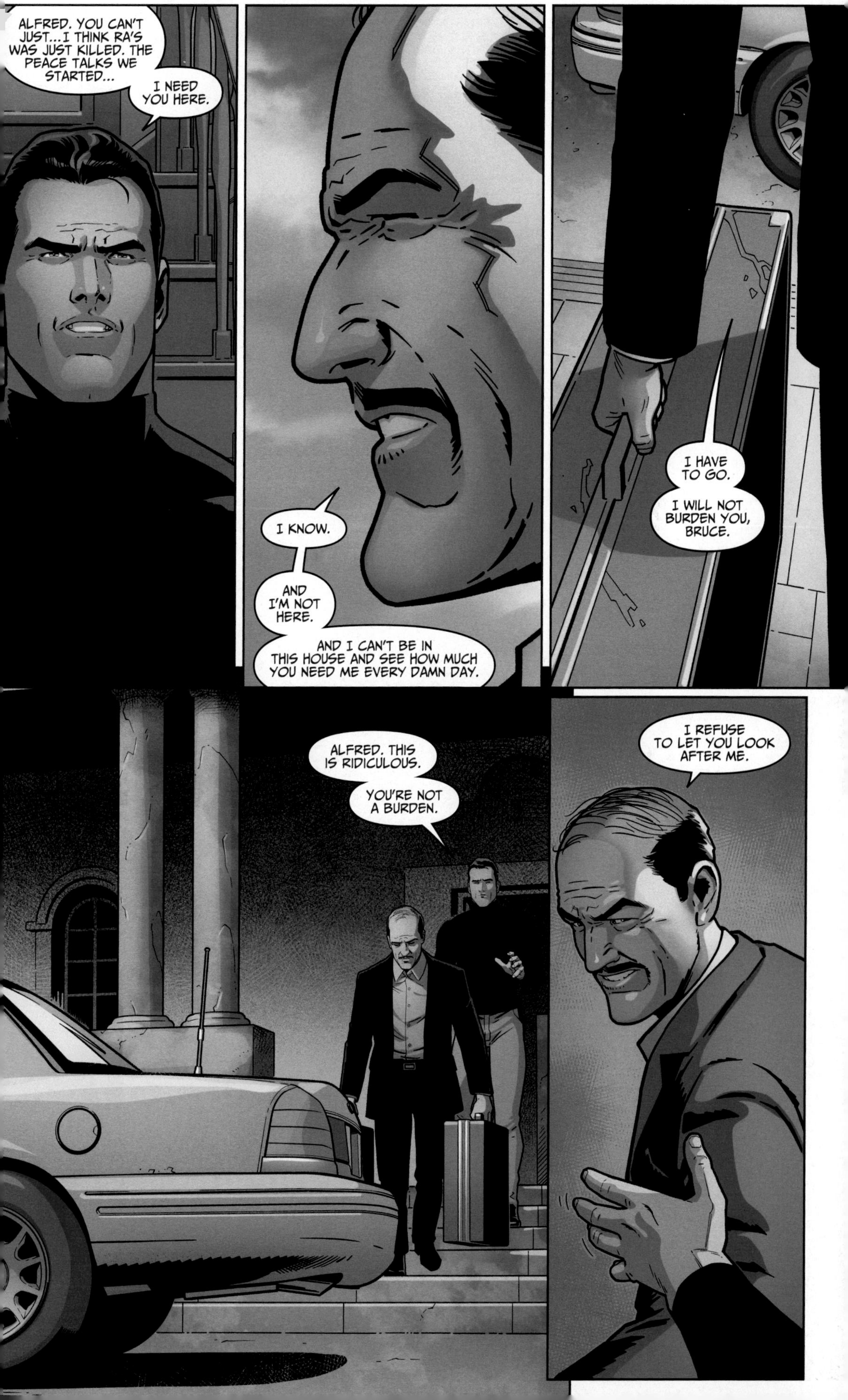

ALFRED. YOU CAN'T JUST...I THINK RA'S WAS JUST KILLED. THE PEACE TALKS WE STARTED...
I NEED YOU HERE.
I KNOW.
AND I'M NOT HERE.
AND I CAN'T BE IN THIS HOUSE AND SEE HOW MUCH YOU NEED ME EVERY DAMN DAY.
I HAVE TO GO.
I WILL NOT BURDEN YOU, BRUCE.
ALFRED. THIS IS RIDICULOUS.
YOU'RE NOT A BURDEN.
I REFUSE TO LET YOU LOOK AFTER ME.

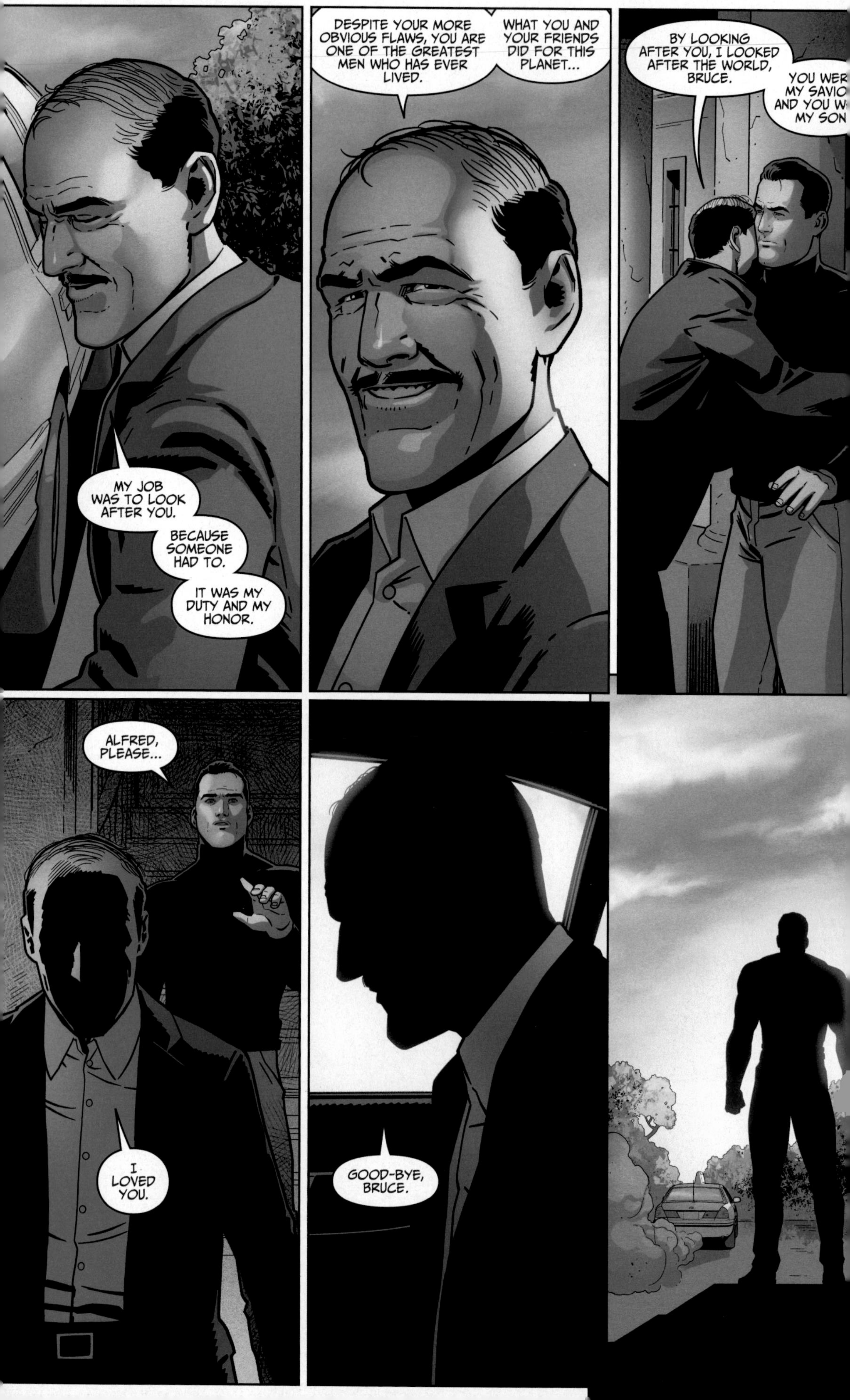
MY JOB WAS TO LOOK AFTER YOU.
BECAUSE SOMEONE HAD TO.
IT WAS MY DUTY AND MY HONOR.
DESPITE YOUR MORE OBVIOUS FLAWS, YOU ARE ONE OF THE GREATEST MEN WHO HAS EVER LIVED.
WHAT YOU AND YOUR FRIENDS DID FOR THIS PLANET...
BY LOOKING AFTER YOU, I LOOKED AFTER THE WORLD, BRUCE.
ALFRED, PLEASE...
I LOVED YOU.
GOOD-BYE, BRUCE.

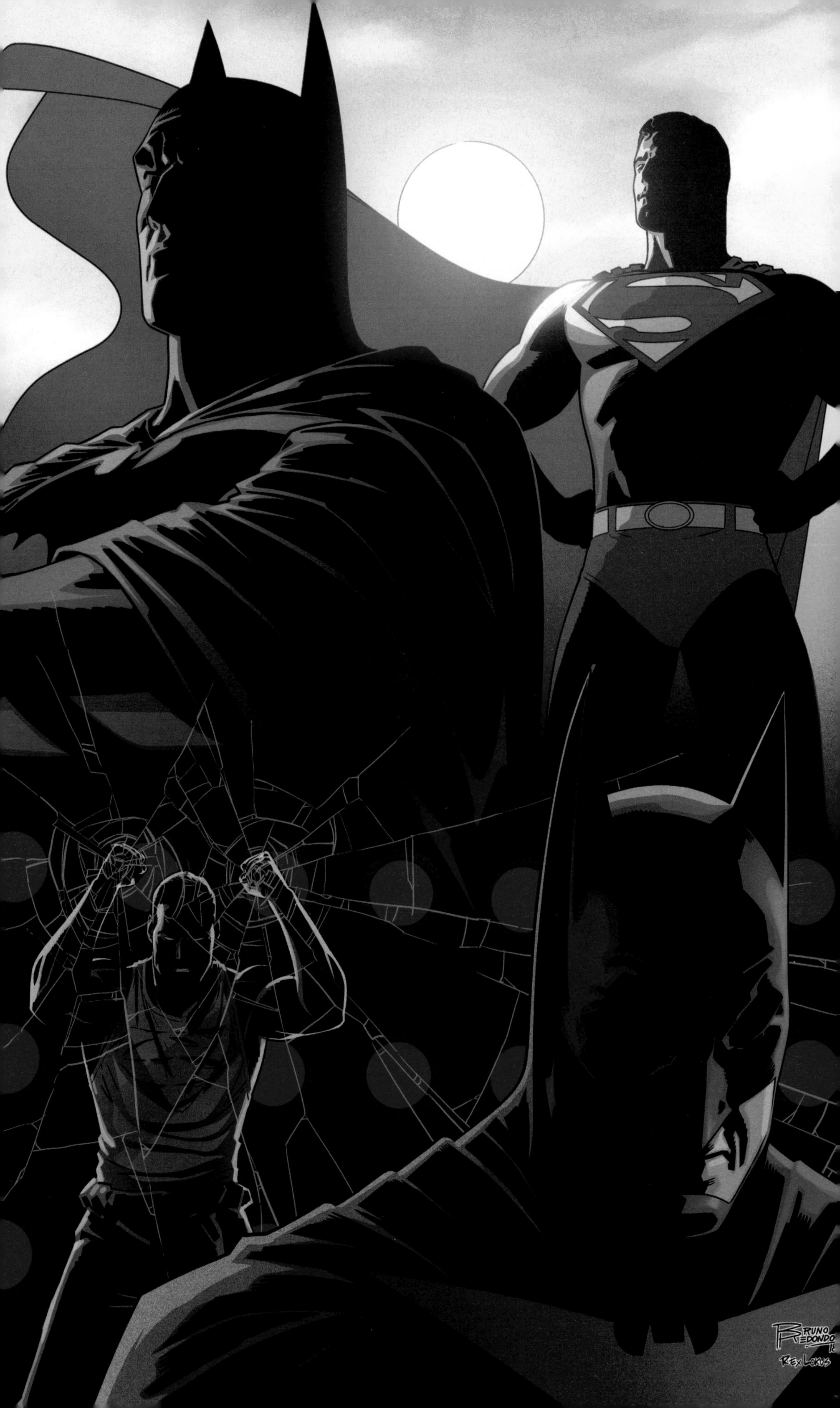
BRUNO REDONDO 18
REX LOKUS

"The World's Finest"

Tom Taylor Writer **Bruno Redondo** Artist **Rex Lokus** Colorist **Wes Abbott** Letterer

Cover art by **Bruno Redondo** and **Alejandro Sanchez**

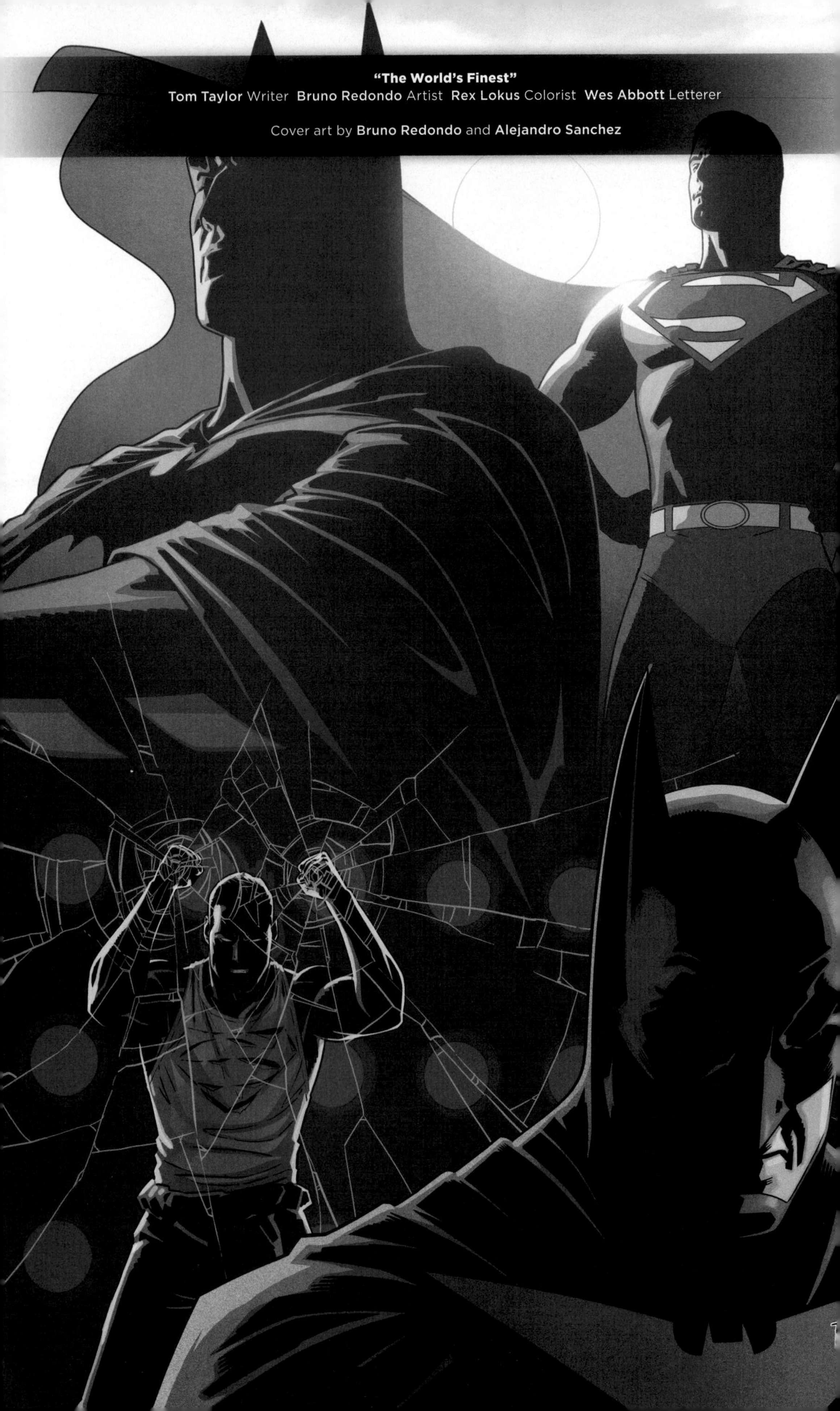

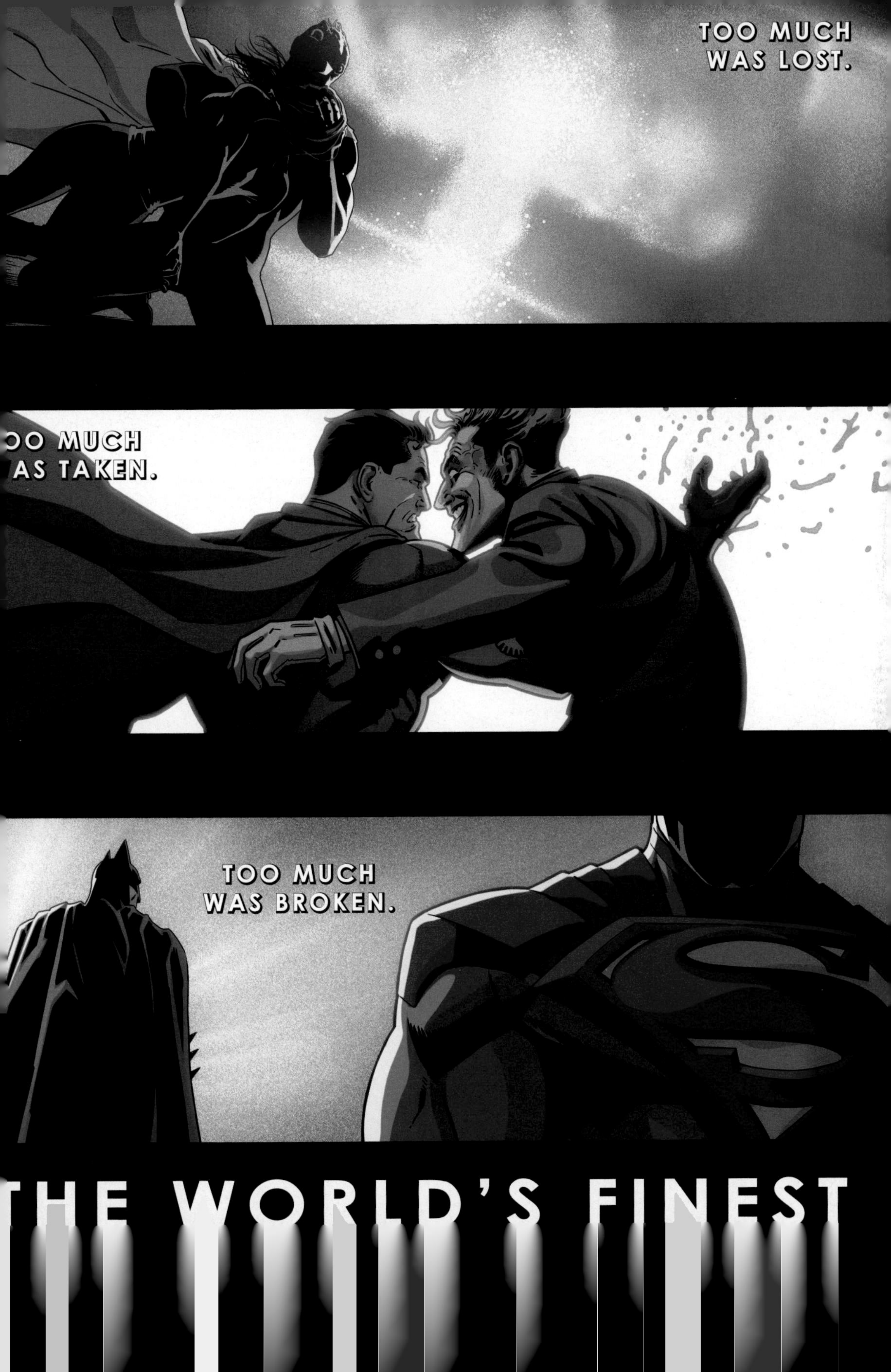
TOO MUCH WAS LOST.
OO MUCH
AS TAKEN.
TOO MUCH WAS BROKEN.
THE WORLD'S FINEST

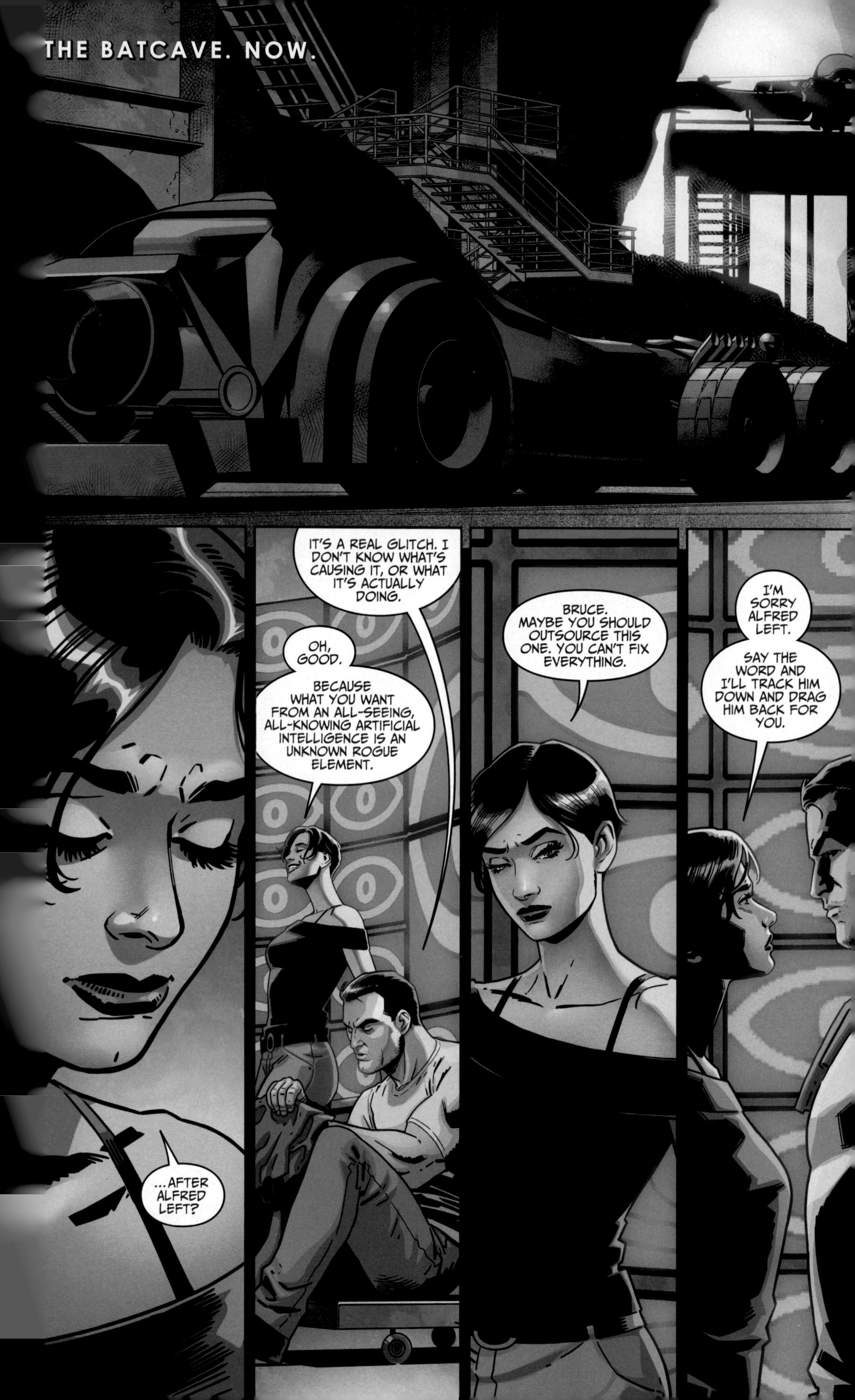
THE BATCAVE. NOW.
...AFTER ALFRED LEFT?
IT'S A REAL GLITCH. I DON'T KNOW WHAT'S CAUSING IT, OR WHAT IT'S ACTUALLY DOING.
OH, GOOD.
BECAUSE WHAT YOU WANT FROM AN ALL-SEEING, ALL-KNOWING ARTIFICIAL INTELLIGENCE IS AN UNKNOWN ROGUE ELEMENT.
BRUCE. MAYBE YOU SHOULD OUTSOURCE THIS ONE. YOU CAN'T FIX EVERYTHING.
I'M SORRY ALFRED LEFT.
SAY THE WORD AND I'LL TRACK HIM DOWN AND DRAG HIM BACK FOR YOU.

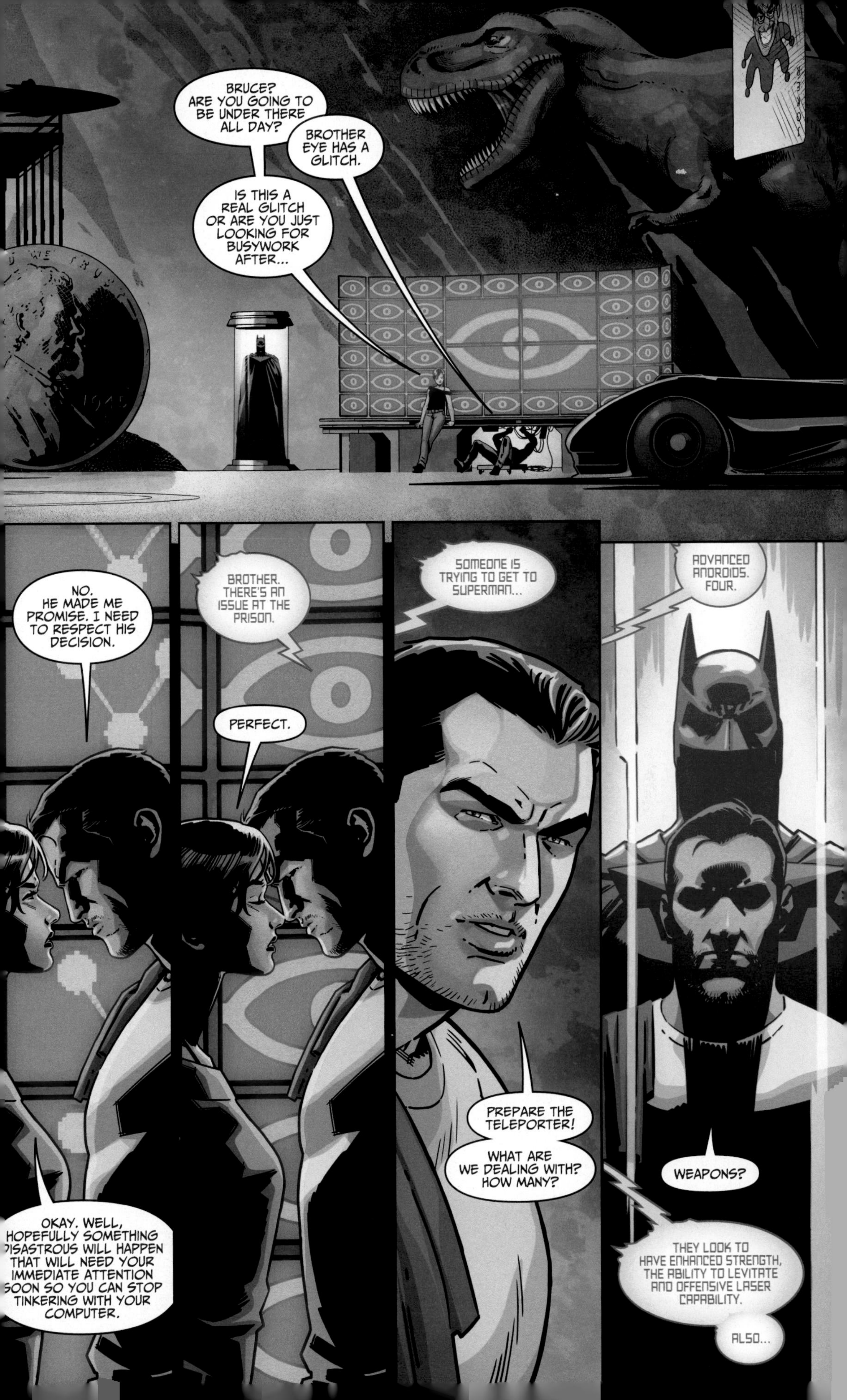
BRUCE? ARE YOU GOING TO BE UNDER THERE ALL DAY?
BROTHER EYE HAS A GLITCH.
IS THIS A REAL GLITCH OR ARE YOU JUST LOOKING FOR BUSYWORK AFTER...
NO. HE MADE ME PROMISE. I NEED TO RESPECT HIS DECISION.
OKAY. WELL, HOPEFULLY SOMETHING DISASTROUS WILL HAPPEN THAT WILL NEED YOUR IMMEDIATE ATTENTION SOON SO YOU CAN STOP TINKERING WITH YOUR COMPUTER.
BROTHER. THERE'S AN ISSUE AT THE PRISON.
PERFECT.
SOMEONE IS TRYING TO GET TO SUPERMAN...
PREPARE THE TELEPORTER!
WHAT ARE WE DEALING WITH? HOW MANY?
ADVANCED ANDROIDS. FOUR.
WEAPONS?
THEY LOOK TO HAVE ENHANCED STRENGTH, THE ABILITY TO LEVITATE AND OFFENSIVE LASER CAPABILITY.
ALSO...

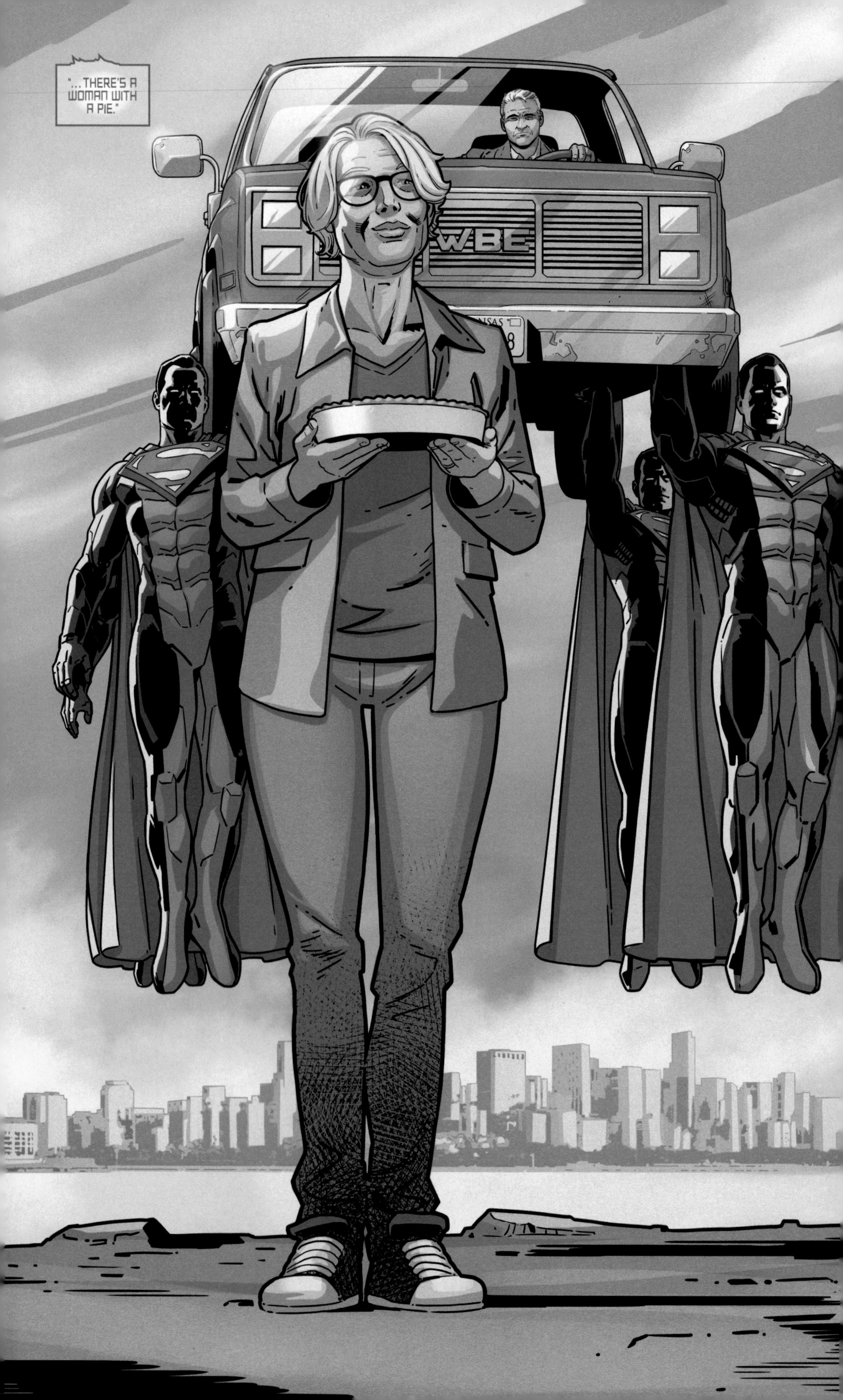
"...THERE'S A WOMAN WITH A PIE."

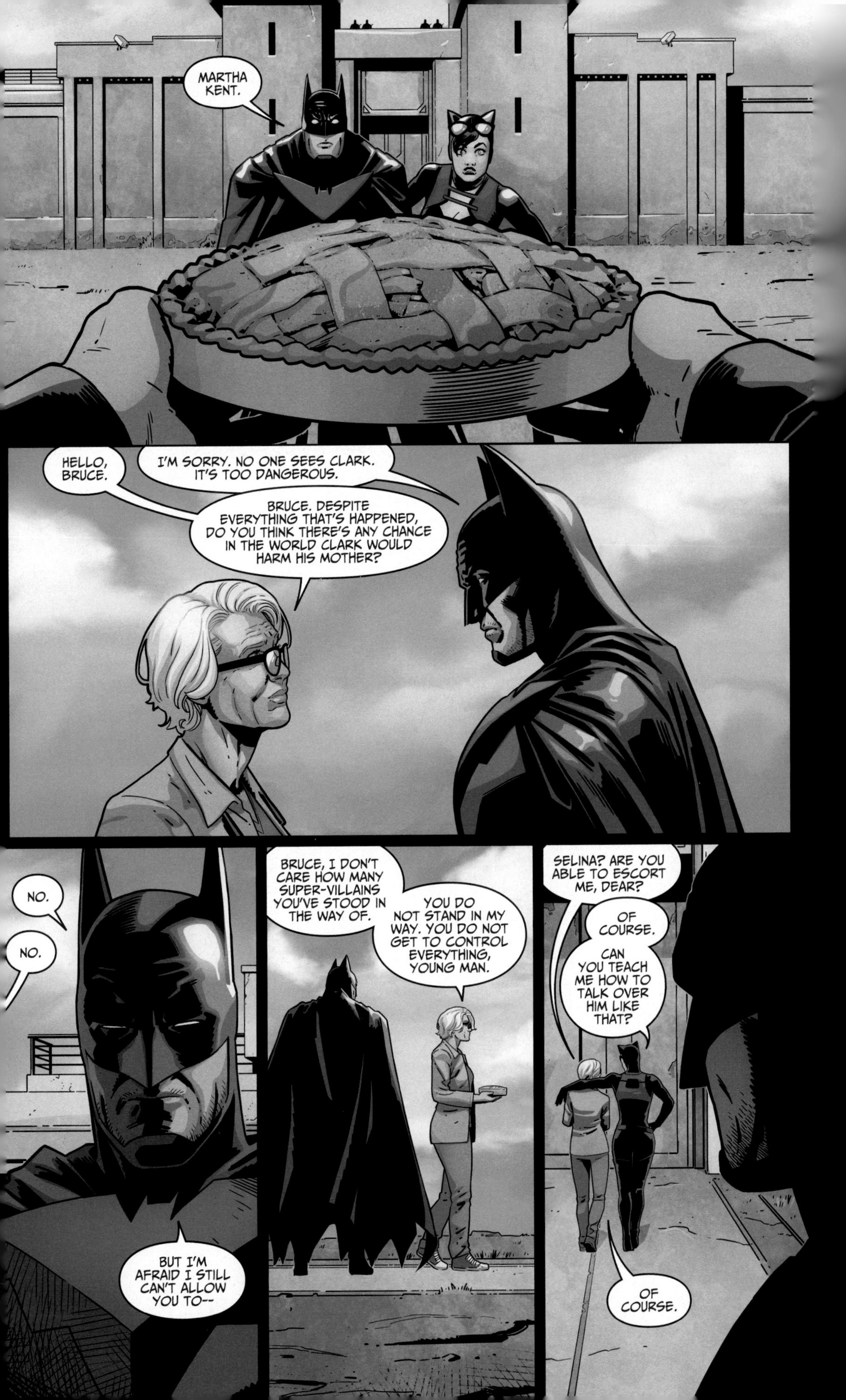
MARTHA KENT.
HELLO, BRUCE.
I'M SORRY. NO ONE SEES CLARK. IT'S TOO DANGEROUS.
BRUCE. DESPITE EVERYTHING THAT'S HAPPENED, DO YOU THINK THERE'S ANY CHANCE IN THE WORLD CLARK WOULD HARM HIS MOTHER?
NO.
NO.
BUT I'M AFRAID I STILL CAN'T ALLOW YOU TO--
BRUCE, I DON'T CARE HOW MANY SUPER-VILLAINS YOU'VE STOOD IN THE WAY OF.
YOU DO NOT STAND IN MY WAY. YOU DO NOT GET TO CONTROL EVERYTHING, YOUNG MAN.
SELINA? ARE YOU ABLE TO ESCORT ME, DEAR?
OF COURSE.
CAN YOU TEACH ME HOW TO TALK OVER HIM LIKE THAT?
OF COURSE.

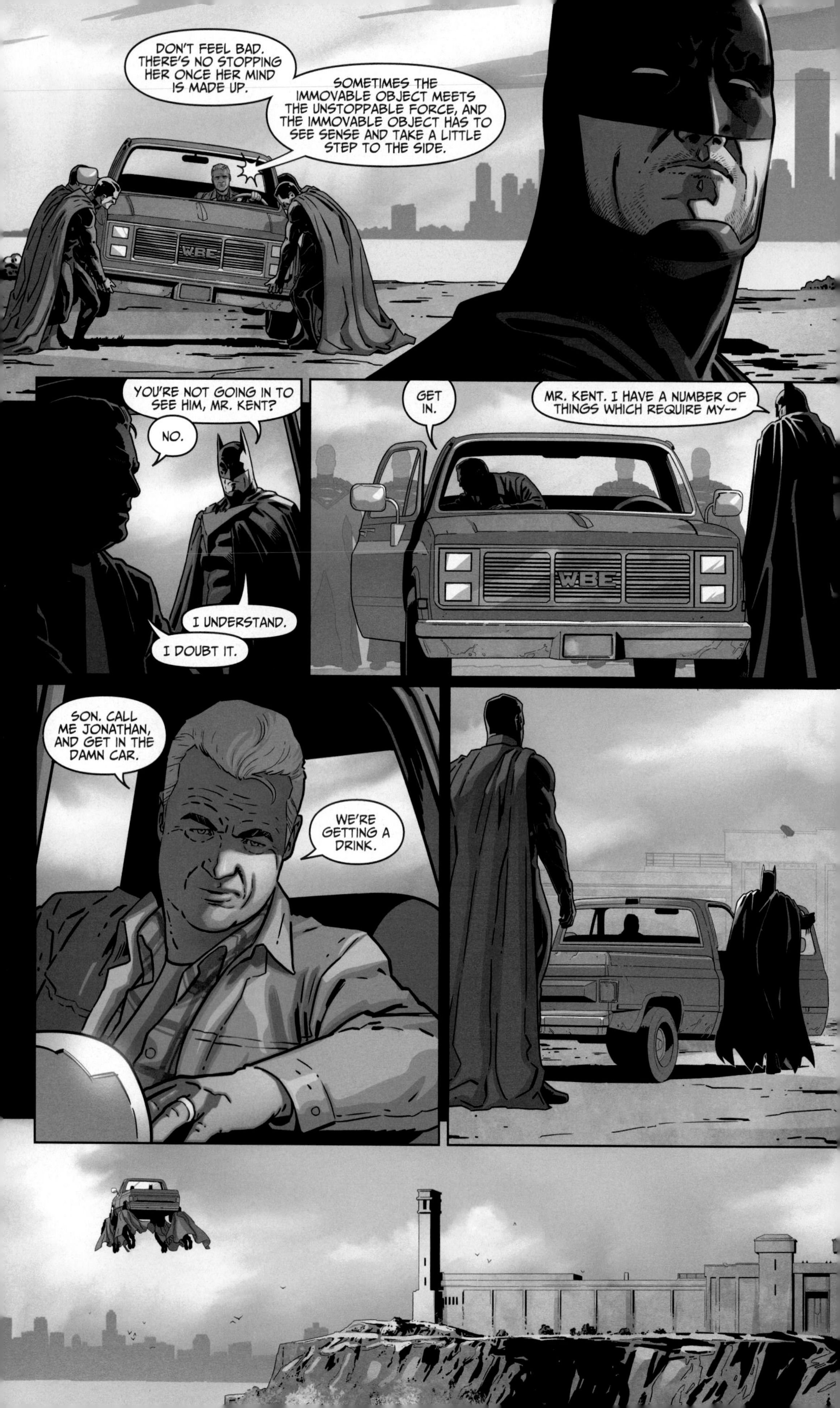
DON'T FEEL BAD. THERE'S NO STOPPING HER ONCE HER MIND IS MADE UP.
SOMETIMES THE IMMOVABLE OBJECT MEETS THE UNSTOPPABLE FORCE, AND THE IMMOVABLE OBJECT HAS TO SEE SENSE AND TAKE A LITTLE STEP TO THE SIDE.
YOU'RE NOT GOING IN TO SEE HIM, MR. KENT?
NO.
I UNDERSTAND.
I DOUBT IT.
GET IN.
MR. KENT. I HAVE A NUMBER OF THINGS WHICH REQUIRE MY--
SON. CALL ME JONATHAN, AND GET IN THE DAMN CAR.
WE'RE GETTING A DRINK.
WBE

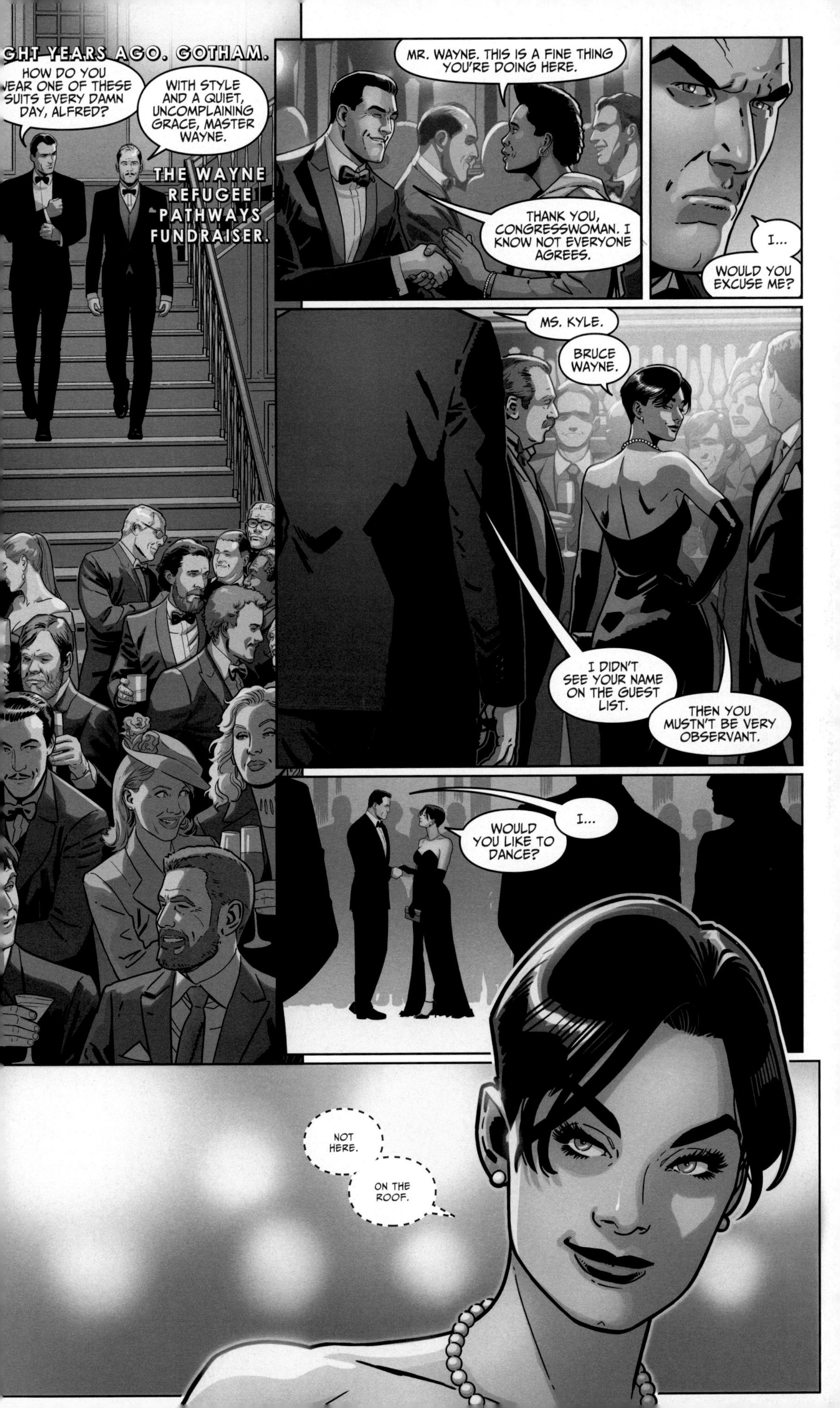
GHT YEARS AGO. GOTHAM.
HOW DO YOU VEAR ONE OF THESE SUITS EVERY DAMN DAY, ALFRED?
WITH STYLE AND A QUIET, UNCOMPLAINING GRACE, MASTER WAYNE.
THE WAYNE REFUGEE PATHWAYS FUNDRAISER.
MR. WAYNE. THIS IS A FINE THING YOU'RE DOING HERE.
THANK YOU, CONGRESSWOMAN. I KNOW NOT EVERYONE AGREES.
I...
WOULD YOU EXCUSE ME?
MS. KYLE.
BRUCE WAYNE.
I DIDN'T SEE YOUR NAME ON THE GUEST LIST.
THEN YOU MUSTN'T BE VERY OBSERVANT.
WOULD YOU LIKE TO DANCE?
I...
NOT HERE.
ON THE ROOF.

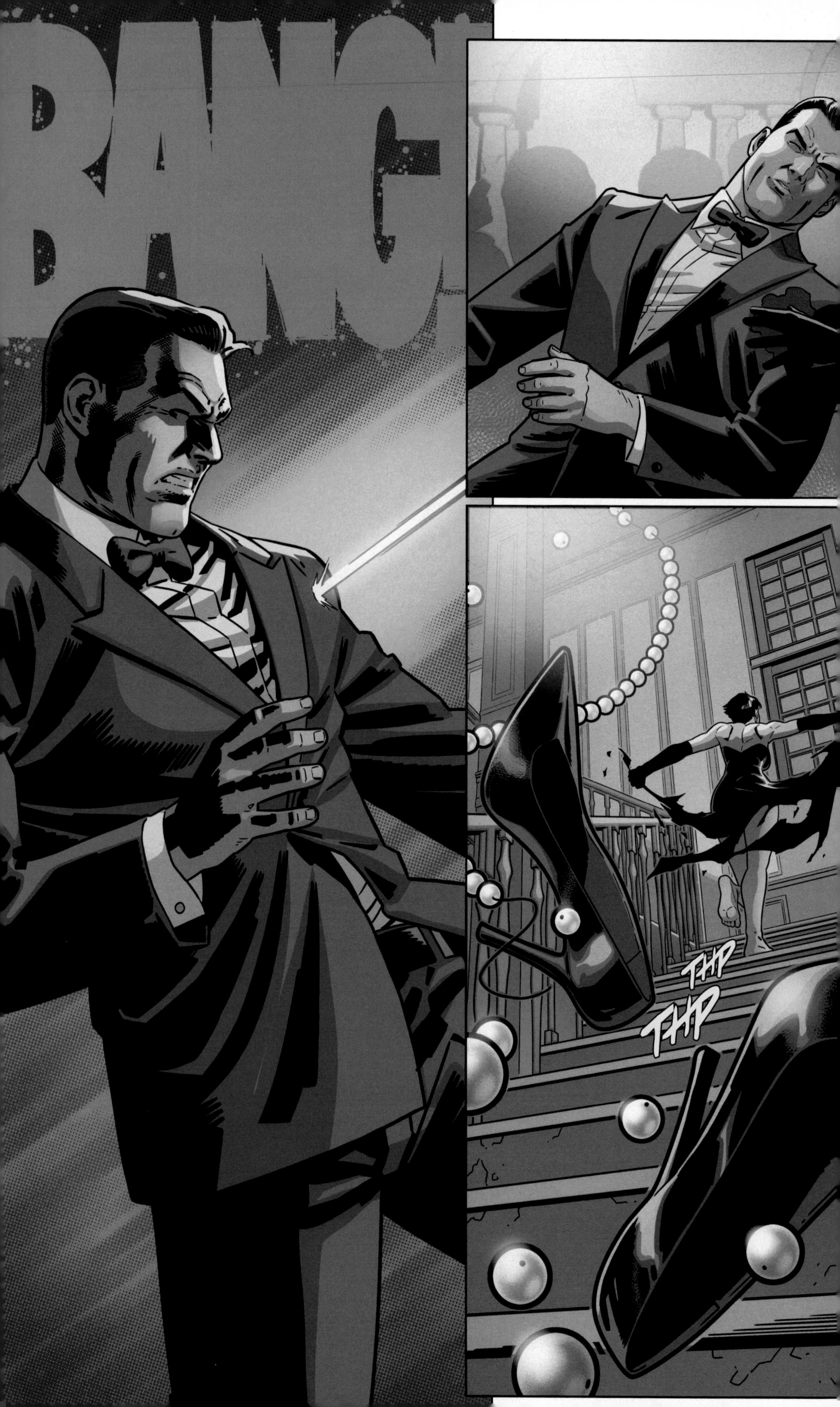
BANG
THP
THP

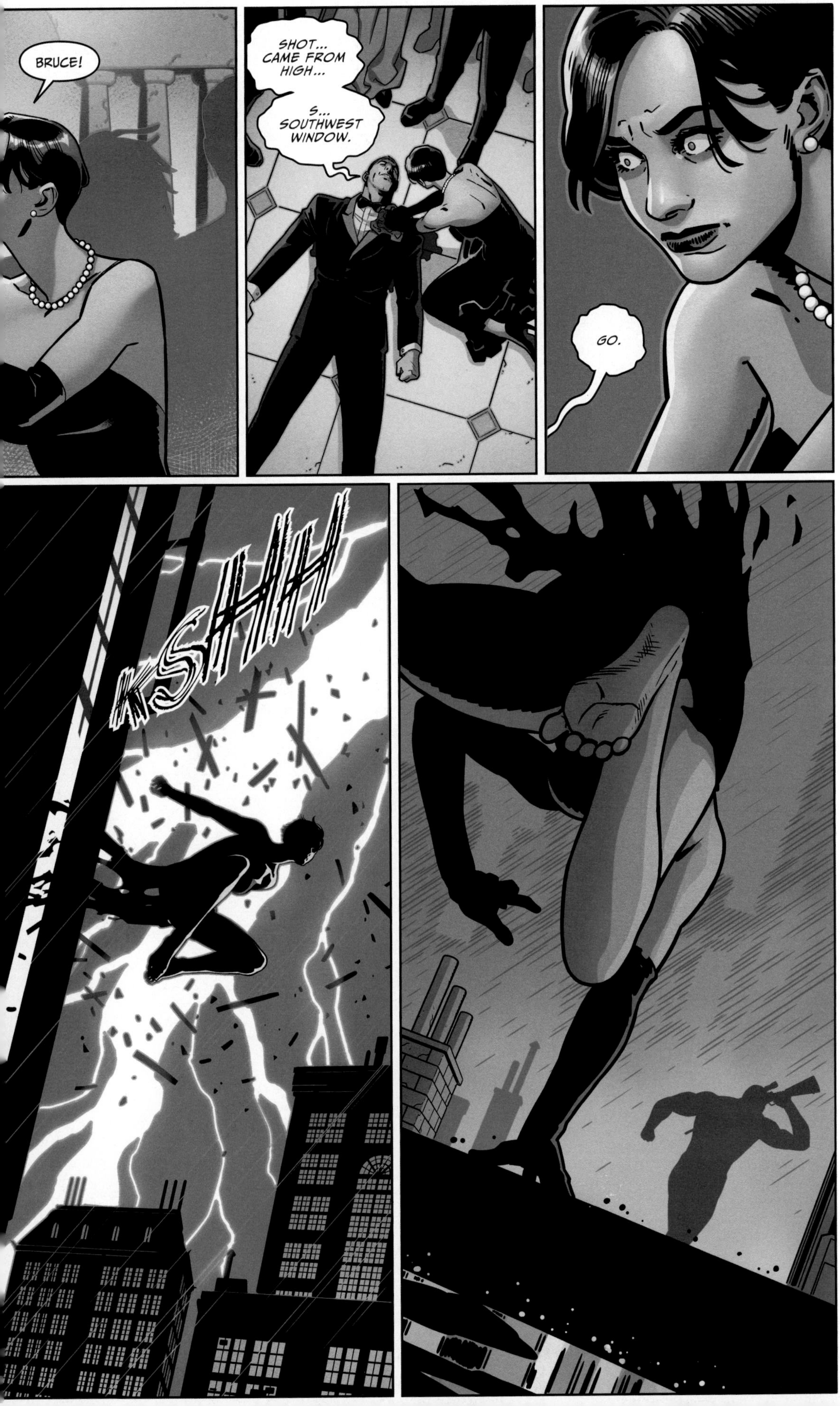
BRUCE!
SHOT... CAME FROM HIGH...
S... SOUTHWEST WINDOW.
GO.
KSHHH

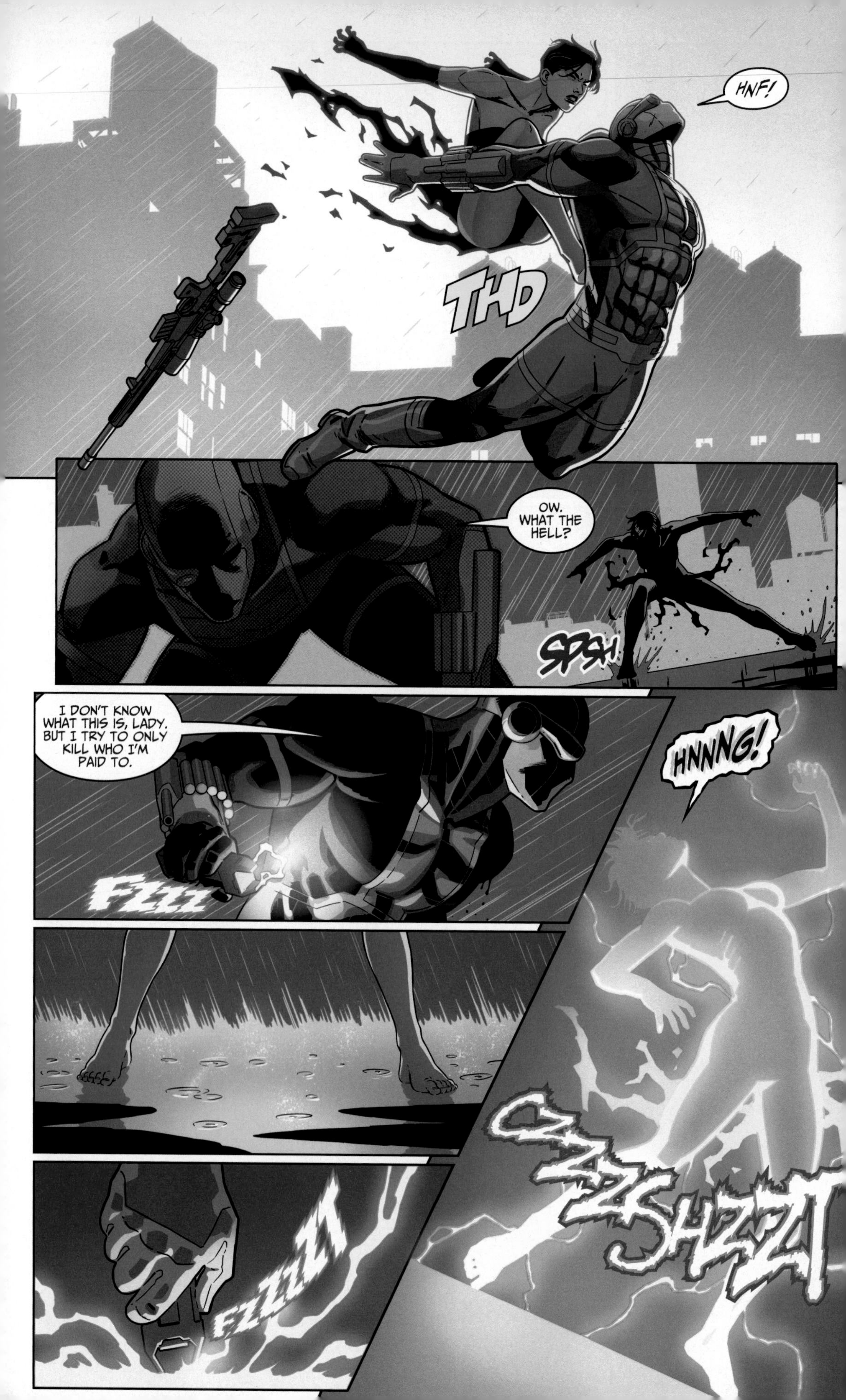
HNF!
THD
OW. WHAT THE HELL?
SPSH
I DON'T KNOW WHAT THIS IS, LADY. BUT I TRY TO ONLY KILL WHO I'M PAID TO.
HNNNG!
FZZZ
FZZZZZT
CZZZSHZZZT

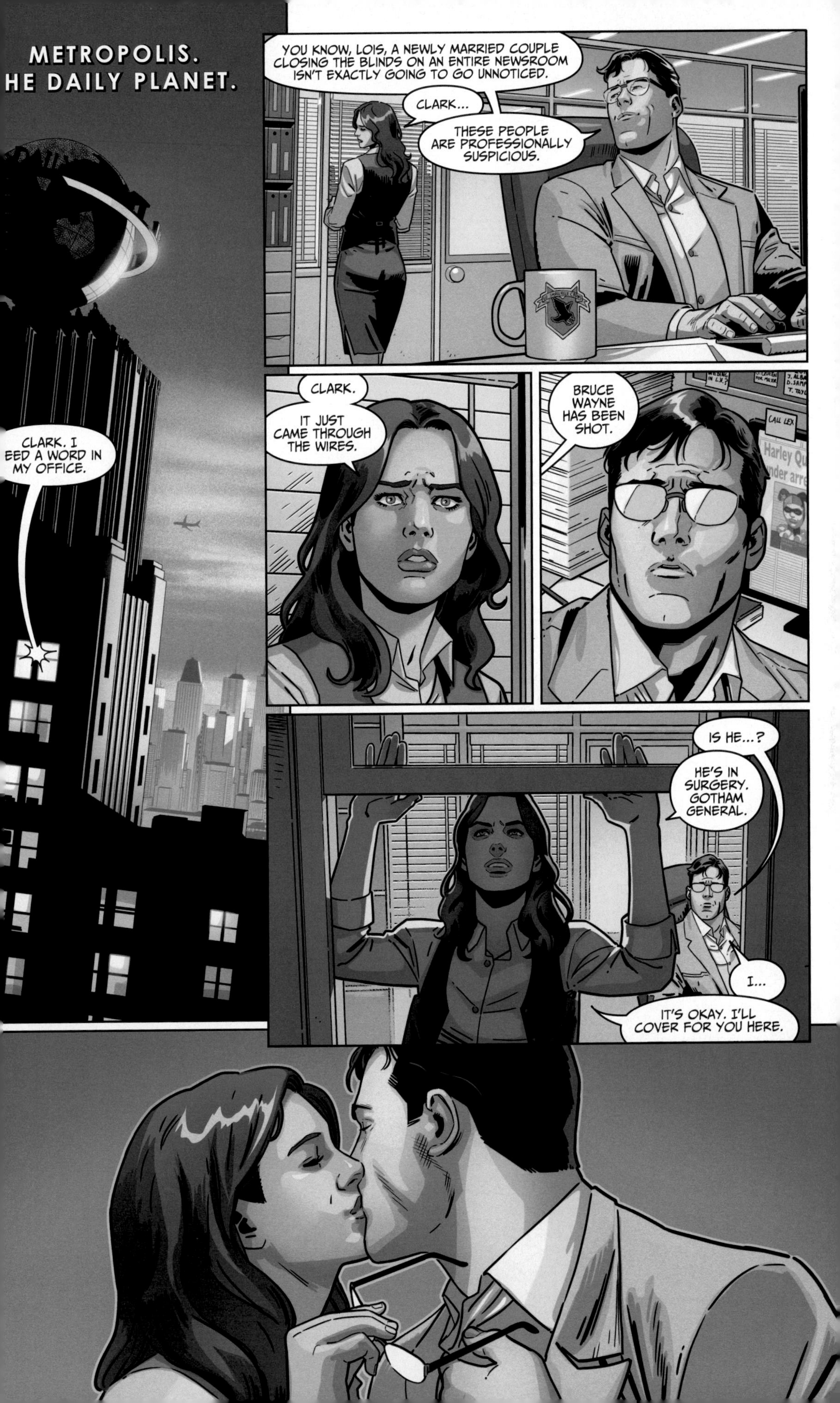
METROPOLIS.
HE DAILY PLANET.
CLARK. I EED A WORD IN MY OFFICE.
YOU KNOW, LOIS, A NEWLY MARRIED COUPLE CLOSING THE BLINDS ON AN ENTIRE NEWSROOM ISN'T EXACTLY GOING TO GO UNNOTICED.
CLARK...
THESE PEOPLE ARE PROFESSIONALLY SUSPICIOUS.
CLARK.
IT JUST CAME THROUGH THE WIRES.
BRUCE WAYNE HAS BEEN SHOT.
CALL LEX
IS HE...?
HE'S IN SURGERY. GOTHAM GENERAL.
I...
IT'S OKAY. I'LL COVER FOR YOU HERE.

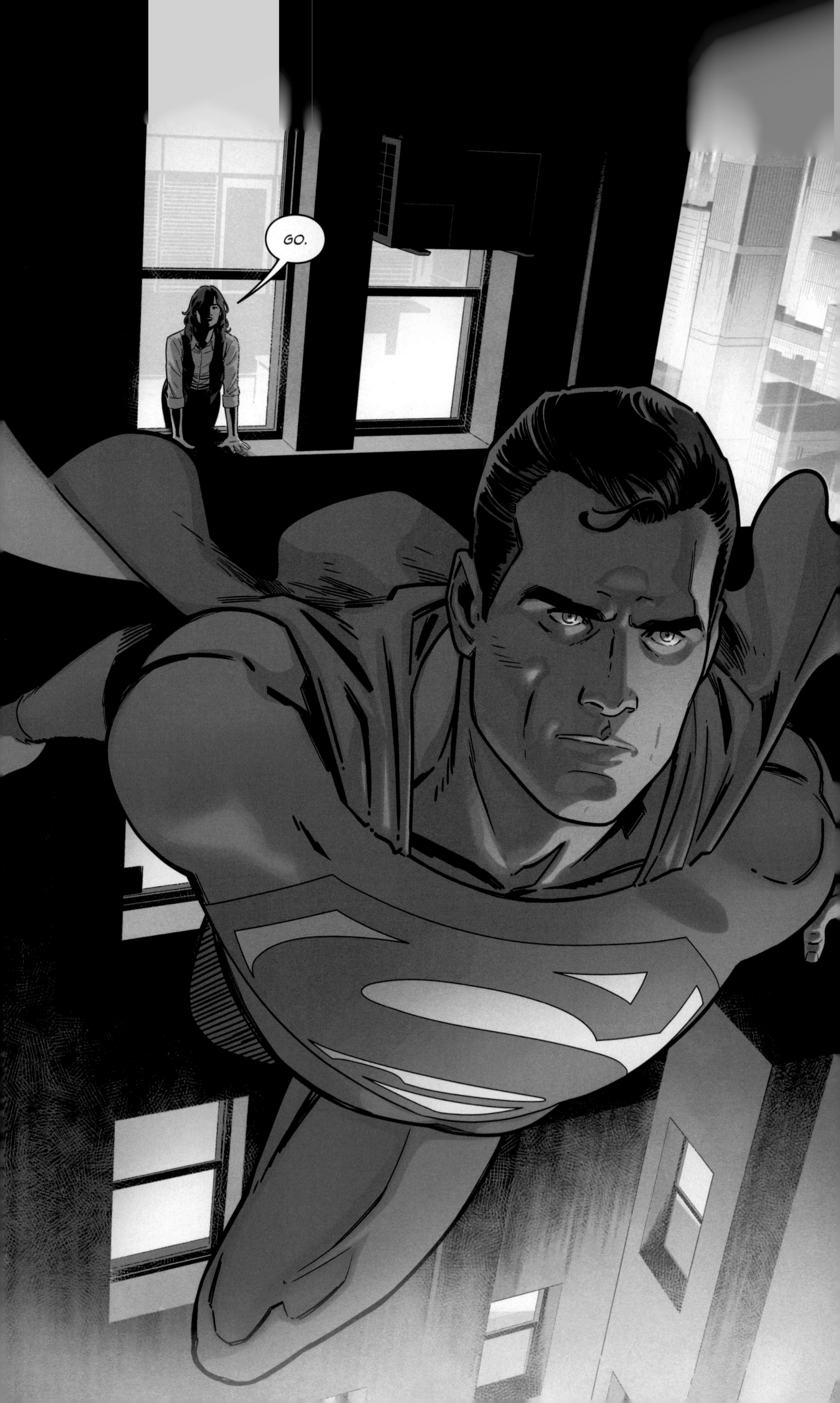
GO.

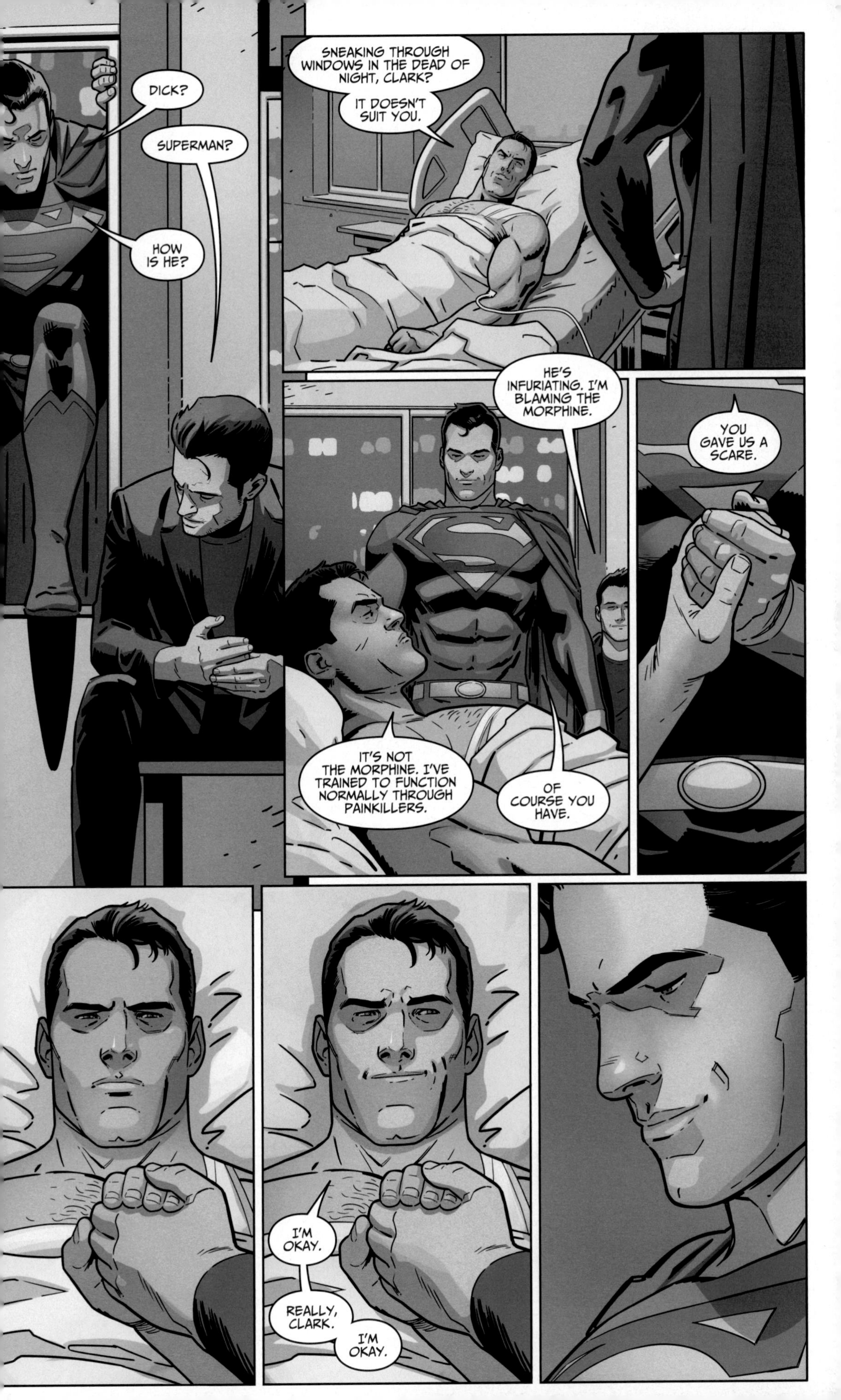
DICK?
SUPERMAN?
HOW IS HE?
SNEAKING THROUGH WINDOWS IN THE DEAD OF NIGHT, CLARK?
IT DOESN'T SUIT YOU.
HE'S INFURIATING. I'M BLAMING THE MORPHINE.
IT'S NOT THE MORPHINE. I'VE TRAINED TO FUNCTION NORMALLY THROUGH PAINKILLERS.
OF COURSE YOU HAVE.
YOU GAVE US A SCARE.
I'M OKAY.
REALLY, CLARK.
I'M OKAY.

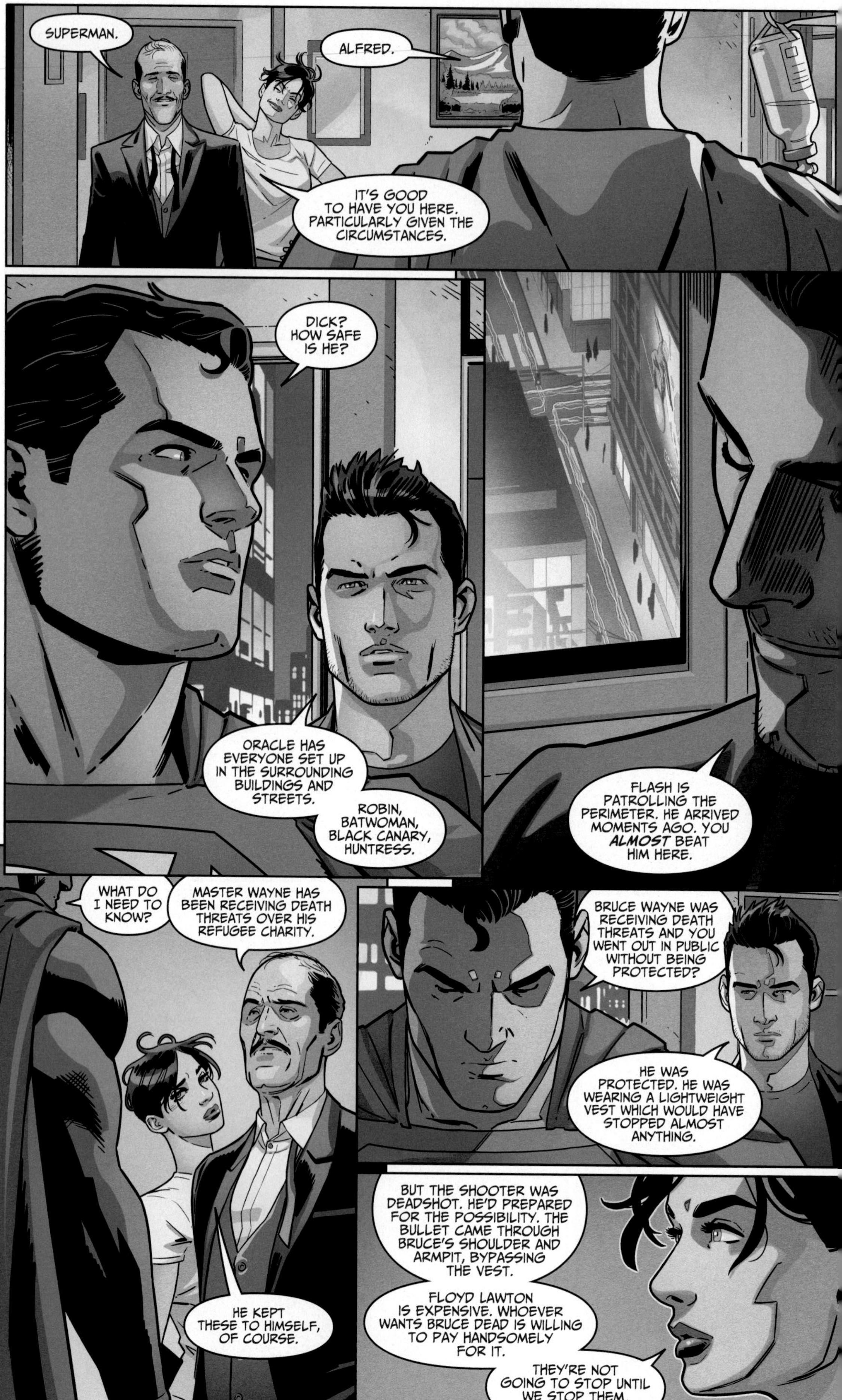
SUPERMAN.
ALFRED.
IT'S GOOD TO HAVE YOU HERE. PARTICULARLY GIVEN THE CIRCUMSTANCES.
DICK? HOW SAFE IS HE?
ORACLE HAS EVERYONE SET UP IN THE SURROUNDING BUILDINGS AND STREETS.
ROBIN, BATWOMAN, BLACK CANARY, HUNTRESS.
FLASH IS PATROLLING THE PERIMETER. HE ARRIVED MOMENTS AGO. YOU ALMOST BEAT HIM HERE.
WHAT DO I NEED TO KNOW?
MASTER WAYNE HAS BEEN RECEIVING DEATH THREATS OVER HIS REFUGEE CHARITY.
HE KEPT THESE TO HIMSELF, OF COURSE.
BRUCE WAYNE WAS RECEIVING DEATH THREATS AND YOU WENT OUT IN PUBLIC WITHOUT BEING PROTECTED?
HE WAS PROTECTED. HE WAS WEARING A LIGHTWEIGHT VEST WHICH WOULD HAVE STOPPED ALMOST ANYTHING.
BUT THE SHOOTER WAS DEADSHOT. HE'D PREPARED FOR THE POSSIBILITY. THE BULLET CAME THROUGH BRUCE'S SHOULDER AND ARMPIT, BYPASSING THE VEST.
FLOYD LAWTON IS EXPENSIVE. WHOEVER WANTS BRUCE DEAD IS WILLING TO PAY HANDSOMELY FOR IT.
THEY'RE NOT GOING TO STOP UNTIL WE STOP THEM.

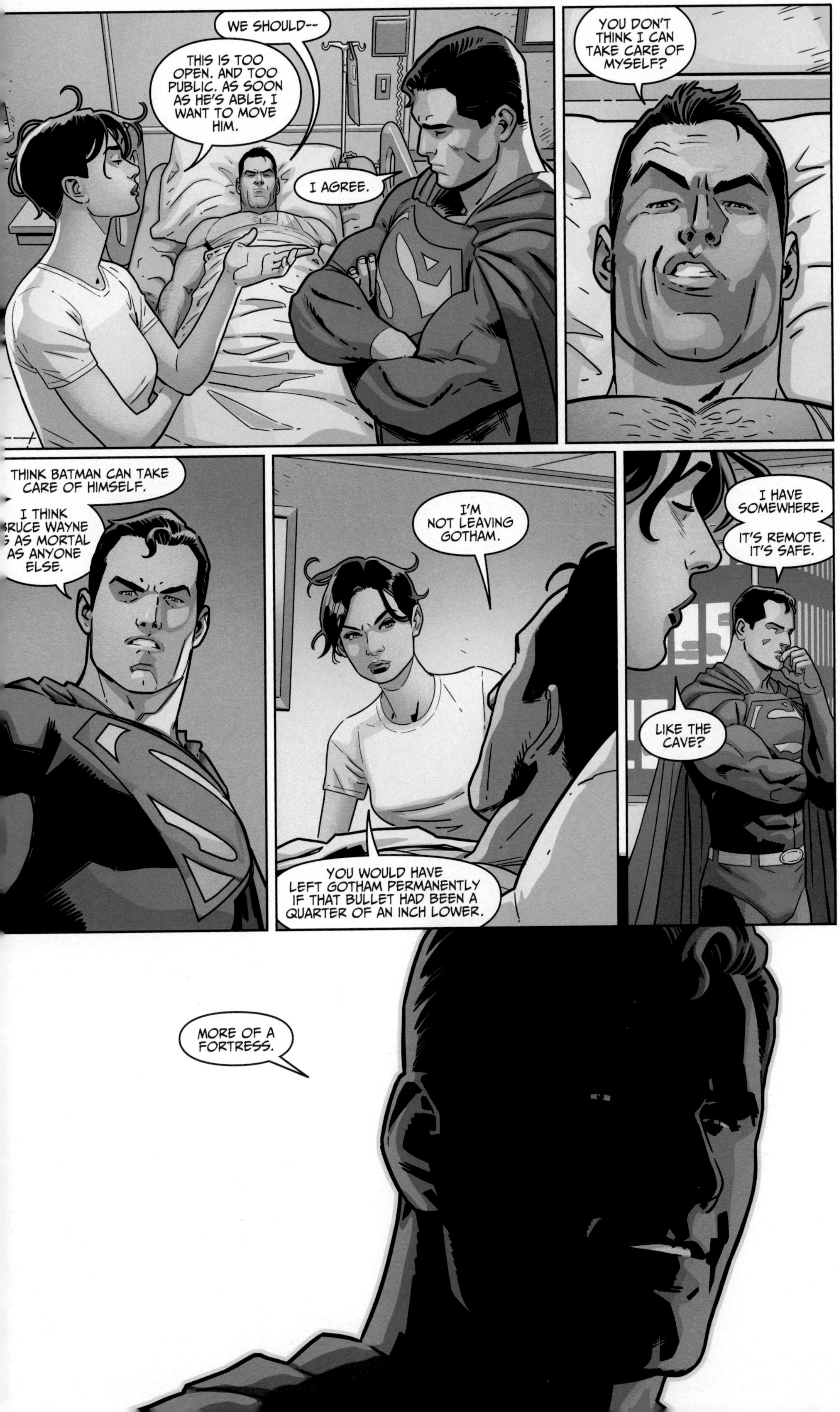
WE SHOULD--
THIS IS TOO OPEN. AND TOO PUBLIC. AS SOON AS HE'S ABLE, I WANT TO MOVE HIM.
I AGREE.
YOU DON'T THINK I CAN TAKE CARE OF MYSELF?
THINK BATMAN CAN TAKE CARE OF HIMSELF.
I THINK BRUCE WAYNE IS AS MORTAL AS ANYONE ELSE.
I'M NOT LEAVING GOTHAM.
YOU WOULD HAVE LEFT GOTHAM PERMANENTLY IF THAT BULLET HAD BEEN A QUARTER OF AN INCH LOWER.
I HAVE SOMEWHERE.
IT'S REMOTE. IT'S SAFE.
LIKE THE CAVE?
MORE OF A FORTRESS.

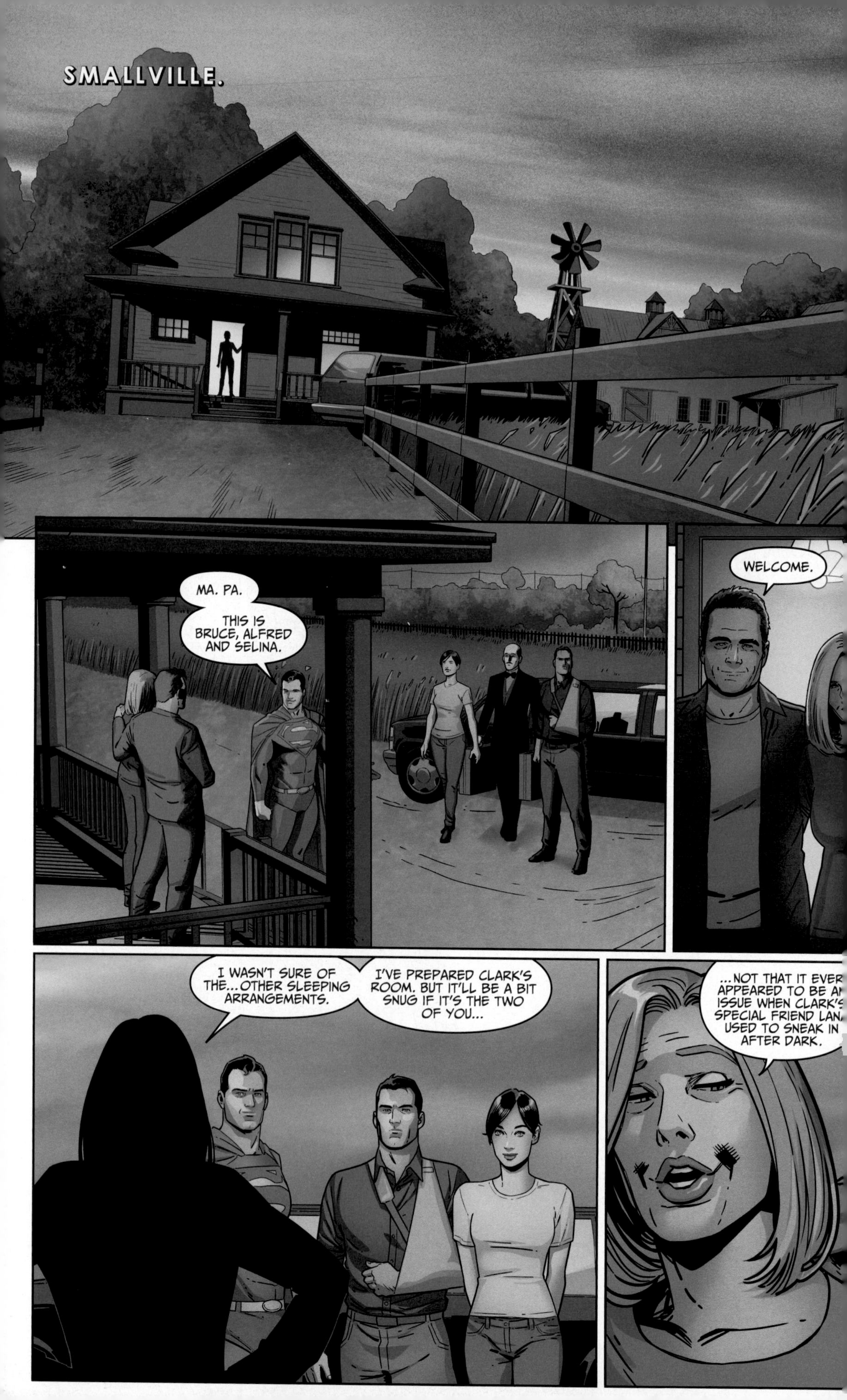
SMALLVILLE.
MA. PA.
THIS IS BRUCE, ALFRED AND SELINA.
WELCOME.
I WASN'T SURE OF THE...OTHER SLEEPING ARRANGEMENTS.
I'VE PREPARED CLARK'S ROOM. BUT IT'LL BE A BIT SNUG IF IT'S THE TWO OF YOU...
...NOT THAT IT EVER APPEARED TO BE AN ISSUE WHEN CLARK'S SPECIAL FRIEND LANA USED TO SNEAK IN AFTER DARK.

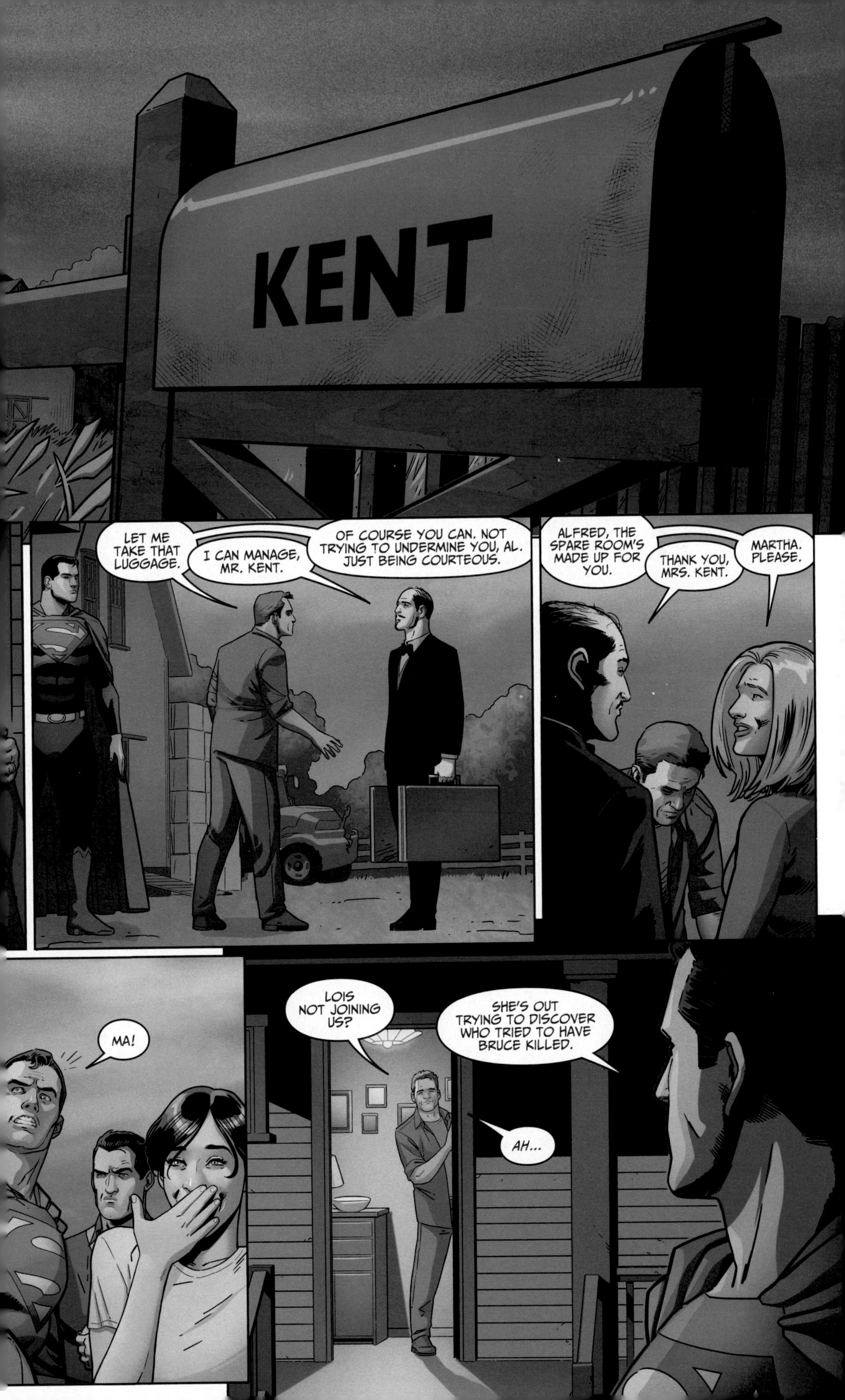
KENT
LET ME TAKE THAT LUGGAGE.
I CAN MANAGE, MR. KENT.
OF COURSE YOU CAN. NOT TRYING TO UNDERMINE YOU, AL. JUST BEING COURTEOUS.
ALFRED, THE SPARE ROOM'S MADE UP FOR YOU.
THANK YOU, MRS. KENT.
MARTHA. PLEASE.
MA!
LOIS NOT JOINING US?
SHE'S OUT TRYING TO DISCOVER WHO TRIED TO HAVE BRUCE KILLED.
AH...

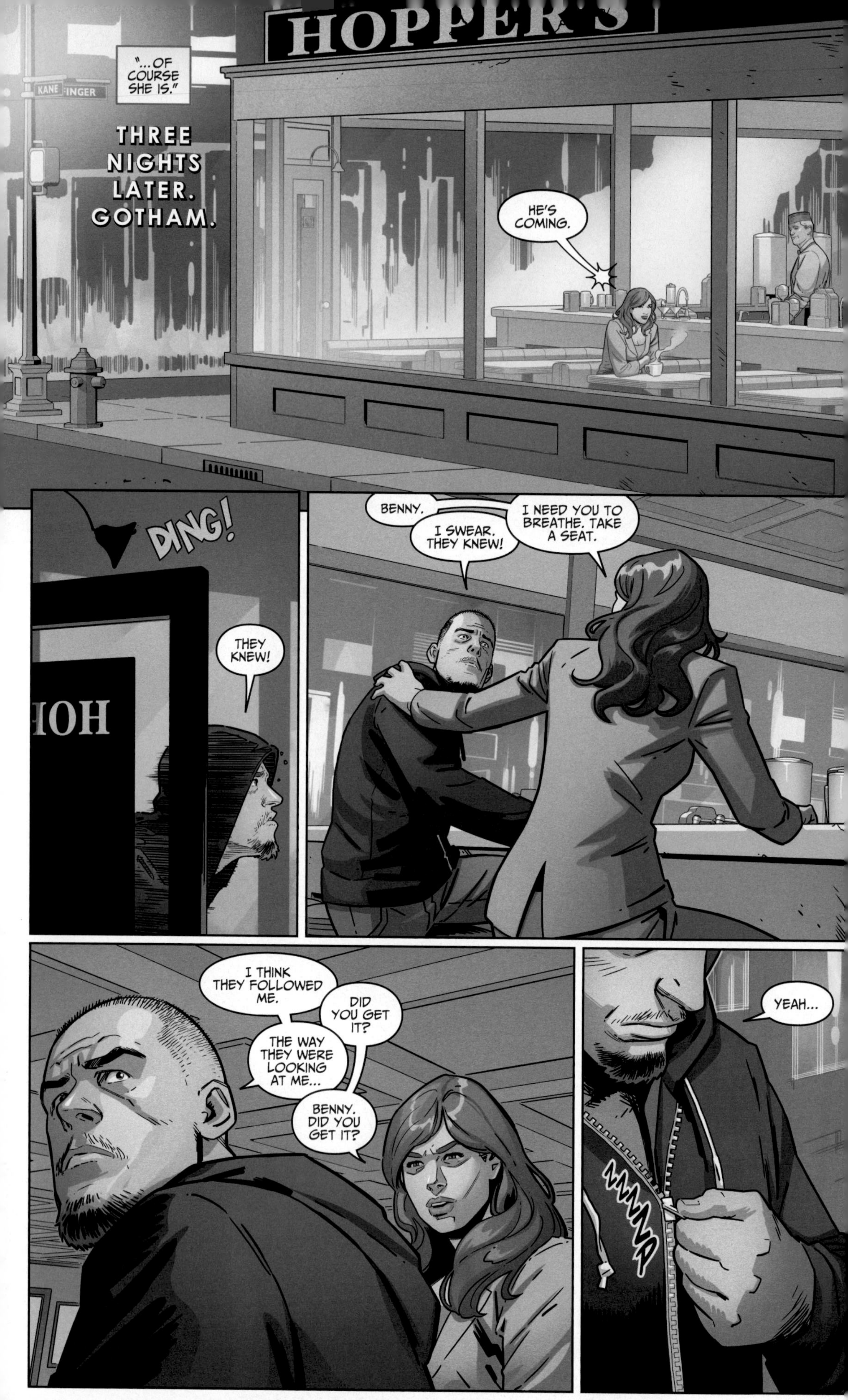

HOPPER'S
"...OF COURSE SHE IS."
KANE
FINGER
THREE NIGHTS LATER. GOTHAM.
HE'S COMING.
DING!
THEY KNEW!
BENNY.
I SWEAR. THEY KNEW!
I NEED YOU TO BREATHE. TAKE A SEAT.
I THINK THEY FOLLOWED ME.
DID YOU GET IT?
THE WAY THEY WERE LOOKING AT ME...
BENNY. DID YOU GET IT?
YEAH...
ZZZZIP

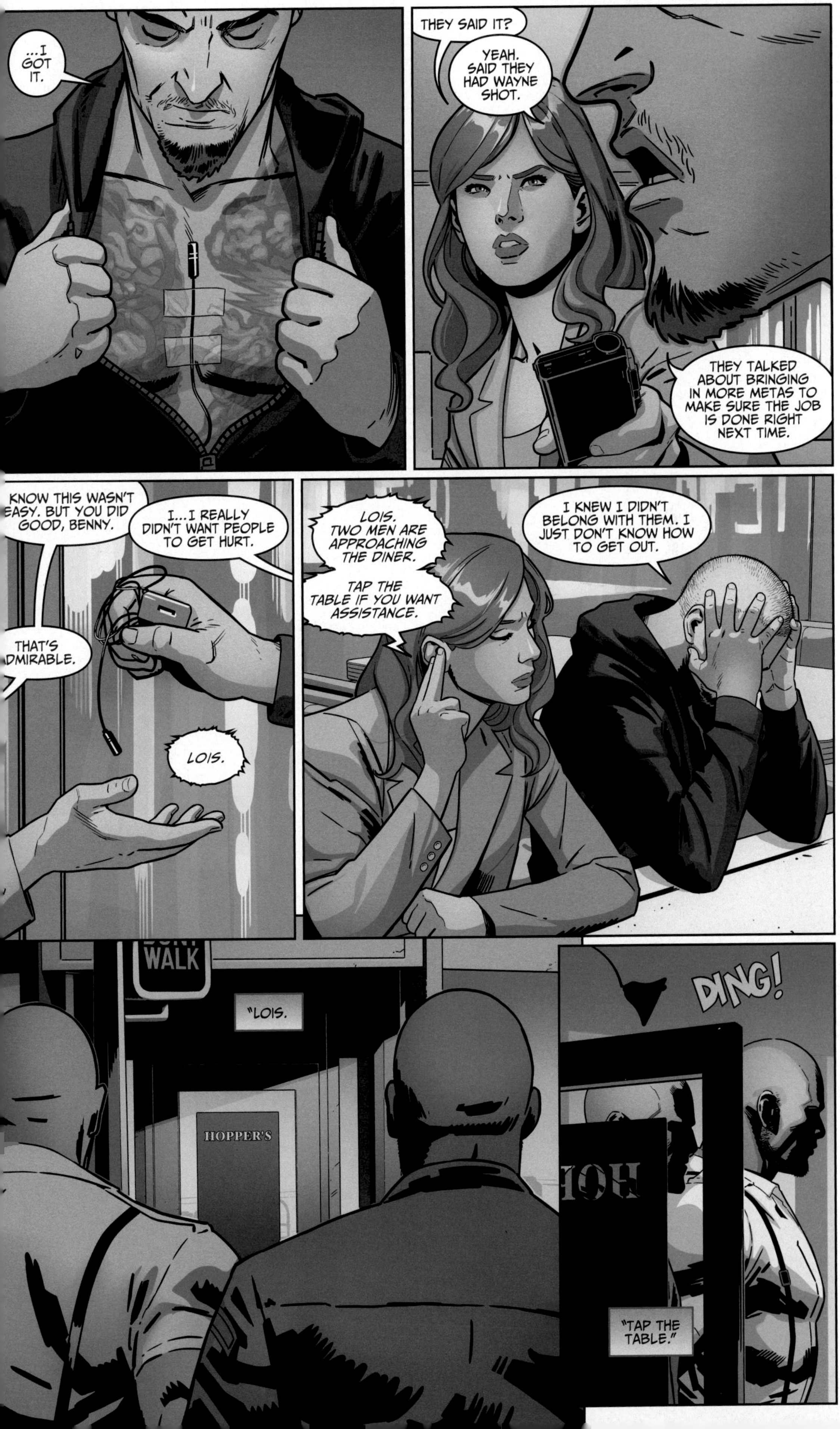
...I GOT IT.
THEY SAID IT?
YEAH. SAID THEY HAD WAYNE SHOT.
THEY TALKED ABOUT BRINGING IN MORE METAS TO MAKE SURE THE JOB IS DONE RIGHT NEXT TIME.
KNOW THIS WASN'T EASY. BUT YOU DID GOOD, BENNY.
I...I REALLY DIDN'T WANT PEOPLE TO GET HURT.
THAT'S DMIRABLE.
LOIS.
LOIS. TWO MEN ARE APPROACHING THE DINER.
TAP THE TABLE IF YOU WANT ASSISTANCE.
I KNEW I DIDN'T BELONG WITH THEM. I JUST DON'T KNOW HOW TO GET OUT.
WALK
"LOIS.
HOPPER'S
DING!
"TAP THE TABLE."

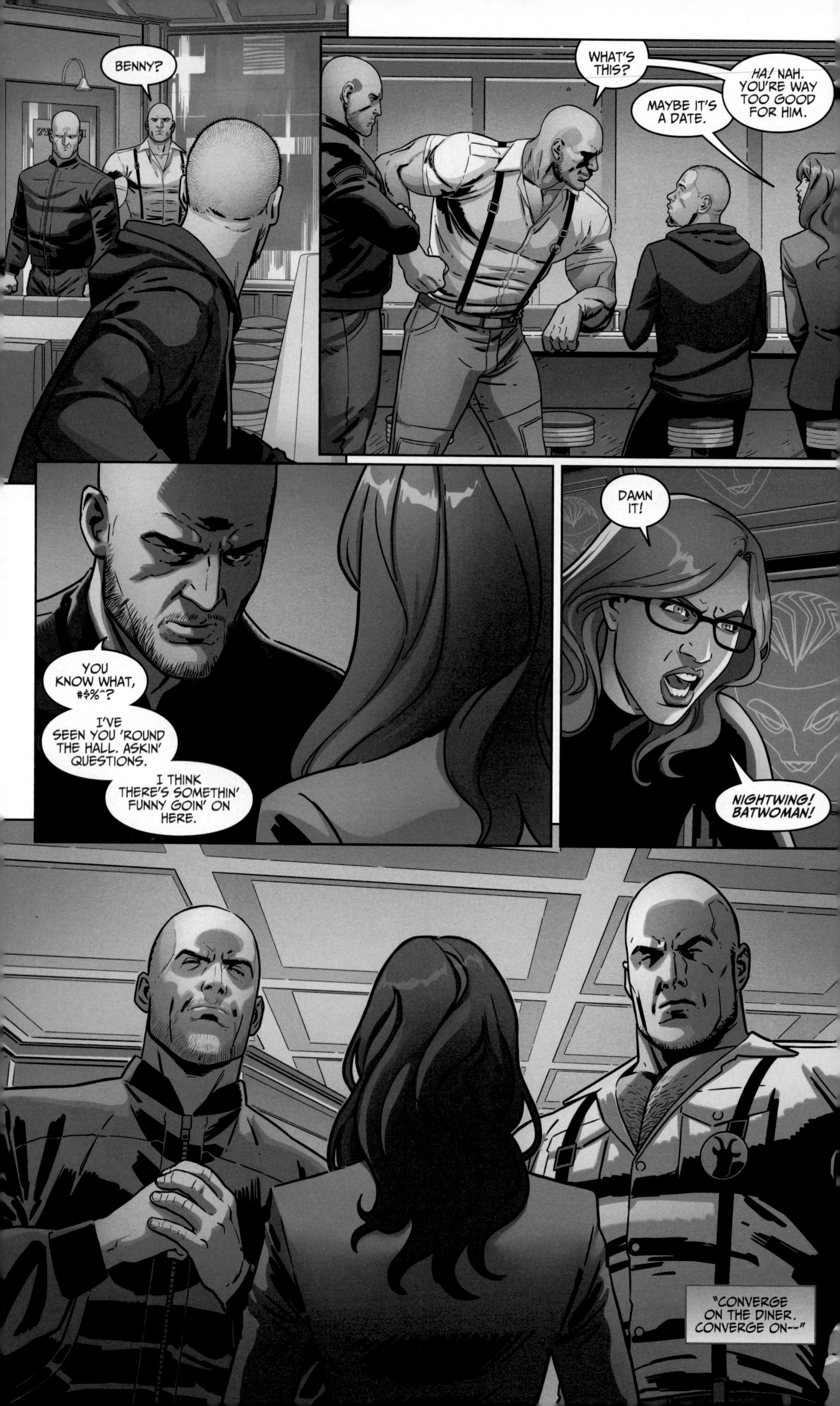
BENNY?
WHAT'S THIS?
MAYBE IT'S A DATE.
HA! NAH. YOU'RE WAY TOO GOOD FOR HIM.
YOU KNOW WHAT, #$%^?
I'VE SEEN YOU 'ROUND THE HALL. ASKIN' QUESTIONS.
I THINK THERE'S SOMETHIN' FUNNY GOIN' ON HERE.
DAMN IT!
NIGHTWING! BATWOMAN!
"CONVERGE ON THE DINER. CONVERGE ON--"

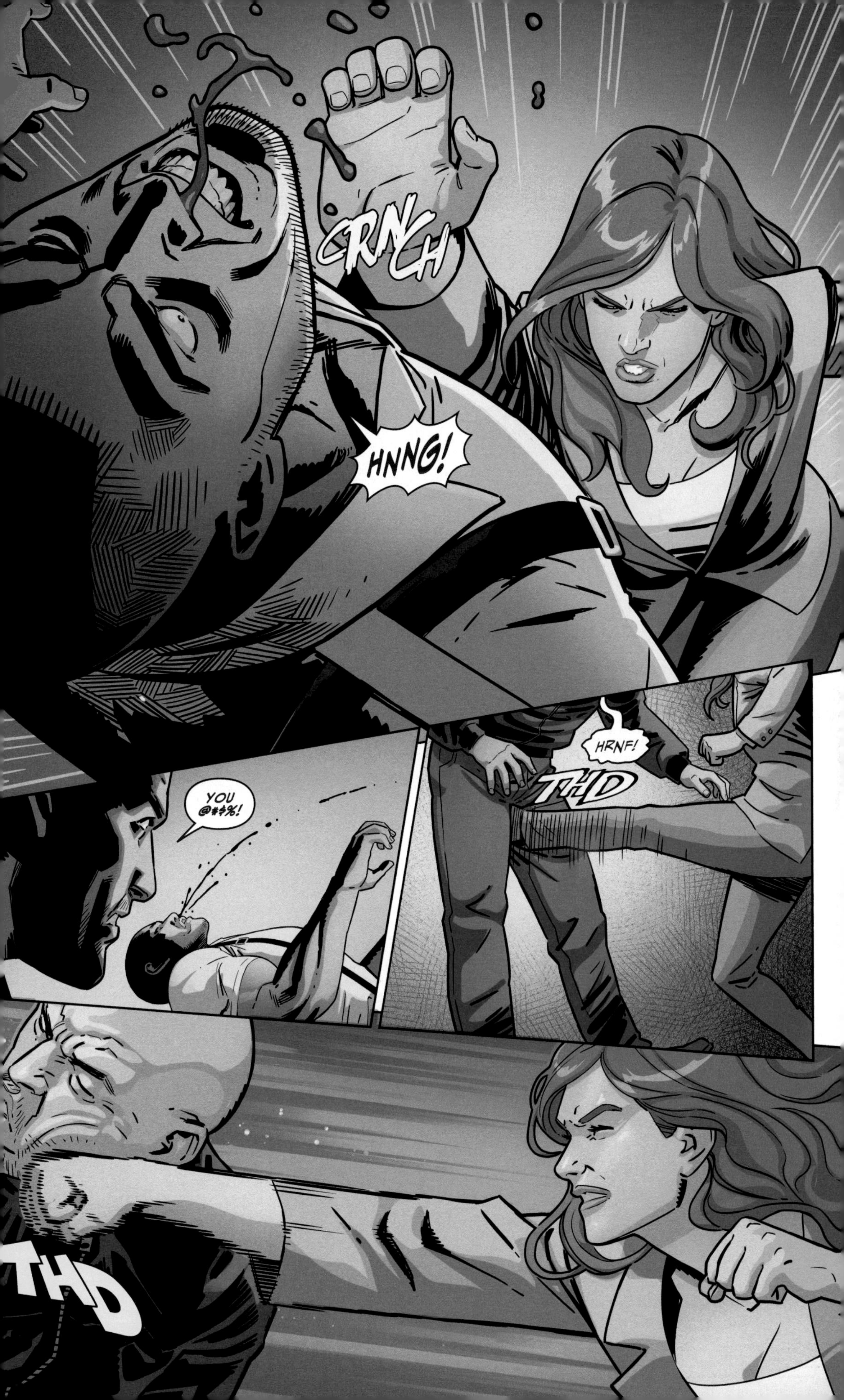
CRNCH
HNNG!
YOU @#$%!
HRNF!
THD
THD

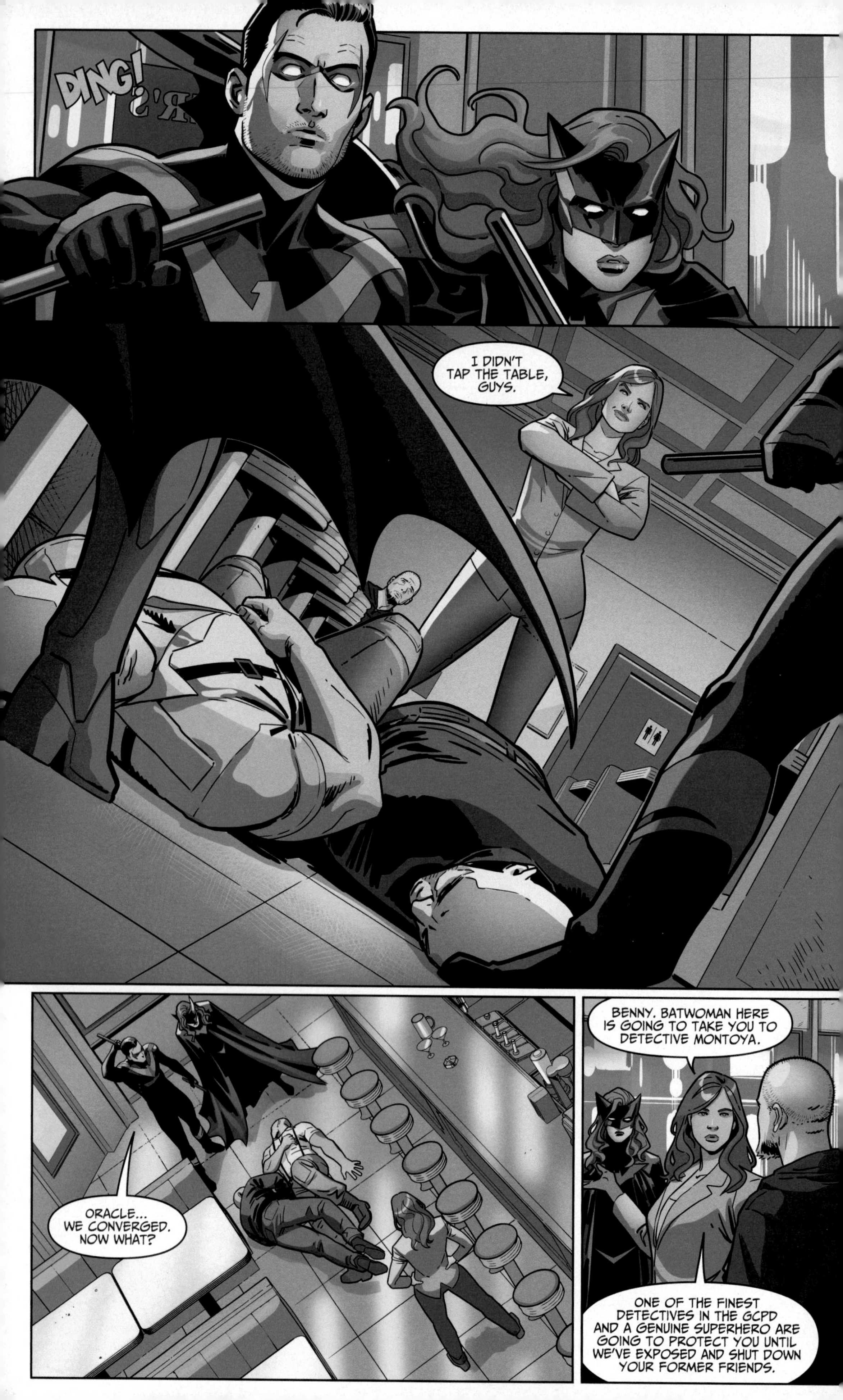

DING!
I DIDN'T TAP THE TABLE, GUYS.
ORACLE... WE CONVERGED. NOW WHAT?
BENNY. BATWOMAN HERE IS GOING TO TAKE YOU TO DETECTIVE MONTOYA.
ONE OF THE FINEST DETECTIVES IN THE GCPD AND A GENUINE SUPERHERO ARE GOING TO PROTECT YOU UNTIL WE'VE EXPOSED AND SHUT DOWN YOUR FORMER FRIENDS.

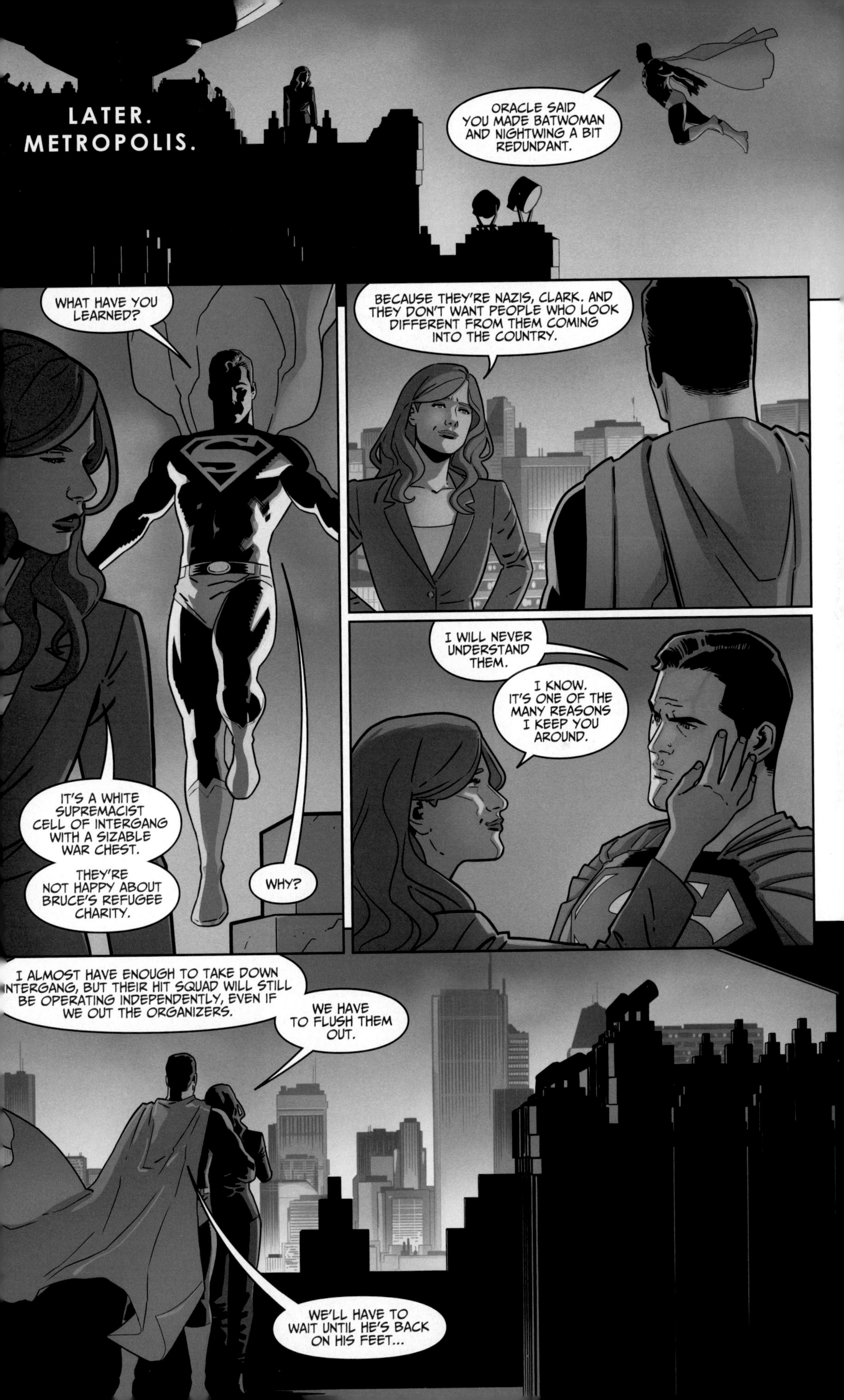
LATER. METROPOLIS.
ORACLE SAID YOU MADE BATWOMAN AND NIGHTWING A BIT REDUNDANT.
WHAT HAVE YOU LEARNED?
IT'S A WHITE SUPREMACIST CELL OF INTERGANG WITH A SIZABLE WAR CHEST.
THEY'RE NOT HAPPY ABOUT BRUCE'S REFUGEE CHARITY.
WHY?
BECAUSE THEY'RE NAZIS, CLARK. AND THEY DON'T WANT PEOPLE WHO LOOK DIFFERENT FROM THEM COMING INTO THE COUNTRY.
I WILL NEVER UNDERSTAND THEM.
I KNOW. IT'S ONE OF THE MANY REASONS I KEEP YOU AROUND.
I ALMOST HAVE ENOUGH TO TAKE DOWN INTERGANG, BUT THEIR HIT SQUAD WILL STILL BE OPERATING INDEPENDENTLY, EVEN IF WE OUT THE ORGANIZERS.
WE HAVE TO FLUSH THEM OUT.
WE'LL HAVE TO WAIT UNTIL HE'S BACK ON HIS FEET...

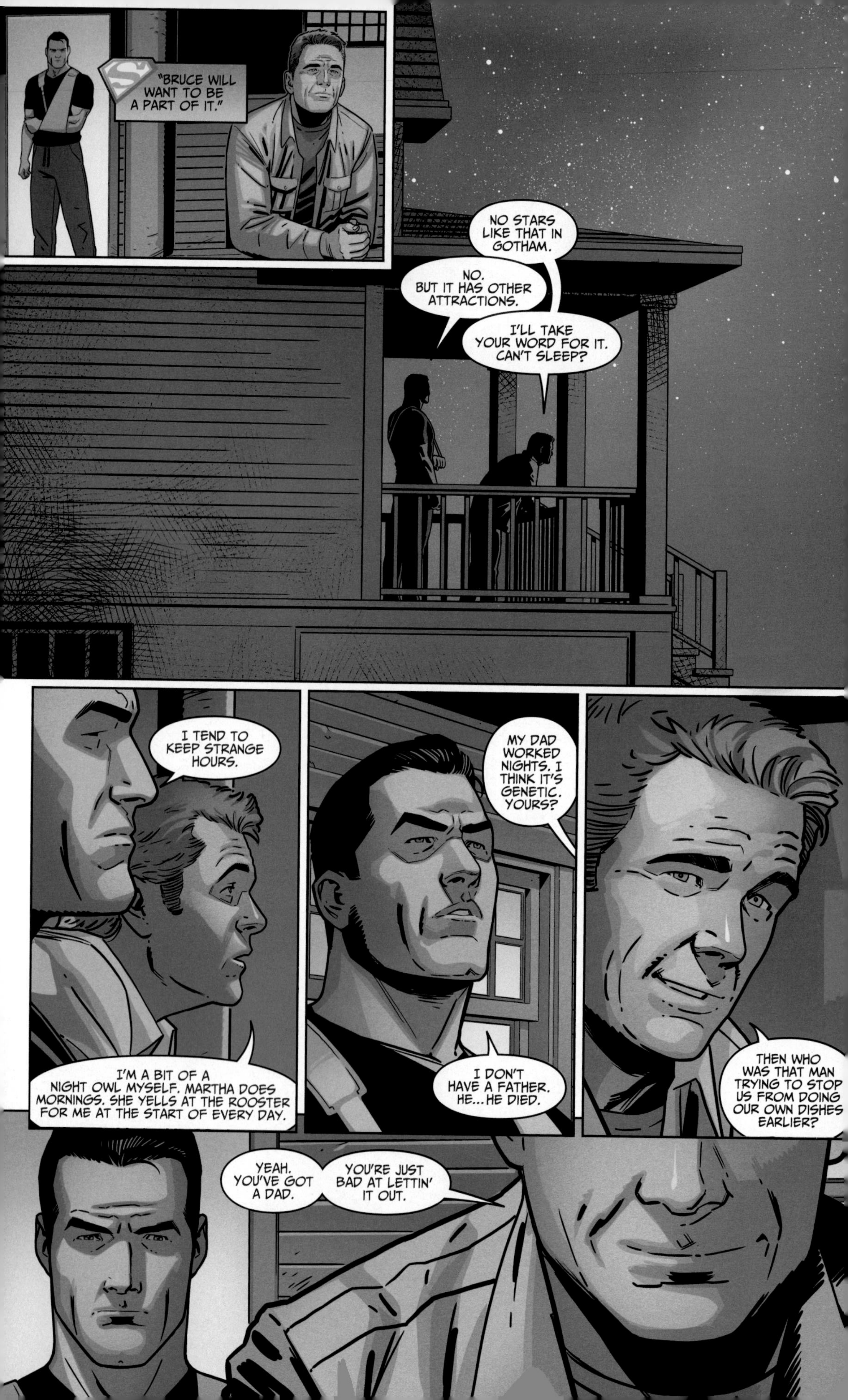
"BRUCE WILL WANT TO BE A PART OF IT."
NO STARS LIKE THAT IN GOTHAM.
NO. BUT IT HAS OTHER ATTRACTIONS.
I'LL TAKE YOUR WORD FOR IT. CAN'T SLEEP?
I TEND TO KEEP STRANGE HOURS.
I'M A BIT OF A NIGHT OWL MYSELF. MARTHA DOES MORNINGS. SHE YELLS AT THE ROOSTER FOR ME AT THE START OF EVERY DAY.
MY DAD WORKED NIGHTS. I THINK IT'S GENETIC. YOURS?
I DON'T HAVE A FATHER. HE... HE DIED.
THEN WHO WAS THAT MAN TRYING TO STOP US FROM DOING OUR OWN DISHES EARLIER?
YEAH. YOU'VE GOT A DAD.
YOU'RE JUST BAD AT LETTIN' IT OUT.

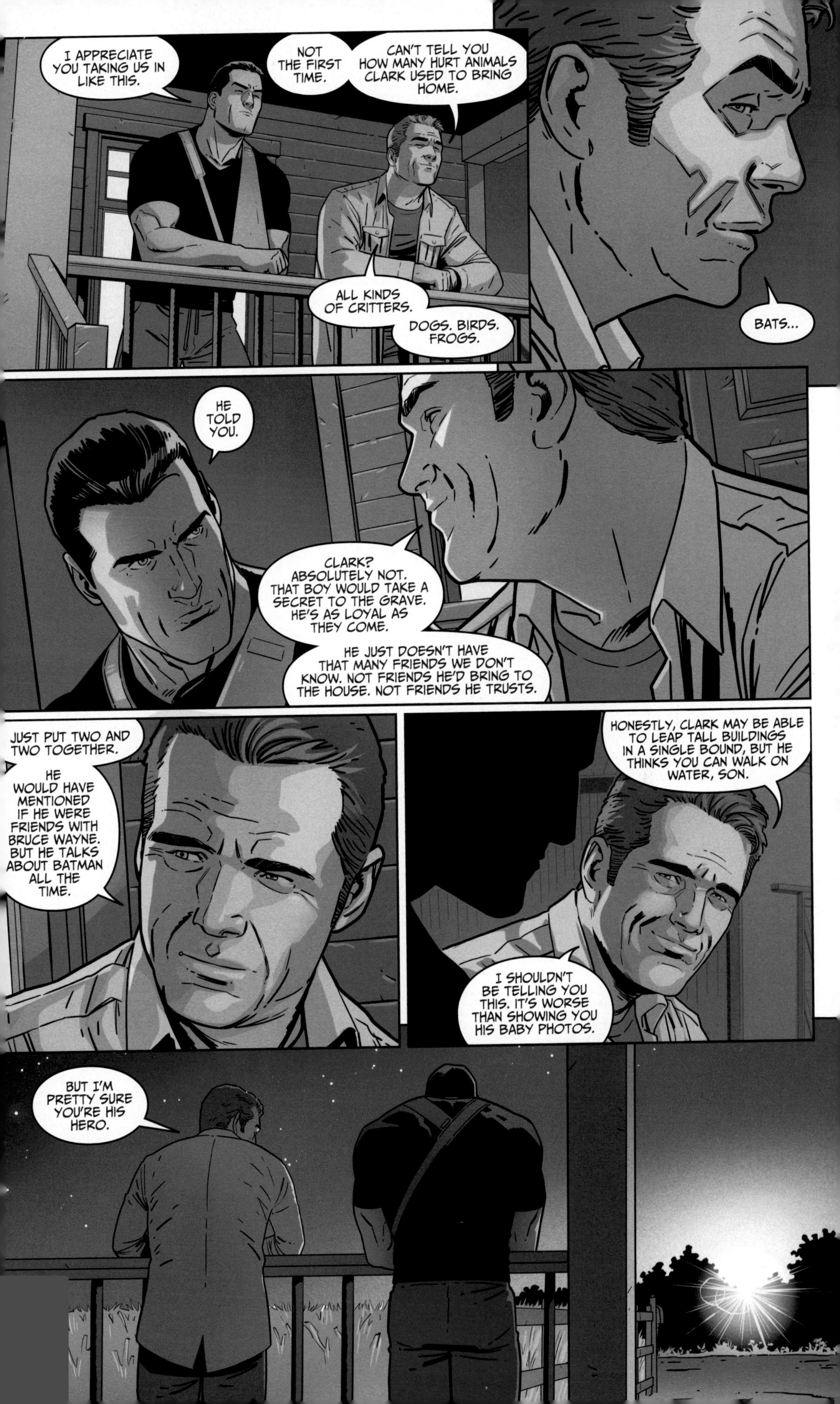

I APPRECIATE YOU TAKING US IN LIKE THIS.
NOT THE FIRST TIME.
CAN'T TELL YOU HOW MANY HURT ANIMALS CLARK USED TO BRING HOME.
ALL KINDS OF CRITTERS.
DOGS. BIRDS. FROGS.
BATS...
HE TOLD YOU.
CLARK? ABSOLUTELY NOT. THAT BOY WOULD TAKE A SECRET TO THE GRAVE. HE'S AS LOYAL AS THEY COME.
HE JUST DOESN'T HAVE THAT MANY FRIENDS WE DON'T KNOW. NOT FRIENDS HE'D BRING TO THE HOUSE. NOT FRIENDS HE TRUSTS.
JUST PUT TWO AND TWO TOGETHER.
HE WOULD HAVE MENTIONED IF HE WERE FRIENDS WITH BRUCE WAYNE. BUT HE TALKS ABOUT BATMAN ALL THE TIME.
HONESTLY, CLARK MAY BE ABLE TO LEAP TALL BUILDINGS IN A SINGLE BOUND, BUT HE THINKS YOU CAN WALK ON WATER, SON.
I SHOULDN'T BE TELLING YOU THIS. IT'S WORSE THAN SHOWING YOU HIS BABY PHOTOS.
BUT I'M PRETTY SURE YOU'RE HIS HERO.

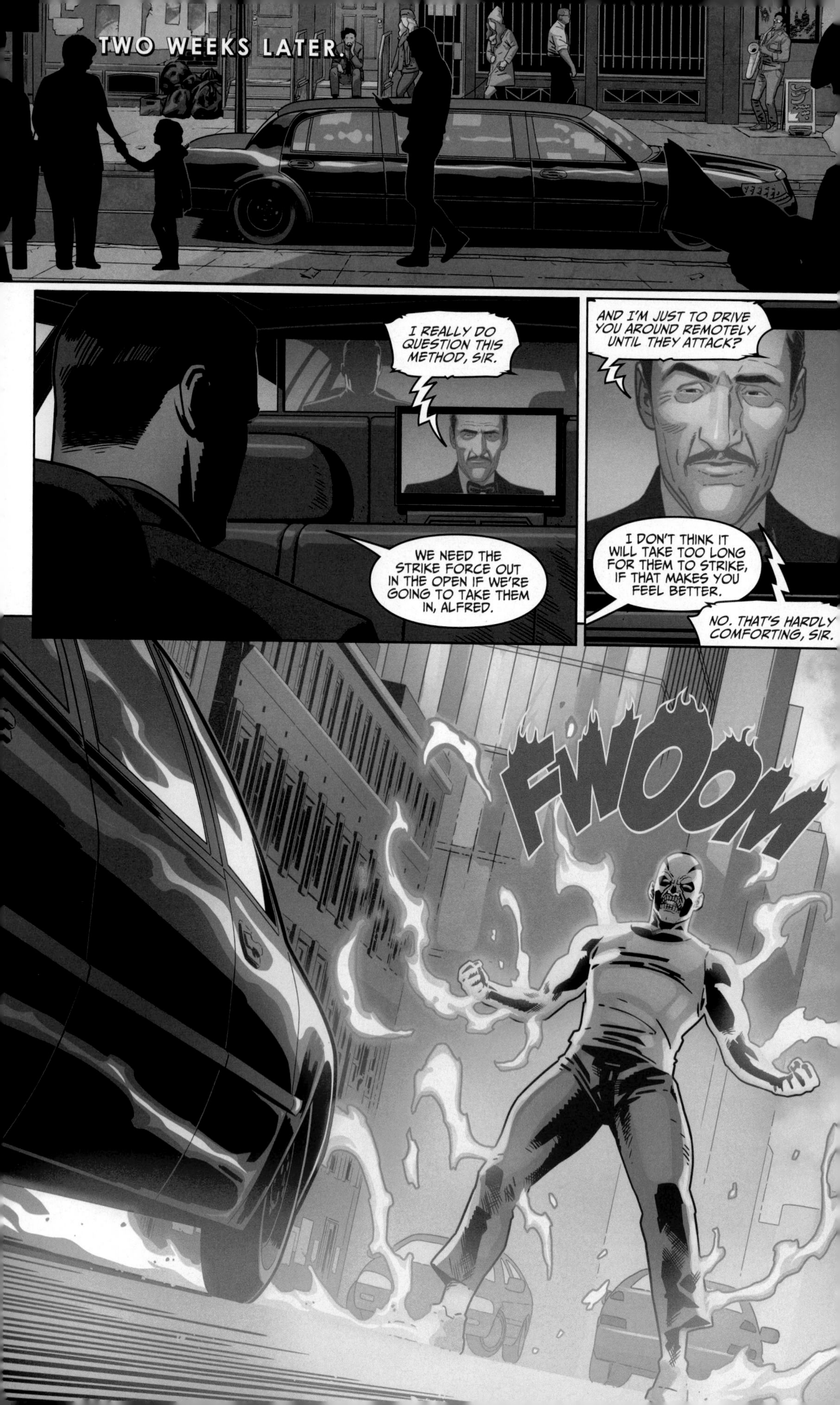
TWO WEEKS LATER.
I REALLY DO QUESTION THIS METHOD, SIR.
WE NEED THE STRIKE FORCE OUT IN THE OPEN IF WE'RE GOING TO TAKE THEM IN, ALFRED.
AND I'M JUST TO DRIVE YOU AROUND REMOTELY UNTIL THEY ATTACK?
I DON'T THINK IT WILL TAKE TOO LONG FOR THEM TO STRIKE, IF THAT MAKES YOU FEEL BETTER.
NO. THAT'S HARDLY COMFORTING, SIR.
FWOOM

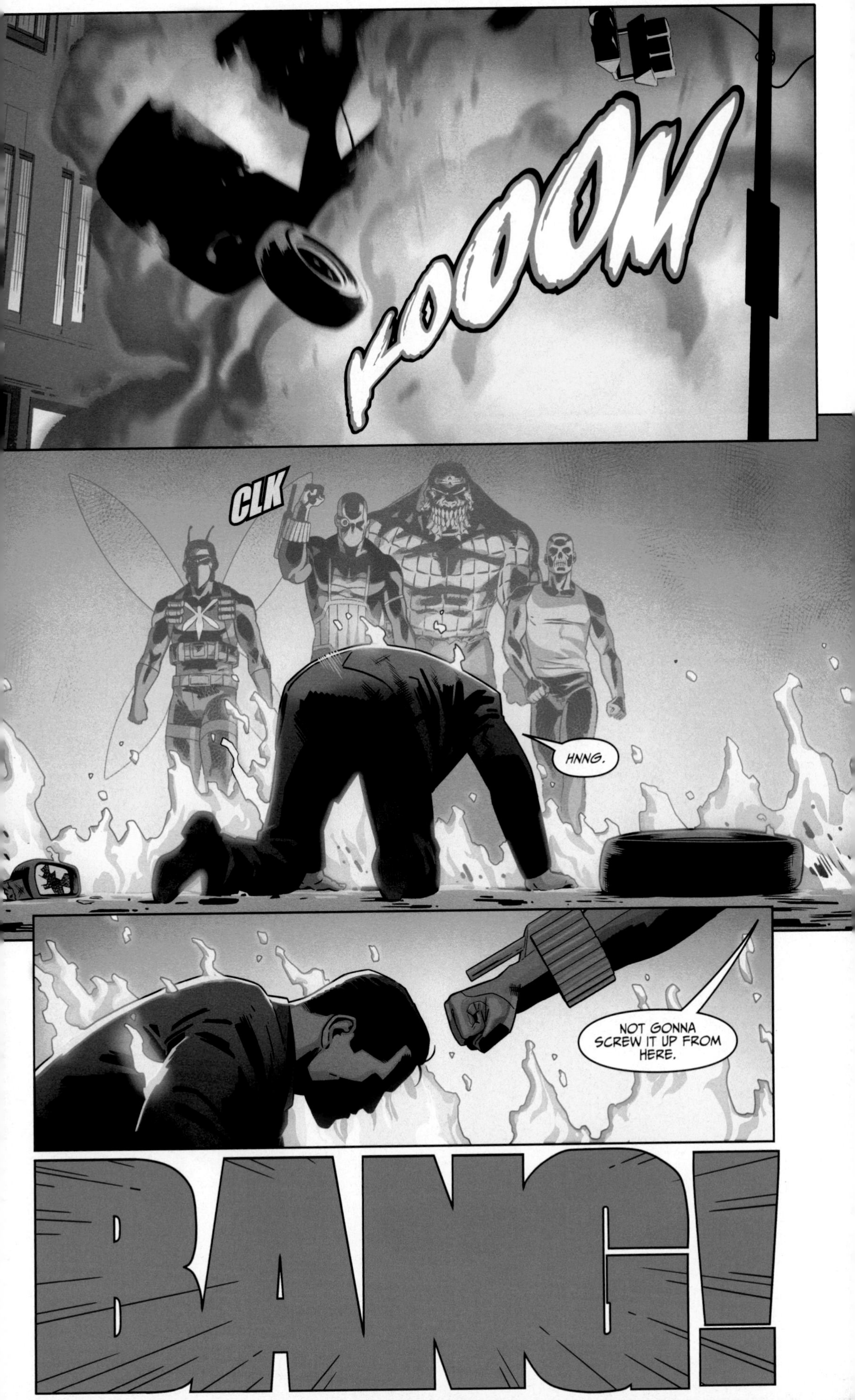
KOOOM
CLK
HNNG.
NOT GONNA SCREW IT UP FROM HERE.
BANG!

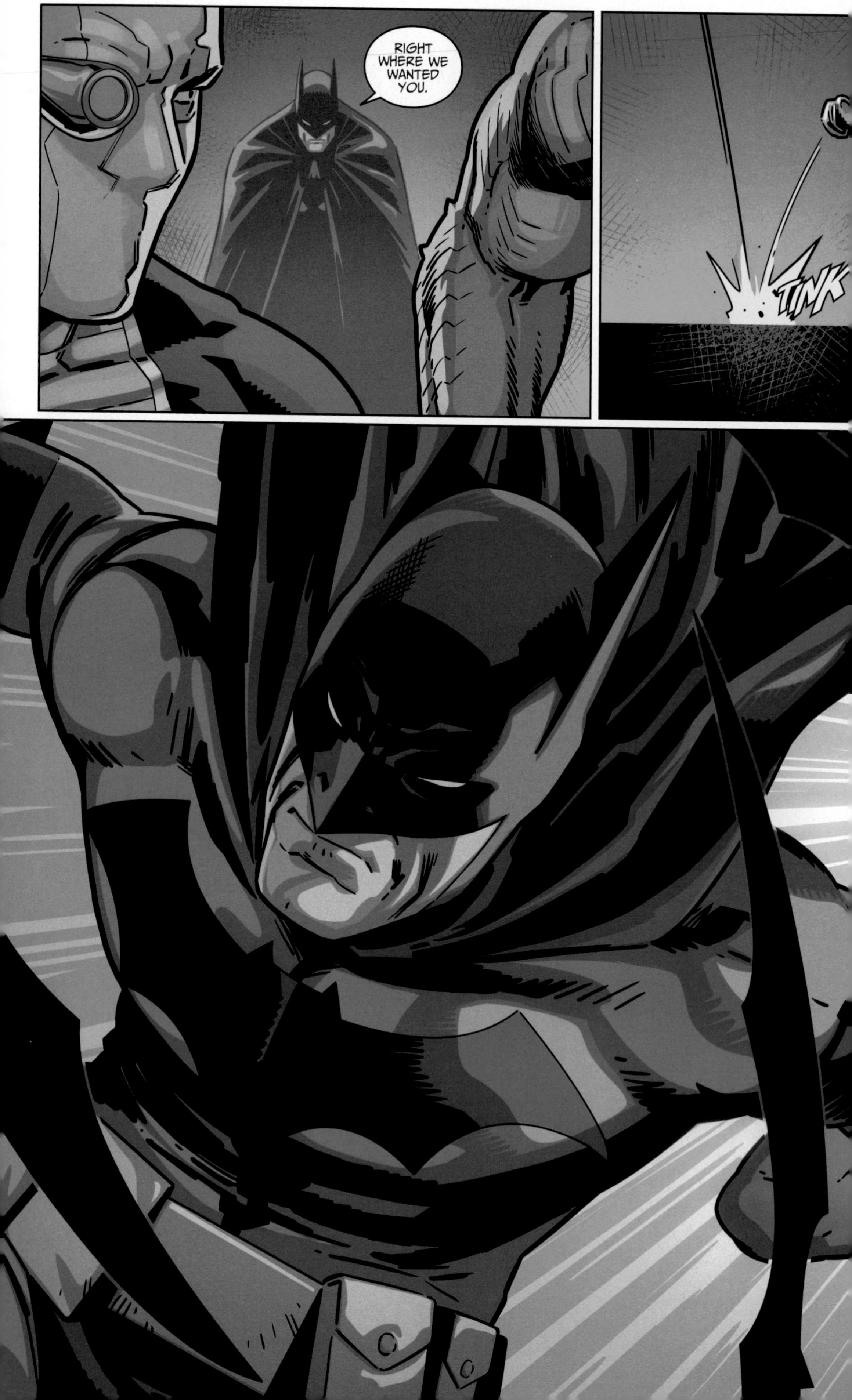
RIGHT WHERE WE WANTED YOU.
TINK

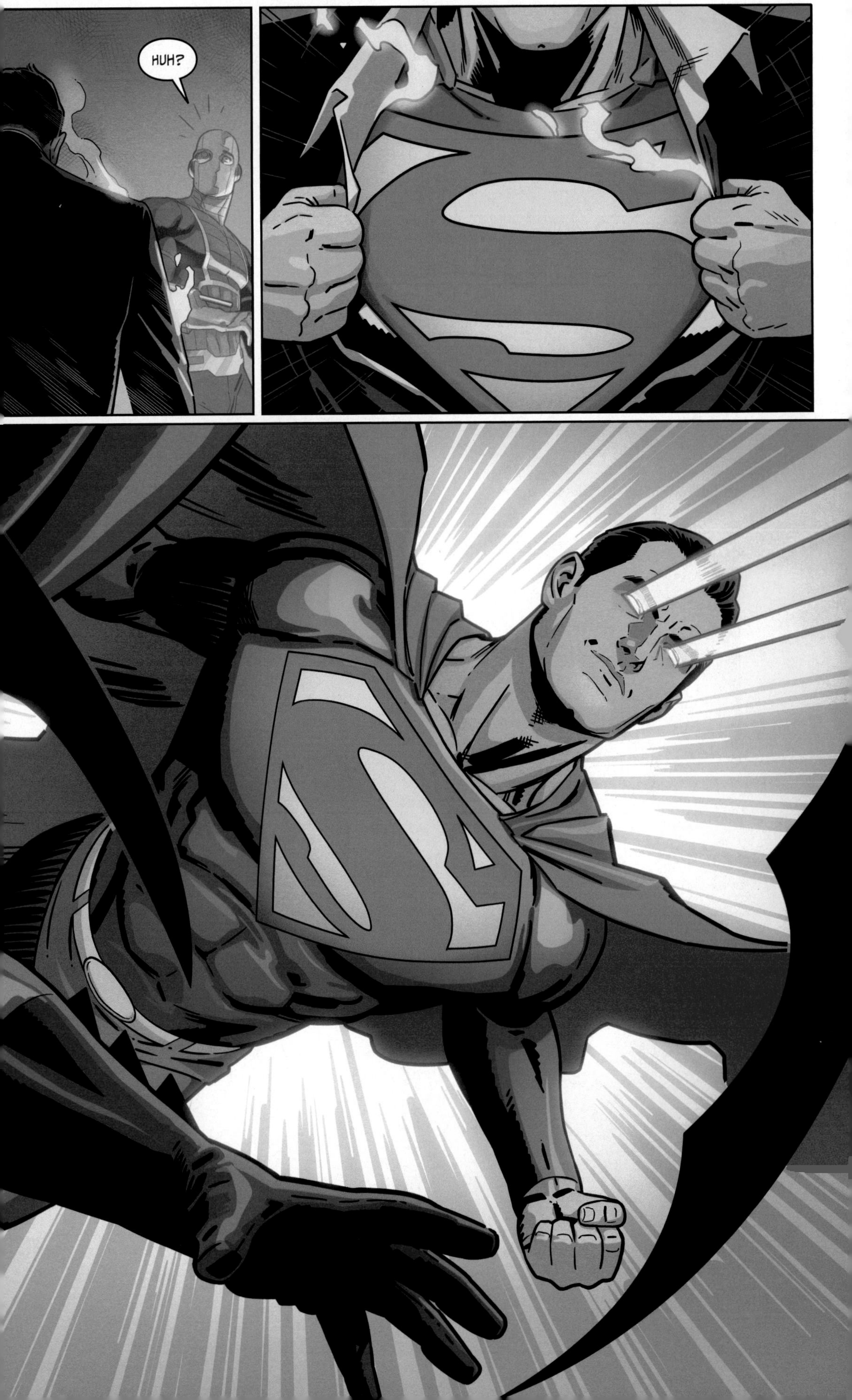
HUH?

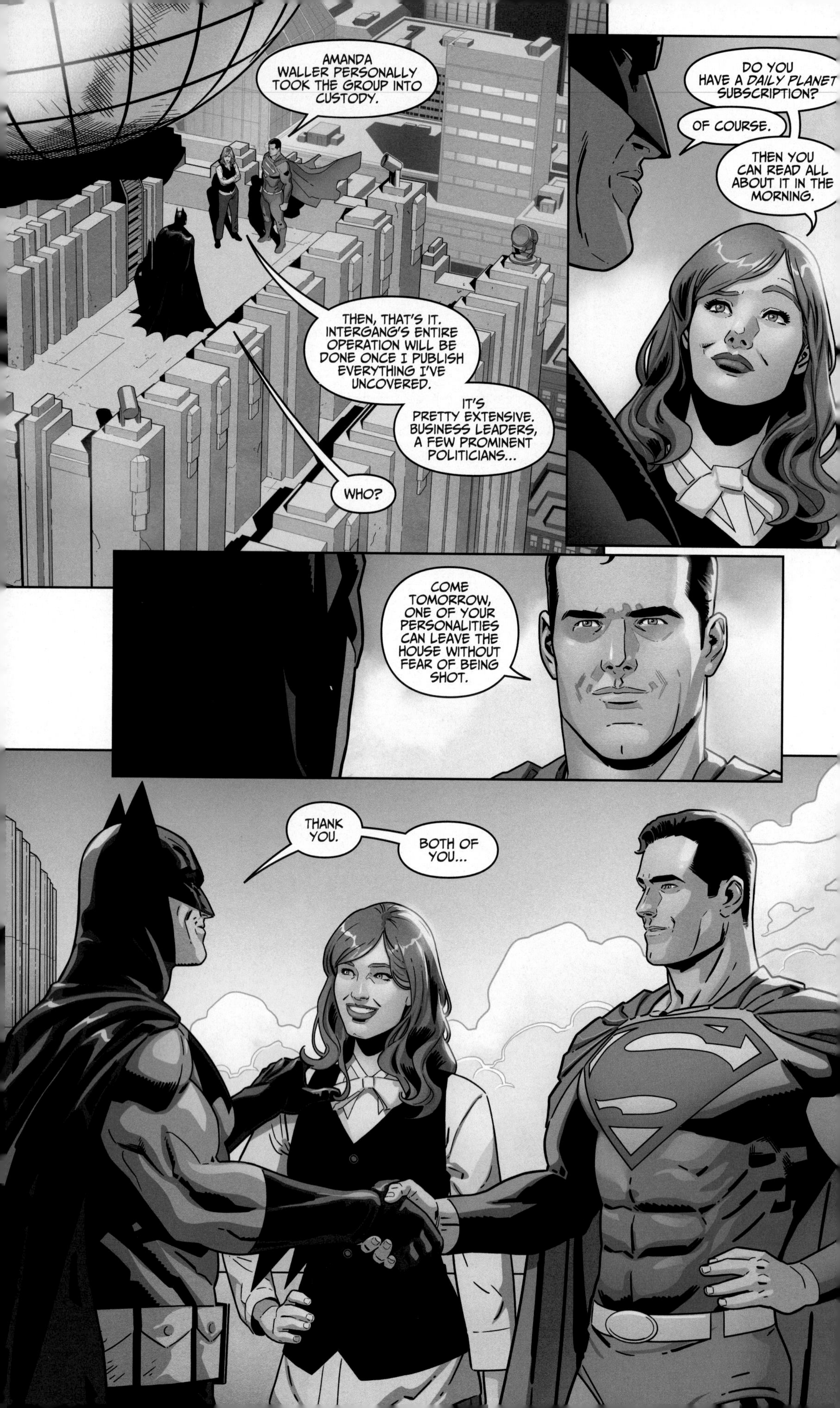
AMANDA WALLER PERSONALLY TOOK THE GROUP INTO CUSTODY.
THEN, THAT'S IT. INTERGANG'S ENTIRE OPERATION WILL BE DONE ONCE I PUBLISH EVERYTHING I'VE UNCOVERED.
IT'S PRETTY EXTENSIVE. BUSINESS LEADERS, A FEW PROMINENT POLITICIANS...
WHO?
DO YOU HAVE A *DAILY PLANET* SUBSCRIPTION?
OF COURSE.
THEN YOU CAN READ ALL ABOUT IT IN THE MORNING.
COME TOMORROW, ONE OF YOUR PERSONALITIES CAN LEAVE THE HOUSE WITHOUT FEAR OF BEING SHOT.
THANK YOU.
BOTH OF YOU...

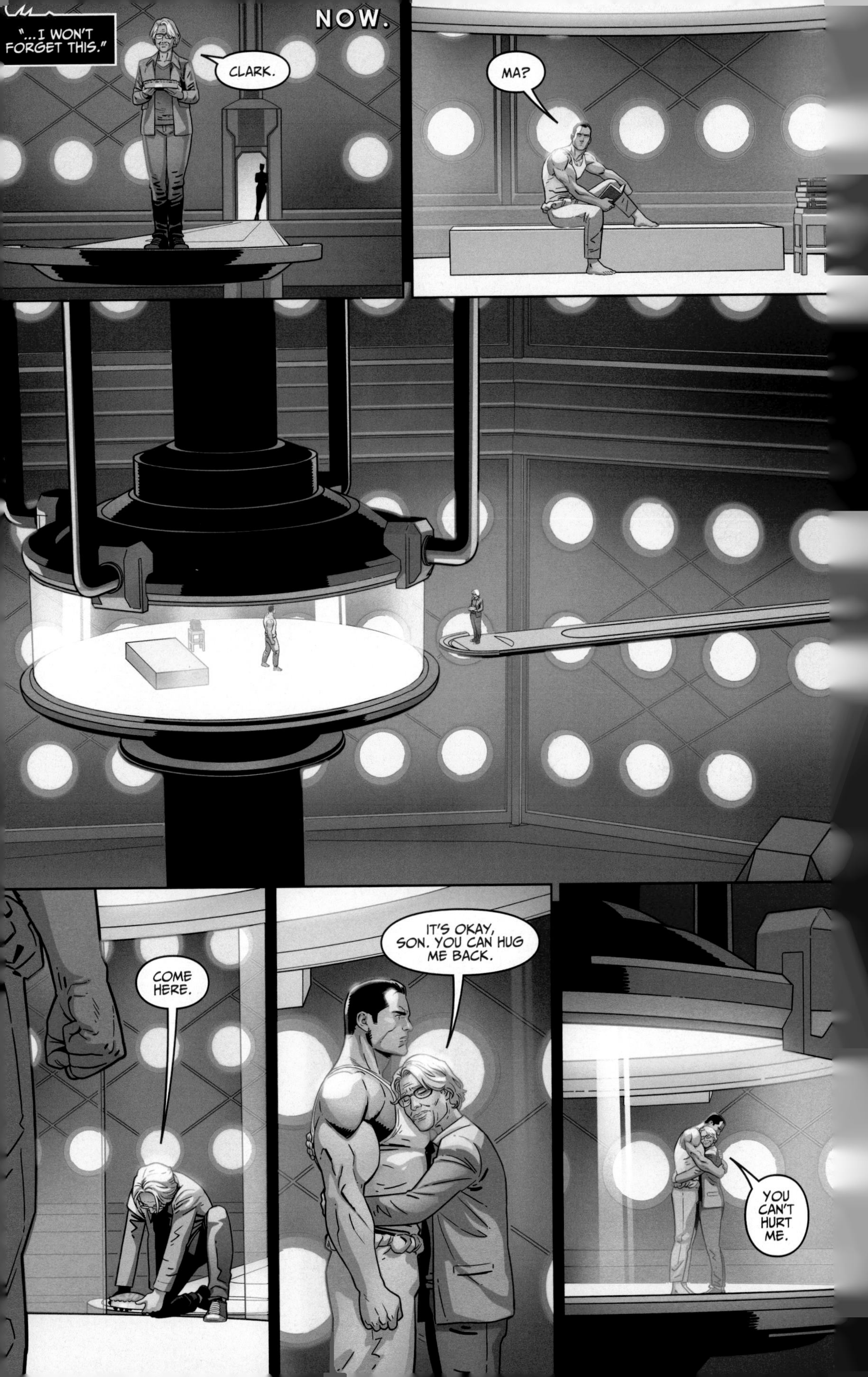
"...I WON'T FORGET THIS."
NOW.
CLARK.
MA?
COME HERE.
IT'S OKAY, SON. YOU CAN HUG ME BACK.
YOU CAN'T HURT ME.

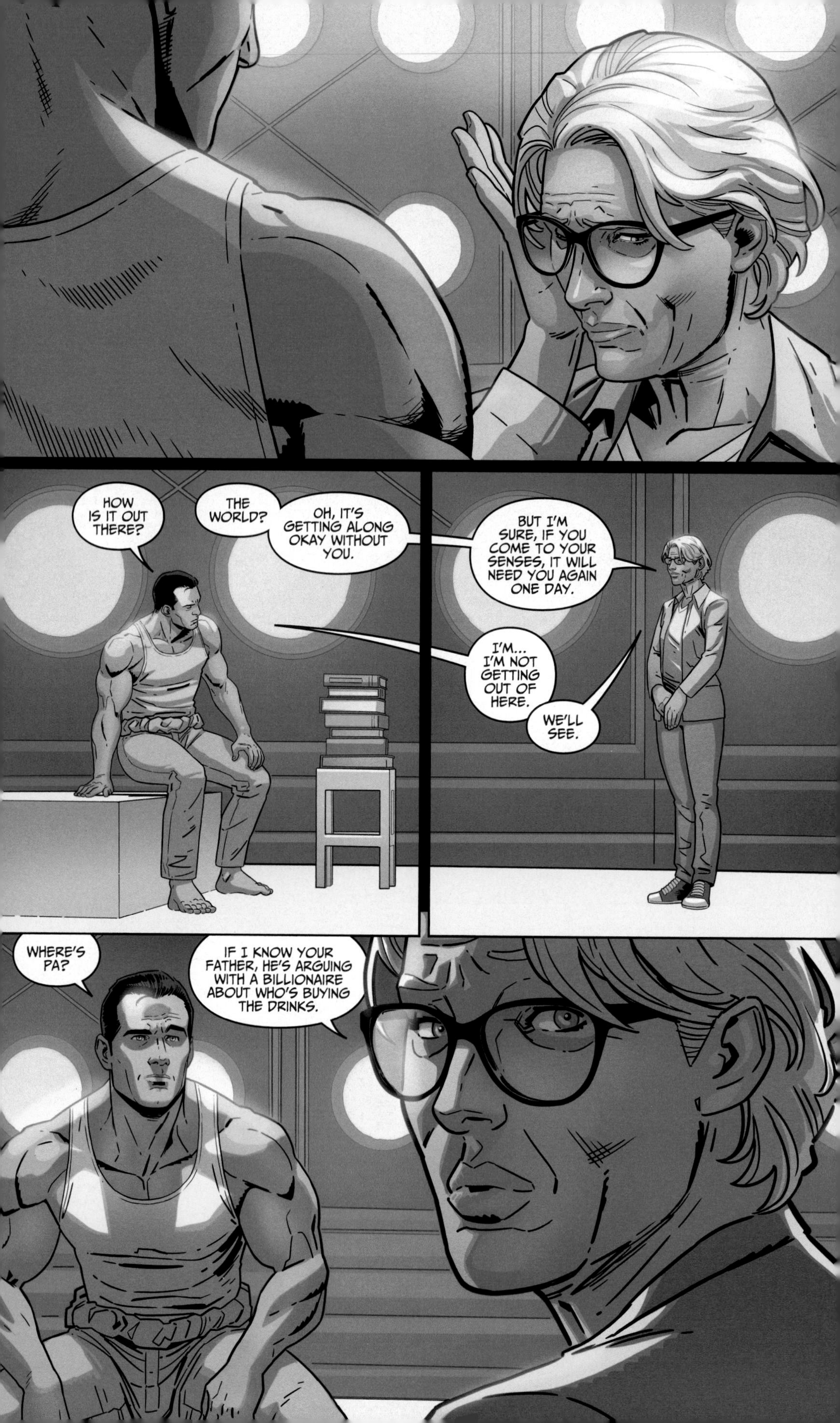
HOW IS IT OUT THERE?
THE WORLD?
OH, IT'S GETTING ALONG OKAY WITHOUT YOU.
BUT I'M SURE, IF YOU COME TO YOUR SENSES, IT WILL NEED YOU AGAIN ONE DAY.
I'M... I'M NOT GETTING OUT OF HERE.
WE'LL SEE.
WHERE'S PA?
IF I KNOW YOUR FATHER, HE'S ARGUING WITH A BILLIONAIRE ABOUT WHO'S BUYING THE DRINKS.

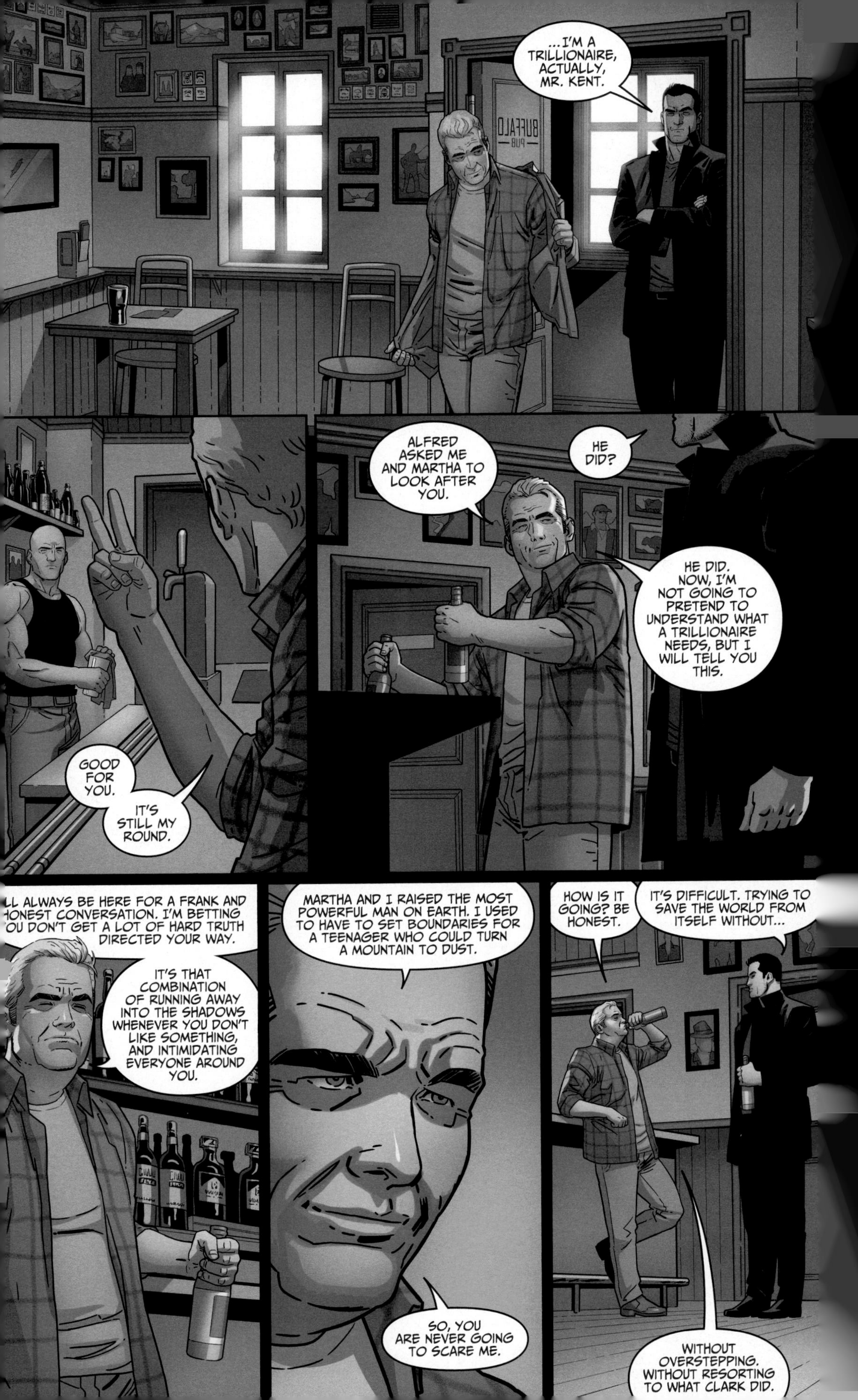
...I'M A TRILLIONAIRE, ACTUALLY, MR. KENT.
BUFFALO PUB
GOOD FOR YOU.
IT'S STILL MY ROUND.
ALFRED ASKED ME AND MARTHA TO LOOK AFTER YOU.
HE DID?
HE DID. NOW, I'M NOT GOING TO PRETEND TO UNDERSTAND WHAT A TRILLIONAIRE NEEDS, BUT I WILL TELL YOU THIS.
LL ALWAYS BE HERE FOR A FRANK AND HONEST CONVERSATION. I'M BETTING OU DON'T GET A LOT OF HARD TRUTH DIRECTED YOUR WAY.
IT'S THAT COMBINATION OF RUNNING AWAY INTO THE SHADOWS WHENEVER YOU DON'T LIKE SOMETHING, AND INTIMIDATING EVERYONE AROUND YOU.
MARTHA AND I RAISED THE MOST POWERFUL MAN ON EARTH. I USED TO HAVE TO SET BOUNDARIES FOR A TEENAGER WHO COULD TURN A MOUNTAIN TO DUST.
SO, YOU ARE NEVER GOING TO SCARE ME.
HOW IS IT GOING? BE HONEST.
IT'S DIFFICULT. TRYING TO SAVE THE WORLD FROM ITSELF WITHOUT...
WITHOUT OVERSTEPPING. WITHOUT RESORTING TO WHAT CLARK DID.

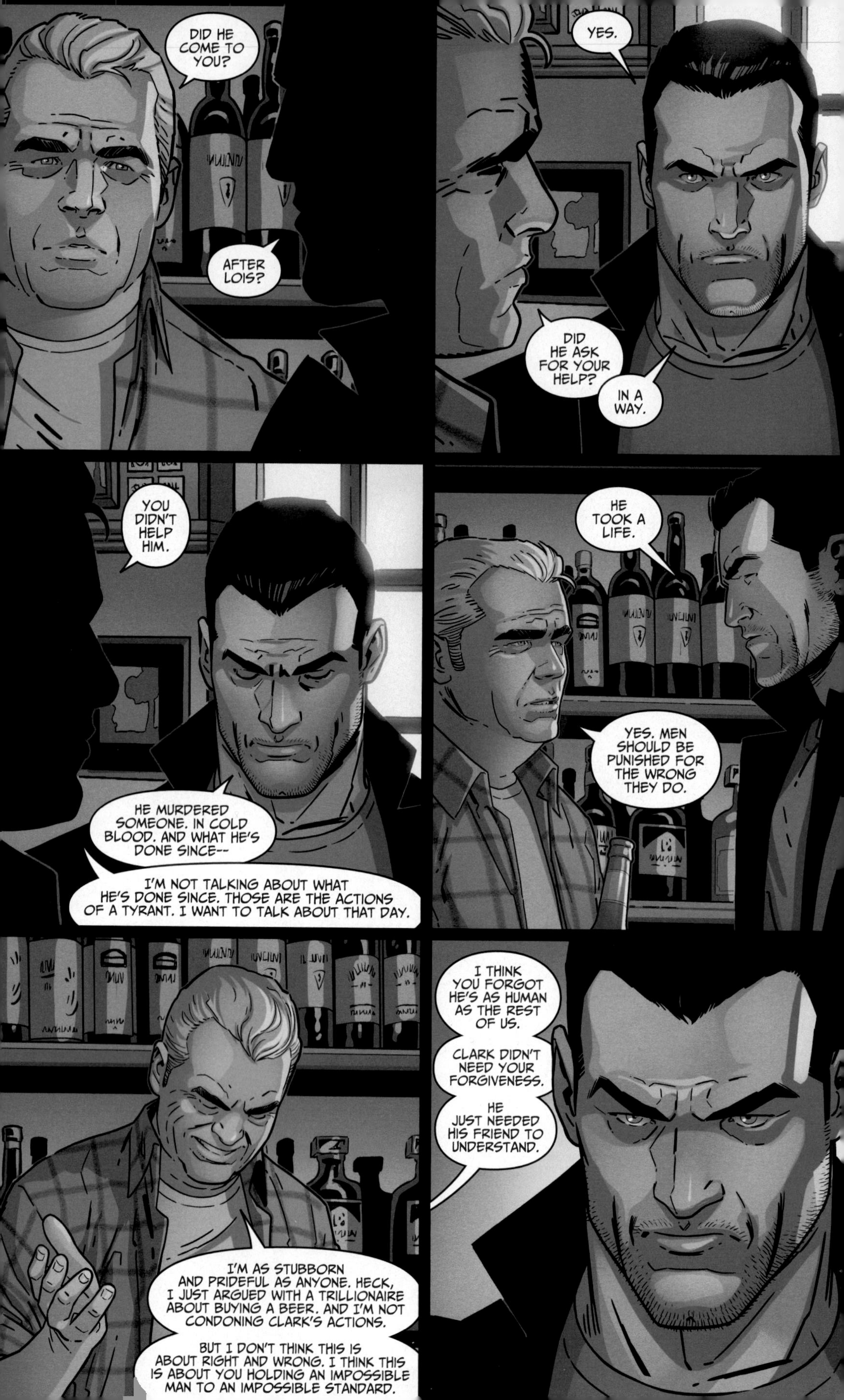
DID HE COME TO YOU?
AFTER LOIS?
YES.
DID HE ASK FOR YOUR HELP?
IN A WAY.
YOU DIDN'T HELP HIM.
HE MURDERED SOMEONE. IN COLD BLOOD. AND WHAT HE'S DONE SINCE--
I'M NOT TALKING ABOUT WHAT HE'S DONE SINCE. THOSE ARE THE ACTIONS OF A TYRANT. I WANT TO TALK ABOUT THAT DAY.
HE TOOK A LIFE.
YES. MEN SHOULD BE PUNISHED FOR THE WRONG THEY DO.
I'M AS STUBBORN AND PRIDEFUL AS ANYONE. HECK, I JUST ARGUED WITH A TRILLIONAIRE ABOUT BUYING A BEER. AND I'M NOT CONDONING CLARK'S ACTIONS.
BUT I DON'T THINK THIS IS ABOUT RIGHT AND WRONG. I THINK THIS IS ABOUT YOU HOLDING AN IMPOSSIBLE MAN TO AN IMPOSSIBLE STANDARD.
I THINK YOU FORGOT HE'S AS HUMAN AS THE REST OF US.
CLARK DIDN'T NEED YOUR FORGIVENESS.
HE JUST NEEDED HIS FRIEND TO UNDERSTAND.

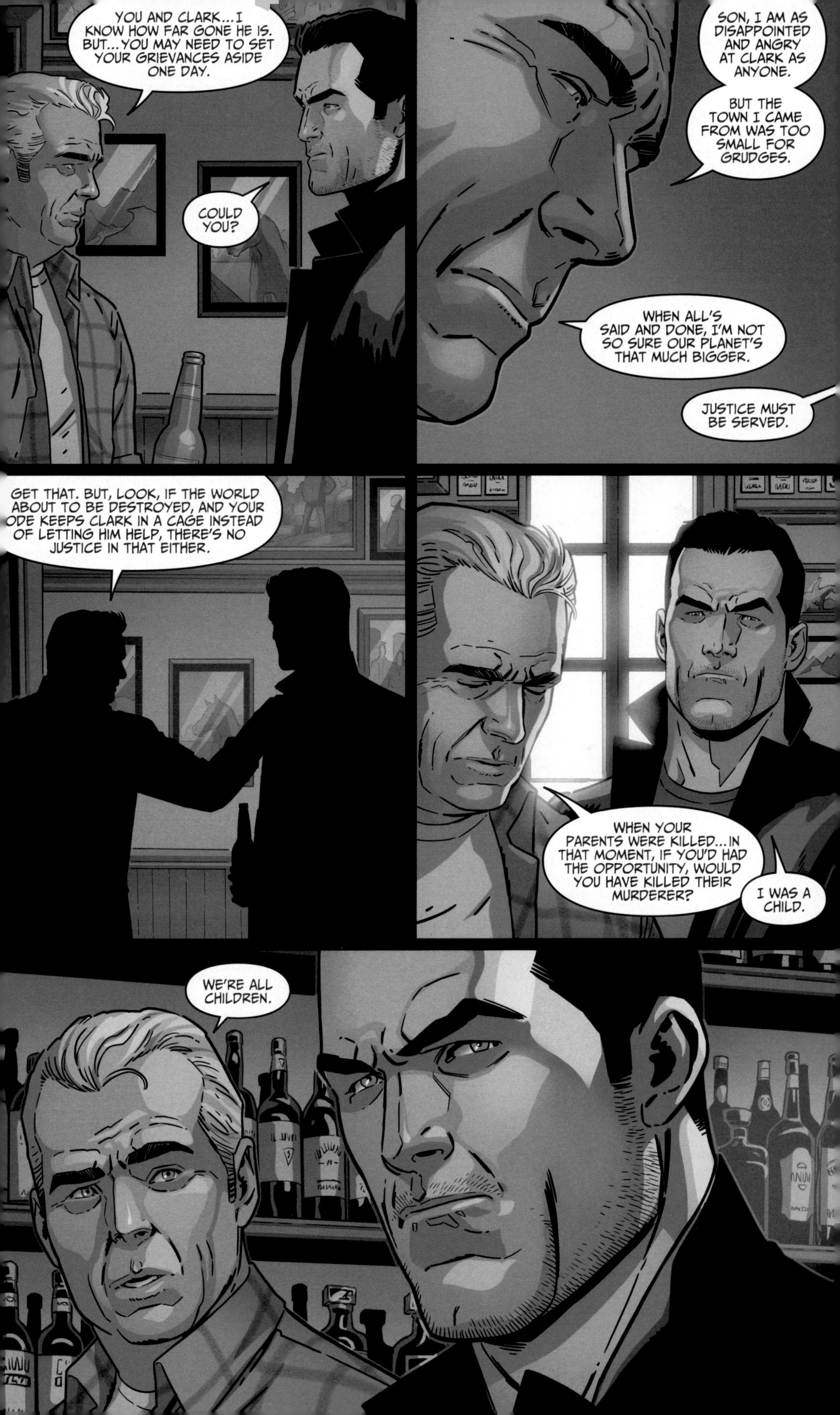
YOU AND CLARK...I KNOW HOW FAR GONE HE IS. BUT...YOU MAY NEED TO SET YOUR GRIEVANCES ASIDE ONE DAY.
COULD YOU?
SON, I AM AS DISAPPOINTED AND ANGRY AT CLARK AS ANYONE.
BUT THE TOWN I CAME FROM WAS TOO SMALL FOR GRUDGES.
WHEN ALL'S SAID AND DONE, I'M NOT SO SURE OUR PLANET'S THAT MUCH BIGGER.
JUSTICE MUST BE SERVED.
GET THAT. BUT, LOOK, IF THE WORLD ABOUT TO BE DESTROYED, AND YOUR ODE KEEPS CLARK IN A CAGE INSTEAD OF LETTING HIM HELP, THERE'S NO JUSTICE IN THAT EITHER.
WHEN YOUR PARENTS WERE KILLED...IN THAT MOMENT, IF YOU'D HAD THE OPPORTUNITY, WOULD YOU HAVE KILLED THEIR MURDERER?
I WAS A CHILD.
WE'RE ALL CHILDREN.

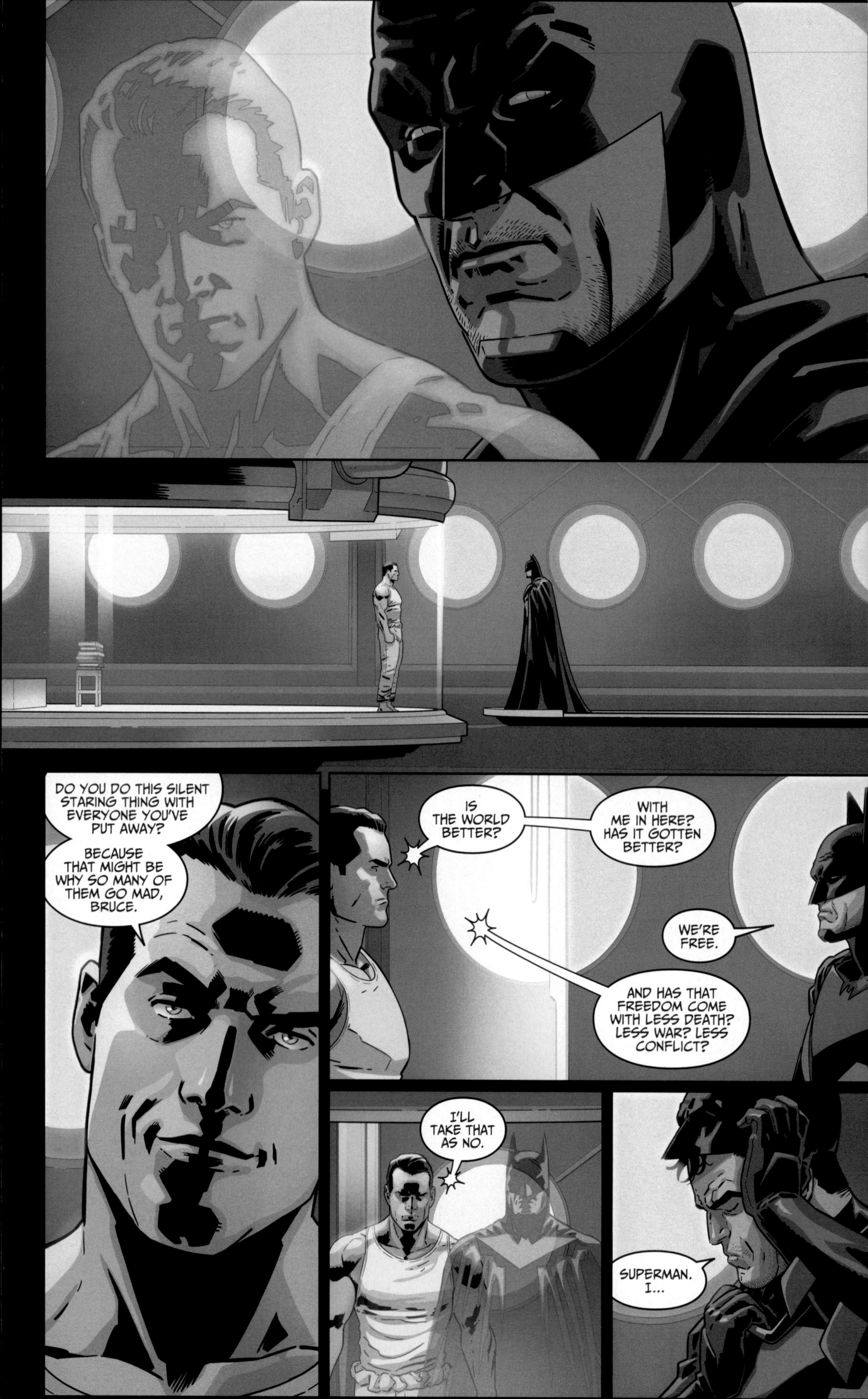
DO YOU DO THIS SILENT STARING THING WITH EVERYONE YOU'VE PUT AWAY?
BECAUSE THAT MIGHT BE WHY SO MANY OF THEM GO MAD, BRUCE.
IS THE WORLD BETTER?
WITH ME IN HERE? HAS IT GOTTEN BETTER?
WE'RE FREE.
AND HAS THAT FREEDOM COME WITH LESS DEATH? LESS WAR? LESS CONFLICT?
I'LL TAKE THAT AS NO.
SUPERMAN. I...

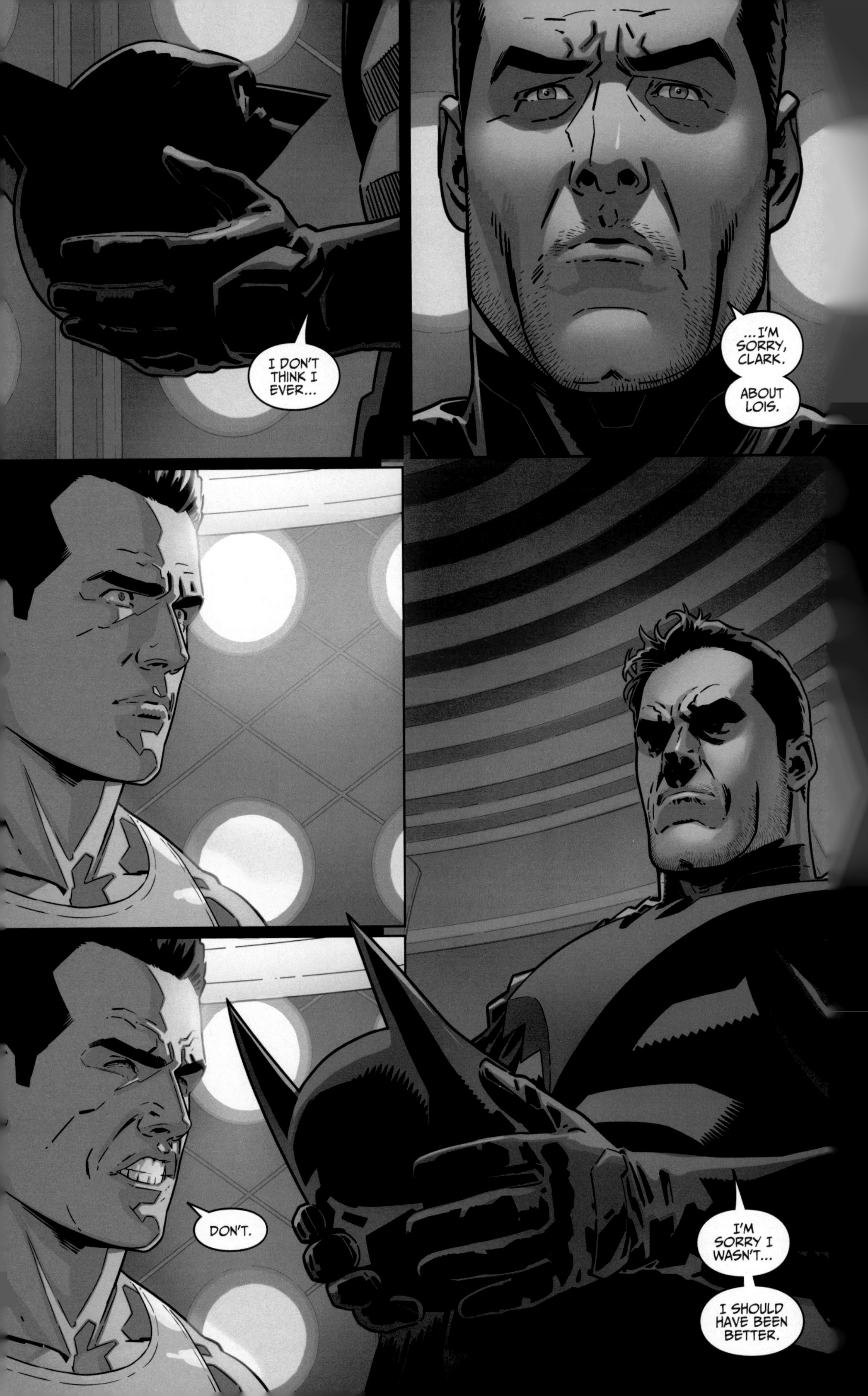
I DON'T THINK I EVER...
...I'M SORRY, CLARK.
ABOUT LOIS.
DON'T.
I'M SORRY I WASN'T...
I SHOULD HAVE BEEN BETTER.

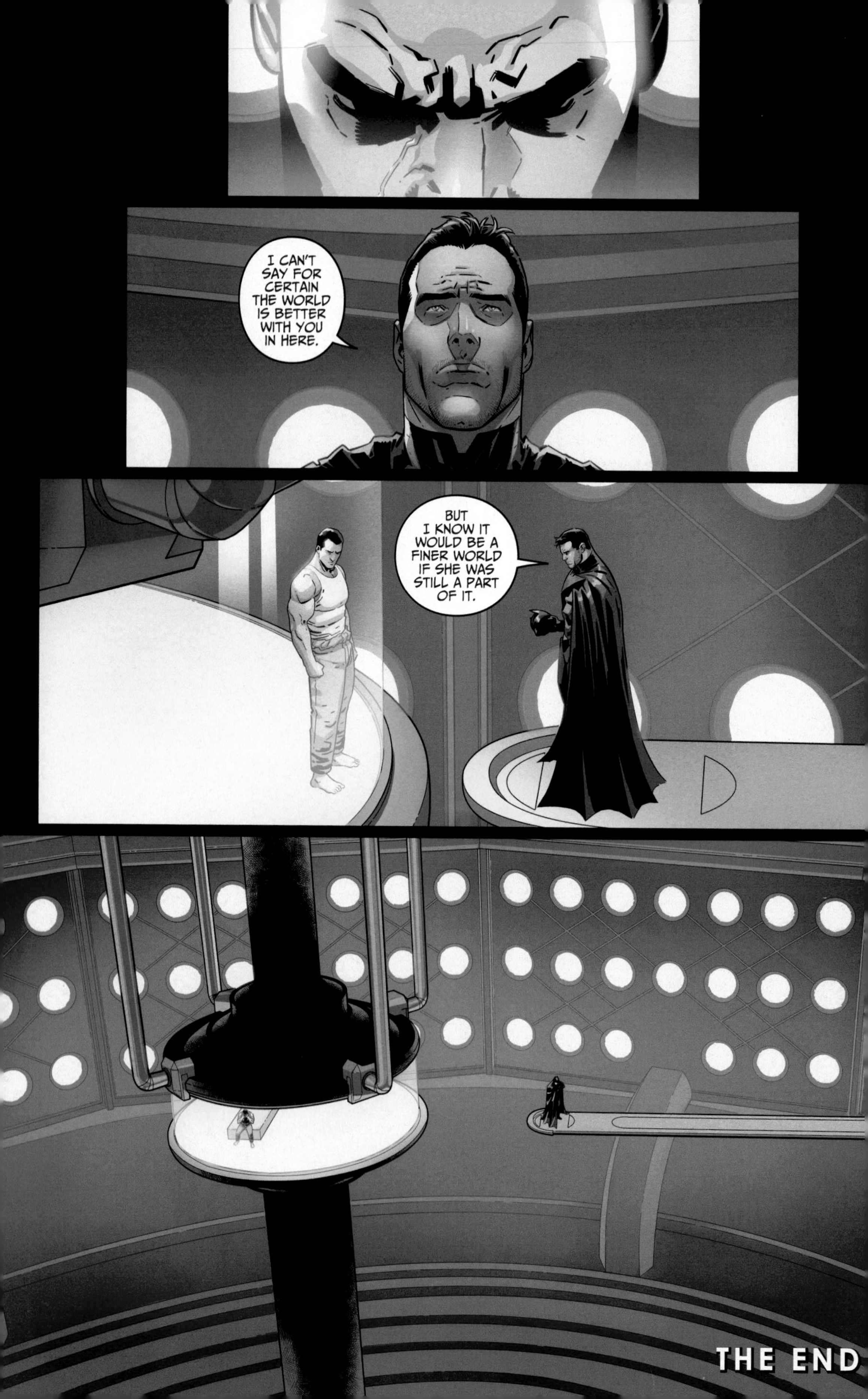
I CAN'T SAY FOR CERTAIN THE WORLD IS BETTER WITH YOU IN HERE.
BUT I KNOW IT WOULD BE A FINER WORLD IF SHE WAS STILL A PART OF IT.
THE END

GREEN LANTERN LOBO character designs by Bruno Redondo

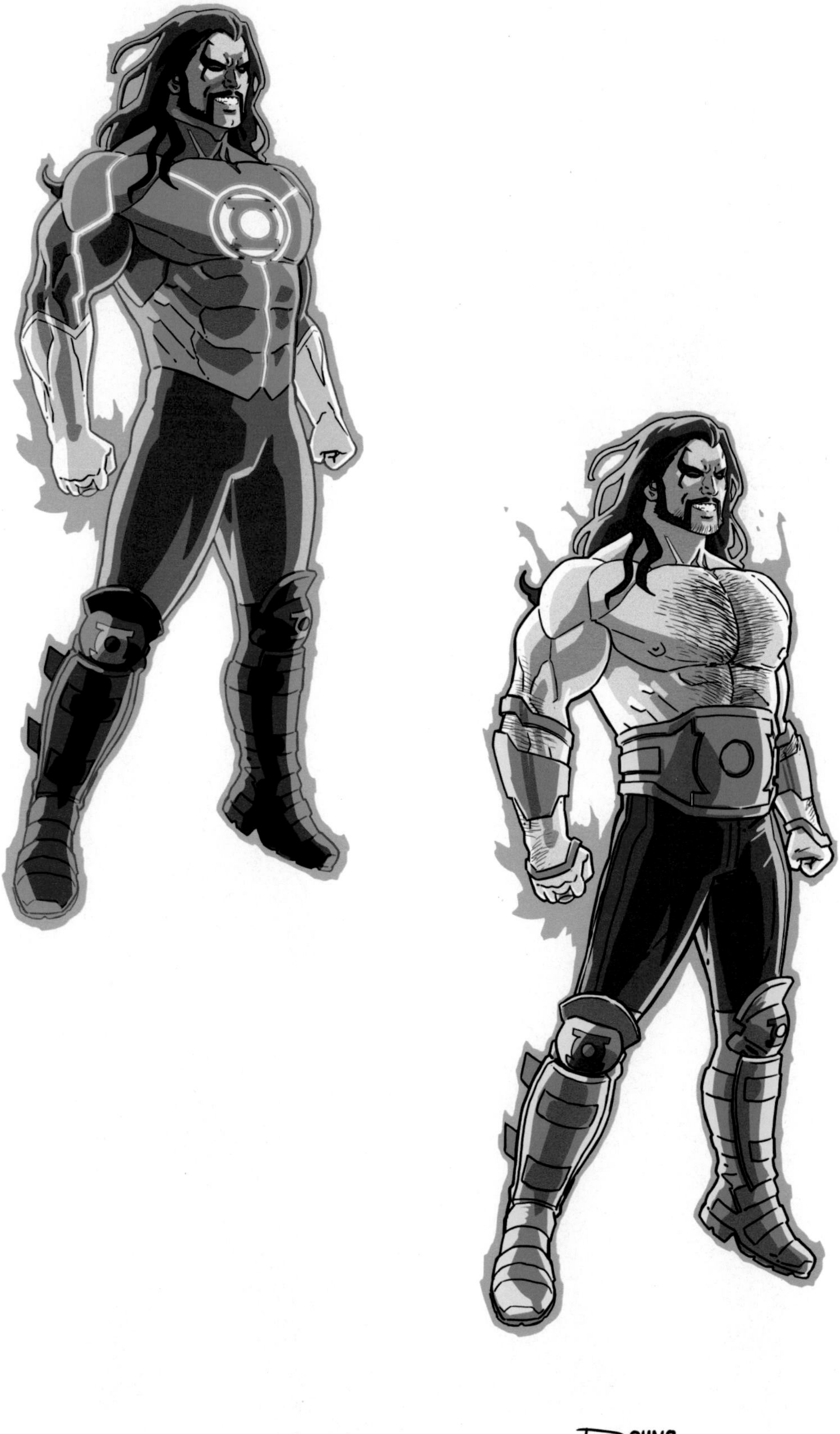
GREEN-LOBO -INJ2
BRUNO REDONDO 18

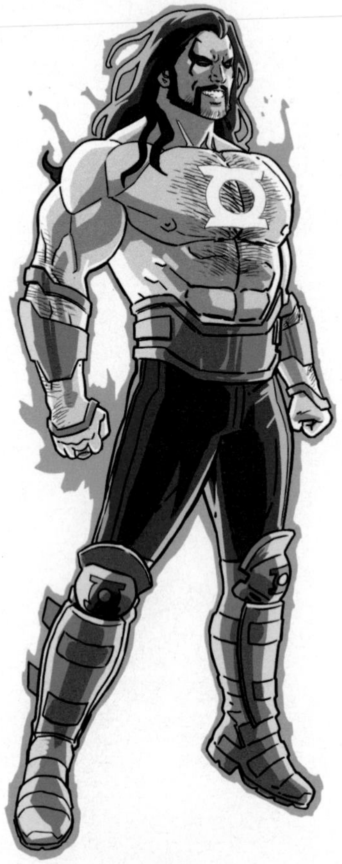
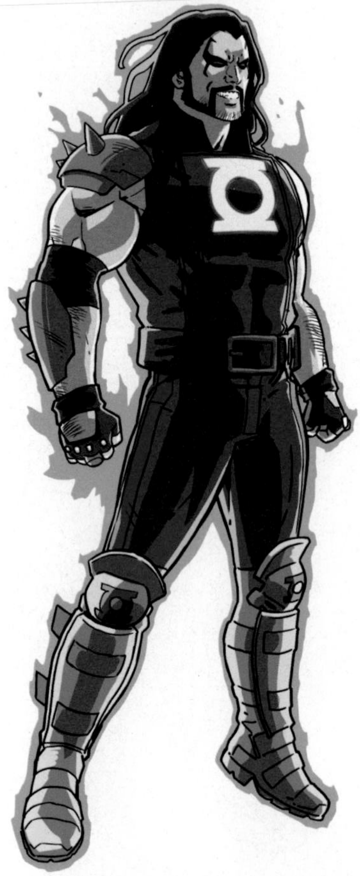
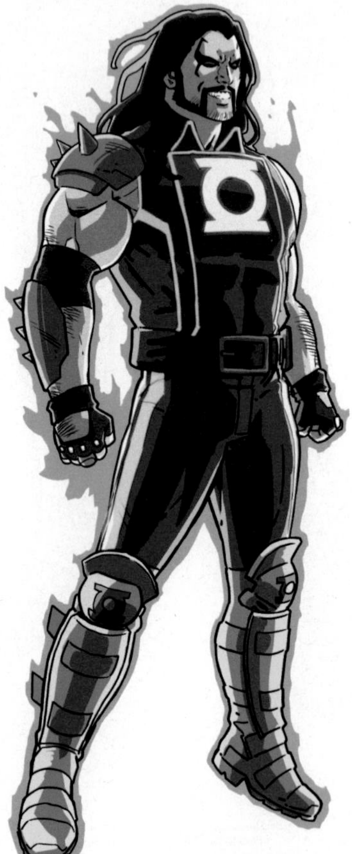
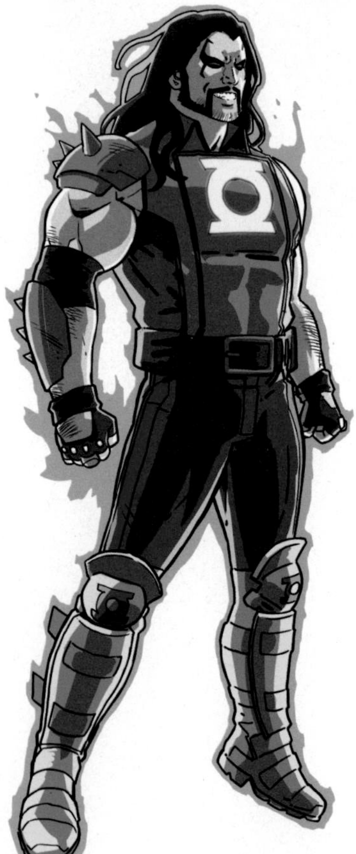

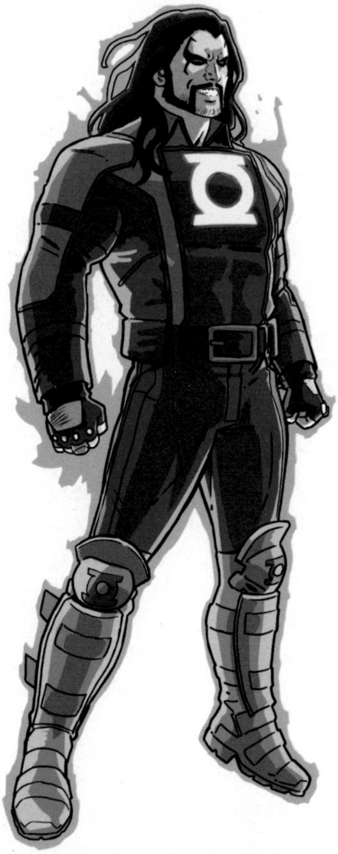
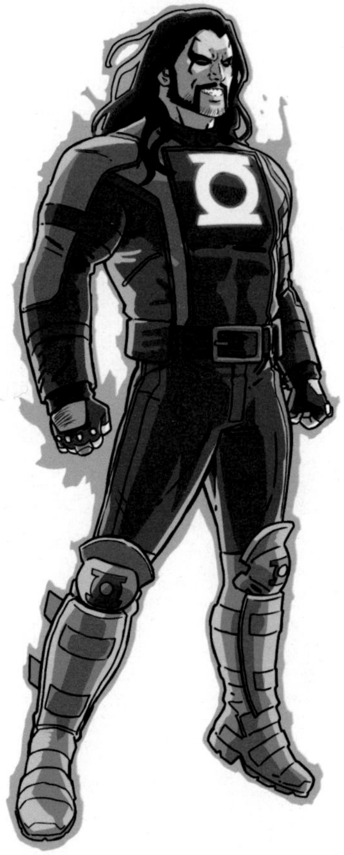
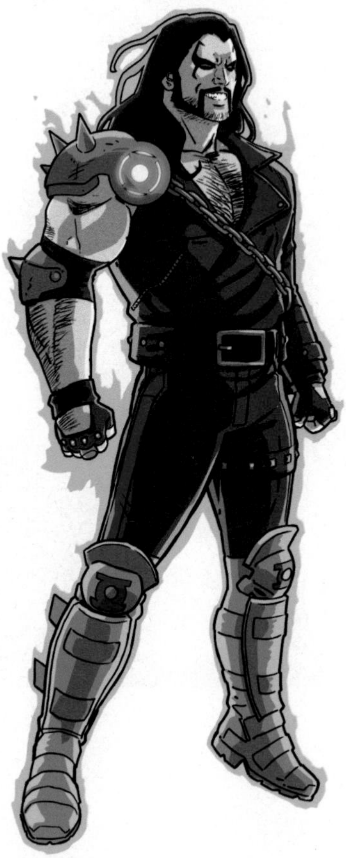
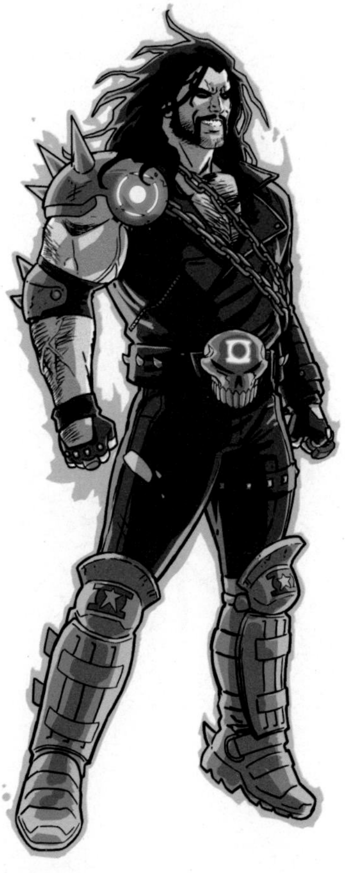

INJUSTICE 2 #31 cover sketches and inks by Daniel Sampere

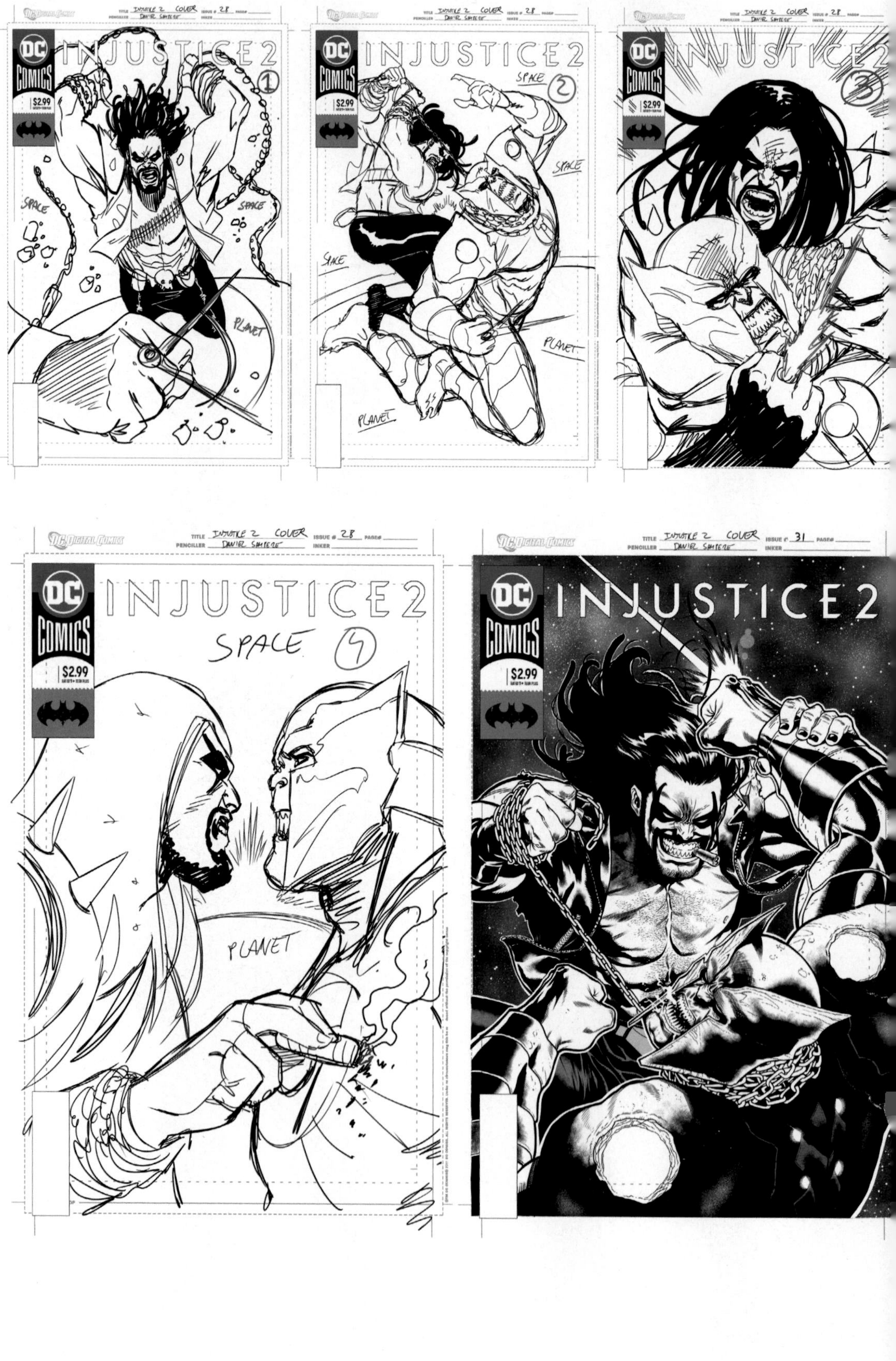
INJUSTICE 2
1
SPACE
SPACE
PLANET
INJUSTICE 2
SPACE 2
SPACE
SPACE
PLANET
PLANET
INJUSTICE 2
3
INJUSTICE 2
SPACE 4
PLANET
INJUSTICE 2

INJUSTICE 2 #32 cover sketches by Bruno Redondo
INJUSTICE 2 #34 cover sketches by Daniel Sampere

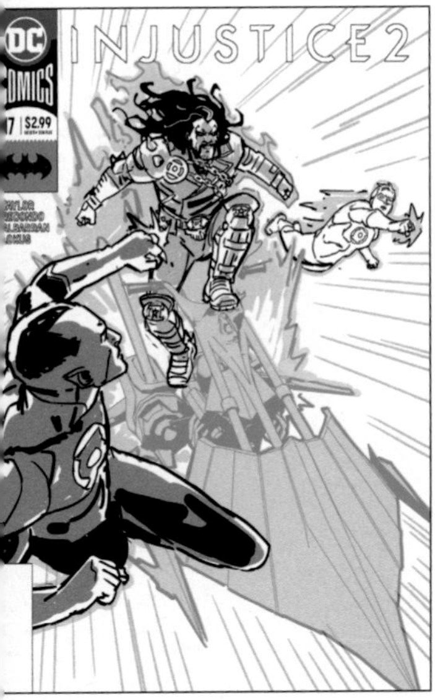
DC COMICS
INJUSTICE 2
$2.99

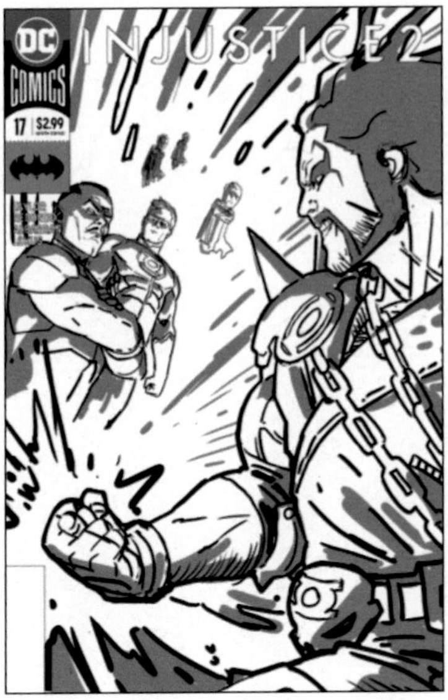
DC COMICS
INJUSTICE 2
17
$2.99

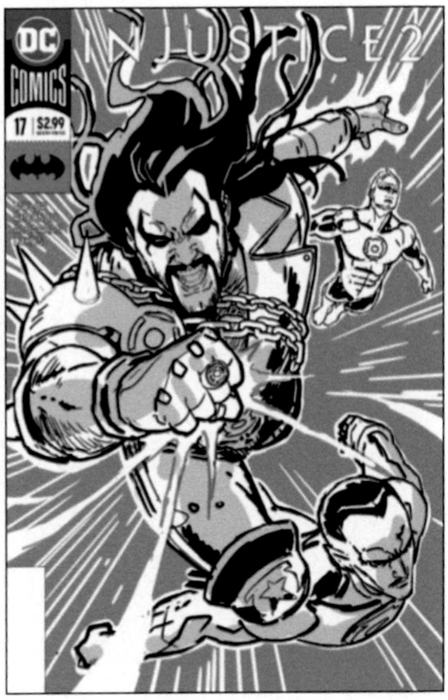
DC COMICS
INJUSTICE 2
17
$2.99

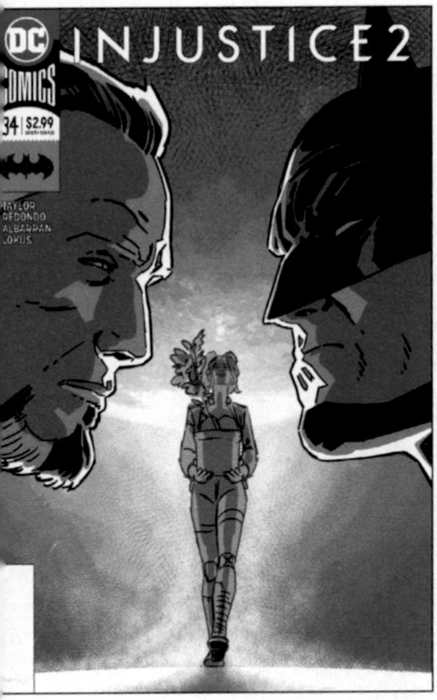
DC COMICS
INJUSTICE 2
34
$2.99

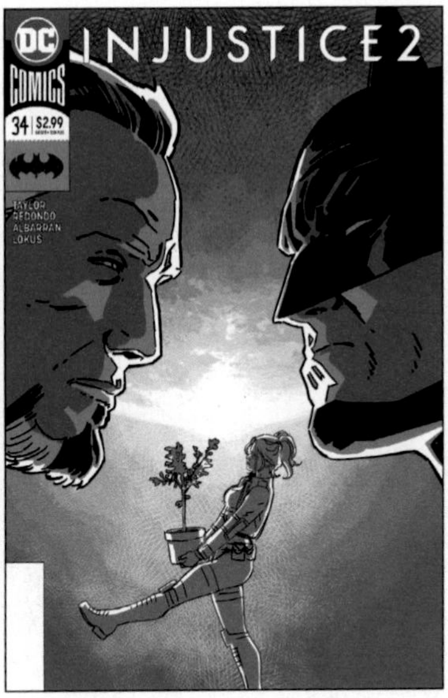
DC COMICS
INJUSTICE 2
34
$2.99
TAYLOR
REDONDO
ALBARRAN
LOKUS

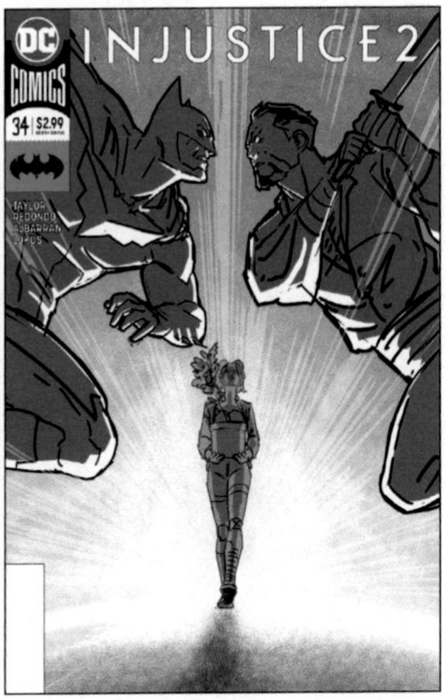
DC COMICS
INJUSTICE 2
34
$2.99
TAYLOR
REDONDO
ALBARRAN
LOKUS

INJUSTICE 2 #35 cover sketches and inks by Daniel Sampere

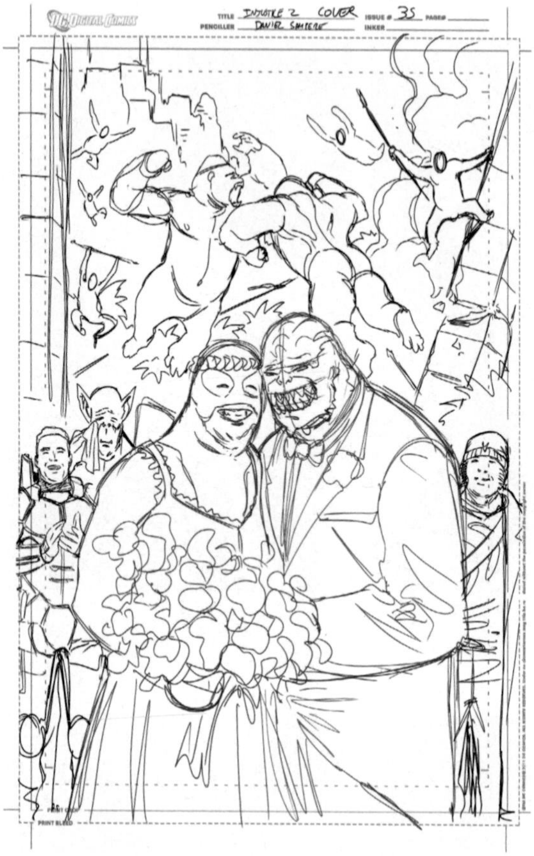

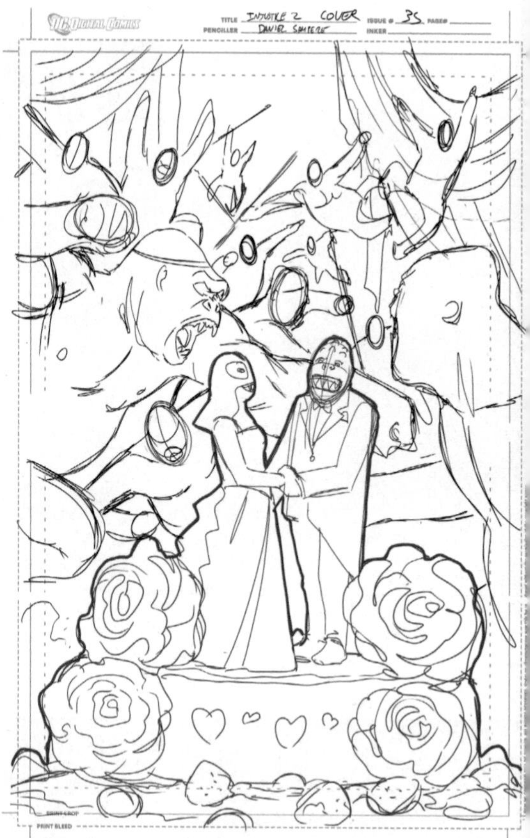

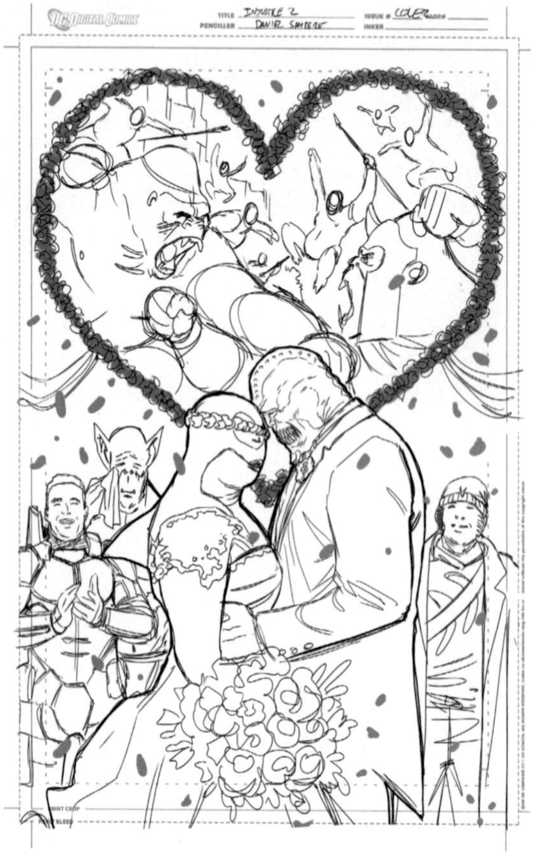

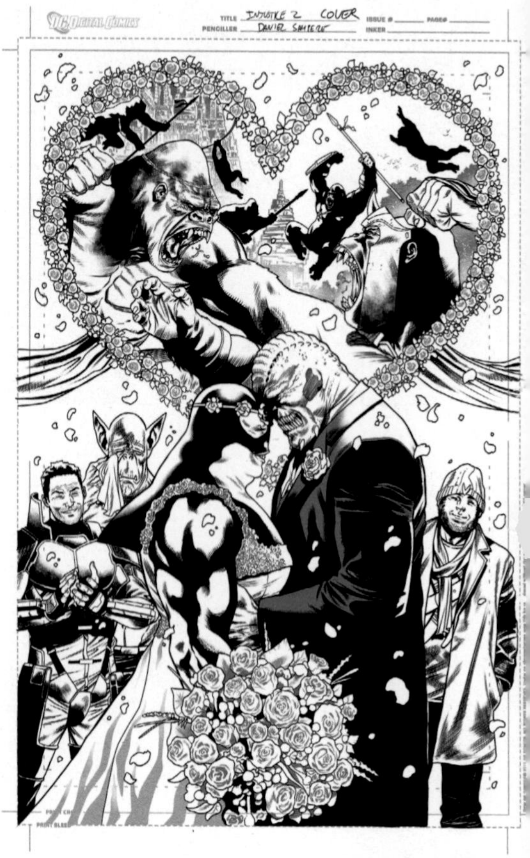

INJUSTICE 2 #36 cover sketches by Bruno Redondo

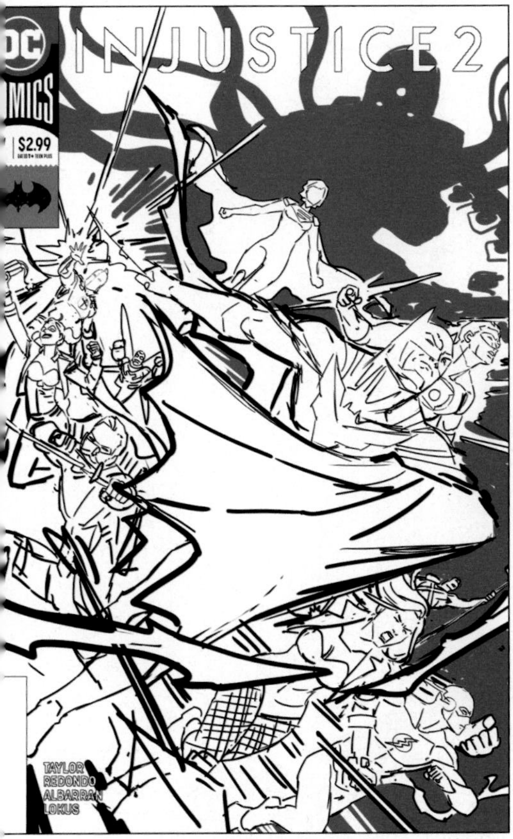
INJUSTICE 2
DC COMICS
$2.99
TAYLOR
REDONDO
ALBARRAN
LOKUS

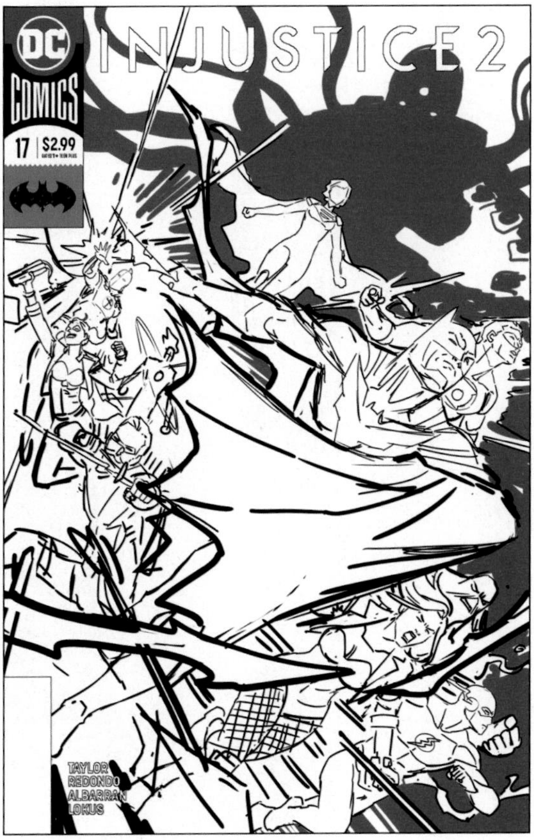
INJUSTICE 2
DC COMICS
17
$2.99
TAYLOR
REDONDO
ALBARRAN
LOKUS

INJUSTICE 2 ANNUAL #2 cover sketches by Bruno Redondo

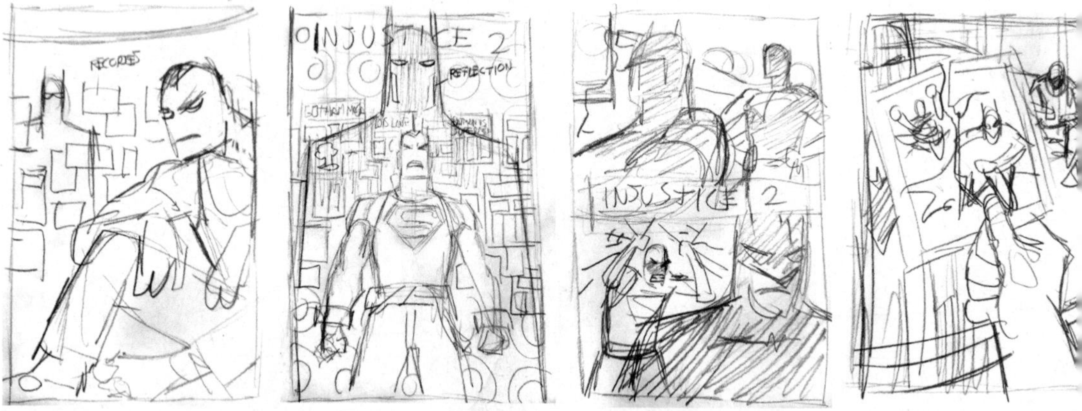
INJUSTICE 2
REFLECTION
INJUSTICE 2

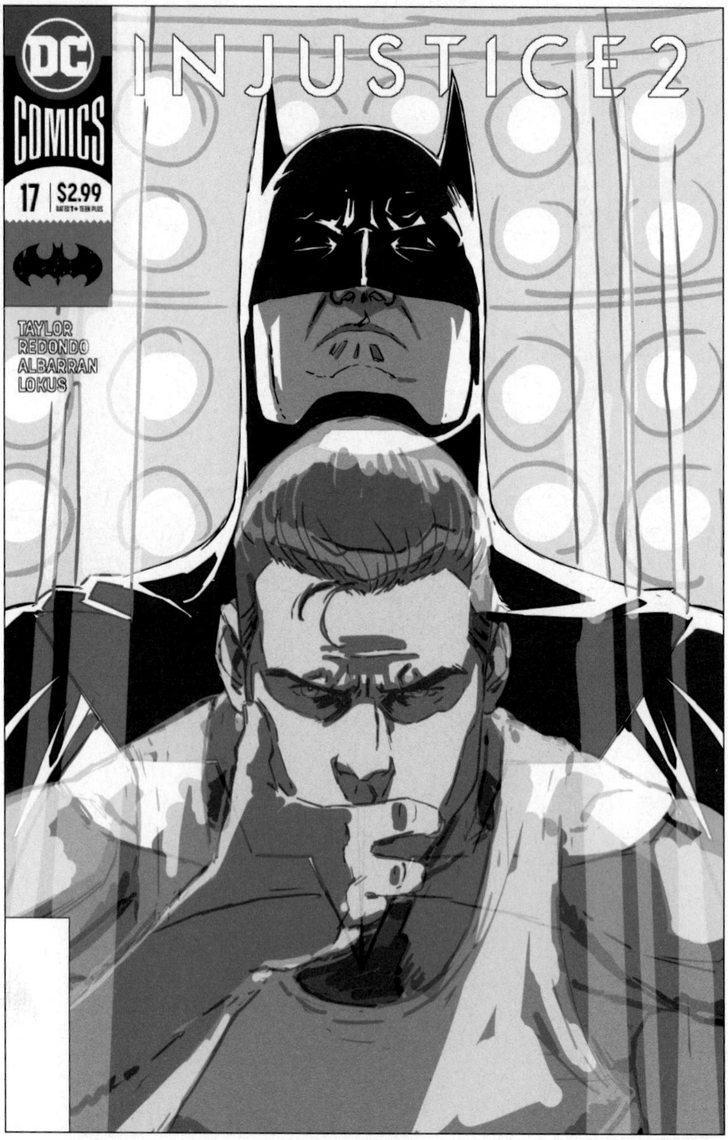
DC
COMICS
17
$2.99
INJUSTICE 2
TAYLOR
REDONDO
ALBARRAN
LOKUS